Also published by Miller Freeman Publications for the forest products industry

Computer Control Systems for Log Processing and Lumber Manufacturing
by Ed M. Williston

Dry Land Log Handling and Sorting
by Charles M. Hampton

Farming the Small Forest
by Laurence C. Walker

The Logging Business Management Handbook
by Ronald R. Macklin

Logging Practices, revised edition
by Steve Conway

Lumber Manufacturing: The Design and Operation of Sawmills and Planer Mills, revised edition
by Ed M. Williston

Modern Particleboard and Dry-Process Fiberboard Manufacturing
by Thomas M. Maloney

Operations Management in the Forest Products Industry
by Richard F. Baldwin

Plywood Manufacturing Practices, second edition
by Richard F. Baldwin

Quality Control in Lumber Manufacturing
edited by Terence D. Brown

Saws: Design, Selection, Operation, Maintenance, revised edition
by Ed M. Williston

Small Log Sawmills: Profitable Product Selection Process Design and Operation
by Ed M. Williston

Timber Cutting Practices, third edition
by Steve Conway

Directory of the Forest Products Industry

FOREST INDUSTRIES Mill Map

FOREST INDUSTRIES North American Factbook

Secondary Wood Products Manufacturers Directory

MANAGING MILL MAINTENANCE

THE EMERGING REALITIES

RICHARD F. BALDWIN

Miller Freeman Publications, Inc.
San Francisco, Atlanta, Boston,
Chicago, New York, Brussels

Copyright © 1990 by Richard F. Baldwin

Library of Congress Catalog Card Number: 89-085008
International Standard Book Number: 0-87930-220-8

All rights reserved. No part of this book covered by the copyrights hereon may be reproduced or copied in any manner whatsoever without written permission except in the case of brief quotations embodied in articles and reviews. For information contact the publishers, Miller Freeman Publications, Inc., 500 Howard Street, San Francisco, California 94105, USA.

Printed in the United States of America

First printing, February, 1990

Our goal is to help our maintenance people reach a degree of proficiency that has been, until now, unheard of... we want to marry maintenance and production... to break down barriers between the two groups.

Charles W. Bingham, 1984

Contents

Preface		xi
Part One. An Overview		1
1.	The Industry Heritage and Changing Needs	3
2.	Defining the Task	12
3.	Creating and Sustaining an Effective Program	22
4.	Building and Developing an Organization	31
Part Two. Managing for Results		47
5.	Maintenance Planning and Scheduling	49
6.	Computers: New Tools for a Tough Task	63
7.	Program Implementation	73
8.	Maintenance Problem Solving	84
9.	Safety and Loss Prevention	95
Part Three. Predictive Maintenance: Tools and Techniques		107
10.	Predictive Maintenance: An Overview	109
11.	Vibration Monitoring and Analysis	116
12.	Infrared Imaging, Ultrasonic Testing, and Other Predictive Maintenance Techniques	128
Part Four. Budgets and Cost Controls		139
13.	The Economics of Maintenance	141
14.	Record Keeping and Cost Tracking	149
15.	Budgeting and Forecasting	157
16.	Rolling Stock Maintenance Scheduling and Cost Control	163
Part Five. Maintenance Support Systems		173
17.	Energy Conservation	175
18.	The Role of the Engineer	187
19.	Total Lubrication	194
20.	Selecting the Vendor	262
21.	Stores and Spares Control	266

Part Six. Worker Participation	277
22. Innovation, Involvement, and Quality Circles	279
23. Designing Away From Maintenance	284
24. The Coupling of Maintenance and Manufacturing: Getting Started	292
Index	297

List of Figures and Tables

Figures

2.1 Managing Maintenance: The Program Elements 14
2.2 Maintenance Program Costs and Benefits 17
3.1 Total Maintenance: The Planning and Implementation Steps 23
3.2 Mission Statement 27
3.3 Objective Statement 29
4.1 Common Features of an Effective Maintenance Organization 32
4.2 Central Maintenance Organization 37
4.3 Area Maintenance Organization 38
4.4 Departmental Maintenance Organization 39
4.5 Maintenance Organizations: A Comparison 41
4.6 Rating System for Skills Evaluation 44
5.1 Major Planning and Scheduling Activities 50
5.2 Maintenance Investment Road Map 51
5.3 The Tradeoff, Maintenance Effort and Commitment Versus Operating Results 52
5.4 Standard Maintenance Work Order 56
5.5 Daily Individual Maintenance Report 58
6.1 A Two-stage Screening Process 69
7.1 Master Equipment List 77
7.2 Georgia Sawmill Downtime Summary 78
7.3 Georgia Sawmill Downtime Summary for a Specified Area of the Mill 79
7.4 Cost/Benefit Curve for CAM Portion of TM Program 82
8.1 Troubleshooting Outline 88
9.1 Unsafe Acts That Cause Lost Workday Cases and Restricted Workday Cases 97
9.2 Lockout Procedures 98
9.3 Cutting and Welding Permit 99
9.4 Vehicle Operator's Checklist 101
9.5 Equipment Safety Analysis Example 104

10.1   Tools and Testing Modes   112
10.2   A Two-stage Screening Process   113
11.1   A Typical Accelerometer   118
11.2   A Typical Velocity Pump   120
11.3   A Typical Non-contact Probe System   121
11.4   Laser Shaft Alignment System   126
12.1   Oscilloscope Display on Test Instrument   133
14.1   Machine or System Card   153
14.2   Simplified Cost Accumulation/Tracking   154
14.3   Newburg Lumber Manufacturing Expense Recap   155
15.1   Maintenance Budgeting and Forecasting   161
16.1   Mobile Equipment Replacement Schedule   165
16.2   Mobile Equipment Maintenance Schedule Board   167
16.3   Mobile Equipment Repair/Cost Form   168
16.4   Mobile Equipment Monthly Repair and Cost Report   171
17.1   High-efficiency Motors Payback versus Operating Time   184
18.1   Steps to Complete Engineering   191
21.1   Mill Floor Schematic Pneumatic Cylinders and Valves   270
21.2   Spares Listing Pneumatic Cylinders and Valves   272
21.3   Critical Spare Parts: A Definition   274
23.1   Investment versus Future Operating and Maintenance Costs   289

Tables

1.1   Repair and Maintenance Costs Over Three Years for Selected Companies   4
1.2   Cost Trends, Combined Repair and Maintenance Costs for Six Selected Companies   5
1.3   Forest Product Companies Annual Sales, Property and Equipment, and Maintenance Costs   6
13.1   Sawmill Survey   146
13.2   Individual Sawmill Survey   147
17.1   Compressed-air Leakage Costs   179
17.2   Air Intake Temperature versus Compressor Horsepower Requirements   180
17.3   Annual Energy Dollars Saved by Reducing Operating Air Pressures   181
19.1   Chart of Interchangeable Lubricants   197
19.2   Commonly Used Industrial Lubricant Viscosity Ratings   255

Preface

> We think that of all the things we do ... maintenance is one that the industry does least well. ... We harp on it, but we haven't done what we need to do!
>
> TOM BUELL, EEO
> Weldwood of Canada
> October 28, 1987

Equipment and facilities maintenance, with an annual price tag in the billions of dollars, is probably the most talked about and least understood management task. The search for understanding has created a demand for seminars and lectures, and many books and magazine articles have been written on the subject.

Everyone seems to have a different perception of what the maintenance task really is. For some, maintenance activities are little more than a downtime avoidance program or the things an operator does to keep running. For others, maintenance activities are the foundation that gives an operator a competitive edge in productivity, quality, and yield.

This book takes the latter view. Its broad framework is intended to help the reader understand and identify the particulars that will optimize each needed maintenance function. In the 1950s maintenance played a secondary role. It was a simpler task then, and my first acquaintance with it occurred in a large West Coast plywood mill.

There were two whistle-chasers in the department on graveyard shift where I worked as an hourly employee. One millwright carried an assortment of wrenches, vise grips, screwdrivers, and a collection of greasy rags in the two back pockets of his Oshkosh-B'Gosh bib overalls. The front pockets were reserved for personal stuff—snuff cans, cigarette makings, and an assortment of vendor-supplied pads and pencils. A soapstone protruded from the narrow middle pocket on the bib.

The other millwright carried a sledgehammer with a handle about as long as he was short. The sledgehammer worked miracles on straightening out damaged equipment, replacing key stock, or fitting errant sprockets back on a shaft. A pull-along wagon transported other hand tools and a portable welding outfit; these tools were about all that was needed in those days.

Maintenance has changed dramatically since then. To document the needs and changes that have occurred during the intervening years, I interviewed active maintenance management and operator participants. The interviews, conducted over the past three years, range from a canter operator north of Munich, to a sawfiler in Maine, to a maintenance manager in Mobile. I also undertook an extensive literature search, utilizing both published and unpublished sources. (These are predominately North American, although European and Asian information is also included.)

A substantial body of maintenance literature directed to other industries applies equally well to the forest products industry. As manufacturing operations increasingly come to depend on high-tech mechanical systems and computerized controls, the various manufacturing industries now share a greater commonality among maintenance tasks. The cost and complexity of the maintenance task continues to grow as each industry adopts more and more space-age technology.

This text is intended for a broad audience. It will be of particular interest to the supervisor or manager, although the individual machine operators or worker will also find specific items to be pertinent. The owner or senior manager can use this book as a tool for understanding a costly and complex portion of the business. A college student will find it useful in preparing for manufacturing management.

The book is organized into six sections. The first, An Overview, traces the evolution from the traditional break it/fix it maintenance effort to the sophisticated technology of today's high-tech mills. This section then identifies the options available and methods that will yield the just right program for a manufacturing operation.

The next section, Managing For Results, describes the planning and goal-setting process. Building and developing an organization, using computers as a manager's program organizer, and implementing an effective feedback method are a few of the topics discussed. I believe that an effective maintenance program is not attainable without an equally effective safety and loss prevention effort, and these methods are also covered.

The third section, Predictive Maintenance, describes both time-tested methods and the newest techniques for identifying equipment needs prior to breakdown or the manufacture of substandard components or products. This chapter describes the various techniques and how each is used effectively.

Budgets and cost controls are the topics for the fourth section. Effective cost accounting tools and equally effective spending controls are necessary to obtain the "biggest bang for the maintenance buck." This section provides a cookbook approach to cost accounting and tracking; it also describes the principles and concepts underlying each.

The fifth section, Maintenance Support Systems, contains four chapters. Each chapter describes the when, why, and what to expect from increasingly more diverse and capable industry support services. These services may be selected inside the local organization, within the company, or within the industry. Increasingly, outside sources common to many manufacturing industries are being employed. The role of engineering services is described, as are other technical services. Lubrication support systems, stores and spares control, and vendor selection are among the other topics discussed.

Section six, Worker Participation, focuses on obtaining more from the mill. These chapters discuss organized innovation, involvement, and quality circles, along with typical results achieved with effectively designed and managed programs. These worker participation programs are uniting the efforts of production and maintenance employees in reducing downtime and simplifying the maintenance effort.

I would like to thank those industry leaders, professors, students, and vendors who read and offered constructive criticism and comments on ideas and the various drafts of those ideas. A special thanks to those who responded with information, photographs, and other editorial needs.

I especially appreciate the contribution of Marie Hyde, a secretary and friend. Thanks also to the Miller Freeman Publications staff, including Charles Baake and Brenda Ordonez, for their assistance and encouragement in the publication of this book. Sterling Platt, as always, supported the efforts with ideas, suggestions, criticism, and photographs—not necessarily in that order. Bill Carter, a former Champion International southern regional maintenance manager, and now on the West Coast with another company, was a sounding board for the original ideas for the book.

Paul Everett, the manager of an employee participation program within Simpson Timber Company and a longtime friend, offered sound ideas and intriguing concepts. Bill Craig, Champion's engineering/mill services manager for Wood Products Eastern Manufacturing, contributed generally, and also offered specific recommendations and technical expertise for sections three and five. John Noffsinger, another Champion, provided additional ideas and assisted with the literature search. John Noonan, John Callas, and Mike Slover provided recommendations for the treatment and materiality of section four. Peggy Barrow was also instrumental in preparing the manuscript.

The patience and support of Betty Baldwin and all eight of the Baldwin family was required to complete this work. I hope this book will be a contribution to an industry that is seeking more efficient mills and lower costs.

Dick Baldwin
Marysville, California
March, 1989

PART ONE

AN OVERVIEW

CHAPTER 1

The Industry Heritage and Changing Needs

The forest products industry is changing, and the change has been dramatic. Credit-sensitive industries such as housing took a terrible beating during the first several years of the 1980s. In response Charles W. Bingham, executive vice president of Weyerhaeuser, concluded, "The medicine that has been forced upon [the forest products industry] is strong indeed and we have reacted to it accordingly."

High interest rates and a tight money supply were used as fiscal antidotes for the nation's monetary and economic ills. As a result housing, which was hitting a robust 2 million starts in 1979, plunged to a meager 900,000 in 1982.

By 1983 industry business conditions had deteriorated so badly that logging and lumbering operations were listed by the Small Business Administration as one of the top four business categories most likely to fail. The resulting failure rate was 207.3 per 10,000 firms versus 39.7 for drugstores and 10.9 for funeral services and crematories. Even structural board plants and paper mills were no strangers to curtailments and closures. Reducing manufacturing costs and particularly maintenance costs were increasingly used as techniques to buck the trend.

Improved Maintenance Equals Lower Costs

Two large companies, International Paper and Weyerhaeuser, have recognized maintenance as a key partner in lowering manufacturing costs. According to the company's coordinator of maintenance services, International Paper began early.

> In the mid-1950s, an evolution was taking place in the paper industry in the development of new paper and paperboard grades that would create markets for industry products. This was necessary in a market economy

to insure survival in the competitive years ahead. During this period of development, maintenance costs were of secondary importance... During the late 1950s and the early 1960s another evolution was taking shape; the generation of 'cost awareness' by manufacturing management.

They began looking at the various items that made up the total manufacturing cost, and evaluating the contribution each was making to the performance of the mill in terms of keeping the mill products competitive. Maintenance came under close scrutiny because this function directly affected the availability and efficiency of the equipment. (Caldwell, 1977, 146)

International Paper has achieved lower maintenance costs compared with similar companies in the industry. Table 1.1 is a graphic illustration. This table identifies the total maintenance costs for a recent three-year period; it then expresses the ratio of these maintenance costs to the average stated value for plant, property, and equipment for the same time period. International Paper has a high ratio, indicating appropriately lower maintenance costs.

Weyerhaeuser has also recognized improved maintenance as a way to improve costs: "We want to marry maintenance and production... to break down barriers between the two groups until we totally blur turf lines and get individuals to think of themselves as people offering complementary skills, which are all needed to keep units running smoothly," explained a Weyerhaeuser executive (Brusslan, 1984, 36).

Table 1.1 *Repair and Maintenance Costs Over Three Years for Selected Companies ($ millions)*

Company	Costs	Ratio[1]
Boise Cascade	732	3.8
Champion International	1,045	4.0
Georgia Pacific	1,031	4.1
International Paper	888	6.2
Louisiana Pacific	268	4.6
Weyerhaeuser	1,242	4.9
Total	5,206	4.6[2]

[1] Ratio of total three-year repair and maintenance costs compared to stated average value of plant, property, and equipment.
[2] Weighted average six companies.

Source: Respective Company Form 10K for years 1983–1985

Weyerhaeuser's intention to break down the traditional barriers between production and maintenance makes cost cutting difficult. Gene Mayers, a Weyerhaeuser senior manager, later told me that "In order to capture the opportunities inherent in improved maintenance we've got to quit looking at maintenance as fixing things when they get broken and see it as a specific part of production . . . a team approach is needed."

The Cost

Today's cost to build, equip, and maintain a mill can be mind-boggling. It is not uncommon for a state-of-the-art paper mill to cost a billion dollars or more as a greenfield project. It is equally common for a new sawmill to cost 30 million dollars, and a structural board plant to cost that or more. A substantial portion of those costs are due to the specialized nature of the process, the sophisticated equipment that is needed, and the ever more stringent environmental demands placed on the newer facilities.

A mill's annual maintenance bill may be from six percent to ten percent of the current replacement cost. And unless a cost-containment program is undertaken these costs mushroom higher each year. Table 1.2 is an illustration.

Table 1.2 *Cost Trends, Combined Repair and Maintenance Costs for Six Selected Companies ($ millions)*

Year	Cost
1983	1,651
1984	1,769
1985	1,786

Source: Company Form 10K for years 1983–1985 (for the six companies cited in Table 1.1)

The total costs for the six selected companies identified in table 1.1 were tallied. Even with major cost-containment efforts by two or more companies, the total dollar amount had grown 8.2 percent in two years over the 1983 base period. In addition the total three-year maintenance cost for the combined six companies was as high or higher than the average annual sales for four of the six. An analysis of the 10K, an annual financial report, provides a key to the combined costs for an individual firm.

Table 1.3 Forest Product Companies Annual Sales, Property and Equipment, and Maintenance Costs Based on Form 10K Report

Company	Annual Net Sales ($ millions) 1983	1984	1985	Property and Equipment[1] ($ millions) 1983	1984	1985	Maintenance and Repair[2] ($ millions) 1983	1984	1985	Maintenance and Repair of Property and Equipment (%) 1983	1984	1985
Boise Cascade	3,451	3,817	3,737	2,399	2,950	3,043	221	241	270	9.2	8.2	8.9
Champion	4,264	5,121	5,770	3,312	4,781	4,314	291	338	416	8.8	7.1	9.6
Georgia Pacific	6,040	6,682	6,716	3,822	4,272	4,741	331	356	344	8.7	8.3	7.3
International Paper	4,367	4,716	4,500	5,129	5,402	6,005	290	309	289	5.7	5.7	4.8
Louisiana Pacific	1,102	1,230	1,261	1,029	1,157	1,220	78	91	99	7.6	7.9	8.1
Potlatch	904	994	950	1,088	1,104	1,153	80	84	88	7.4	7.6	7.6
Union Camp	1,687	1,974	1,800	2,511	2,783	2,986	116	141	144	4.6	5.1	4.8
Weyerhaeuser	4,883	5,550	5,206	5,904	6,107	6,217	419	434	389	7.1	7.1	6.3
Willamette	1,046	1,182	1,152	744	745	822	NA	NA	NA[3]	NA	NA	NA

[1] Gross cost when acquiring asset; is not net book value; excludes timber and timberlands.
[2] Includes expenditures to restore assets to fit condition upon breakdown (repairs); and expenditures to maintain assets in fit condition to perform their work (maintenance) when expenditures are ordinary and recurring.
[3] Maintenance and repair information not reported on 10K.

Source: Company Form 10K for years 1983–1985

For example, in 1983 Weyerhaeuser spent nearly 400 million dollars on its total maintenance spending (see table 1.3) (that is, everything the company reportedly spent for the cited year). Georgia Pacific spent nearly 350 million dollars; Union Camp, a much smaller corporation, spent 100 million dollars; and other companies reported costs to be over 100 million dollars.

Effective maintenance only comes with the full involvement of the company, the mill, and the traditionally separated mill functions. Statistics show that even in a well-run manufacturing operation less than 50 percent of the maintenance cost and activity is directly controlled by the maintenance department. Major functions with control over or impact on the other 50 percent are production, purchasing, accounting, and engineering. Within each corporation the individual and combined costs are high and getting higher. And because of the competitive nature of the forest products business the producer cannot assume that higher product prices will cover the cost increases; the manager's task is to get more with less maintenance dollars in order to survive.

The Changing Expectations of the Effort

Controlling and reducing maintenance costs while getting more from the mill requires greater knowledge, initiative, and different skills for accomplishing the maintenance task. The manager's task is to figure out how to get the most from the equipment and his people resource.

According to George H. Kuper, who heads the Manufacturing Studies Board, a research arm of the National Academy of Sciences, "Many managers are reluctant to run the kind of social revolution at work that is needed to make technology pay for itself" (Naisbitt, 1986, 71).

This so-called revolution rejects authoritarian management and narrow craft skill in favor of more open relationships with supervisors as leaders and employees as participants. Thinking, doing, and personal initiative are expected from both maintenance people and their production counterparts. Macmillan Bloedel mill at Powell River, British Columbia, is an example of the benefits.

Management installed a quality-awareness program at this operation to improve production, quality, and maintenance. This mill previously had relied heavily on emergency maintenance, and as a result the maintenance crew was stretched to the limit to keep downtime within control. Jerry Southern, a production supervisor, said, "There's been drastic improvement in the whole operation . . . we have a lot fewer mechanical breakdowns, our kerfs are narrower, and the sizes are much more accurate."

"Since the... program began," commented an edger operator, "there's been a better atmosphere of cooperation between hourly people and management... There's a feeling that we are being taken seriously when we come up with new ideas." These comments were further reinforced by Kevin Kirkham, a millwright. "There's much less of an 'us and them' attitude between the production and maintenance departments now... with the result that the operators are really looking out for mechanical problems and letting us know... Their input is very valuable" (Westergaard, 1986, 27).

The role of the supervisor and worker is changing; authoritarian management and narrow craft skills are being replaced with more open management and broader yet job-specific skills.

Increasingly, managers are finding that an employee's input is valuable; it can be even more valuable when this input is enhanced through the development of added skills and knowledge.

According to futurist John Naisbitt, "The skills to maintain high-technology systems are becoming as important as the creative skills that design the systems. All across the country, buses, planes, utilities, even sewage treatment plants, miracles of modern science, are breaking down and proving unusable because we are unable to provide the companion miracle of modern maintenance" (Naisbitt, 1982, 49).

These added skills are obtained by concerted on-the-job-training by qualified experts, and classroom sessions. Commented a maintenance manager: "It's a struggle to keep up with the new stuff that is being introduced all the time. My knowledge and skills can become obsolete almost overnight if I don't make a conscious effort to ask questions and learn."

The knowledge and skills are not just needed to keep the equipment running, but to have the equipment perform and maintain the available benefits: "Usually the problem with the newer more sophisticated equipment after the initial debugging is not one of uptime but figuring out how to maintain the actual benefits, and the benefits can no longer be easily measured visually or with pocket tools."

These newer systems are maintained properly only when the mill operator and the maintenance personnel:

- recognize that the maintenance function is something more than a task that is learned on weekends as a helper. The maintenance worker now needs extensive training and retraining just to keep up

with the task.
- understand that effective maintenance must be partnership; a partnership that includes the equipment designer, equipment operator, and maintenance person.
- accept the concept that the accuracy of a machine function may be in 0.001 inches rather than fractions. Ongoing audits are necessary; these audits frequently require equally sophisticated measuring devices.

The service manual plays a key role in operating and maintaining these newer systems. First, it documents the correct methods for operating and maintaining the equipment. Second, it catalogs the features of the machine that the operator needs to know to manage the process.

In addition, the service manual is usually written on two levels: the technical level and the management level. The former is intended to explain the technical aspects of operation and maintenance; the latter explains the features and the benefits attainable.

The newer equipment features computers and complex electromechanical components. For example, a stacked cylinder positioner commonly used in numerous mill applications is now being replaced with computerized linear positioners for added accuracy. The former costs several hundred dollars a copy; the latter costs anywhere from eleven hundred to five thousand dollars a copy depending on the end use. The added expense is justified in added accuracy and repeatability, but the cost in parts and attention to detail is significantly higher.

Attention to detail is the way to obtain design performance from sophisticated equipment. Byron Brookhaeuser, a long-time mechanical engineer and noted inventor, commented on the shortcomings of the current maintenance efforts: "Often a well-tuned-up mechanical system will outperform or perform equally as well as the newer computerized systems. The problem is that neither the mechanical systems nor the control subsystems are being properly maintained."

Brookhaeuser reached his conclusion after auditing more than a dozen installations of computerized positioners. In most instances the customer had spent over a million dollars per copy. His audit indicated that a number of the customers were getting little value from the positioner. In fact some were getting so little added value that the new equipment wasn't performing much better than the equipment it replaced. The resulting less-than-optimum performance is often masked by the remarkable dependability built into the design and construction of this type of equipment.

Wanda Maxey of Maxey Electronics tells this story about visiting a sawmill with a potential customer who was looking at trimmer optimizers. The potential customer stepped up to a rough mill man and asked, "How much downtime does this equipment give you?" The mill man responded, "I don't know—I've only been here two years."

Changing Expectations of the Machine

Reducing maintenance costs often means running a mill harder, longer, and more effectively. Frequently, the throughput of a single machine or manufacturing system has doubled or tripled as a result of speedup, tuneups, and the addition of more modern equipment.

For example, "The manufacturer said we could only go to about 200 fpm, we are running consistently at 230 . . . it costs us a gear set every now and then, but look at the benefits," commented Reggie McQueen, Champion International's Camden Lumber manager.

The output of this canter machine was nearly doubled with the increase in the infeed speed and a corresponding decrease in downtime. McQueen went on to say that he was tempted to return to the former mode of operation because of maintenance problems, but he determined that differing throughput rates require different maintenance demands. A bearing, gearset, or transmission system that performs well at one level may be obsolete at another.

A machine or system speedup frequently requires a change in design or an innovative idea when solving a maintenance problem. For example, turning the green veneer clipper knife so that the knife bevel became a veneer shear, and modifying the veneer infeed holddowns, resulted in a feedspeed increase from 320 fpm to 450 fpm.

The task is to identify the need and then shop for a solution. Often the solution may be an innovative idea such as the green clipper example, or it may be a one-of-a-kind prototype that is designed and redesigned in a continuing sequence until the need is satisfied. The subsequent trial and error usually leads to a higher plateau of performance. The higher levels of performance are due to a combination of innovative ideas, a new appreciation for detail, more sophisticated equipment, and a search for a better way to perform the maintenance function.

References

Brusslan, C. 1984. Maintenance Is Serious Business. *Paper Trade Journal* (January): 34–36.
Caldwell, M. H. 1977. Maintenance Management System Saves Mill $1.2 Million Annually. *Pulp & Paper* (February): 146–47.
Lannon, T. 1986. New Technologies Challenge Maintenance Organization—*Plant Engineering* (June 19).
Lerner, M. 1983. A Dead Stick at 23,000 Feet. *Newsweek* (May 16).
Moslemi, A. A. 1986. Strong Medicine for the Forest Industry: Has It Healed the Patient? *Forest Product Journal* 36, no. 5 (May): 9.
Naisbitt, J. 1982. *Megatrends*. New York: Warner Books, 49.
———. 1986. Special Report, Management Discovers The Human Side of Automation. *Business Week* (September 29): 70–80.
———. 1986. Timber Processing. *Newsfeed* (January): 6.
Westergaard, B. 1986. MB's Innovative Quality Program Saves $28 Million in Just Two Years. *Logging & Sawmilling Journal* (February): 25–28.
———. 1979. Plant Maintenance—How to Manage Maintenance for Higher Profits. *Wood & Wood Products* (June).

CHAPTER 2

Defining the Task

The forest products industry is a commodity business with mature markets and relatively low margins. The maintenance effort is an essential function that can be an operator's companion in obtaining the attainable yield from the log or wood furnish, the optimum productivity, and the most and best product from the mill.

The maintenance effort requires substantial planning, control, and follow-up. Unfortunately, too often maintenance programs are unplanned. Studies indicate that such maintenance costs are increasing at a level substantially higher than the rate of inflation.

Nearly twenty years ago John T. Wilkinson commented, "Judging from personal experience with a wide variety of companies, I would estimate that most manufacturing companies today are in a position to reduce their maintenance costs by one-third or more and to improve substantially the level of work productivity" (Wilkinson, 1968, 100). The same holds true today; only the product and the state of the art have changed.

Recent forest industry studies correlate closely with overall industry findings. These studies indicate that 75 percent to 80 percent of all maintenance can be routine, predictable, and planned, but that only about 20 percent to 30 percent was actually planned based on a tally of maintenance man-hours expended. The cyclic nature of the forest products business can make the maintenance task more difficult.

Good years are when we purchase equipment; down years are when we stretch out the wear cycles on rolling stock, structure, utilities, equipment, and related components. The variable business and spending cycles that result make the maintenance task more difficult. Even worse are the common misconceptions about maintenance:

- Maintenance work is different and does not lend itself to planning and controls.
- Maintenance work just can't be measured. Maintenance workers must be allowed to do their work in their own way.

Defining the Task 13

- Maintenance work does not lend itself to method changes; each job is different.
- Every maintenance dollar is a good investment; or the flip side of the coin, every dollar spent on maintenance takes away from the bottom line.
- When the plant is running well and there are no whistles to chase, the plant is being maintained properly.

Each of these has some basis in experience. But each also presumes that a maintenance program should be based on random occurrences such as downtime, rather than uptime based on planned and predictable events.

"Maintenance work can be measured and controlled just as other functions can, and its effectiveness can be improved in a systematic way," stated John T. Wilkinson in a 1968 *Harvard Business Review* article entitled "How to Manage Maintenance." This article and the author's conclusions were later reinforced within a maintenance effectiveness study conducted during 1975 and 1976 by Weyerhaeuser. This study concluded,

> Effective maintenance has several common elements across the forest product industry, whether in pulp paper, lumber, plywood or fiberboard. The basic principles are applicable even in the smallest of operations and provide the base case for these principles. The larger the mill, the more necessary it becomes to formalize the organization and the supportive system. The larger the plant the more difficult it is to achieve effective maintenance. (Schille, 1976)

Managing Maintenance: The Program Elements

Wilkinson's comments and Weyerhaeuser's conclusions reinforce each other: The maintenance task and the work connected with that task can be planned, accomplished, and the results measured just as other functions of the forest products business. The program elements of planning, organizing, leading, and controlling are basic to the maintenance effort. These are outlined in figure 2.1 and further described as follows.

Planning

A successful maintenance planning effort has two prerequisites. The first—top management approval, appreciation, and support—is necessary prior to committing resources. This should be defined in a maintenance mission statement. In addition there should be an agreement on objectives, and tactics and timetables to achieve those objectives for the facility and its component parts.

Figure 2.1 *Managing Maintenance: The Program Elements*

Program Elements	Tactics
Planning	• Establish goals, policies, and procedures. • Identify permissible tolerance and variances. • Seek basic causes for unacceptable deviation. • Determine and schedule corrective action.
Organizing	• Publish maintenance plan and communicate with understanding to each participant. • Marshall the needed resources on a timely basis. • Schedule the right resources to be in the right place at the right time.
Leading	• Implement corrective action within scope and within budget in a timely fashion. • Follow-up during and after the planned and unplanned activities.
Controlling	• Measure equipment performance against established norms or goals. • Provide feedback in terms of the recipient's needs. • Provide information for effective forward planning.

Second, the resulting top management approval and support presumes that an annual budget will be prepared as part of the planning effort. An approval mechanism and the spending parameters should be agreed upon in advance. An occasional multiyear planning effort should also be expected; although short-term updates, usually quarterly, will provide the tactical planning.

These two prerequisites provide the basis for planning. The following four management principles are the underpinning for further planning:

1. The planning and doing activities must be separated, otherwise the doing tasks will always take precedence over the planning effort. Maintenance is often managed as a reactive response to everyday events when the doer is also the planner.
2. A good organization is essential for good performance. The best results occur when each participant has a definite role with specific tasks to accomplish within a definite time frame and in a definite manner.
3. The more narrow and shallow the skill level of the individual maintenance person, the more difficult it is to match the time,

Defining the Task

task, and skill requirement with the available maintenance person.
4. There is direct correlation between the time spent planning and the results achieved. Detailed planning will result in efficient and effective use of man-hours and other resources.

The effective maintenance programs will have accurate performance and condition assessments available for planning. Planning will be further discussed in chapter 4.

Organizing for Results

Organizing is the make-ready step in the maintenance effort. It can be as simple as lining out the work and materials for the upcoming shift activities, or as complex as organizing the major restructuring of the maintenance effort in an entire plant.

Purchase orders are written, commitments from outside contractors or service people are finalized, in-house resources are assigned, and the schedule or plan published. The organizing task is effectively accomplished when unnecessary nonproductive time is held to a minimum — that is, when materials and people are in the right place at the right time with the appropriate resources as the maintenance plan unfolds. Symptoms of a poorly organized plan include unnecessary travel time to the job, a millwright chasing tools or parts during the job, or make-ready activities such as cleanup being done by a skilled craftsman after the machine is offline and available.

Leading

Planning and organizing provides the foundation for the do-it activities; leading is the task that translates these earlier efforts into results. Leading encompasses the activities that allow the planned maintenance tasks to be completed on time, within budget, and with the intended scope.

Ideally, changes will be anticipated as the work is opened up, with contingency plans implemented in a timely fashion. The leadership activities should not be reserved for one or two supervisors or an engineer. This function should be built into each participant's role with accountability and authority equal to the task.

Controlling

Controlling, the fourth program element, encompasses the other three. This element covers the before, during, and after time frame for the

maintenance activities. It includes such jobs as measuring performance to established guidelines, providing feedback on machine performance, and determining the success of current maintenance projects.

Controlling specifics may include ongoing documentation of maintenance and downtime at a machine center, physical measurements of a machine component or process device, and auditing of lubrication checklists achieved. A well-laid-out control system, coupled with planning and do-it activities, will transform uptime and downtime into planned events rather than random occurrences.

The Maintenance Program

Maintenance programs vary from the simple to complex; each has particular attributes and each generally represents discrete points on a continuum of maintenance practices. This continuum ranges from the break-it/fix-it tactics so common in many mills to the more complex optimization methods which comprise the total maintenance program (TM). Programs that use preventive and predictive maintenance are situated somewhere in between.

These programs, from least effective to most effective, are break it/fix it, preventive maintenance, predictive maintenance, and total maintenance. The benefits of each are illustrated in figure 2.2. Out-of-pocket maintenance costs are reduced as the operator moves toward the total pro-

Defining the Task

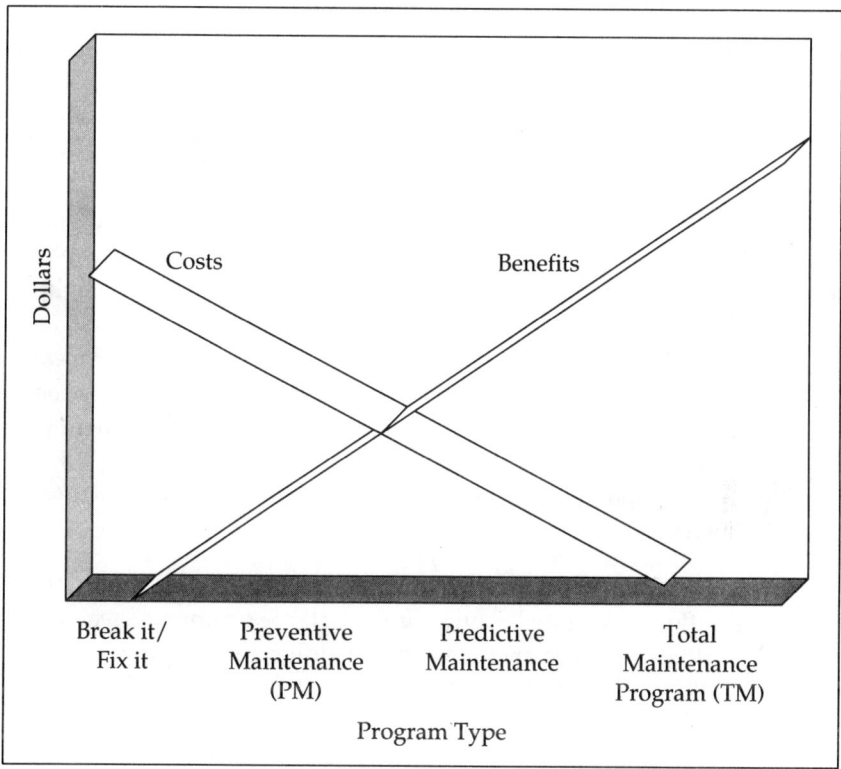

Figure 2.2   Maintenance Program Costs and Benefits

gram; the tangible and intangible benefits increase in direct proportion to the effort made to move away from the break-it/fix-it activities.

Break It/Fix It

Maintenance is often done as a reactive response to everyday events. Few records are kept; planning becomes little more than a questioning attitude, which is usually reinforced by the latest in a continuing stream of breakdowns. The mill worker then asks, "What can I expect to break down next?" The answer is usually not long in coming. One southern sawmill offered a prime example.

Four broken or worn-out pillow block bearings – the newest two of the four still retained the stick-on stocking label – were scattered adjacent to an identical bearing currently in service. Close examination revealed a well-greased replacement, but silver-colored fine metal filings were evident. Further examination revealed that the cause was a misalignment of the drive sprockets and bearings.

An operator's first reaction would be, "How come the mill allowed such dumb millwrights to work the floor?" The answer in this mill provided a lesson for others: The available maintenance personnel, including their supervisor, had gotten locked into a system of "breakdown hopscotch." The ongoing effort to keep the mill running no longer allowed time to determine the cause, just to repair the systems.

This costly system has many variations, which occur too frequently. Another was described by a maintenance supervisor in a structural board plant: "We grease it and run it until it quits, then hope we or our neighbor plant has the right parts to fix it."

Another operator further stated, "We witness the lift truck or pickup that stays in service and then incur higher and higher maintenance costs. We are presently trapped with the fact that every piece of equipment that stays in the mill must be maintained."

How do the operators and their people cope? There are three ways, each very expensive:

1. Periodically replace the equipment or restore to a like new condition after downtime becomes unacceptable or unmanageable.
2. Use the mechanics axiom as an overriding philosophy:
    When in doubt
    Make it stout
    Out of something
    You know about (Bloch and Geitner, 1983, 6)
   This axiom fails to include something about who pays the bills for the extra "stout"; the ongoing costs can be prohibitive.
3. Build a highly reliable system using redundant or second systems wherever possible. Expensive high-reliability components are included.

Each of the three will minimize breakdowns, and indeed each of the three has merit in the correct situation. Unfortunately, too often a mill will evolve into each by way of mill floor decisions made under pressure. When the mill manager balks at the resulting costs, the usual response is, "We have got to spend money to keep the mill running, so do you want it to go back to the way it was?"

Preventive Maintenance (PM)

Preventive maintenance is like virtue: Most folks insist that they have it, but the observer is sometimes hard pressed to figure out the who, what, and where. A kinder observation was offered in a recent publication: "In many plants, a carefully structured and monitored preventive maintenance (PM) program has yet to become standard practice, although more than likely preventive maintenance exists in some form" (Singh and Allen, 1986, 46).

The objective of a preventive maintenance program is to reduce costs and stop functional failure through systematic inspection and lubrication, repair and replacement of components prior to a breakdown or failure, and establishing correct maintenance and operating practices. Equipment checklists, sophisticated lubrication schedules, work orders, and equipment histories are some of the preventive maintenance tools used.

Although a preventive maintenance program focuses on cost and downtime reduction, the operator making the transition from the break-it/fix-it mode may notice an initial increase in both. During this transition period the operator may be tempted to revert to a simpler program and may even be encouraged to do so by the production results obtained or the complaints of excess paperwork by the crew.

The resulting complaints are usually accompanied by the admonition, "We don't have time to keep the mill running if we do all that!" Within recent years a variety of computer-assisted maintenance (CAM) software has been used to simplify the preventive maintenance task and reduce the time needed to trace a preventive maintenance program. (CAM and the software used is described in chapter 6.) A well-managed preventive maintenance program will have the following advantages:

- A gradual decrease in overall maintenance costs, first man-hours and then material costs. Cost savings of 15 percent to 30 percent and more are attainable.
- Fewer large repairs and a lower frequency of unscheduled downtime occurrences.
- Fewer dollars tied up in inventory; delivery cost premiums such as so called hot-shot deliveries are minimized. Overall there is a more cost effective management of materials and parts inventories.
- More useful equipment records, which identify when a machine or component has reached the end of its economic life. Replacement can be scheduled as a budgeted expenditure.
- Improved data and cost collection resulting in improved budgeting and forecasting. Management credibility is improved.
- Senior management discovers that maintenance is a controllable cost and is not a mysterious black hole into which potential profits are sucked.

Overall, the morale of both the maintenance and manufacturing personnel is improved as management attention is more closely focused on improving the overall business rather than the task of just keeping the mill running.

Predictive Maintenance

The inspection function—touched on in the description of break-it/fix-it maintenance, and more fully developed within a preventive maintenance program—is further enhanced with predictive maintenance. Predictive maintenance focuses on reducing maintenance costs and increasing uptime, but also has an important by-product: the auditing of tolerances related to quality and process requirements.

Vibration meters, heat sensors, contaminant monitors, and similar devices are used at predetermined times and places to audit ongoing equipment operation. (The tactics and tools used are more fully described in chapters 10, 11, and 12.)

Total Maintenance (TM)

Total maintenance (TM) takes the best from the programs described earlier and molds each into a program that not only maximizes maintenance costs and downtime but enhances the overall mission of the mill and business. Equipment, materials, parts, and job functions are each identified with the company's mission. Machines and processes must then not only run efficiently but must contribute to the quality requirements and other goals of the business.

The emphasis shifts from a downtime and cost-control program to a proactive program designed to prevent opportunity losses and gain additional benefits. A distinct maintenance function remains, however; the maintenance effort becomes a team effort with each line and staff participant having a role to play. The result is a clear demarcation of who does what, but a blurred distinction between maintenance and operations.

The following are common features of a functioning total maintenance program:

- A clean mill with low downtime and high worker productivity that produces quality products at relatively low costs.
- An operating manager with maintenance appreciation who exerts leadership within a participative management framework.
- A well-developed questioning attitude throughout the organization. Effective communication and cooperation is a norm between production and maintenance personnel. Complaints and an adversarial attitude are largely eliminated.

A recent in-house unpublished study of a large forest products company said this about the introduction of a total maintenance program: "Ideally, effective maintenance will have the correct economic balance between maintenance costs and equipment . . . this happens only by the actions and decisions of effective people having adequate supportive resources (reporting systems and controls) tailored to the particular needs of a particular plant."

This quote simply describes the task for the operator seeking to survive and compete in today's business environment; and that's the mission of this chapter and the ones that follow.

References

Bloch, H. and F. K. Geitner. 1983. *Practical Machinery Management for Process Plants.* Houston: Gulf Publishing.

Coleman, M. 1980. *Maintenance Methods for the Pulp and Paper Industry.* San Francisco: Miller Freeman.

Criswell, J. W. 1983. *Planned Maintenance for Productivity and Energy Conservation.* Atlanta: The Fairmont Press.

Dhillon, B. S. 1983. *Reliability Engineering in System Design and Operation.* New York: Van Nostrand Reinhold.

Herbaty, F. 1983. *Cost-Effective Maintenance Management, Productivity Improvement and Downtime Reduction.* Park Ridge, NJ: Noyes Publications.

Hicho, M. D. 1986. *Six Steps to Reducing Machinery Maintenance Costs.* Vitec, Inc.

Higgo, M. 1985. Managed Maintenance. You Can't Have One Without the Other. Forest Industry 1985 Clinic and Machinery Show.

———. 1984. Focus. The Mission Statement; Chapter for Successful Maintenance Performance. *Weyerhaeuser Maintenance Journal* 3 (March-April).

Singh, J. B. and R. M. Allen. 1986. Establishing a Preventive Maintenance Program. *Plant Engineering* (February 27): 46.

Wilkinson, J. T. 1968. How to Manage Maintenance. *Harvard Business Review* (March–April): 100.

CHAPTER 3

Creating and Sustaining an Effective Program

"Too much money being spent with too few results" is an apt description of many current maintenance programs. The goal is to do better, the task is to get started and to move along in a purposeful fashion. This may be the toughest challenge: getting started, moving along, and doing better.

According to one author, "Because the potential for maintenance improvement is recognized, many efforts have been made to optimize maintenance cost, but usually without much success. The reason is that usually one element of maintenance performance is addressed at a time, rather than the total function" (Pierce, 1986, 101).

The more successful programs address all elements of the total function. The management method for establishing such a program will recognize the individuality of each location but will use common techniques for creating the results. Figure 3.1 outlines the required steps for creating the results. These steps are described throughout this chapter.

Getting Started

Communicating a commitment, creating a sense of purpose, and making resources available is the function of senior management. Understanding the changes and adjustments that will be required is also included in that function. These individuals, who will create the program and make it work, must also share that commitment and sense of purpose.

Decisions will be based on the premise; help is defined in the terms of the recipient. The recipient is the selected manufacturing facility or department. Help can be corporate or division assistance, local leadership with the necessary background and skills, or outside consultants.

The outside consultant's role can be active or passive; an active role will create, install, and maintain a program. In a passive program the outside consultants act as coaches and advisors to local management. Each approach and variation of those extremes has been used successfully in a variety of situations. The option selected will be the preference of the company and the background and skills of the personnel at the selected location.

Weyerhaeuser is an example of one approach. Six experienced staff members—engineers, computer application experts, powerhouse specialists, and others—were formed into a full-time maintenance support group in February 1983. The group, supported in principle and fact by senior management, helped local management set up systems, advised on questions of maintenance, assessed skills and training needs, helped measure local maintenance performance, represented maintenance functions to corporate decision makers, and also became a clearinghouse for information. "We're taking maintenance seriously, real seriously, much more than in the past. A measure of the first year's progress is heightened awareness of the need to handle maintenance in less traditional ways," cited an original team member.

Figure 3.1 *Total Maintenance: The Planning and Implementation Steps*

Getting Started	• Establish senior management support. • Select an implementor, such as a consultant. • Identify an implementation approach. • Evaluate the selected location's organizational strengths and weaknesses.
The Mission Statement	• Organize the task group. • Draft the mission statement. • Obtain senior management concurrence.
Establishing Objectives	• Continue work of task group. • Identify objectives that correlate with the mission statement.
Facility Assessment	• Audit the selected location in relation to the objective statements. • Identify specific areas of opportunity. • Obtain local management commitment.
Implement Results	• Select tasks to implement. • Prioritize, identify resources, and establish time frames. • Implement the selected projects. • Follow-up through established controls.

Burlington Industries, a textile manufacturer in a highly competitive world industry, is another example. This company, with eighty-five plants, the majority located in North Carolina, also used a corporate group to get effective programs in place. A maintenance committee was formed in April 1983 under the direction of senior management. Composed of senior operation managers from the corporate level and the plants, it was charged with upgrading Burlington's maintenance function. The committee, assisted by an in-house consultant, provided two functions: the leadership to install local programs, and an interface with senior management.

A Japanese manufacturer has an even more pervasive resource help available. An industry trade organization, the Japan Institute of Plant Maintenance (JIPM), will set up a program upon a member's request and then make regular follow-up visits to assure that the implementation plan is on schedule and that the expected results are being achieved. Each maintenance consultant benefits from continued training; the consultant spends an average of one week a month updating and learning management skills to assure that the manufacturer is benefiting from the latest and best technology in managing maintenance.

The individual forest products manufacturer may not have access to a corporate assistance group like those at Weyerhaeuser and Burlington, or to a trade organization like JIPM. The skills and resources must then come from qualified outside consultants who are available in most producing regions. These consultants will provide tailormade programs at turnkey installations, or advice and counsel to those locations capable of installing a program on their own. An interested manufacturer should seek presentations from several, and then select the one that best answers the needs of the location.

Answering the maintenance management needs of a particular location will require more than just a qualified outside consultant and senior management support, however; the location manager is the key. What's needed is an involved, supportive management atmosphere, with technically trained and committed personnel. The location manager must be able to communicate the benefits that an improved maintenance program can provide, and then develop the commitment within the organization to move in that direction.

The location manager in smaller locations, and the maintenance manager or plant engineer supported by the location manager in the larger locations, must each have the following attributes:

- Business oriented, cost effective not just cost conscious, and aware of the bottom line.
- Technically competent, knows the basics of maintenance and the requirements for getting a job done.
- Personally involved, with hands-on participation as required.
- Well-developed appreciation for reporting and control; prepared to follow up and have audits performed as tools to measure the successes achieved.
- Ability to develop people, doesn't carry the whole load, and delegates activities and accountability effectively.

These attributes are essential to the initial and continuing success of a total maintenance (TM) program. The strengths of the local organization, the commitment of senior management, and the availability of a maintenance management resource group provides the foundation for the activities that follow.

The Mission Statement

No single maintenance program definition can fit all situations. Ideally, each maintenance program will have the correct economic balance between costs and equipment performance. The balance only occurs as a result of decisions and actions taken by effective people; the basis is the mission statement.

Each mission statement should be tailored to the particular plant. It must consider business strategies, people skills, and program expectations. This uniqueness should be further defined in terms of technical complexity of the manufacturing process, size of the operation, capital intensity of the investment, and geographic location as related to outside support services.

The team that will write both the mission statement and the objectives should consist of both staff and line members, inside and outside specialists, and maintenance and nonmaintenance personnel. The location manager, the production superintendent, the maintenance manager, purchasing manager, and other local specialists should be included. The team will meet to draft the mission statement and the companion objectives; the resulting discussions also establish the individual roles of both the maintenance and nonmaintenance team members.

"Given the nature of our particular operation, what should be the mission of the maintenance department?" This question will prompt and guide the group. The discussion leader, usually the operation manager or staff specialist, should appoint someone to take notes so that he or she is allowed to interact with the participants and guide the discussions. No single individual should be allowed to dominate the exchange of ideas.

The ideas should be free flowing; each sentence in the final draft of the mission statement should be developed as a result of lengthy discussions and a final consensus agreement. The resulting consensus agreement becomes a recommendation to be further reviewed with the senior manager at that location (if he or she is not a party to the discussions) as well as senior management. The statement will address equipment maintenance; it will also address safety, operating performance, uptime, quality, and other maintenance-related issues.

Figure 3.2 is an example mission statement developed by a West Coast company. This mission statement is brief, just four sentences. Each sentence is broad enough to cover the areas to be addressed, yet specific enough to allow for the development of more detailed and measurable objectives. The mission statement should:

Creating and Sustaining an Effective Program

- provide a consistent direction for the maintenance program
- serve as a statement of agreement and understanding
- flow logically into the objective statements
- become a resource document for each year's profit planning.

The mission statement should be revised or amended only after a real need has been identified. This usually occurs because of significantly changed conditions. The most careful deliberation, ideally with the original participants, should precede any changes.

Establishing Objectives

The objective statements flow from further discussions as the mission statement authors continue their assigned task. Each objective becomes a follow-through step and should be sufficiently detailed to be measurable.

The statements should detail objectives that can improve profitability and results. If the list is short it could be included in the mission statement. The following key questions will provide the basis for preparation of the individual objective statements:

- How is the mission statement to be achieved? (the tasks)
- What are the objectives of the maintenance function within a given time period? (the fiscal year, for example)
- What are the measurements to be used to judge how each is carried out?

Each objective statement should be evaluated carefully to ascertain that each fits under the umbrella of the mission statement. Each objective

Figure 3.2 *Mission Statement*

The primary objective of maintenance is to maintain equipment as designed in a safe, effective, operating condition to ensure that production targets are met economically and on time. Maintenance will also support project work as required. In addition, maintenance will maintain buildings and facilities and provide support services such as boiler or compressor operation. Maintenance will also ensure the satisfactory performance on constructural maintenance services.

Date _____

Location _____

may address one or more of the five basic categories of maintenance needs:

1. Machine centers: headrigs, paper machines, forming lines, and so on.
2. Transfer stations: log decks, load conveyors, and so on.
3. Process systems: chip conveyors, pneumatic dust systems, compressed air, and so on.
4. Basic facilities: buildings, grounds, utilities, and so on.
5. Rolling stock: log loaders, forklifts, trucks, and so on.

These basic maintenance categories can be further detailed as follows: planned routine maintenance, daily breakdowns (including poor sizes or undetected worn-out components), and abuse of equipment (that is, using equipment in excess of design limitations, careless handling, or unsuitable use).

The following example objective statements fit within the framework of the mission statement and detailed maintenance needs (see figure 3.3):

- Set up an engineered lubrication program.
- Begin using a work order system.
- Establish and improve downtime and performance tracking systems.
- Involve machine operators in maintaining their equipment.

The identified objectives along with the mission statement then become a basis for a mill assessment, which will determine the specific tasks to accomplish. The assessment process will also be the basis for selecting priorities and required completion times.

Facility Assessment

The next step is to prepare an assessment of current conditions. A traditional method is to have a third-party team, either a consultant or corporate task team, make an on-site evaluation and then report current conditions. The recommended steps to achieve the planned objectives are also detailed. This assessment activity may be conducted periodically as the need is identified.

Union Carbide uses a team of three or four senior maintenance people to conduct a survey over three to four days at the selected facility. This team reviews the operation of the location's maintenance department; the team also reviews the procedures and activities of other departments that service or affect the maintenance effort. The survey scope includes the following:

Creating and Sustaining an Effective Program 29

Figure 3.3 *Objective Statement*

What	Who	By When
Set up an engineered lubrication program.	Lee Smith, Maintenance Superintendent	March 31, 1990
Begin using a work order system.	Wes Alden, Maintenance Planner	May 15, 1990
Establish and improve downtime and performance tracking systems.	Bill Brown, Maintenance Coordinator	July 31, 1990
Involve machine operators in maintaining their equipment.	Sam Woods, Production Superintendent	Sept. 15, 1990

Date _____

Location _____

- organization, personnel, interdepartmental relationships
- workload, planning effort, and the scheduling activity
- preventive, predictive, corrective maintenance
- purchasing and stores
- plant engineering and contracting
- cost-control efforts.

The Union Carbide team begins the survey by initiating discussions with the location's management to develop specific areas of concern. Next maintenance supervisors and technical personnel complete a questionnaire concerning their perspective on current maintenance activities.

Group meetings with selected plant personnel further assist in evaluating the comments and concerns developed during earlier discussions. Thirty to forty individual interviews then follow to provide additional input. Job-site interviews and inspections complete the survey.

Team members conduct an exit interview with the plant management to discuss the findings, clarify issues, and resolve questions. They issue a final written report within two weeks, which is then used as the basis for establishing an action plan that documents the specific improvement goals and activities.

Some other companies use a self-assessment questionnaire that is filled out by a cross-section of the location's personnel. Each individual questionnaire takes about four hours to complete. They are then evaluated by a maintenance support group. A comprehensive evaluation and recommended corrective activities are forwarded back to the location within ten days. This self-assessment tool has been tested against the traditional evaluation methods with a reported high degree of correlation.

The goal of both the outside group and the formal or informal self-assessment is to:
- examine the location with a questioning attitude
- evaluate the results against the attainable
- provide a benchmark for assessing improvement
- document the specific opportunities that will provide the first steps toward planned objectives
- allocate limited resources and recognize obstacles to be considered in planning and implementation.

The resulting facility assessment then becomes a working document to establish the location's version of a total maintenance program.

Implementing Results

The implementation schedule should be based on manageable chunks once the assessment is completed and the specific tasks are identified. It is tempting to try to accomplish the tasks quickly, but the risk is failure, lost momentum, and wasted resources.

Only a few critical activities should be implemented initially, as the organization and its resources are tested. The number will increase as the mill achieves successes and increases project capability.

The operator should avoid the common failures that result when managers institute corrective programs without providing adequate maintenance control systems such as reports, on-site audits, and effective follow-up supervision. The task is to get started, use resources wisely, measure results, and move along with a sense of purpose.

References

Pierce, F. R. 1986. Maintenance: Do More with Less. *Hydrocarbon Processing* (June 1986): 101.

———. 1986. Profile: Japan Institute of Plant Maintenance. *Plant Engineering* (June 12).

Schille, W. L. 1976. *Maintenance Effectiveness Study*. Weyerhaeuser (October).

Singh, J. B. and R. M. Allen. 1986. Establishing a Preventive Maintenance Program. *Plant Engineering* (February 27).

Uskavitch, S. 1984. Maintenance Management. *Timber Harvesting* (July).

Wilkinson, J. J. 1968. How to Manage Maintenance. *Harvard Business Review* (March–April): 100–111.

CHAPTER 4

Building and Developing an Organization

Building and developing a maintenance organization has never been easy; and it is becoming increasingly complex as new manufacturing technologies are introduced and plant automation trends continue. The maintenance tasks are different, the needs are greater, and the expectations of what a maintenance program should do has changed. And then there are the participants: the people who make the program work.

The People Ingredient

Total maintenance (TM) requires the participation of both production and maintenance personnel. Each has a role to play. Purchasing, accounting engineering, and other specialized staff services are playing an increasingly participative role in the maintenance process. In addition, outside participants supplement the effort when completing specialized one-time assignments smoothing out the peaks of a periodic maintenance overload.

The required maintenance skills, broader yet more specialized, are transforming predictable craft-oriented career paths into lifelong assignments where flexibility in doing tasks and a desire to learn are necessary prerequisites. Apprenticeship programs have become an introduction to a lifetime of continuous learning and skill upgrading.

Each participant in turn expects and even demands more communication, less supervisory control, and a broader input into how the program functions. The leader's task is to harmonize the sometimes conflicting needs and demands into a maintenance program that will achieve the mission of the business. The resulting maintenance organization, the staffing decisions for that organization, how that staff functions as a team, the when and what of outside assistance, and the ongoing development of the organization and the individuals within the organization are critical issues that need to be faced not once but periodically as the business, its technology, and its scope of activities change over time.

Elements of an Effective Maintenance Organization

Effective maintenance organizations have a number of common features (see figure 4.1). These features are readily apparent whether pulp, paper, lumber, plywood, or reconstituted boards such as the newer oriented strand boards (OSBs) are being manufactured.

Manufacturing Leadership with Strong Maintenance Appreciation

"The most common denominator found in the highly rated plants was the technical and/or a supportive awareness of plant management towards maintenance," cited a 1976 unpublished multicompany report.

Flat Organization Structure

There is a short line of vertical authority. The traditional low ratio of workers to supervisors, which is designed for control and close supervision, is being replaced with improved crew selection, tighter communication, and greater participation and additional training opportunities. Poor performers or those requiring close supervision are systematically weeded out.

Central Shop Deemphasized

Central shops are only used in the larger multiproduct complexes to supply common specialized services such as machine shop work, plumbing, pipe fitting, fire protection, specialized electronic repair, and mobile equipment maintenance. These shops are used as if they were outside

Figure 4.1 *Common Features of an Effective Maintenance Organization*

- manufacturing leadership with strong maintenance appreciation
- a flat and lean organization structure
- central shops deemphasized
- multicraft skills
- formalized rather than standardized methods
- employee involvement and participation in decision making
- coordination with the mission of the firm

contractors and are set up, where possible, as profit rather than cost centers. Each shop is then forced to defend its existence before and after each budget period.

Multicraft Skills

Multicraft skills are sought and developed. Selective hiring, continuous training, and performance incentives are some of the tools offered to obtain and enhance these multicraft skills.

The more successful companies are replacing rigid, narrow maintenance skills with broader ones that serve to motivate workers and enhance operating flexibility.

Formalized versus Standardized Methods

Job content and responsibility is clearly spelled out and enunciated. Tasks such as preventive maintenance checks, lubrication/oiling, and planning activities are formalized; the mechanics of accomplishing a task are not. Tasks and programs are designed to achieve results, not as an end unto themselves. Core values are formalized; the ways to sustain these core values are not formalized unless standardized procedures are required. Flexibility is allowed within the system to achieve results. Innovation and finding the better way is not only tolerated but expected.

Employee Involvement and Participation in Decision Making

There is a results-oriented interface between maintenance and production at the lowest level. "Sound participation is a tough, no-nonsense relationship that places great demands on subordinates through the skillful use of profit, cost, or production center concepts, performance evaluation systems, financial incentives, and other means of ensuring accountability," stated a researcher in a management journal. "A sound strategy for implementing participative management should first aim to control performance outcomes effectively, which then permit subordinates greater freedom to employ their discretion" (Cal Management Review, 40).

Commented Gene Meyer of Weyerhaeuser, "As we push decision making downward, we owe it to our operators to give them the resources they need... we can only upgrade the efficiency of our maintenance to the extent people in production understand the needs of maintenance workers and work closely with them. I'm not talking about making each machine center a cottage industry. I'm talking about achieving an optimum blend of operations and maintenance considerations" (Meyer, 1984, 10).

Participation and involvement is most effective and satisfying where individuals understand the parameters of their operating environment and feel that a valid contribution can be made and accepted.

Coordination with the Overall Mission of the Firm

There must be an equitable balance of priorities between production, maintenance, and other considerations. According to John Teresko in *Industry Week*, "Most companies are in the dark about the relation between business strategy and maintenance."

He went on to quote maintenance consultant Michael E. Mora of A. T. Kearney, Inc.: "The goal is not in technological achievement, but rather in the business purpose of becoming the least-cost producer in a defined market. That means the presence of a successful maintenance philosophy and practices. This is the only road to business success" (Teresko, 1987, 41, 42).

Benefits

The obvious benefits of these common features grow over time. This is clear in the results of other industries, which appear to be ahead of the forest products industry in designing and shaping the maintenance function. For example, "At some IBM plants, the workers on the lines are even responsible for doing their own maintenance, while the new layouts were motivated by the company's desire to speed the production cycle and reduce work-in-process inventory, the arrangement gives accountants a clearer picture of which costs are associated with which products" (Worthy, 1987, 50).

Maintenance becomes a tool both to lower and accurately track the resulting manufacturing costs. That's a competitive edge for IBM, and a way of thinking that offers exciting possibilities for the forest products producer.

Organizational Renewal

Good maintenance performance is the result of a well-thought-out organizational structure designed to use people effectively. People doing the right thing at the right time becomes a planned and rehearsed event rather than a chance occurrence. Maintenance programs designed to upgrade the maintenance effort can only be implemented and sustained within an organizational structure that is just right. Here's an example of one such successful program:

"Equipment reliability is a maintenance program involving the operators, line supervision, maintenance, engineering, and purchasing," stated Charles E. Geisel, industrial engineering manager for Container Corporation of America (CCA) (Geisel, 1985, 136). "Under this system, the operators and operating departments are responsible for the care and upkeep of their equipment. Maintenance personnel repair, modify, and make detailed inspections of the equipment."

The lines of responsibility, the authority to take action, and the duties assigned are defined within the framework of the CCA organization. This in turn insures the success of the program. These are three primary considerations in the redesign and renewal of an organization. These considerations include the scope of the organization structure used to take care of the first two.

The scope of the maintenance function is divided into primary and secondary functions; each is further categorized into further definable parts.

Primary functions may include all or part of the following:

- existing equipment maintenance
- inspection and lubrication of equipment
- equipment renovation and modification
- new equipment installation

Secondary functions may include such diverse activities as loss prevention and control—for example, the upkeep of the fire system; environmental compliance to local, state, and federal mandates; storage and salvage of excess or unused components and equipment; and disposal of waste materials. The scope of activity at the primary aluminum reduction plant of Alumax of South Carolina is one example. "Here, equipment not only has to work right, but it has to look right as well. This applies to buildings, vehicles, and grounds. The belief is that people will do a better job and take better care of assets when equipment and facilities are good looking and in good condition" (Piper, 1984, 50).

The maintenance program scope at this Mt. Holly facility encompasses the preservation and upgrading of the total plant asset. Cleanliness and "look right" are recognized as important results that enhance employee attitudes toward the equipment and how it is maintained. The importance of this is not lost on the forest products industry.

"We all know that 'cleanliness is next to godliness,' particularly in wood mills and pulp mills, because our maintenance costs skyrocket rapidly in areas that are not kept clean," emphasizes an observer. This is also true in all sectors of manufacturing, from the block preconditioning area of a softwood plywood plant to the recovery boiler operation within a paper mill complex.

The role of maintenance in the plant or complex is conditioned by the following:

- The type, age, and layout of the manufacturing plant and surrounding site.
- The character, variety, number, and technology level of installed equipment.
- The skill types and levels, and where each is available under what circumstances.
- The types of services required to maintain the facility within the framework of the maintenance program scope.

Generally, the larger the scope, the more diverse and complex the role within that scope, the greater the need for a formalized way to focus and allocate resources toward needed outcomes. Hence the organization structure.

Organization structures will range from the simplest (for example, the hourly maintenance leadman reporting to the young vice president of operations in a small family-owned sawmill in central Oregon) to the large multilayered multicraft paper mill maintenance organization with narrow job skills and hundreds of maintenance personnel. The task is to recruit or develop the needed skills and talents and to organize these human capabilities into a functioning work group that responds effectively to the mission of the department and business.

The three dominant organizational structures are central, area, and department. Each has its adherents, each adherent will cite various advantages and disadvantages; the favorable or unfavorable characterization will often depend on the perspective of the observer. There is considerable overlap and apparent grey areas in actual practice. The following is a description of these traditional forms; each will be used as a reference point in describing the emerging trends in maintenance.

Central Maintenance

Figure 4.2 is an illustration of the central maintenance organization type. The entire maintenance for the manufacturing site including its equipment, buildings, and grounds are the responsibility of one person. This one person reports to the business head at that location. A plant engineer usually runs the program on a multiproduct complex and

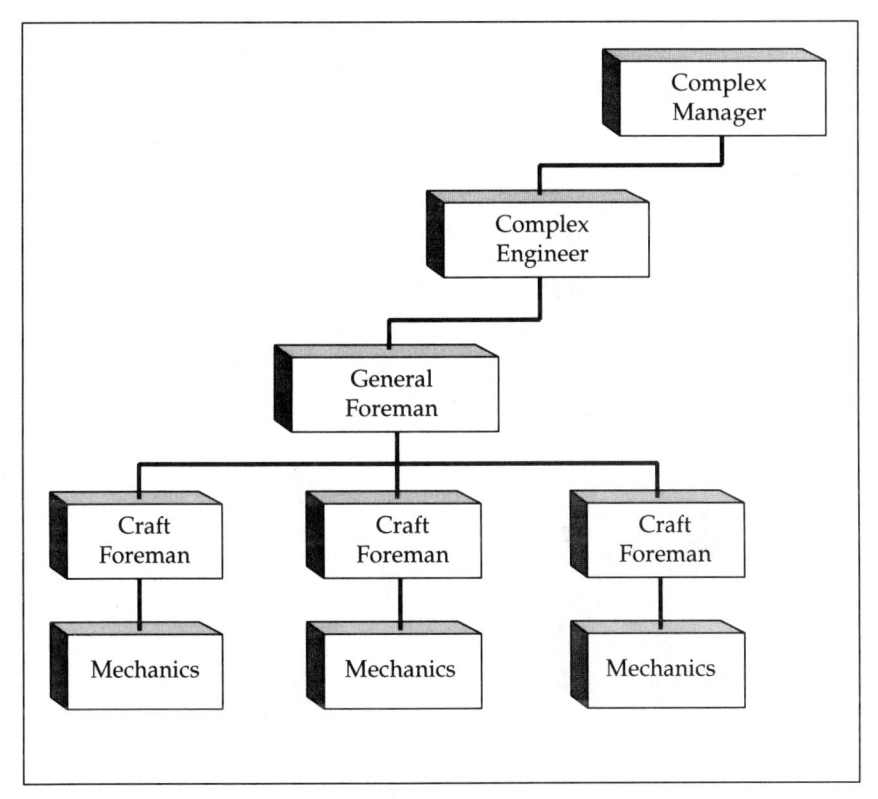

Figure 4.2   Central Maintenance Organization
Source: Plant Engineering Library, 1983

reports to the complex or regional manufacturing manager. This structure allows for economies of scale and specialization; but job priorities are a headache, particularly when two or more production departments or mills begin competing for resources. And travel can also be a headache.

The perfect skill never seems to be available when a breakdown occurs. In addition, the maintenance foreman and the individual craftsman have a reduced opportunity to know a production process; each becomes a generalist in the process and a specialist in the craft. Effective preventive maintenance programs just seem more difficult to set up and maintain.

Area Maintenance

Figure 4.3 illustrates the area maintenance organization type. The entire maintenance program reports to one person, who in turn reports to the manufacturing manager of that business or process. The area may be

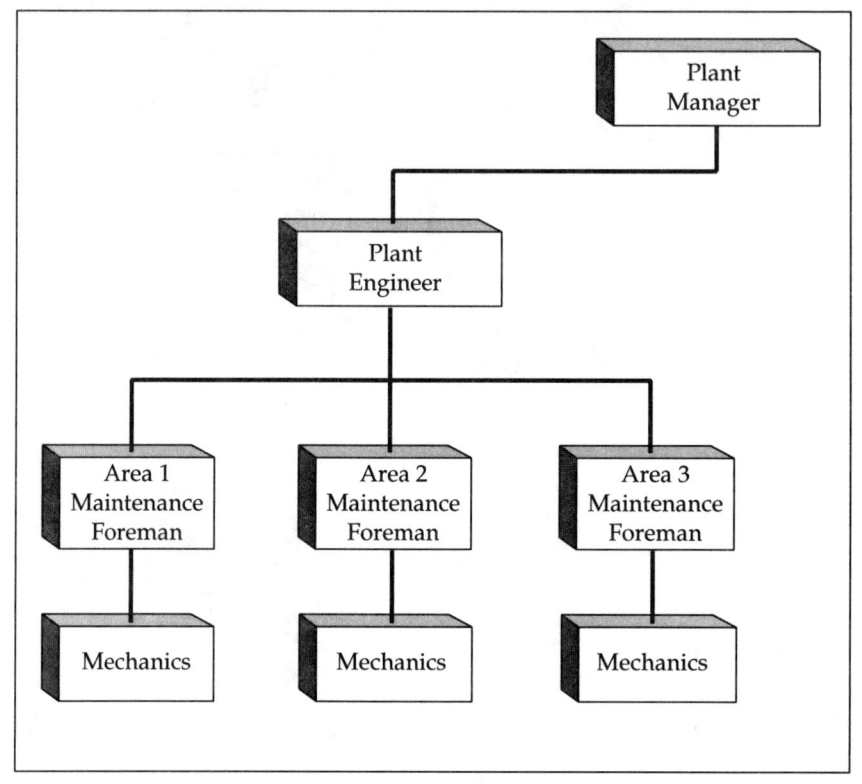

```
                        ┌──────────┐
                        │  Plant   │
                        │ Manager  │
                        └────┬─────┘
                             │
                        ┌────┴─────┐
                        │  Plant   │
                        │ Engineer │
                        └────┬─────┘
         ┌───────────────────┼───────────────────┐
    ┌────┴─────┐        ┌────┴─────┐        ┌────┴─────┐
    │  Area 1  │        │  Area 2  │        │  Area 3  │
    │Maintenance│       │Maintenance│       │Maintenance│
    │ Foreman  │        │ Foreman  │        │ Foreman  │
    └────┬─────┘        └────┬─────┘        └────┬─────┘
    ┌────┴─────┐        ┌────┴─────┐        ┌────┴─────┐
    │Mechanics │        │Mechanics │        │Mechanics │
    └──────────┘        └──────────┘        └──────────┘
```

Figure 4.3   **Area Maintenance Organization**

Source: Plant Engineering Library, 1983

defined geographically; by product group such as lumber, plywood, and pulp; or by production department or service function such as boilers and utilities. A central service is maintained for special skills such as electronics, rolling stock, and machine shop.

The maintenance personnel assigned to a specific area generally begin to acquire multicraft skills and develop intimate knowledge of the production process. They become specialists in the process and generalists in the maintenance crafts.

Departmental Maintenance

The maintenance personnel, usually multicraft-skilled, are assigned to a definite area or function and report directly to a production supervisor. Often a maintenance foreman will act as a level between the maintenance and the production supervisor. Figure 4.4 highlights the departmental maintenance organization type.

Building and Developing an Organization 39

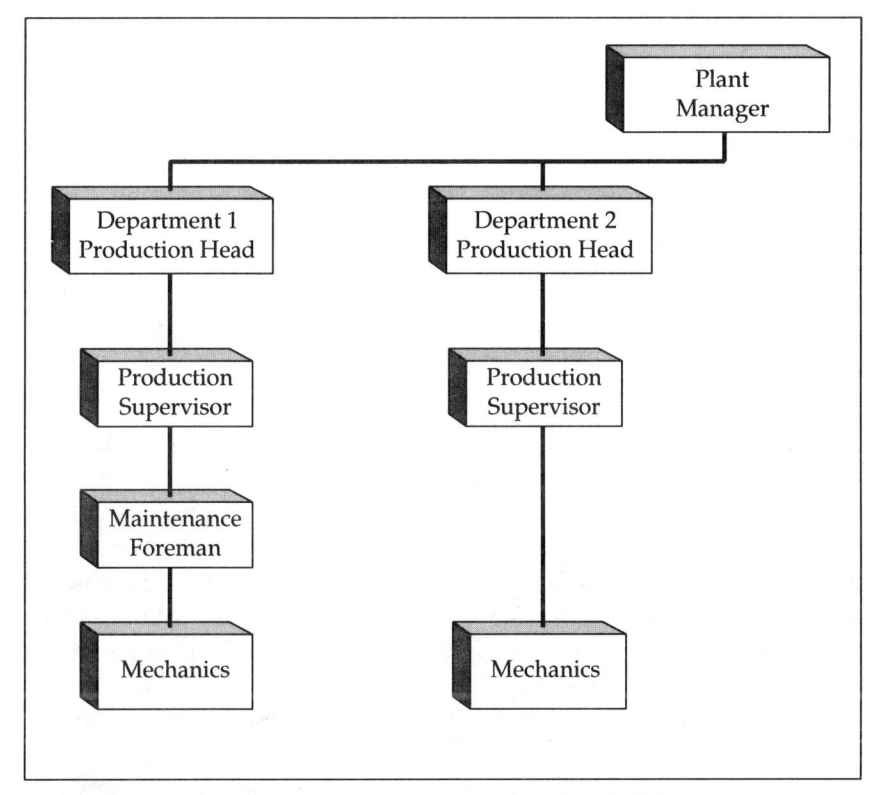

Figure 4.4   Departmental Maintenance Organization
Source: Plant Engineering Library, 1983

The production person has complete responsibility for an important factor affecting production and costs. There is no problem of priorities; however, the operation has to rely on informal lines to obtain the outside resource people needed to complete the maintenance task. And there are other cited disadvantages.

Production supervisors are required to know and understand maintenance; the time required to become knowledgeable may not be available with the press of other supervisory activities. The equipment may be repaired improperly or operated with minimum maintenance because of other priorities or lack of the requisite skills.

Emerging Organizational Structures

The mill will pay a heavy price for a maintenance organization structure that doesn't get the job done right, as graphically described by a Canadian author: "A paper machine crash during a production run is an expensive way to discover a problem. Downtime can be excessive, because such failures usually cause substantial damage to machine parts, roll surfaces, felts, wires, etc. amounting to tens of thousands of dollars" (Pemberton, 1987, 43).

The average age of a Canadian paper machine is estimated to be around forty years. The trend is to a faster, more demanding operation; an upgrade can result in a 1,500 fpm machine stepped up to 2,100 fpm and more. The necessity for the perfect organization form will continue to increase.

The emerging maintenance organization forms will depart markedly from the traditional norms. The organizational structure, the assignment of work, the control of the task, and the relationship to management and the decision-making process are all different. Figure 4.5 compares the features of the traditional and emerging organizations.

The emerging organizations are less structured, and many participants are outside the formal maintenance group. Job assignments depart from narrowly defined craft tasks and extend into the multicraft concept, becoming intermingled with the hands-on production process. Greater participation of both maintenance and production employees is not only invited but expected.

"In a conventional manufacturing plant, maintenance procedures don't really have to work well, and employees don't have to be involved. Instead, the operating policy is to try to build in enough safeguards so that production will be kept humming in spite of problems. But safeguards don't come cheap. To remove downtime risks in conventional manufacturing, managements typically resort to such costly practices as buffer stock," commented *Industry Week's* John Teresko. He then emphasized the need for operator involvement. "Does this mean that the operators must be able to fix all of the machine outages? Not necessarily. Even minimum participation, such as getting machine operators involved with lubrication, can have a big effect on downtime."

Teresko then quotes another expert: "Employee involvement should gravitate toward a sense of ownership . . . The machine should become his machine and the operator should be allowed a sense of responsibility that will spot machine trouble and initiate action before it becomes a work stoppage."

Maintenance personnel often become trainers and resource people, and each becomes a partner in the process. "The idea is to consider maintenance as part of the single system called the operating business. The challenge is to use maintenance to achieve the business goal" (Teresko

Figure 4.5 *Maintenance Organizations: A Comparison*

Factors	Traditional	Emerging

Organizational forms	• Self-contained hierarchical forms with three essential organization types.
	  • central
	  • area
	  • departmental
	• Well-defined organization structure and tasks.
		• Less structured organizational forms with loose/tight operating methods.
		• Outside resources replace in-house functions where practical.
		• Many participants outside the formal organization.

Job assignments	• Narrowly defined by crafts. • Prescribed routine of when, what, and how. • Some initiative encouraged on whistle-chasing calls.	• Broadly defined by ability and availability. • Formalized versus standardized task assignments.
Skills	• Traditional craft-type jobs such as welder, electrician, millwright, machinist, and pipe fitter. • Mostly on-the-job training, including an apprenticeship; some outside training. • Individual career advancement based on a narrow career ladder within a craft.	• Multicraft-based skill. • On-the-job training supplemented with ongoing formal off-the-job, in-house, and outside training in both maintenance and related soft skills. • Individual career advancement based on skills acquired and results achieved.
Control of the work	• Prescribed routine of what, when, how, and who. • Initiative required in emergencies. • Little input in planning and methods.	• Prescribed routine of what, when, and who; the how is changed through involvement as appropriate. • Initiative is expected, communication is required. • Active resource person and frequent participant in planning.
Labor/Management	• Employee provides time, skills, and effort. • Me/you relationship; complaints and grievances are used to effect change.	• Employee is participant who can and does participate in the task-related decision-making process. • Group participation is used to resolve complaints or concerns.

1987, 42). Weyerhaeuser's southern pine lumber operation at Bruce, Mississippi, is an example of what is currently happening in the industry. A maintenance group, comprised of a salaried team leader, five hourly team leaders (two of whom are also production leaders), and the maintenance planner, makes most of the decisions regarding maintenance at the Bruce facility. This group deals with the usual maintenance tasks but expands into cost-control issues, cost effectiveness, and overall productivity. The operation superintendent then deals only with major issues; these are often discussed, with recommendations provided as each reaches his desk.

Forward planning, training-needs identification, and key-issue resolution activities that tended to be placed on the back burner because of the urgency to address immediate needs are now an important management activity.

Training and Development

Training has always been important; now it is essential as well. According to a recent article in *Plant Engineering*,

> The quality of maintenance determines availability and dependability of complex equipment. And a key factor in providing quality maintenance is the level of skill with which craftsmen carry out their work. Factors affecting the level of training at a specific plant include location, rate of employee turnover, corporate policy on training, educational resources within the community, average age of maintenance workers, and complexity of plant equipment. (Peele and Chapman, 1987, 52)

The need becomes visible when planning a new mill startup or upgrading the old one. New production, yield, and quality targets that were originally used to justify the new equipment can only be achieved through training and development. And of the two kinds of crews to be trained, production and maintenance, it is important not to forget the latter group.

"If it's an electrician and he's not up on program logic control, you try to give him courses—formal training. Try to have him present during the installation, or have him install it himself. Give him as much time as possible with the installers, and buy a spare unit that he can play with in the shop," states Cliff Bowering, a veteran of four mill startups (Baker, 1987, 20). The development of a training and development program will focus on development of a training concept, preparing a training plan, develop-

Building and Developing an Organization 43

ing or locating the necessary resource material and trainers, and carrying out the plan.

The training concept statement simply states the commitment to training and development and identifies training requirements ahead for at least one year and up to a five-year planning cycle. The needs of the operation are assessed; in-house skills and readily and economically available outside resources are also identified. A timetable is then prepared to match the two.

Figure 4.6 is an example of a rating system used to evaluate millwrights' and electricians' skills. Individuals are first audited in relation to their primary maintenance skills. The question is then asked, "What else does this individual need to know?" The answer may be a course in advanced electronics for the electricians; or it may be the need to obtain a class B electrical rating for a millwright seeking to broaden his or her skills.

An operation manager may also have a vision of the future in which optimizers are introduced onto the sawmill floor. The training of the mill personnel should precede the reality. The resulting skills and needs inventory is used as a basis for the training plan.

The training plan should cover a continuum in time with a multiyear overview. The annual plan, usually based on calendar quarters, should be

Figure 4.6 *Rating System for Skills Evaluation*

Millright	Electrician
D Mechanical aptitude; willingness to learn; adaptable; good judgment; ability to work safely; basic knowledge of hand tools and portable equipment; serve as a helper.	**D** Electrical aptitude; willingness to learn and follow instructions; good judgment; safe work habits; show initiative; basic knowledge of tools and equipment; serve as a helper.
C Basic knowledge of fundamentals of millwrighting, including welding, burning, measuring devices, lubrication. Basic machine repair, maintenance and troubleshooting. Basic knowledge of oils and greases; some shop math; able to work safely.	**C** Basic knowledge of fundamentals of electricity. Knowledge of electrical tools, ability to thread conduit, hang lighting fixtures; assist electrician as needed.
B All of C plus more advanced skill level with troubleshooting capability. Show initiative. Floor man on routine shift with ability to handle routine problems. Basic knowledge instrumentation repair.	**B** Ability to read blueprints, make splices, hook up wires from blueprints; basic knowledge of electrical troubleshooting procedures. Knowledge of electrical meters. Basic knowledge of and ability to test motors and generators; ability to change out motors.
A All of B plus advanced skill levels in welding, couplings, pumps, shafts, etc. Able to set bearing tolerances, high level of burning skills. Advanced troubleshooting ability. Advanced knowledge of blueprint reading and sketching. Basic knowledge of pipefitting, working knowledge of temperature and pressure controls. Ability to plan materials, work time and equipment necessary to complete job; utilize people effectively. Ability to install air control of valves and fittings.	**A** All of B plus advanced skills in reading prints; some knowledge of solid state equipment. Generally able to wire panels and electronic systems; advanced troubleshooting capability. Able to handle high voltage distribution problems; install electronic automatic control valves. Knowledge of repair and maintenance of motors and generators; knowledge of motor settings, drives, coupling devices, manual and automatic controls including magnetic and solid state. Basic knowledge of environmental metering devices. Ability to lead others. Basic knowledge of local and state electrical codes.
A+ All of A plus basic knowledge of electricity; exceptional ability in welding and troubleshooting. Leadership ability; ability to set priorities.	**A+** All of A plus complete knowledge to design and install motor circuits as required; ability to operate electrical shop, take charge and make decisions; ability to lead people; experienced troubleshooting abilities, identify problems quickly and take action, basic knowledge of electronics, DC circuiting, drives and controllers. Ability to organize and set priorities.

Figure 4.6 *(continued)*

Millright	Electrician
Leadman All of A plus ability to organize many projects; coordinate the various trades. High level of leadership ability. Full understanding and appreciation of management goals. Ability to evaluate people.	**Leadman** All of A plus ability to organize work assignments for crews; line up work. Ability to take charge in foreman's absence. Generally high level of leadership ability. Full understanding and appreciation of management goals. Ability to evaluate people.

Source: Baldwin, 1984

prepared no later than the latter part of the third quarter of the year preceding the actual implementation. The remainder of the year is then available to plan, organize, and set in motion the training plan.

"A master training plan will spell out who gets training, when it will take place, what kind of training, and how it will be presented," explains Thomas Westerkamp of H. B. Maynard and Company. The training activity should not only focus on craft skill but may include planner training, safety training, stockroom management, material and tool control, various computer-assisted management program elements, and training in involvement and participative management. The actual selection will represent a variety of training topics and activities designed to further the competitive position of the firm.

Training course development can be accomplished in three phases: analysis, design, and development. Each job or related skill to be taught is analyzed and compared to the skill and knowledge level of the group or individual to be taught. The body of information should focus on needs. This keeps the interest level of the participants high. Lesson plans for each session focus on the objectives to be accomplished; specific criteria is then targeted to be observed to indicate successful completion.

These training methods are but an overview of a much larger topic. The task is to blend the correct training and development with the equally correct organization structure. The result is the foundation upon which focused and cost-effective maintenance practices can be developed.

References

Baker, K. 1987. In Search of a Perfect Mill. *Logging & Sawmilling Journal* 18, no. 4 (April): 20–21.

Baldwin, R. F. 1984. *Operations Management in the Forest Products Industry*. San Francisco: Miller Freeman, 196.

Barnett, K. W. and J. K. Blundell. 1981. *Trade in Maintenance: Determination of Optimum Crew Sizes by the Monte Carlo, Simulation Technique*. Amsterdam: Elsevier Scientific Publishing Co.

Geisel, C. E. 1985. Get the Operator in on the Act. *TAPPI Journal 68*, no. 5: 136.

Griffin, G. 1985. Contract Maintenance, Is It an Emerging Trend? *Forest Industries* (August).

Kay, D. H. and L. A. Peters. 1987. Maintenance Crew Dynamics. *Plant Engineering* (April 23).

Meyer, G. 1984. On the Stump. *Weyerhaeuser Maintenance Journal* (March/April): 9-10.

Peele, T. T. and R. L. Chapman. 1987. Designing a Maintenance Training Program. *Plant Engineering* (August 13): 52-55.

Pemberton, R. 1987. Predictive Maintenance Program for Maintenance in the Pulp & Paper Industry. *Pulp & Paper Canada 88*, no. 1: 43.

Piper, J. 1987. Training for Advanced Technology. *Plant Engineering* (June 18).

———. 1984. Making Planned Maintenance Pay Off. *Plant Engineering* (August 9).

Plant Engineering Library. 1983. *Maintenance—Managing and the Maintenance Function*. Part A. Organization A. Barrington, IL: Cahner's Publishing Co.

Rantala, J. W. 1983. Organizing and Using a Maintenance Training Program. Plant Engineering Library. Division of Cahner's Publishing Co.

Teresko, J. 1987. Modernizing Maintenance. *Industry Week* (June 29): 41-44.

Tichy, N. M. and M. A. Devanna. 1986. The Transformational Leader. *Training and Development Journal* (July).

Westerkamp, T. A. 1985. How to Test Maintenance Productivity. *Plant Engineering* (September 22): 43.

Weyerhaeuser Maintenance Journal. 1984. (March-April).

Worthy, F. 1987. Accounting Bores You? Wake Up. *Fortune* (October 12): 43-49.

PART TWO

MANAGING FOR RESULTS

CHAPTER 5

Maintenance Planning and Scheduling

Currently, only about 20 percent of all maintenance work done in American industry is done on a planned basis. All too often maintenance manages the manager; this is completely opposite from the way it ought to be. As a seasoned heavy equipment troubleshooter said, "Owners are so production oriented that they often ignore the importance of maintenance, and this is one area that'll eat your lunch" (Knight, 1984, 3). But it doesn't have to be that way.

Ninety-one percent of the maintenance work of Alumax at Mt. Holly, South Carolina, is planned in advance; only 8.3 percent are breakdowns or trouble cases (McCormick, 1984). Maintenance costs at Mt. Holly run about 40 percent less than those for other facilities of the same size in the primary aluminum industry.

A Vision of Success

Whether it is aluminum or lumber, basic manufacturing is pretty similar. An effective maintenance program must have a vision of success, such as at Mt. Holly. "If there is a problem to be worked on, a solution to be found, everybody works on it," said John Day, engineering and maintenance manager (McCormick, 1984). The key is mental rehearsal and planning of each step.

Planning identifies the elements required to perform a task in advance of the job start time. Scheduling relates the resulting elements with a sequence in time and then proceeds to order the work. Each contributes to the vision of success.

The Task

The maintenance task covers a wide range of activities that require planning, scheduling, supervising, and follow-up. Figure 5.1 clarifies and

Figure 5.1 *Major Planning and Scheduling Activities*

- Determine the project scope and what resources are required.
- Identify priorities among competing demands.
- Identify resources (people, time, materials, and dollars).
- Assign resources to do the job.
- Communicate results expected to participants and stakeholders.
- Organize the work before the job starts.
- Track work in progress.
- Follow-up to determine variance to plan.

expands upon these major activities. The activities begin with the determination of what needs to be done and concludes with an evaluation of results achieved.

"Planned maintenance is an investment as much as a capital project is an investment," commented the Mt. Holly plant manager. "You cannot expect to get anything out of maintenance unless you invest in it. Repairing breakdowns is not an investment" (McCormick, 1984).

Figure 5.2 is a schematic of this investment road map. The maintenance investment can be as minimal as an unstated strategy to run it until it breaks (RB); or it can be as elaborate as an optimized program that considers preventive maintenance (PM) as a key ingredient but achieves even more benefits by extending the scope to include other considerations.

These considerations include optimizing and balancing sometimes competing objectives such as initial cost, production, and quality—which are something more than having the equipment operating or not operating. Sizes, basis weight, color, and the overall cost and quality of the resulting finished or in-process goods are just some of the considerations that are not covered by measuring downtime and maintenance costs as the primary scorecard.

Figure 5.3 is a graphical representation of this maintenance strategy. The vertical axis represents the level of maintenance employed; it ranges from the break-it/fix-it (RB) mode, to preventive maintenance (PM), on to condition maintenance (CM), and through to total maintenance (TM), where the optimization mode begins. The results are indicated on the horizontal axis.

The horizontal scale represents a continuum that ranges from unpredictable equipment operation in degrees to totally predictable equipment uptime. Further progress in degrees leads to additional benefits as some-

Maintenance Planning and Scheduling 51

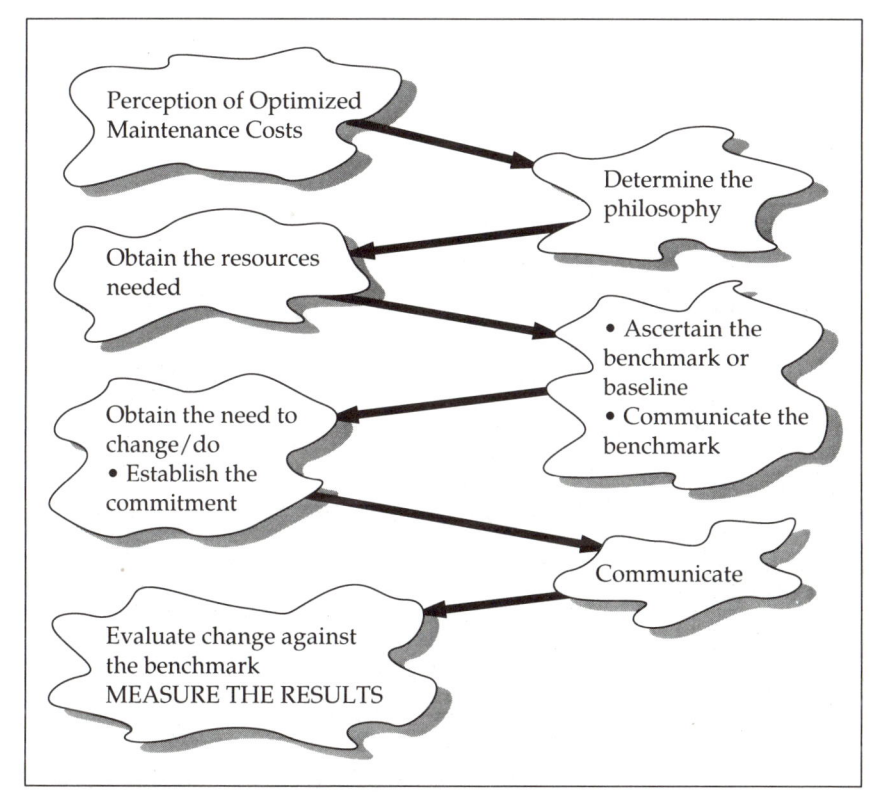

Figure 5.2   **Maintenance Investment Road Map**

thing more than predictable run time is achieved. The maintenance strategy will provide the underpinning for all that follows, beginning with the planning function.

Planning and the Planner

The planner must be well qualified to function effectively. Full-time planners are usually selected based on experience as machinists, millwrights, electricians, or welders. Craft ability in one or more skills is important; the knowledge and respect that follows are perquisites for getting the job done.

It is difficult to justify a full-time planner for a crew of less than twenty-five. The usual compromise is for the maintenance crew leader or supervisor to be the planner with the help of a key crew member.

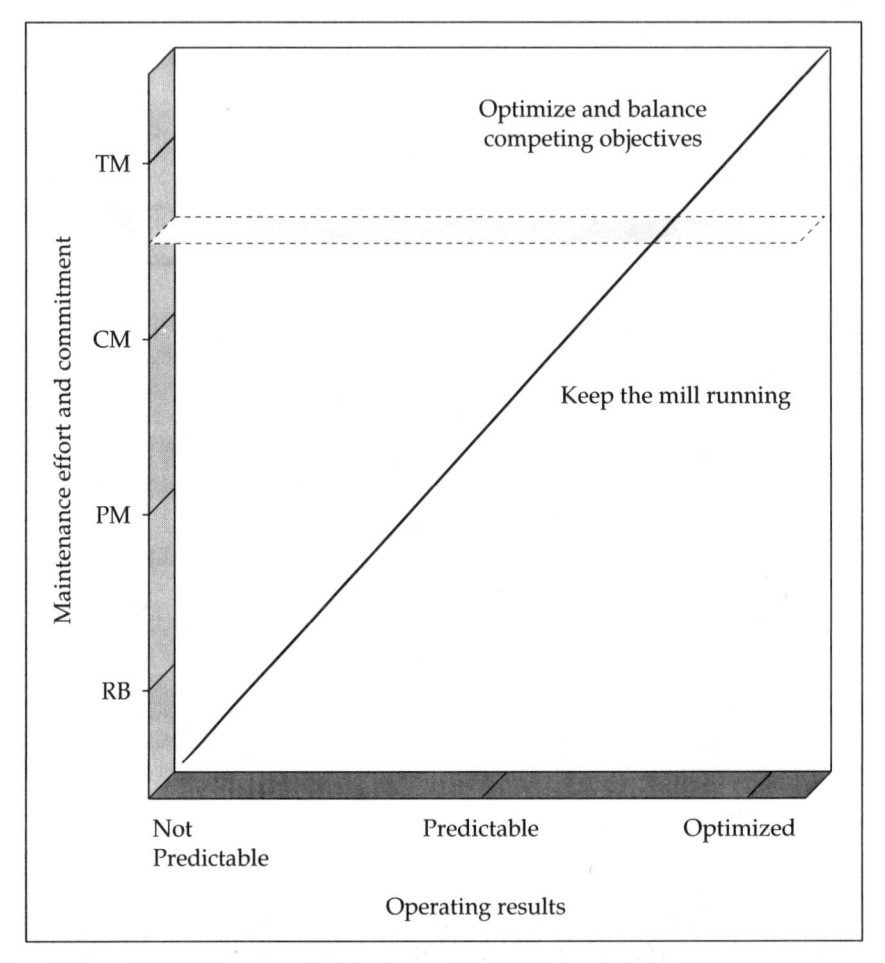

Figure 5.3   **The Tradeoff, Maintenance Effort and Commitment Versus Operating Results**

Mt. Holly planners, for example, are craftsmen with an average work experience of twenty years. Each planner is assigned to one, two, or three of the twelve-person crews, and each works closely with the supervisor of those crews. The major responsibility for monitoring the maintenance needs of an area and for planning and scheduling the workload falls to the supervisor and the planner.

Planning and scheduling can also be a development activity for new graduate engineers, perhaps as part of a training process that rotates them through various disciplines in a plant or field organization.

Communication skills are the tools of the trade. Writing clearly and concisely are important qualifications, along with pragmatic experience in maintenance practices. The planner must also have the ability to get along with others while projecting a good attitude toward company supervisors and working associates. The foundation for the planner's efforts will center on the following:

- Goals, policies, and procedures as established for the planning effort.
- Current conditions as identified as a tool to establish benchmarks.
- Available resources as identified and some judgment made whether each is adequate for the task ahead.
- In-plant communication as a vehicle to recognize tasks.

The planner must determine the current state of planning for people and things. He or she must know who is doing what, or who is not doing anything at all. Harold Geneen cites this example in his book, *Managing*:

> We first had to take an inventory of all the maintenance men and their jobs in each of the departments, and in so doing we found plenty of waste. In fact, we discovered one maintenance man who for twenty years had done no work at all and had gone undetected. He simply picked up a pail at one plant, carried it across a bridge to another plant, sat down out of sight all day, carried the pail back at the end of the day, and went home. (Geneen, 1984, 73–74)

Every plant has similar war stories; the task is to sort the fact from the fiction to find out what people are available and what each is doing or could be doing to contribute to the maintenance effort.

Some folks just waste time in an honest attempt to contribute. For example, some crew members may take more time deciding how they are going to do the job than it takes them to perform the task. The journeyman who does the job may plan the sequence of activities in his head, or discuss it with his helper, or sometimes even work it out on a piece of scrap paper or a soapstone on the concrete floor. Soapstone engineering and discussions between participants is helpful; but these activities should be the supplements to planning, not the primary means.

The planner leads the way in planning, although participative involvement of others in the maintenance and production staffs, including hourly employees, will enhance the effort and build commitment. Above all, the planner needs to obtain the facts.

For example, if piping work is to be done, pipe fitters cannot be scheduled on the job until it is known if scaffolding is needed, if pipe coverings have to be removed and if these coverings contain asbestos, or if steam has to be shut off by the operator. It also must be known if material is available and how long it should take to do the job.

The Planning Ingredients, a Recipe for Success

An effective planning system includes all and more of the following core ingredients: equipment records, parts and materials lists, process information, work orders, and daily individual maintenance reports.

Equipment Records

Equipment records should include manufacturer's information, specifications, and the maintenance and downtime history. A machine safety analysis should also be part of the package.

The downtime and repair history provides the planner with a great deal of useful information. For example, the planner may recognize the need for a change in the PM or overhaul schedule, or an adjustment in the lubrication program. He or she can also determine how much money is being spent on the equipment and what type of work has been done on it, such as routine repairs or breakdown maintenance.

Parts and Materials Lists

Parts, supplies, and component lists are kept and periodically updated. Cross-references to manufacturers' catalog numbers are a necessity for timely reordering and procurement, or to prevent unpleasant surprises such as having the wrong part when the machine is down for repair (a frequent occurrence that is not often talked about).

The parts selected for a job should be ordered by the planner and delivered to the job site at least five days before the work is scheduled. This allows for double checking and final scheduling of the job.

Process Information

Process information includes operator manuals with formal updates from the vendor or informal updates from in-house and industry sources. The resulting information allows the reader to refresh his or her understanding of how the machine or process should operate before making repairs and adjustments.

Work Orders

The work order, frequently preceded by a work request, is prepared or submitted to identify a needed repair or modification. The basic purposes of the work order are to:

- provide a means for screening and authorizing work
- segregate cost data in a logical manner
- gather feedback information on repetitive failures
- facilitate planning and scheduling of maintenance work
- enhance productivity by timely communication of equipment or process needs

A work order planning system allows the generation of purchase requisitions, cost estimating, committing or allocating stores stock, and writing safety or other important cautions. A work order system will also include a cost system for tracking labor, materials, and outside services costs.

A typical form is shown in figure 5.4. This form is produced with at least two copies. The first is a hands-on work copy to be used to organize and follow through the jobs; and the second is retained by the planner as a backup follow-up tool to ascertain that the work is done, done in a timely and cost effective fashion, and done within the scope and manner expected.

Maintenance Work Order

Chk Priority			
E	5	W+	Date _____

E = Emergency
5 = This Week
W+ = Week or More

Hard card back copy to maintenance
Paper top copy retained by originator

Req. By _____
Dept _____
Chg To _____

Cost center code

Description _____

Estimated man hours by maintenance superintendent

Est M.H. _____

Noted by millwright

Work Done _____

Actual man-hours determined from assignment sheet sign on/off times

Act M.H. _____

Parts & Mat. _____

Parts and material costs

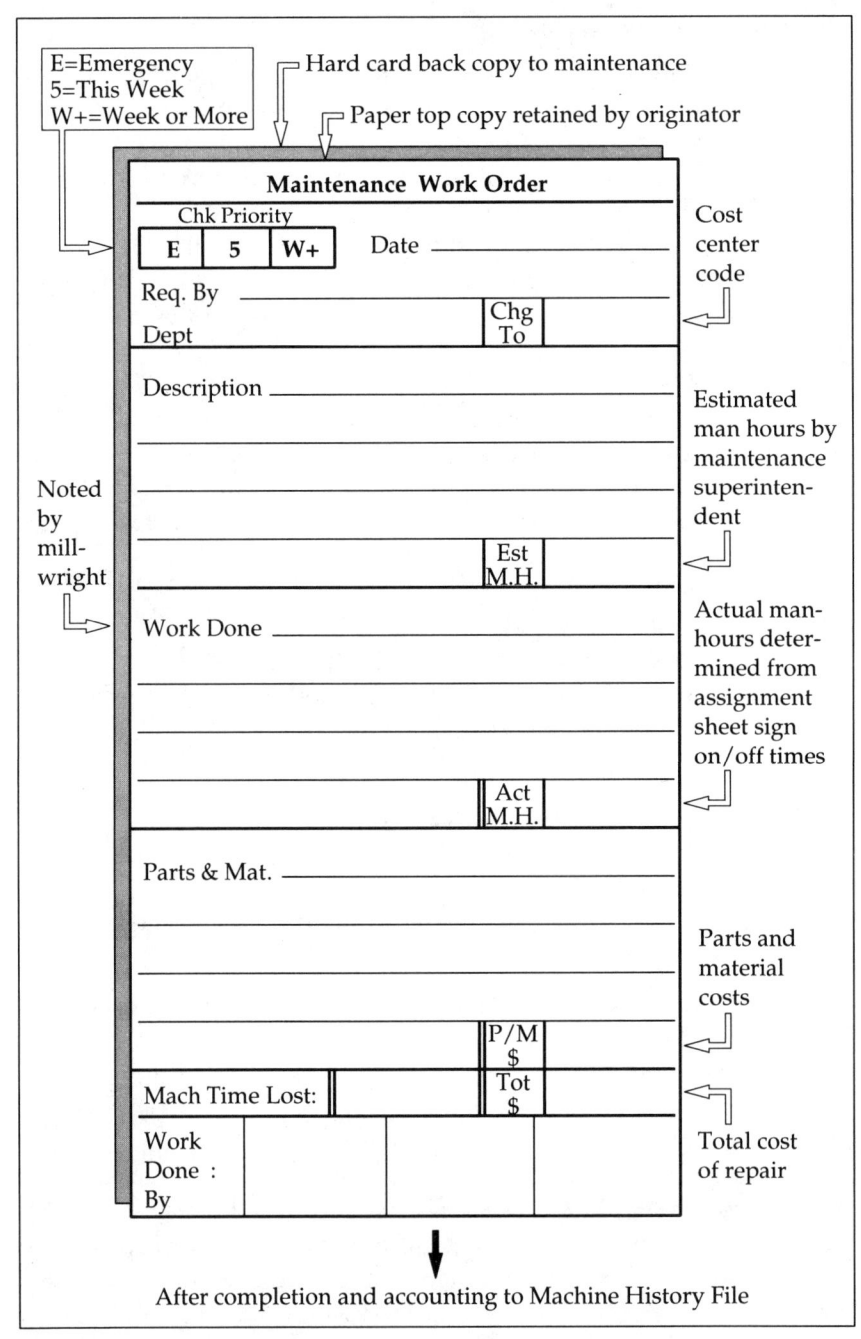

P/M $ _____
Tot $ _____

Mach Time Lost: _____

Work Done : By

Total cost of repair

After completion and accounting to Machine History File

Figure 5.4   Standard Maintenance Work Order

The date, priority, project description and name of the originator is filled in. Work order is filled in by the originator; this could be the maintenance person, supervisor, or machine operator. The planner checks and clarifies the information, seeks any required approvals, identifies the work to be done along with necessary parts and materials, and identifies the particulars of costs and repair schedules.

The priority designation is of major importance. It indicates the time left before a repair need becomes a serious problem. A repair need becomes a serious problem when it is likely or certain to create unacceptable downtime, costs, or operating variances; or cause damage or injury to someone or something.

Figure 5.4 lists three priorities: emergency, this week, and week or more. This priority listing may be adequate for most situations; a large or complex facility may prefer a further listing that adds additional definition.

The work order can be used as a general request such as, "Repair the air leaks in the woodyard"; or as a special work order prepared for a specific task such as, "Re-pack the air cylinder on the Number 3 log kicker." The former is usually done for routine jobs that are simple and repetitive. The latter is used to ascertain that a certain task is done in a certain way with certain results; the completed work order then becomes part of the machine history upon completion of the task.

Daily Individual Maintenance Report

A daily individual maintenance report (see figure 5.5) is prepared for each individual maintenance person before the shift. The planner's steps are as follows:

1. Enters the worker's name, the date, and circles the appropriate shift.
2. Identifies one or more work orders for each individual. Removes one copy of each work order (hard copy) and places it with the individual maintenance report. Marks the assignment on both work order copies; the follow-up copy serves as an on-shift people locator in a large operation.
3. Enters work order numbers in the same sequence in the top-left-hand section of the daily individual maintenance report.
4. Clips work orders to individuals' daily reports and sets the package aside for the incoming maintenance person. The incoming

58　　　　　　　　　　　　　　　　　　　　MANAGING MILL MAINTENANCE

		Date _____
Craftsman _____		Shift (circle) 1 2 3

Assigned W.O.#	Description and or special instructions
Assigned W.O.#	Description and or special instructions
Assigned W.O.#	Description and or special instructions

Shift hour	Activities-Jobs performed, delays	Time Spent	Charge To
1			
2			
3			
4			
5			
6			
7			
8			
9			
10			

Figure 5.5　　　　**Daily Individual Maintenance Report**

Maintenance Planning and Scheduling 59

   maintenance person picks up the package and reports to the first assignment.
5. Upon completion of the repair the maintenance person contacts the production supervisor or machine operator, who approves the repair and signs off the hard copy of the work order.
6. The lower half of the daily individual maintenance report is provided to record hour-by-hour activities, including any emergency interruptions (chasing whistles) and the time spent on these activities.
7. An uncompleted work order should be reassigned and so noted on the daily individual maintenance report.

Planning Tool

Custom report-writing capability is available for most personal computers. This capability can be used directly to plan maintenance, or it can be used to identify trends and measure performance. Further information is presented in chapter 6.

Planning Horizons

The planner then combines the developing information with communication from other participants into four planning horizons: the emergencies, the daily job plan, the short-range plan (within one year), and the long-range plan (more than one year). Classifying each developing task into one of the four will assist in scheduling and allocating resources.

Emergency Management Planning

Emergency management planning is unplanned work that requires an immediate response. Emergencies can be classified as follows: Type A, machine or component is not operating (downtime); or Type B, machine or component is not operating within the bounds or specifications required and risks damage to people or equipment.

A certain amount of emergency preplanning can and should be performed:

- Listing, by each foreman, typical emergencies that may take place, with emphasis on emergencies concerned with critical equipment and safety hazards.
- Writing emergency procedures covering items that cannot be handled by normal knowledge and skills of incumbent personnel within reasonable time frames.

- Training personnel in managing critical situations (fire-drill-type training).
- Determining the availability of materials either to stock or from readily available nearby vendors. Set up a critical spares program (discussed further in chapter 21).
- Locating available special tools, fixtures, and equipment. This search will seek special repair aids such as custom-designed tools and jigs.
- Creating troubleshooting aids. Certain items of equipment are easy to troubleshoot; others are complex and difficult. Trouble analysis charts should be made and hung up in plastic envelopes on the respective machine. These charts should follow this format: (1) trouble or symptom, (2) probable cause, (3) remedy. The troubleshooter can quickly identify the trouble, its probable cause, and how to fix it.

Unfortunately, training and preplanning will not cover every expected emergency, particularly in the beginning of a program. That's where the postmortem comes into play. People directly involved should ask these questions within twenty-four hours of the emergency:

- What happened?
- What was the cause?
- What can we do to prevent it?
- If it happens again, how can we improve our response?

The results of this meeting, and the answers, must then be followed up.

Daily Job Planning

The planner and the maintenance supervisor meet twice each day, first thing in the morning and again at the end of the day. They discuss the work orders completed the day before and review and screen the tasks for the next twenty-four hours. Input data includes work orders, checklists, notes from the oiler or machine operator, and additional information from any number of sources.

Daily job planning provides the following:

- Job instruction, including drawings and specifications as required.
- Material required, including a checklist of those obtained.
- Labor required by skill type and level, crew size, and man-hours.
- Special tools and equipment, such as specialized devices.
- Safety instructions, including a review of any unusual safety hazards involved and how to deal with each.
- Required completion date, including design or planning time, work

order approval time, material delivery time, shop backlog time, and actual time required at the machine to effect the repair.

At the end of the shift or day the planner takes the package of work orders for the next day to the supervisor; the maintenance supervisor in turn gives the planner the work orders completed that day.

Weekly Job Planning

Daily jobs are planned along with forward planning for the weekend or other shutdown periods for a seven-day operation. The usual sequence is as follows:

- Monday: Look at weekend results (sometimes called the game films), determine the successes, and also determine what was learned that can be useful in the future.
- Tuesday: Make up a weekly prioritized maintenance list that identifies what people will do and what the maintenance people will do by project for the coming week. Much of this information will have been developed from the daily planning sessions.
- Wednesday: Prepare for and have the weekly planning meeting, which includes hourly and salaried and maintenance and production representatives.
- Thursday: Complete the weekly planning cycle, with special emphasis on the upcoming weekend work. Make sure that previously ordered supplies and last-minute needs either are or will be available.
- Friday: Coordinate and communicate with maintenance for weekend and new needs.

Short-range Planning

This is the annual plan of operation. It consists of the following:

- A general plan of how people should be distributed throughout the various departments.
- Detailed planning and scheduling of major events taking place during the year, such as major overhauls, large construction jobs, major preventive maintenance tasks, and plant shutdowns.

The basic purpose of the annual or short-range plan is to provide adequate lead time to plan all elements of very large jobs and budget resources for the year. Lack of such a plan will inevitably lead to misunderstanding with senior management and lack of preparation for the bigger jobs.

Long-range Planning

Long-range planning of the maintenance requirements is closely allied with and dependent on long-range business prospects and capital funds availability. Long-range planning takes into consideration the changing technology and prepares plans to meet the maintenance needs of new equipment and new processes. Identification of training and development needs are also an important part of the long-range planning process.

The Goal

These planning horizons and activities comprise the dynamic cycle around which a maintenance program will evolve. They are the time frame over which the planner and other participants in the planning process work their craft. Planning activities are the early steps in a cycle of change and challenge. Successful planning with a committed crew can translate the business into something more than a vision of success; success becomes a reality on a continuing basis.

References

Cooling, W. 1973. Low Cost Maintenance Control—A Division of American Management. AMACOM.

Criswell, J. W. 1983. *Planned Maintenance for Productivity and Energy Conservation*. Atlanta: The Fairmont Press.

Dhillon, B. 1983. *Reliability Engineering in Systems Design and Operations*. New York: Van Nostrand Reinhold.

Geneen, H. with A. Moscow. 1984. *Managing*. Garden City, NY: Doubleday, 73–74.

Hannon, J. W. and R. E. Cowie. 1971. *Practical Operator-Training Methods. Industrial Engineering Handbook*. New York: McGraw Hill, 164–170.

Herbaty, F. 1983. *Cost-Effective Maintenance Management—Preventive Maintenance*. Park Ridge, NJ: Noye Publishing.

Humphries, J. B. 1987. Measuring Maintenance Planning Success. *Plant Engineering* (October 8).

Knight, D. K. 1984. The SWAG Concept Lives. *Timber Harvesting 32*, no. 7 (July): 3.

McCormick, L. B., Jr. 1987. Measuring, Planning & Scheduling Effectiveness. *Plant Engineering* (March 12): 192–194.

———. Making Planned Maintenance Pay Off. *Plant Engineering* (August 9): 50–56.

Robinson, C. 1987. Designing a Master Equipment List. *Plant Engineering* (January 8): 76–78.

———. 1984. *Weyerhaeuser Maintenance Journal 3* (March-April): 6.

CHAPTER 6

Computers: New Tools for a Tough Task

An estimated $250 billion is spent annually on repair and maintenance in the aggregate of all North American industrial plants, and forest products operations probably receive more than their share. This amount constitutes about 6 percent to 11 percent of a typical operating budget—up substantially both as a percent and total from a decade ago.

"The cost of maintenance is only part of the picture," a maintenance expert recently stated. "A larger part is the cost of lost production and broken equipment caused by poor maintenance. With the rise of the factory of the future, maintenance will become even more important. As production becomes more and more automated, maintenance workers are the only ones sure to remain and, if they don't do their job right, production is stopped" (Williams, 1987).

Forest products manufacturing plants are not likely to become that automated anytime soon. But it is likely that equipment failures, which can and do bring whole plants to a stop, will continue. Occasionally, a dramatic plant stoppage such as a boiler accident will become national news. The resulting media coverage focuses on the event as if it were an act of God. Sometimes it is; but most times it is not. Too frequently it is an equipment malfunction, maintenance problem, or operator error. The sophistication and complexity of the newer equipment combined with the demands of the older systems will increase the probability.

"The North American practice of running plants at or beyond design capacity to maximize short-term output aggravates the maintenance problem," a speaker explained to a maintenance conference at Mont Gabriel, Quebec in 1984. "This is further compounded by the tendency to cut manpower when market demand is down" (Fleming and Kawaja, 1984).

One supervisor in industry with production and maintenance problems similar to those faced by the lumber, paper, or structural panel producer stated, "Management now sees computerization as necessary and has provided our department with several thousand dollars to purchase new, state-of-the-art equipment. In today's market, it is certain suicide for any company to continue without at least some degree of computerization" (Williams, 1987).

Computer Tasks

The computer has suddenly become commonplace. New uses are initiated so frequently that it is difficult to keep abreast of even the most significant developments and applications, and the number of useful applications has mushroomed. Weyerhaeuser's experience provides an example of this phenomenon.

Weyerhaeuser has installed numerous maintenance-related systems, ranging from computer-aided design (CAD) programs that create electrical system schematics and process-control drawings, to many and varied computer-assisted maintenance (CAM) applications. CAM software is being used at manufacturing locations such as Weyerhaeuser's softwood lumber operation at North Bend, Oregon.

This thirty-four-year-old tidewater mill produces about 100 million board feet annually of Douglas fir and hemlock lumber and employs about sixty maintenance craftsmen. A CAM-type program purchased from Decision Dynamics Inc. was installed to bring order to an involved planning, scheduling, and tracking process. According to the vendor, "The system leads to improved personnel productivity by improving the scheduling practices." Frank Babcock, the maintenance superintendent, concurs: "One day, we started keeping a backlog and generating work schedules immediately" (Fleming, 1987).

Manual methods such as those formerly used at North Bend are being overwhelmed with the volume of data that has to be assembled, processed, updated, and retrieved in order to make the optimum ongoing decisions. Maintenance management (defined as the direction and control of resources to ensure the optimum continuing availability of plants and equipment) is well served by the computer systems, which can do many of the maintenance documentations and planning tasks. CAM-type software is and continues to be the predominant computer assistance available to the plant operator at Weyerhaeuser and like-situated forest products companies.

Computer-Assisted Maintenance (CAM)

A 1982 survey of North American industry identified thirty systems classified as CAM-type programs. The three important functions—maintenance planning, scheduling, and control; machine history and data base; and spare parts inventory control and purchasing—were only integrated on two of the thirty vendor offerings. About two hundred software packages were on the market by late 1984 along with numerous proprietary in-house systems. A current census would reveal at least a doubling of maintenance-related systems with a far larger choice of features and greater specialization.

Falling prices, ease of use, and fast payback have made these systems popular with the user. Five years ago most maintenance programs were minicomputer based and command driven; today's user can choose a micro, mini, or mainframe computer-driven package. The architecture of today's menu-driven software makes the program user friendly—that is, little training is required. The user then concentrates on manipulating data and obtaining results rather than becoming a computer hacker.

The programs, with imaginative names that range from ABC/MM to WORKSMART, cover almost every imaginable aspect of maintenance management. Work order scheduling and form generation for preventive maintenance are covered along with parts inventory control, equipment history recording, and other aspects.

User success, however, hinges on more than low cost and ease of use. A company and its individual manufacturing locations will find it necessary to decide the overall direction of the total maintenance (TM) program and where they want to go in computer systems. In addition, the user needs to focus on what to expect in terms of effort and results. Let's look at two companies as an example.

The Proctor & Gamble Cellulose, Ltd., pulp mill located near Grande Prairie, Alberta, Canada, developed its own computerized maintenance management system beginning about 1980. The development of work order-related information systems and work order management were the initial primary functions. The original authors also envisioned a totally integrated information system, which was to be expanded over the subsequent years. Parts information by machine number, engineering drawing control system access, automatic preventive maintenance scheduling, equipment history reporting, and maintenance task analysis, were only a few of the features added. The minicomputer that ran the CAM-type programs was then accessed into the main computer.

Payroll, stores information, and purchase order systems are available by access to the mainframe. The maintenance program user is provided maximum flexibility in obtaining information; all that is needed from the mainframe is available. This powerful combination of mini and mainframe provides the user with convenient and timely access to all related performance and cost information.

A vendor-supplied CAM-type system was introduced into Kaibab Forest Products' sawmill in Fredonia, Arizona, over a period of years beginning in 1982. The vendor, Dubal, Beck, Harris & Humphries, Inc., worked with the mill to design and implement an upgraded manual system and then later streamlined into a full-blown CAM system.

The vendor first developed detailed service instructions for each machine or production component. The vendor then organized these instructions into a scheduled preventive maintenance program, with other management functions later added. A machine history file, work order system, and spare parts inventory control were subsequently introduced. The computer monitor or the selected screens (the latter duplicated on a printer) are available immediately upon request.

"Our computer-based maintenance management system has really helped us improve our operations," relates Greg Honey, the maintenance superintendent. "Since we started the program, we've had a big improvement in production and downtime. The computer is essential" (Beck, 1986, 27). Honey also likes the Chargeable Time Summary, a report that identifies where the maintenance personnel are spending the most time—that is, on present or potential trouble spots.

Both Kaibab and Procter & Gamble have identified the direction they want to go and what they feel is realistic in terms of effort and results. Kaibab chose a vendor-supplied product; Procter & Gamble chose a sophisticated in-house designed system. Both have sharply reduced costs and upgraded the respective mill operation. These two locations demonstrate that a CAM system is useful for a plant whose maintenance work detail and quantity of information has grown beyond the normal capability of a manual cost effective system.

Electric motors and mobile equipment are two such specific examples within a mill. Union Camp has expanded a ten-year-old manual electric motor-tracking system into a computer-aided PM program. The CAM system is divided into two files, a motor inventory file and a motor history file.

The motor inventory file assigns a five-digit code that identifies the motor's specifications and its current location. Each location is also assigned a six-digit code; the first three digits identify its location within the mill.

For example, the motors and generators on No. 1 paper machine have the same three digit prefix: 401. Motors and generators on No. 7 machine are assigned 407. These numbers directly correlate with other cost center numbers such as 200 series woodyard, 300 series pulpmill, and 400 series paper machines. Other numerical and alphabetical coding is also used.

The maintenance history of each motor is tracked, and a preventive maintenance program is enhanced with predictive occurrences for each motor type and application. Critical motors are part of the whole, but facts are readily available on an ongoing basis for routine and downtime decisions.

Diagonal Data Corporation has created a comprehensive vehicle software package that can track upwards of ten thousand vehicles—and the status and maintenance needs of each. Work order generation and control, fuel and oil reporting, equipment status reporting, warranty recovery, and cost-per-mile reporting are some of the features tracked for each vehicle in the fleet. The Diagonal Data Corporation product, GEMS Systems, is typical of the systems-development efforts that have focused on the high-payoff operational aspects of the business, not just the bookkeeping. But these systems have limitations: a system will not turn a wrench, inspect a piece of machinery, input data, or act on what it recommends.

Further, a CAM-type program just will not function and be useful if an effectively organized and managed manual program is not in place or capable of being put into place and accompanied by an adequate staff count providing the needed skills for data input and file maintenance, planning and scheduling, and the repair and maintenance task accomplishment in the mill.

Selecting an Approach

"A great deal has been published about the benefits of computerizing the maintenance management function," states *Engineer's Digest*. "Painfully little has been written about the first step . . . that is . . . how to decide if you need such a system" (Donnell, 1987).

A team of four or five people, usually a mix of potential users and systems people, are selected to audit the mill or operation. Their task is to identify and further define the requirements for the short term and long term.

Short term is eighteen to twenty-four months into the future; long term extends to a time frame consistent with the operating future of the plant. And the best way to define the needs is to go to the source: the people who are going to use the system. These people may be called "users" or "stakeholders." They are easily recognized by jobs and positions entitled millwrights, electricians, foremen, leadmen, planners, schedulers, and maintenance managers.

An approach rather than a recipe is needed to aid the selection or design of a CAM program tailored to a user's expectations. A two-stage screening process (see figure 6.1) follows the needs identification and analysis.

The first stage is an initial screening of various programs available from vendors and consultants. This initial screening is a go/no-go procedure for choosing systems that meet the plant's minimum standards. The list of candidate programs is obtained from available sources such as referrals, trade journal articles, and software directories published by various sources.

The first step separates the wheat from the chaff; the examination of the wheat comes during the second screening. The list of desired systems

Computers: New Tools for a Tough Task 69

components is evaluated against the potential candidates singly and in aggregate. Those with the requisite features are held for the second-stage review. The result may be only three or four probables, or as many as twenty and more.

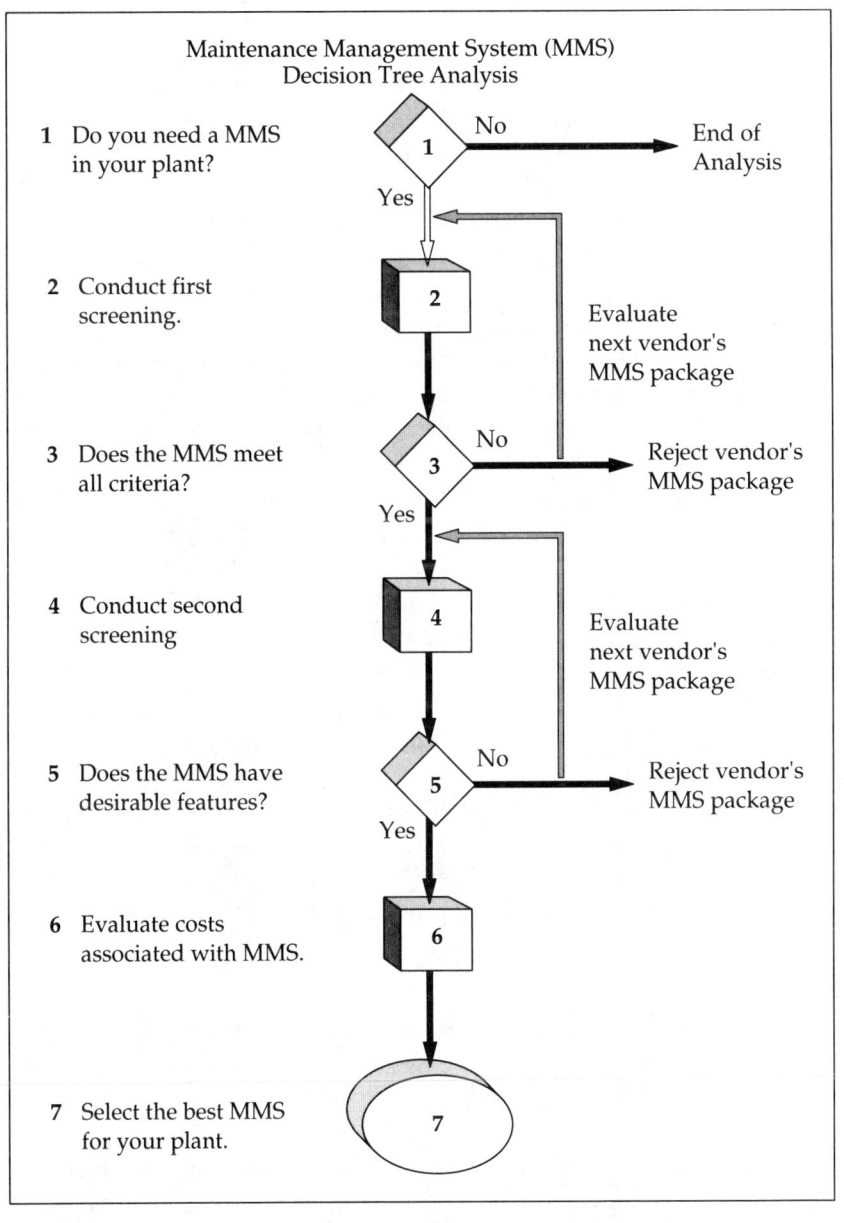

```
Maintenance Management System (MMS)
         Decision Tree Analysis
```

1. Do you need a MMS in your plant? — No → End of Analysis / Yes ↓

2. Conduct first screening. → Evaluate next vendor's MMS package

3. Does the MMS meet all criteria? — No → Reject vendor's MMS package / Yes ↓

4. Conduct second screening → Evaluate next vendor's MMS package

5. Does the MMS have desirable features? — No → Reject vendor's MMS package / Yes ↓

6. Evaluate costs associated with MMS.

7. Select the best MMS for your plant.

Figure 6.1   **A Two-stage Screening Process**

The candidates are then evaluated as the second stage of the screening process proceeds. Each desired feature is carefully examined, as are the subtle aspects of the entire program. All things being equal or near equal, the combination of initial and installation costs may weigh heavily in the selection.

The vendor's reputation, track record, and service history may also rank high on the list of priorities. System compatibility and hardware needs are another consideration. Planners may want to ask these questions: What are our incremental hardware needs? Is the software compatible to currently used systems? System complexity is also a factor. Planners should ask themselves the following questions: What computer skills will be required to run the system? Is it user friendly? What are the time requirements for inputting and maintaining the system? Will the vendor adequately support our training and troubleshooting needs? What type of documentation comes with the system? (user's manual, troubleshooting guide, program documentation, and so on). How flexible is the system? How interconnected are the components? It is essential to answer these questions satisfactorily, and closely match the needs to the software and hardware.

Many mills have already replaced the hardware once or twice as a result of having underestimated their requirements. The hardware system should be capable of at least a fourfold growth in data storage, which otherwise may require a progression through several models of computer hardware and components. The software and file storage techniques must remain compatible through all hardware upgrade.

Provision should be made for the eventual installation of terminals in production areas, shops, and maintenance offices, although initial application may be limited to staff areas such as maintenance planning and scheduling, engineering, and the storeroom. The ideal system could consist of an online system, with the maintenance department controlling and providing the impetus for the action and interface with stores, purchasing, accounting, payroll, personnel, engineering, and manufacturing.

The Make or Buy Decision

The user has a wide-ranging choice between make or buy software. The software choices, along with provisions made for future needs, will narrow down the hardware choice.

The hardware choice will be based on obtaining the biggest buy for the buck considering initial and continuing costs, capability, and capacity; and whether or not the software will be part of a stand-alone system or whether it will be a component for a larger integrated system. An integrated system may need to rely heavily on the in-house tailoring that is the hallmark of a custom system to provide the tie-ins and interfaces that may be peculiar to a particular operation.

An in-house program has other advantages. For instance, company personnel become very familiar with the logic and architecture of the software system and the hardware components. They also gain a thorough understanding of the principles and objectives upon which the CAM is based. There is usually a knowledgeable relationship between maintenance and other business functions. The control of the program standards used in its development are also thoroughly understood along with the long-term mission of the program.

These advantages, however, can also be outweighed by disadvantages. An outside supplier or vendor has generally become an expert over time with the work to be performed; the vendor has acquired focused and skilled programming and consulting expertise. This expertise can translate into lower system costs and less trial and error efforts. More rapid debugging can mean the expected savings come quicker and more surely. In addition, menu-driven software offers such a sophisticated program interface that most users require little training and can concentrate on manipulating data without understanding the computer system.

The outside systems are usually designed broadly enough to apply to a relatively wide range of applications with little or no modification. But an advantage may also be a disadvantage. The particular software may be too broad or too narrow to be a perfect fit, although the broader offerings are rapidly offsetting this potential disadvantage.

Frequently, the copyrighted log is hard-coded, or it is difficult to gain access to a vendor's proprietary information. This can make revisions slow and costly, a particular headache when the operations maintenance program becomes dependent upon the outside-supplied system.

Chances are that a vendor-supplied product will win out over the in-house program. There is just too much development work already accomplished; most desired features have already been written and developed, or the jumping-off place already established, and the talent is in place to extend the hardware and software programs into the future.

References

Armstrong, C. N. 1984. Computerized Maintenance Management. *Western Miner. Maintenance 57*, no. 3 (March): 16.

Barre, D. L. 1985. Wrenches and Keyboards: Does Maintenance Need a Computer? *PIMA* (June): 36–37.

Beck, T. L. 1986. Computer-Assisted Maintenance Management. *Forest Industries* (February): 27.

———. 1985. Managed Maintenance: Software Tools of the Trade. 1985 Sawmill Clinic (March).

Churchill, E. 1987. "It's Suicide to Continue without Some Computerization." *IMPO* (October).

Cooner, N. C., D. P. Sheridan, G. Lundin, and D. L. Willis. 1987. Computer Use in Millwide Maintenance. *TAPPI Journal* (June): 190–191.

Cortes, T. 1986. Using a Minicomputer for Motor Maintenance. Computer-aided Motor Maintenance. *TAPPI Journal* (September): 72–74.

Donnell, R. 1986. Opening Faces. *Timber Processing* (November): 32.

———. 1987. Should You Computerize? *Engineer's Digest* (February).

Fleming, G. K. and D. J. Kawaja. 1984. *Computerized Maintenance Management*. Maintenance Conference. Mont Gabriel, Quebec: 145.

———. 1987. Issue Focus: Maintenance. Maintenance Software Offers Payback. *Forest Industries* (November): 37.

Hodgkenson, A. 1979. *Aspects of the Use of Computers in Maintenance Management: Two Case Studies. Case Study 2: Application of Computers to Maintenance Control.* Abstract: Terotechnica 1 (1980). Amsterdam: Elsevier Scientific Publishing Co., 197–205.

James, L. R. 1984. *Maintenance Management Information Systems*. 1984 Maintenance Conference. Mont Gabriel, Quebec (May): 77–80.

Katzel, J. 1987. Maintenance Management Software. *Plant Engineering* (June 18): 124.

———. 1987. Microcomputer Applications Software. *Plant Engineering Software Directory* (May 14): 68–69.

———. 1986. Modular Maintenance System Controls Work Order, Inventory. Software Review. *Plant Engineering* (March 27): 74–78.

Peele, T. T. and R. L. Chapman, 1986. Automating Maintenance Management. *Plant Engineering* (October 23): 76.

———. 1987. Putting Personal Computers to Work at Weyerhaeuser Co. *Plant Engineering* (March 12): 134–136.

Sage, D. 1985. Computing for Profit. Case Study: Kaibab Forest Products. *Forest Industries* (December): 83–84.

Williams, T. D. 1987. Higher Maintenance Cost Spur Development of New Software. *IMPO* (October).

CHAPTER 7

Program Implementation

The implementation phase of a total maintenance (TM) program is the bridge between the plan and results. An old expression from drag racing aptly describes the expectations of the maintenance manager and the other stakeholders: "We'll see what happens when the rubber meets the road!"

The rubber meets the road when the plan is set in motion. The action steps are selected, each is prioritized, sufficient resources allocated, and time frames established. Then each step is translated into action. A follow-up and tracking system provides feedback on progress. This chapter will take a look at the building blocks managers can use to implement such a plan.

People Selection and Placement

These common issues of people selection and placement need to be resolved at the beginning of the implementation process:

- The job or position description that defines the tasks of each team member, including participants outside the formal maintenance organization.
- A structure that identifies the intended people relationships and how these relationships will work in actual practice.
- A selection and placement process to fill the designated jobs and positions.
- Team-building activities that will mold team members into a cohesive group, that can effectively address the maintenance task overall.

Resolving these issues may be the toughest task facing the manager who is implementing change. Entrenched management forms and relationships, common in many older mills, combined with a union contract with rigid craft skills and detailed work rules, may doom the implementation process. Fortunately, the preparation of the mission statement and objectives (described in chapter 3) required a buy-off from the other major stakeholders, the senior managers. Now it's time to put that buy-off to work.

This buy-off, secured well before the implementation process begins, should be a demonstrated commitment to support change. This support may require tough-minded decisions and the commitment of time and energies. This will resolve difficult people issues that can generate vocal and sometimes costly employee complaints and concerted labor actions. The task is to ascertain that the benefits outweigh the costs, and then proceed.

Specific Task Assignment

The planning and scheduling functions described in chapter 5 are designed to determine who does what when, with what results, at what cost. It's the job of the planner/scheduler to bring substance and visibility to the activity of task assignment. The following discussion of planning and scheduling a lubrication program is a good example of task assignment and follow-up.

The planner/scheduler reevaluates the current lubrication program in terms of form and results. This includes performing an on-site evaluation of the work being done, auditing the oiler activities, and screening the records used to document oiling/lubrication at each machine center. The planner/scheduler then evaluates the current regimen and determines what else needs to be done in conjunction with the input of the lubrication products vendor, the manufacturer of equipment to be maintained, and the actual operating experience of the mill. Specific task assignments can now be made. The planner/scheduler then:

- defines the task and what needs to be done to optimize the lubrication program.
- determines who is to do it. Will this be a combination assignment in conjunction with other maintenance and/or production work? When can it be done, what intervals, and what is to be used?
- walks through the resulting tasks with the assigned individual to determine the effectiveness in time, methods, and coverage.
- periodically audits performance through record checks and on-site inspections.

This format can be used universally for other maintenance processes. Planning and scheduling is the heart of the formal total maintenance (TM) program, and specific task assignment is central to that effort.

Equipment Record System and Downtime Reporting

An equipment record system is the base of any effective maintenance program. It is something more than a dog-eared collection of vendors' manuals, old purchase orders, long-completed work orders, a collection of notes in a soiled manila folder, and assorted repair logs. It is a comprehensive documentation of the facts used as a basis for informed maintenance.

The first question to ask when developing an equipment record list is, What should it contain? The answer is simple: every item that is to be maintained as a separate item, whether a machine or a significant component. Does the item justify the tracking of costs, performance, and downtime? If the answer is yes, it should be included within the master list.

One writer explains how to decide what to include. "In every case, the decision to identify and list equipment and components depends on size, criticality, and the plant's maintenance philosophy. There are no absolute rules about what should or should not be included in a master equipment list. Each plant must draw up guidelines based on its maintenance philosophy and the goals set for the system being installed. Established guidelines ensure that all personnel involved in database development make consistent decisions about specific listings" (Robinson, 1987, 77).

The following broad guidelines should help make this decision easier:

- List all major items that have maintenance costs tracked and performance measured, such as headrigs, paper machines, and veneer lathes.
- List components that are duplicated elsewhere or for which spare parts are stocked.
- List all motors above 5 hp so that maintenance tracking occurs for repair, replacement, or borrowing in the event of a greater need somewhere else in the plant.
- List repairable instruments and components for which insurance or regulatory agency records must be kept, such as an opacity meter on a boiler stack.

When the equipment list is completed, identify the data to be documented about each item (see figure 7.1). Give each item an identification number. Then identify the equipment by type, manufacturer, model number, serial number, location (department, area, and/or processing center), and importance (criticality). Next describe the service use, along with the purchase history and specifications.

Other information, such as a description of past repairs, can also be added to the file. The file should also list either the technical data or a reference for obtaining the need-to-know information. It may also include service and repair recommendations and methods to carry out those recommendations.

As repairs are completed, the system collects and organizes repair information such as cause of failures, total downtime, and repair costs. This information will highlight trends and recurrent breakdowns. Some software, such as Hewlett Packard's Maintenance Management, also provides capabilities for highlighting trends graphically.

The downtime report is an important ancillary document; it provides source information for the equipment record history. This downtime information can either be collected manually or collected automatically at a machine center. The computer can assist with either method of collection. The newer more automated downtime collection systems will fea-

```
┌─────────────────────────────────────────────────────────────┐
│                                                             │
│   Equip. ID No. : _____   Equip. Type : _____ │
│                                                             │
│   Department: _____   Manufacturer: _____ │
│                                                             │
│   Area: _____   Model Number: _____ │
│                                                             │
│   Criticality: _____   Serial No: _____ │
│                                                             │
│                                                             │
│   Service Use: _____ │
│                                                             │
│                                                             │
│   Vendor: _____   P.O. Number: _____ │
│                                                             │
│   Date Purch.: _____   Data Ref.: _____ │
│                                                             │
│                                                             │
│   Specs: _____ │
│   _____  │
│   _____  │
│                                                             │
└─────────────────────────────────────────────────────────────┘
```

Figure 7.1   **Master Equipment List**

ture automatic or semiautomatic collection for frequency of occurrence, length of each, and cause. The semiautomatic systems require the operator or attendant to visually identify the cause and punch it into the collection system.

Figures 7.2 and 7.3 are simple yet effective downtime compilations that are used in a sawmill in southeastern Georgia. The resulting report features a five-day summary of downtime by shift by area or machine. Note the prioritized listing of downtime by source.

For example, the gang saw was the culprit of the week (figure 7.2), having accumulated 24.2 percent of the total downtime or 2.2 percent of the total operating hours. More than two-thirds (32 minutes day shift, 88 minutes night shift) occurred on the night shift. This report further lists

Figure 7.2 Georgia Sawmill Downtime Summary From 04-Aug-86 to 08-Aug-86

Area	D Shift Minutes Downtime	N Shift Minutes Downtime	Total Minutes Downtime	D Shift Occurences Downtime	N Shift Occurences Downtime	Total Occurences Downtime	Percent of Total Downtime	Percent of Total Oper Hrs
GANG	32	88	120	3	6	9	24.4%	2.2%
TRIM SAW	112	0	112	3	0	3	22.8%	2.1%
SORTER	46	34	80	3	3	6	16.3%	1.5%
C-N-S	0	62	62	0	5	5	12.6%	1.1%
WASTE CONV.	0	53	53	0	3	3	10.8%	1.0%
CHIP CONV.	21	0	21	3	0	3	4.3%	0.4%
MISC.	16	0	16	1	0	1	3.3%	0.3%
TIPPLE GATE	0	12	12	0	1	1	2.4%	0.2%
DEBARKER	9	0	9	1	0	1	1.8%	0.2%
EDGER	0	7	7	0	1	1	1.4%	0.1%
LUCKY	0	0	0	0	0	0	0.0%	0.0%
STACKER	0	0	0	0	0	0	0.0%	0.0%
BUCK SAWS	0	0	0	0	0	0	0.0%	0.0%
RAIL SWITCH	0	0	0	0	0	0	0.0%	0.0%
CHIPPERS	0	0	0	0	0	0	0.0%	0.0%
TAYLOR	0	0	0	0	0	0	0.0%	0.0%
DIP VAT	0	0	0	0	0	0	0.0%	0.0%
LOGDECKS	0	0	0	0	0	0	0.0%	0.0%
LOG CONVEYOR	0	0	0	0	0	0	0.0%	0.0%
ROLLCASES	0	0	0	0	0	0	0.0%	0.0%
TEREX	0	0	0	0	0	0	0.0%	0.0%
LOG SHORTAGE	0	0	0	0	0	0	0.0%	0.0%
LOG CRANE	0	0	0	0	0	0	0.0%	0.0%
TOTAL MINUTES	236	256	492	14	19	33	100.0%	9.1%

	D Shift	Percent of Total Downtime N Shift	Total	D Shift	Percent of Total Operating Time N Shift	Total
OPERATIONAL	20.3%	44.3%	33.0%	1.8%	4.3%	3.1%
MECHANICAL	71.2%	42.8%	56.2%	6.2%	4.2%	5.2%
ELECTRICAL	8.5%	12.9%	10.8%	0.7%	1.3%	1.0%
	100.0%	100.0%	100.0%	8.7%	9.8%	9.3%
OPERATING HOURS:	45	45	90			

Program Implementation 79

the areas or machines in sequential order from the next greatest downtime (trim saw) to the least. Only the downtime that caused a production interruption was tallied. Maintenance tasks or problems that could be taken care of "on the fly" or during scheduled downtime were excluded from this record.

Figure 7.3 provides more detail on the gang saw; each of the other areas (machine center or process) and individual pieces of equipment also have a separate listing. For example, the gang saw summary of downtime categorizes the machine stoppages by operational, mechanical, and electrical based on a predetermined definition of each. Saw problems on the bottom arbor of the double arbor gang is the apparent cause, the operator or maintenance person then confirms the real cause and solves the problem.

"Even when a maintenance job looks minimal, we consult the records and look up the equipment history," commented Lufkin Industries employee Darvin Dominey, as he described a problem-solving approach similar to the one used in the Georgia sawmill (Steiner, 1987, 34). The equipment history, including the downtime portion, assists in determining both the cause and solutions for downtime and maintenance problems.

Dominey's thoughts were reinforced by Kevin Baker in an article entitled "Fixing the Breakdown Blues": "If managers can track the history of individual pieces of forestry equipment, they can ensure maintenance is performed before a breakdown happens" (Baker, 1987, 18). An equipment record and downtime reporting system is the key to making that happen.

Figure 7.3 *Georgia Downtime Summary for a Specified Area of the Mill*

			Minutes	Percent
		D SHIFT:	32	26.7%
04-Aug-86	AREA OF MILL:	N SHIFT:	88	73.3%
TO		OPERATIONAL:	91	75.8%
		MECHANICAL:	11	9.2%
08-Aug-86	GANG	ELECTRICAL:	18	15.0%
		TOTAL:	120	100.0%

Date	S	Reason	O	M	E
04-Aug-86	D	PRESSROLL CHAIN OFF & REPAIRED	5		
06-Aug-86	N	FEEDROLLS KICKED OUT & WOULDN'T RESTART			18
07-Aug-86	N	CHANGED BOTTOM SAWS/ LAYED DOWN	10		
06-Aug-86	N	CHANGED BOTTOM SAWS 2 TIMES/LAYED	17		
08-Aug-86	N	CHANGED BOTTOM SAWS 2 TIMES/LAYE	19		
07-Aug-86	N	CHAIN OFF INFEED PRESSROLL & REPAIRED		6	
06-Aug-86	N	CANT HUNG IN SAWS	18		
31631	D	BOTTOM SAWS CHANGED/ LAYED DOWN	5		
08-Aug-86	D	BOTTOM SAW CHANGED 3 TIMES	22		

Stores and Inventory Control

Stores and inventory control keeps track of parts both on hand and on order, identifies their location, and determines available quantities in-house and outside the location. Timely identification of maintenance needs provides time to shop an item and still get it to the job site or storeroom in time. (Chapter 21 provides additional information on this maintenance basic.)

Computer-assisted Maintenance (CAM)

Who needs a computer-aided maintenance (CAM) management system? Edwin L. Marshall, president of Chicago's Marshall & Little Inc., a maintenance management consultant firm, gives this answer:

"It is useful for any plant whose maintenance-work detail and amount of information have grown beyond the normal capability of manual system. There are no hard and fast rules other than economic justification . . . but experience suggests that plants with a maintenance crew as small as four people can justify computerization."

He added, "A computer-aided maintenance-management system is not magical, it does nothing by itself. What it does is schedule and help plan an already functioning maintenance system" (Bose, 1984, 69–71). The rule of thumb is organize, and implement, then computerize.

A successful CAM startup begins before the computer is even plugged in. The stakeholders—vendors, outside consultants, or company systems specialists, as well as the on-site participants—need to familiarize themselves with the plant and its facilities.

Next the equipment record system (see figure 7.1) should be audited to ascertain that the listing is accurate and up to date, and that the current numbering system is adequate for the equipment grouping and sequential numbering required with a CAM program. Training mill people—the users—in the use of basic hardware and software should proceed concurrently with other preparation activities.

An installation checklist is also developed as part of the overall plan to automate the information system. This comprehensive checklist will include the entire sequence of activities that occur during the installation process; this sequence of activities includes the installation plan for introducing the various modules that make up the total software package.

The resulting computerized information system provides three tiers of information:

1. First tier: Basic information about machines, maintenance routines, personnel, and parts inventory.

2. Second tier: Daily information, such as work order status, scheduling information assignments, job and machine reporting, and parts and material information.
3. Third tier: Reports on time and cost accounting, machine history, personnel performance, and inventory status.

The third tier of a well-designed program allows the user either to stop and print the results for manual analysis, or to go on and allow the computer to analyze and provide whatever visual aids are needed to identify trends and variances. These features are usually extras that are purchased as an add-on, or are recognized as the upscale feature of the computer and the software selected.

Pitfalls

There are pitfalls to even the most well thought-out CAM management system. Introducing a software program as an answer to a need as yet unidentified is one; introducing a complex and difficult to maintain system is another.

Data input forms need to be designed with the millwright in mind. Filling out too many forms that are too complicated to use is a program killer. This was recognized early on: "It should be noted that if many forms have to be filled out to make a maintenance planning program work, the system will fail. Therefore, the system designed for use on the computer should require as few forms as possible" (Richardson, 1980, 84).

A yes/no or multiple-choice data input is preferred to original phrases or numbers. Simple checkmarks or other indicators should be used where practical. Where original input is required it should be keyed off well-accepted terminology for that organization or manufacturing process. It is all right to use specialized words or phrases (for example, "changed bottom saws/layed down"), as long as each has a recognized meaning for the participants.

The output of the software can also yield pitfalls. Too little feedback is an infrequent problem; but its cousin, too much feedback, happens too often. This pitfall is characterized by voluminous screens or printouts that require excessive study and manual data manipulation to provide understanding. A few selected facts are better than too many.

The Benefits

A total out-of-pocket cost reduction of one-third and more may be possible when achieving greater uptime and improved quality. The actual figure will depend on the state of the existing maintenance program when

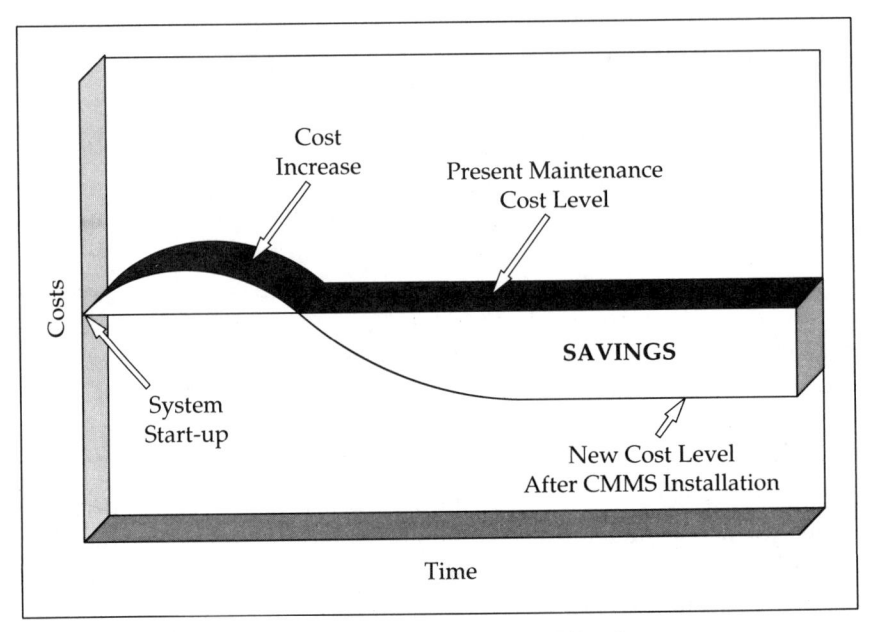

Figure 7.4   **Cost/Benefit Curve for CAM Portion of TM Program**

Source: Reprinted with permission from July 1986 issue of *Engineer's Digest Magazine*. Copyright 1989, Intertech Publishing Corp., Overland Park, Kansas.

the TM program was initiated. The actual amount will depend on the skill of the operator and the crew, and the status of the maintenance effort — that is, whether the plant was on a break-it/fix-it mode of operation, or whether it had graduated into a PM phase of the maintenance effort.

The payback rate for a TM program with a CAM-type system may not happen immediately. In fact, the total maintenance bill may increase during the installation and transition period (see figure 7.4).

Cost increases are likely at the beginning of the program. The actual cost behavior for the total program is similar to a capital investment, a sometimes costly startup curve is soon translated into sharply improving results. That's the rule rather than the exception with a well-implemented program.

References

Baker, K. 1987. Fixing Breakdown Blues. *Logging & Sawmilling* (March).
Barton, W. D. and R. Warburton. 1980. *Aspects of the Use of Computers, in Maintenance Management; Two Case Studies. Case Study 1: Application of Computers to*

Prevention Maintenance Schedulings. Abstract: Terotechnica 1 (1980). Amsterdam: Elsevier Scientific Publishing Co., 187–96.

Bose, P. P. 1984. Moving Maintenance toward Prevention. *American Machinist* (December): 69–71.

Geisel, C. E. 1985. Get the Operator in on the Act: A Maintenance Program That Makes Equipment Reliable. *TAPPI Journal 68*, no. 5 (May): 136–38.

Herbaty, F. 1983. Cost Effective Maintenance Management. Park Ridge, NJ: Noyes Publications. 183–203.

Lewis, G. W. 1986. Don't Overlook Electronics Basics. *Timber Processing* (November).

Mayer, P. 1985. Installing and Starting Up a Computerized Maintenance Management System. *Practical Lubrication and Maintenance 8*, no. 3 (September): 9–10.

Patton, J. D., Jr. 1983. *Prevention Maintenance Computer Assistance. Instrument Society of America.* NY: Publishers Creative Services Inc., 113–20.

Richardson, D. C. 1980. Maintenance Management System Can Increase Plant Availability and Reliability. *Power Engineering* (July): 84.

Robinson, C. J. 1987. Designing a Master Equipment List. *Plant Engineering* (January 8).

Sainas, J. 1983. The Evolving Sawmill: Computer Assisted Maintenance – Slash Costs, Paperwork With CAMS. *Logging and Sawmilling Journal* (October): 24–25.

Steiner, V. 1987. Facilities Engineering Improving Maintenance Reporting with Personal Computers. *Plant Engineering* (November 25): 30–31.

———. 1987. Computerized Maintenance Tracking Cuts Downtime and Inventory. *Plant Engineering* (May 14): 34.

Wells, A. 1984. Computer Aided Maintenance Keeps Production Flowing. *Petroleum Review 38*, no. 447: 31.

Wigmore, C. E. 1980. Computerized Maintenance Management System. Abstract from CPPA Maintenance Conference.

CHAPTER 8

Maintenance Problem Solving

This chapter is all about problem solving, especially when the answers are difficult to obtain. It presents a systematic approach to problem prevention, detection, and solution. The goal of this and succeeding chapters (particularly chapters 10, 11, and 12) is to provide the reader with the tools to prevent poor performance and costly results.

The Problem

What should the mill expect in performance and ease of operation? When do we really have a problem? These questions become more and more difficult to answer with the introduction of space-age machinery and state-of-the-art retrofits. Managers must employ trained personnel and advanced analysis and problem-solving techniques to overcome each new problem as it occurs: "The reliability of electronics systems in a mill rests on the ability of electrical and electronic maintenance personnel to read electronic schematics and troubleshoot systems. Correspondingly, the reliability of hydraulic systems depends on the ability of maintenance personnel to read hydraulic schematics and effectively troubleshoot systems" (Smiley, 1987, 30).

Traditionally, downtime—defined as an element of time in which a system or component could not operate during scheduled operating hours—was the prime indicator of equipment efficiency. The lower the downtime, the higher the equipment performance. It was as simple as that. Today increased complexity, costliness, and heightened expectations have begun to replace the term downtime with a broader term: failure.

Failure describes a condition in which a machine or system component is not operating within the bounds or specifications set forth; that is, it is unable to carry out its intended function satisfactorily. Sometimes failure isn't even understood until it is too late, as the following story illustrates.

Maintenance Problem Solving 85

> Several years ago a large bank loaned a Northwestern sawmill a little over five million dollars to modernize its plant. Despite the new equipment, the mill ran into serious problems with the loan and filed for Chapter 11 bankruptcy. The mill management was experienced and sales were brisk, yet continuous operating losses were putting the mill into default.
>
> Observation of the mill operation showed considerable downtime. A study of the downtime records confirmed the hunch that downtime was the problem. The sawmill was experiencing 30% "unanticipated operational downtime" (UDO), and management didn't even realize that the downtime was eating up its profits. (Mater and Mater, 1987, 26)

This mill had downtime in the traditional sense—the mill was not operating. However, the actual nonrunning time was probably the tip of the iceberg. The real culprit was machine and system failure; downtime was only the symptom. Chances are that the equipment was not performing its intended function satisfactorily when it was operating and manufacturing lumber the other 70 percent of the time.

This mill is not unlike others in the lumber and other wood-based businesses, which usually experience a problem cycle after initial startup and debugging. The progressive stages of the cycle eventually lead to the blowout—unexpected major downtime. The various stages are detectable; the trick is to understand the stages and correct the causes early on. The problem cycle consists of the following six stages:

1. Gestation: Barely detectable, usually precipitated by changing demands of the process; introducing unsuitable components, neglect, or improper maintenance.
2. Incipient failure: The machine or system appears to operate well, but its ability to maintain attainable tolerances begins to wane. Hydraulic usage and amperage demand may increase.
3. Incipient damage: Telltale symptoms begin to appear—heat, vibration, or a change in the composition of the lubricating oil are common.
4. Distress: The signs become audible and visible—for example, an uncharacteristic sound of a gear train in operation, or evidence of spalling at the base of a bearing.
5. Deterioration: Unscheduled downtime begins to occur; repair is only what is needed to get by, and is done only in reaction to an apparent cause.
6. Blowout: Major downtime, requiring extensive repairs and replacements.

It's easier to define the problem later in the cycle. Unfortunately, the blowout is probably a serious indicator of what is happening elsewhere in the mill. The operator's gut reaction is usually to play maintenance hopscotch—that is, to solve each problem as it occurs. New parts, usually secured on an emergency basis, and extraordinary maintenance man-hours are thrown at the developing problems. If the operator is lucky, enough of the downtime problems will be licked before the money or patience runs out. But sometimes luck runs out. The compelling task for the operator is to spot the problem in its initial stages and cure it there. It can be done.

Problem Prevention

Problem prevention begins with the selection and design of equipment, and proceeds through the layout, installation, training, startup, and debugging phases of the project. Each is important to failure prevention.

Much can be done to design away from maintenance problems. Design considerations can be as simple as placing the grease fittings where each is readily accessible; or implementing structural redesigns that will beef up and simplify the machine while eliminating high maintenance components. Scrapping little-used features, sometimes called whistles and bells, will add a great deal to the problem- and failure-prevention effort.

Failure prevention is a way of thinking and doing on a continuing basis. The remarks of a complex maintenance manager in Western Washington make this clear:

> A prime management objective for the maintenance function should be to maximize production by minimizing the maintenance caused downtime. The production manager of the plant should keep asking the maintenance people over and over again, "Why did the breakdown occur and what have you done to see that it doesn't occur again? What could have been done to prevent it?" If the maintenance man can look at this job in this light then he's open minded to a preventive maintenance and repair program.

Preventive maintenance and condition-based monitoring are proven helps in identifying a problem early on. Preventive maintenance has been described in earlier chapters; condition-based monitoring (or predictive maintenance, as it is frequently called) is described at length in chapters 10, 11, and 12. And then there is the ultimate: the helicopter maintenance policy suggested by a Northern California sawmill owner, who also owns a helicopter crane service:

"I would like to get a helicopter preventative maintenance-type program into the sawmill. You have to keep a helicopter in service to pay its way. Helicopter maintenance is organized by section. We periodically work our way through each section of the helicopter on a systematic and planned way without waiting for problems to show up. We need to figure out how to do that in a sawmill."

Section-by-section coverage may not be attainable for the typical forest products operation, but the concept and the follow-up thinking can add a new dimension to problem prevention.

Problem Solving

Traditionally, problems have been singled out for correction on the basis of empirical data such as downtime, parts usage, hydraulic oil consumption, work orders, production reports, customer complaints . . . and the list goes on. The tendency is to focus on the visible, and then deal with each problem as it is observed. The key to problem solving, however, is troubleshooting, more of an art than a science.

Troubleshooting defines the problem results and then works backward to identify the cause of failure. The resulting troubleshooting and problem solving can be simplified by the following guidelines:

- Problems have causes. Separate the apparent symptoms from the real cause before trying to solve for the latter.
- Problems will occur. It's better to plan and anticipate them rather than to be surprised.
- Problems are best solved one at a time. Always prioritize and allocate resources of time and money on those that will yield the biggest bang for the buck.
- Analyze problems before taking action. Know what you want to accomplish and how you will measure the results.
- Small problems become progressively larger as the failures are allowed to continue. Each tends to become more complex and the root cause more difficult to recognize as time goes on.

The following quote is from a hardcover manual on machinery failure and troubleshooting. It aptly describes the task for the maintenance person: We need to gear our thinking patterns to allow us to be efficient and successful. "Machinery failure analysis and troubleshooting is really the process of understanding what causes machinery to fail or malfunction.

Figure 8.1 *Troubleshooting Outline*

---

1. Identify problem or failure symptom.
   - observed changes from normal such as those observed by sensors or human senses
   - internal inspection results
   - postmortem analysis
2. List possible cause of each problem or failure symptom.
3. Search for tie-in between symptom and cause.
4. Rank the probability of each symptom/cause relationship.
5. Begin and continue the remedial procedure in a systematic fashion.
6. Follow up to ascertain that problem or failure symptoms and results have been corrected.

'Understanding is thinking,' and as one successful troubleshooter once said, troubleshooting is knowing when to think and when to act. If failure analysis and troubleshooting at times are not successful, it may be that our thinking patterns do not allow us to be efficient and successful" (Bloch and Geitner, 1983, 214). Becoming thoroughly familiar with the functional characteristics of the machine/system, the interaction of the parts, the operating and failure modes, and have an overall understanding of the process: These are initial steps to gearing our thinking patterns for success.

Figure 8.1 is a simplified troubleshooting outline. First, the trouble symptoms are identified and quantified where possible. Symptoms will usually appear as observed changes from normal—something may look different, or smell funny, or sound wrong. Internal inspections and postmortem analysis are part of that inspection and sensing process.

Sensors are increasingly taking the lead in identifying failure symptoms. Sophisticated conditioning-monitoring equipment, either operated continuously or at discrete intervals, identifies a signature for a particular failure mode that appears as vibration, heat, sound, or image even before the problem is detectable within the threshold of the human senses.

Next the troubleshooter lists all the possible causes of the problem or failure symptom. The knowledge of the equipment or the ability to have readily available resource information then comes into play. Usually the vendor or the vendor's representative will back up the on-site troubleshooter or at least act as a sounding board for problem discussion.

For example, most bearing failures can be attributed to one or more of the following causes: defective bearing seats on shafts and in the housing, misalignment, faulty mounting practices, incorrect shafts and housing fit, an unsuitable bearing type or size, and inadequate lubrication. The symptom or symptoms may appear as spalling, misalignment to shaft, corrosion, scoring, and excessive thrust load (the latter is often readily apparent as the bearing is placed under full load).

The troubleshooter then searches for a tie-in between the symptoms and the possible causes. The next step is to rank probability by cause, remedy the problem systematically, and then ascertain that the problem and failure cause has been corrected. Occasionally, the solution is only found after repeated trial and error; sometimes radical solutions, such as a major engineering redesign, may be required. Replacement of the entire piece of equipment may even turn out to be the least costly solution.

The troubleshooting process outlined in figure 8.1 can be used effectively to obtain relatively simple solutions, such as with bearing problems. It can also be used with more complex maintenance problems, which require advanced problem-solving techniques.

Advanced Problem-solving Techniques

The increased complexity and cost of the manufacturing process has hastened a new era in problem solving and troubleshooting: the need to do it rapidly. Manual problem-solving techniques are fast being supplemented by more automated methods.

The self-diagnostic features of the newer electromechanical systems are a step in that direction. However, powerful and more advanced techniques have added a new dimension to the problem-solving process. One such technique, sneak analysis (SA), was initiated by the National Aeronautics and Space Administration (NASA) in the 1960s and further refined in the years that have followed.

Sneak Analysis (SA)

Sneak analysis (SA) is a term applied to a group of analytical techniques that identify design oversights. These design oversights may cause the occurrence of one or more unwanted functions. SA is generally structured using the documentation prepared in designing, engineering, and manufacturing the system.

SA searches out and identifies any unexpected path of logic within a system that, under certain conditions, can initiate an unwanted function or inhibit a desired function. It can operate alone and/or in combination with the hardware, software, and operator actions.

The resulting sneak circuits trace the paths of current, energy, or logic sequence and determine whether or not the path travels along an unexpected route or in an unintended direction. SA also searches the timing sequence to ascertain that planned events do not occur in an unexpected or conflicting sequence. SA traces system control board indicators to make sure there are no ambiguous or false displays of system operating conditions that could mislead the operator to take an undesired action. Conversely, SA also examines the control labeling to ensure against incorrect or imprecise labels that could result in the activation of undesired control system functions.

SA is used primarily as a troubleshooting and failure prevention tool; it was originally designed to examine the electric/electronic systems and computer programs for hard-to-detect errors. It since has evolved so that it can be used to evaluate other systems, such as mechanical, pneumatic, hydraulic, and others.

Expert Systems

Expert systems are computer programs, primarily designed for training and troubleshooting, that draw on the organized expertise of one or more experts plus the other resource material available. Each system covers a specific topic or particular subject matter. The knowledge base of the system has two components, the facts and the rules. (1) Factual information about the equipment or system is entered into the factual database.

(2) The rules of thumb for diagnosing problems, which the expert participant has accumulated during years of experience, are entered into the heuristic database.

The development of each system hinges on the acquisition of accurate information, which is then organized into factual and heuristic reasoning rules. These in turn are inserted into a so-called expert software shell. The resulting software can either be run on a mainframe or easily adapted to a desktop personal computer. The system is a natural for problem solving and troubleshooting.

An expert system, tailored to a particular piece of equipment or process, can reduce the time required for repairs by correctly diagnosing the failure cause and providing repair recommendations. An expert system is interactive with the user; it requests information about the case from the user and in turn provides a recommendation based on the data provided. It even explains the basis for its recommendations upon request.

The resulting knowledge base synthesizes the information into a cohesive whole that can be used by many parties within a user-friendly format. The user needs to know little more than the most basic computer operating knowledge. Perhaps the expert system's greatest contribution occurs prior to the need for maintenance repairs. The expert system:

- provides a training tool to continuously update the knowledge and skill level of the maintenance personnel. Practical advice and on-the-job training is readily available for each equipment operator or maintenance person as an aid in honing their repair and troubleshooting skills.
- creates an environment that promotes practical preventive maintenance (PM) rather than reactive repairs. The useful operating life of the equipment is thus extended.
- develops many experts rather than a few; minimizes the communication and call-out burden on senior plant maintenance personnel. There is less opportunity for one or two individuals to become virtually indispensable.

Five additional characteristics make the expert system even more attractive as a maintenance tool:

1. It utilizes a natural language. Ask in English, it responds in English.
2. It draws upon multiple areas of expertise. The facts and the rules will be as extensive as needed; the depth and breadth will depend on the need and the multiple sources of information available.

3. It explains the reasoning to the user upon request. It provides a transparent knowledge basis that can be examined and challenged.
4. It can provide recommendations based on incomplete data, then follows with a probability expression, such as, "I'm 85 percent certain of this recommendation."
5. It offers more than one solution to the problem when requested; the user then selects the most desirable option.

Currently, expert systems are not widely used in the forest products industry; but it's just a matter of time. As plant equipment and systems become ever more complex, keeping the staff up to date can become a serious problem. There just may not be enough human experts to go around. The expert systems are an answer to that need.

Automated Expert Systems

The expert systems described above rely on the user to provide the information about the case; the software then diagnoses the failure cause and provides repair recommendation. Expert systems, so useful in training and troubleshooting, tend to be used after the fact by the troubleshooter and can create a situation described by Pierre Dersin (1987) as "autopsy rather than diagnosis."

Dersin's company, Transimatics, Inc., has developed and produces an online system that provides a special niche between the manual expert systems and the device diagnostic features of most PLCs (Programmable Logic Controller) and many custom microprocessor controllers. The resulting product provides an online diagnostic expert system for automated fault detection and monitoring in industrial machinery and processes.

The site-specific uses of the automated expert systems require a discrete body of knowledge with accurate sensing devices to determine when the system falls out of the desired norm. The ambiguity, so tolerated in the manual expert systems, cannot be present for the automated devices to function effectively.

Ambiguity is partially compensated for by high-resolution signals that allow for generation of signature curves. These signature curves are used for calibration and setup verification of the equipment or process. Trend analysis occurs as the system or equipment operates and immediately signals out-of-spec performance, which reduces the amount of time and effort spent making bad product before a problem is detected and the failure cause identified. Repairs begin immediately.

The automated diagnostic system focuses on process diagnostics rather than the device diagnostics of the PLCs and similar computerized control systems. Automated expert systems enhance the built-in diagnostic features of the PLCs which often simply check the controller I/O modules, power supply, and like components.

These newer controllers, PLCs, and microprocessors are simply too slow and too focused on the control function to be much value as system monitors unless specifically overlaid onto the system. However, the diagnostic features of these systems combined with the simplicity of the ladder diagram tracking, inherent in the PLCs, have been so much more efficient at failure identification than the troubleshooting required with the ratchet relay systems of the pre-1980 era that the mill operator is still dazzled by their use. Automated expert systems now offer something better.

Other Maintenance Problem-solving Aids

The newer problem-solving and troubleshooting techniques are taking trial-and-error out of maintenance. The challenge for the forest products operator is to keep up with the exponential growth of these knowledge-based skills. Each year brings something more.

For example, Apple Computer's Hypercard software is making it easier for Apple computer users to organize and sort through huge amounts of information. This will allow the user, including the maintenance professional, to glean through and categorize information heretofore relatively untouched because of the time and effort required.

This will affect the operator and maintenance professional in at least two ways: It will spawn ideas for even more sophisticated equipment and process systems; and it will provide a way for the mill operator to keep up. Keeping up has been no easy task, and it will be even more difficult in the years ahead. And how does one keep up?

First participants in the industry, both individually and collectively, determine that "keeping up" is a priority and "keep on keeping on" is not. Resistance to change will be replaced with a questioning attitude; habits will be transient, each will change as the demand requires. And the end result? Problems that are not real problems but opportunities in disguise—sometimes deep disguise—are resolved in a timely and economical fashion.

References

Bloch, H. P. and F. K. Geitner. 1983. *Practical Machinery Management for Process Plants. Vol 2, Machinery Failure Analysis and Troubleshooting.* Houston: Gulf Publishing.

———. 1987. A New Approach to Equipment Diagnostics. *CIM Strategies* (September).

Dallimonti, R. 1987. Computers in Maintenance: Smarter Maintenance with Expert Systems. *Plant Engineering* (June 18): 51–56.

Dersin, P. 1987. Process Diagnostics Beyond Real-Time: The Detective™ Expert System. Paper. Control Expo. '87. (Session XII), Chicago, May 19–21.

Mater, M. H. and M. S. Mater. 1987. Preventive Maintenance Key to Profitability. *Forest Industries* (November).

———. 1987. New Product Showcase. December 15–17, 1987–Anaheim Convention Center. *Plant Engineering* (November 25): 64.

———. 1987. Putting Personal Computers to Work at Weyerhaeuser Co. *Plant Engineering* (March 12, 1987): 134–136.

Schlender, B. R. 1987. New Software Beginning to Unlock the Power of Personal Computers. *Wall Street Journal* (November 16): 27.

Smiley, C. A. Correct Pressure Settings Reduce Hydraulic Downtime. *Forest Industries* (November): 30.

Transimatics. 1987. Product Note. The Detective™; A Tool For Automated Fault Detection and Statistical Quality Control. Burlington, MA: Transimatics, Inc.

CHAPTER 9

Safety and Loss Prevention

The traffic reporter's screams, "Hit the water! Hit the water! Hit the water!" were her last words as the helicopter dropped sharply, struck a sidewalk and chainlink fence, and then plunged into the Hudson River. A million listeners, mostly rush-hour commuters, were stunned as they listened to what later was reported as a maintenance mishap. Paul Harvey, while delivering a postscript in a broadcast from Chicago several days later, stated, "The mechanic installed the wrong clutch...he [the mechanic] resigned."

Safety errors can kill, maim, and seriously injure employees, even the maintenance worker. Mistakes are costly, as this accident in a South Carolina lumber operation demonstrates: Repairs were required at a log conveyor. The power was cut off, and the maintenance man crawled onto the conveyor to investigate the problem. Suddenly, the machine restarted, the worker sustained severe head and chest injuries and died instantly. Why? The required safety lockout was not in place.

These two stories point out two errors that are more common than the industry would like: failure to use the correct parts and to double check the completed work, and failure to use a secure lockout device. It doesn't have to be that way.

E.I. duPont de Nemours, a company known worldwide for the manufacture of explosives and chemicals, rarely has a lost-time injury. Its Kinston, North Carolina, synthetic-fibers plant completed 66 million manhours over a thirteen-year period without a lost-time injury. Howard A. Kress, manager of the Kinston plant, explains. "The basic premise is that the company will produce materials only if they can be manufactured, transported, used, and disposed of safely" (Teresko, 1981). This basic premise is also becoming more widespread in the forest products industry.

Dick Parrish, Boise Cascade's vice president of timber and wood products, recently stated, "Several years ago we looked at the individual plant numbers, and we decided that we needed to change." Parrish later described the efforts made in creating believers throughout the organization. "It is not uncommon for a Boise Cascade plant to go a year or more without a lost-time injury, the emphasis and commitment is there. The maintenance personnel are an important part of the commitment . . . and effort."

How do others get to the commitment phase in the transition to safe work and maintenance practices? Safety-related educational material is printed and distributed in an almost endless stream; this material ranges from posters and visual aids with catchy phrases to almost indecipherable rules and regulations printed in the *Congressional Record*. The task is to sort out the vital few and use them as a foundation for promoting safety in a maintenance department and the mill. The following is not a guide to OSHA regulations; it is a no-nonsense guide on how not to burn down a mill or seriously impair or kill a worker.

The Millwright as a Missionary for Safety

Millwrights and other maintenance personnel do more than pack tools and fix things; each has a unique role to play in setting the pace for the mill's safety and loss-prevention efforts. Training is a key to that effort. Each maintenance person should be a card carrier: One card indicates first aid training certification with a current date; another card indicates the completion of a program such as the DuPont Safety Training Observation Program (STOP), which stresses safe work habits. Figure 9.1 illustrates the premise of the program, which is based on extensive research.

About 96 percent of lost workday cases and restricted workday cases are the result of unsafe acts. Two classes of unsafe acts, tool-related causes and positions of people, account for a half of all the injuries. Personal protective equipment and actions of people together with the former two make up more than two-thirds of the total mishaps.

A safety trained millwright often buttresses the skills that may be (and often are not adequately) represented in the overall work force. The maintenance person generally has access to all parts of the mill, and is usually the first to respond to an unusual occurrence that can and does result in injury. As a trained observer, each has the opportunity to assess their own skills while assessing the skills of those around the work or problem area. In addition, the opportunity to observe and talk with others can sometimes prevent tragedies. The following incident in a western Washington mill demonstrates the need for improved communication skills.

Figure 9.1 *Unsafe Acts That Cause Lost Workday Cases (LWCs) and Restricted Workday Cases (RWCs) Typical 10-Year Period*

Class of Unsafe Acts	LWCs and RWCs (%)
Personal protective equipment	12
Positions of people	30
Actions of people	14
Tools	20
Equipment	8
Procedures	11
Orderliness	1
Total injuries caused by unsafe acts of people	96
Total injuries from other sources	4
	100

Source: Baldwin, 1984

Dan was a graveyard-shift millwright with a Class A certification. He was also working on his electrical certification and had become an excellent troubleshooter and multiskill maintenance person. However, he also had family problems, which he took onto the job with him. He was getting little rest between shifts and had to do a lot of coping.

Early one morning, Dan answered a trouble call at the veneer-edge gluer machine center. The "grasshopper" transfer between the jointer and storage trays was not functioning properly. A series of air-activated valves controlled the function. Dan locked out the jointer but kept the transfer system activated to test fire the air valves. He crawled under the machine as a companion observed nearby. His coworkers could only guess what Dan had on his mind when he manually fired the wrong valve; but it was too late. A crushing blow ended his life.

"If we had only known," lamented several of his coworkers. Training, knowledge, and simply thinking ahead to what might happen can enable maintenance workers to save their coworkers or a nearby production worker as well as themselves.

The Essentials, Tasks, and Protective Devices

Wearing an approved hard hat, safety glasses, gloves, safety shoes, and hearing protection when needed is essential for maintenance workers in most forest products plants—even when such devices and apparel are not mandated. The resulting safety habit will become an important barrier to an accident.

This protective equipment is designed to prevent injuries caused by striking against, being struck by, being caught in, and falling onto machinery. Other specialized safety devices, such as those used for cutting and welding, are also needed from time to time.

Safety tasks are another important barrier to injury. The death of the South Carolina worker cited earlier could have been avoided with a foolproof lockout device. Figure 9.2 identifies the core features of failsafe lockout procedures.

Following these procedures, it is usually sufficient to lock out the main disconnect switch in the "off" position. On machines with hydraulic or pneumatic power sources, the lines and reservoir tanks are either relieved or bled to zero pressure. The controls are then locked out with a personal padlock to prevent accidental reactivation of the system.

The lockout procedures should be used at all times; the employee who places the tag should remove the lockout at the completion of the job or when transferring the uncompleted job to another. There should be a clear penalty for noncompliance.

The cutting and welding permit illustrated in figure 9.3 provides a one-over-one review of the fire- and loss-prevention efforts prior to the job. The maintenance person originating the cutting and welding permit makes certain that the site is clear of debris and combustible materials; and also ascertains that fire protection equipment such as hoses, water

Figure 9.2 *Lockout Procedures*

1. Alert the operator.
2. Before starting work on an engine or motor, line shaft of other power transmission equipment, or power-driven machine, make sure it cannot be set in motion without your permission.
3. Place your own padlock on the control switch, lever, or valve, even though someone has locked the control before you. You will not be protected unless you put your own padlock on it.
4. When through working at the end of your shift, remove your own padlock, or your own sign and blocking. Never permit someone else to remove it for you, and be sure you are not exposing another person to danger by removing your padlock or sign.
5. If you lose the key to your padlock, report the loss immediately to your supervisor and get a new padlock.

Source: National Safety Council, 1974

Safety and Loss Prevention 99

CUTTING AND WELDING PERMIT	DATE	
FIRE CONTROL SECTION	DEPARTMENT	
BUILDING		LOCATION ON FLOOR
TIME STARTED	FINISHED	
NATURE OF JOB		

ALL PRECAUTIONS HAVE BEEN TAKEN TO AVOID ANY POSSIBLE FIRE HAZARD. AND PERMISSION IS GIVEN FOR THIS WORK.

SIGNED _____   SIGNED _____
OPERATION SUPERVISOR   CRAFTSMAN

                             _____
                             FIREWATCH

Figure 9.3 Cutting and Welding Permit

buckets, and fire extinguishers are on site. The fire hose will be charged with adequate pressure and laid down adjacent to the work being performed.

One southern plywood producer discovered what happens when the workplace has not been adequately prepared for cutting and welding: A millwright was called to one of two hot presses on a trouble call. The fix required cutting and welding. A spark ignited a build-up of dust and wood volatiles, and the resulting fire traveled up into the overhead structure. Someone quickly grabbed an adjacent hose and turned it on. Unfortunately, he was not quick enough, and the resulting response combined with a lack of water pressure turned a simple repair job into a disaster.

Within twenty minutes the fire spread throughout the building, aided by an overhead draft; four hours later the wood and metal structure was little more than a concrete foundation and smoldering debris. The millwright lost his job; so did about 250 others.

The originator of the cutting and welding permit presents the completed form to the area supervisor, who double checks the preparation efforts and signs off when assured that the fire risk is minimal. Constant watch for a stated interval during and immediately after the job should occur, with additional arrangements made for periodic inspections at progressively longer intervals for at least the next forty-eight hours. Sparks from cutting and welding have been known to reside forty-eight hours or more before igniting the adjacent area.

Fire and accident prevention also includes rolling stock. Figure 9.4 is an example of a vehicle operator's checklist. The operator should check the critical items that could lead to breakdown, accidents, and fire before operating the vehicle. The vehicle should be taken out of service immediately if unsafe. If it is serviceable but needs repair, the operator's checklist becomes the basis for a work order and prompt follow-up repairs. Management, after installing the vehicle operator's checklist procedures, assures that the program is in place through unscheduled and unannounced random inspections of vehicles in service.

Routine and periodic service checks also become the basis for more thorough inspection of each vehicle. Ansul Company, a well-known manufacturer of a fire suppression system, offers these recommendations:

1. Check all oil, hydraulic fluid, and gas lines for cuts, abrasions, or undue wear. Replace as needed.
2. Inspect all oil, hydraulic, and gas line fittings for tightness. Clean off all residue and tighten.

Safety and Loss Prevention

OPERATOR CHECK LIST
MATERIAL HANDLING EQUIPMENT
GAS AND ELECTRIC

FLEET NO.	DATE
SHIFT	DRIVER

HOUR METER READING _____ HRS.

CHECK IF:
✓ SATISFACTORY
X UNSATISFACTORY

ENGINE OIL	☐	ENGINE	☐
HYD. OIL	☐	CONTROLS	☐
TRANS. OIL	☐	HOIST	☐
BATTERY	☐	TILT	☐
RADIATOR	☐	HYD. HOSE	☐
HORN	☐	HOSE REEL	☐
BRAKES	☐	TRANS.	☐
EMERGENCY BRAKE	☐	TIRES & WHEEL POSITION	☐
LIGHTS	☐	FORKS	☐
GAUGES	☐	ATTACHMENTS	☐
HOUR METER	☐		

FIRE EXTINGUISHER REQUIREMENTS?
　　　　　　　　　YES ☐　　NO ☐
IS UNIT DAMAGED?　YES ☐　　NO ☐
ALL NECESSARY SAFETY GUARDS IN PLACE?
　　　　　　　　　YES ☐　　NO ☐

OTHER _____

REMARKS _____

_____

_____

FOREMAN _____

Figure 9.4　　　**Vehicle Operator's Checklist**

3. Inspect and clean the engine area. Depending upon the operation of the vehicle, use water or steam to clean it. Schedule cleaning for the end of the workshift, when heat buildup may occur after the engine is shut down.
4. Check the braking system for proper adjustment—especially if the brakes overheat when not engaged.
5. Check all possible ignition points (such as engine block, exhaust manifolds, turbochargers). Make sure oil, hydraulic fluid, and gas lines are not in contact with these ignition points.
6. Clean the vehicle of all combustible debris—such as vegetation, particles, dust. Also remove any oil and fuel drippings.
7. Check all electrical lines and connections for tight fit, wear, or abrasion. Replace any defective electrical equipment or wiring.

These minimum recommendations are additional safeguards to prevent destructive fires. They are particularly important for larger vehicles, such as yard equipment. Large log loaders, frequently costing $350,000 and more, have elevated operator stations that make fires particularly hazardous and costly.

Maintenance Role in the Safety Inspection

Maintenance and safety are often inseparable. The mill safety inspection is one such activity.

At the DuPont Kinston plant, "Safety inspections are made so regularly that it is a safe assumption that, at almost any given time, an inspection is taking place somewhere in the plant." Safety inspections as an accident-prevention tool work equally as well in forest products facilities. Maintenance workers should be:

- participants in the walkabouts, which are a part of the formal safety tour.
- leaders in identifying and correcting safety deficiencies as each is identified during the normal flow of activities—the prevention maintenance checks and the oil and lubrication rounds will reveal safety deficiencies.
- doers in correcting facility- and equipment-related deficiencies in prioritized fashion.

The maintenance planner or designated supervisor should report the status of pending safety items on at least a weekly basis. He or she will reestablish a priority listing frequently to assure that the most critical items are taken care of immediately. A priority listing may be as follows:

- Emergency: The recognized deficiency constitutes an existing and immediate threat to life and limb; to be done immediately. May require a shutdown so the work can proceed with haste.
- Urgent: The safety item also constitutes a threatening situation but can be contained until adequate planning and preparation has occurred to effect repairs.
- Noncritical: Safety projects or items that need to be done within a reasonable time frame but constitute no immediate threat to life and limb.

Often a facility will use work orders for the safety items with an urgent or noncritical priority listing. These safety work orders may be earmarked in some way for special attention.

Job Planning

Job planning is critical to the safety and loss prevention effort. Maintenance personnel frequently encounter:

- equipment and systems they do not fully understand.
- first time or infrequent repair or modification activities.
- work environment and conditions with lighting, temperature, working surface, or other extremes that make work arduous and/or hazardous.
- pressure to get things completed quickly.

Dealing with these conditions requires planning and preparation prior to arriving at the work site and additional on-site planning and preparation before, during, and after the job is done. The equipment history file is a good source for prejob planning.

The equipment history for each machine center should have a safety analysis as a key part of the information readily available. Figure 9.5 is one such example for a plywood layup line. This safety analysis, covering one portion of the overall line, documents the correct operation of the machine and then alerts the maintenance or production worker to the particular operating characteristics that need to be understood to avoid accidents. "Accidental tripping will cause the main-line chain to start automatically and run 1–3 feet, even though a *safety stop* push button may be pushed off," is an example of need-to-know or need-to-be-reminded-of information that has to be understood prior to working on the machine.

This type of safety analysis is becoming increasingly important as the machines and production systems are becoming more complex and sophisticated. Even the most knowledgeable maintenance person should

Figure 9.5 *Equipment Safety Analysis Example*

Equipment: Plywood Lay-Up Line
Component: Main Lay-Up Line Chain Conveyor

The "Main Line Chain," which is nonreversing, is powered with an electric or hydraulic drive and is electrically controlled by selector switches and limit switches throughout the line. Under normal operation this chain will run continuously.

The "core layers" or "line supervisor" can stop or start the line at any time from one of 15 different "Stop-Start" stations.

Therefore "beware" the line can stop or start at any time without warning.

Do Not walk under or work under the line while it is in operation.

Do Not stand on the main chain conveyor.

Stand Clear and keep hands clear of the main chain flights when the line is in operation.

Lock Out the Drive before doing any maintenance on the line. The man making the lock out must remove his lock out, when maintenance is complete and all workers are in the clear.

Remove Guards only to do maintenance.

Replace all Guards prior to operation.

Safety Stop Push Buttons are provided at "key" locations throughout the Glue Line. Learn these locations for your safety.

When electrical and hydraulic power are on, care must be taken not to inadvertently trip the lug-actuated limit switches under each sheet station, because of internal electrical interlocking circuits provided to insure a positive sheet drop at the sheet station. Accidental tripping will cause the "main-line chain" to start automatically and run 1–3 feet, even though a *Safety Stop* push button may be "pushed off."

Care must be taken to be sure the main line valve is electrically disconnected or the hydraulic pump driving the main chain is either "valved off" or electrically locked out prior to working inside of the main line chain guides or drive guards.

The Motor Control Relay (MCR-1) located inside the Channel 1 control cabinet provides an interruption in electrical power to all inputs and outputs. Shutting off the MCR-1 will stop all the motor and cylinder operations.

Before shutting off the MCR-1 to stop the main line chain, check with the main line supervisor, in order to prevent damage to the glue processing system. The glue pump module filters and heat exchangers could become plugged due to uncontrolled temperature changes in the glue heating system.

run through the safety checklist before using the equipment.

Housekeeping is important before and after the job is done. The job is never completed until the guard is in place and the maintenance materials are cleaned up. Discarded bearings and metal parts, plus bolts and other unused components, are often responsible for a seemingly endless sequence of fix and repair. Discarded materials are often intermingled with wood or fiber process debris and then swept into by-product or cleanup conveyors; or debris may become entangled in sprockets, belts and pulleys, or seriously damage chippers, flakers, hogs, and feeders. The result is more work, more downtime, more costs, and more overtime.

Safety as a Culture

Safe work practices have to become a part of the culture of the workplace, as is the case at DuPont and Boise Cascade. These and other companies are making safety a key part of the operating culture. FMC, a supplier to the forest products industry, is another example of a company that has achieved a safety culture.

"Our employees firmly believe that safety is an important part of every job. Our safety program is action-oriented, it's not just talk," says Tom Yeater, FMC's corporate safety manager. "Everybody's involved in safety at FMC from the top on down the line. Strong measures are taken if an employee at any level does not abide by the established safety procedures." The company president reinforced Yeater's views: "We simply don't have jobs at FMC for people who disregard our safety standards" (National Safety Council, 1984).

Some years ago an obsolete West Coast mill provided an example of how a work culture also reinforces a safety culture. This mill, built in the mid-1920s as a stud mill and later converted to a small plywood plant, was at and beyond its useful life. The dedication of the crew, both production and maintenance, had managed to keep the doors open; safety was an ingrained part of that dedication.

The crew, typically with service of twenty years and more, had extensive vacation time off accrued each year, which they took during a four-month summer period. New hires or temporaries, usually undergraduate students from a nearby college, were recruited to fill in for production and maintenance relief, the latter as helpers. One young man was nearly crushed between a load of plywood when he stepped unexpectedly between a forklift and a load. The instant response of his coworkers prevented the accident.

What happened to prevent future unsafe acts? His senior coworkers were clear: "We told him if he got hurt and ruined our safety record we would break his leg!" The word got around to the other new hires. The following year the mill surpassed five years without a work-related lost-time accident.

Safety as a culture can prevent young workers from getting hurt, and it can also prevent skilled maintenance workers from the same fate. When safety is combined with effective loss-prevention activities, it can mean a secure future for forest products workers and their families.

References

Baldwin, R. F. 1984. *Operations Management in the Forest Products Industry*. San Francisco: Miller Freeman.

———. 1984. Safety Training Observation Program. Course Unit #1. E. I. DuPont de Nemours Co. Wilmington, DE.

———. 1982. G. P. Manual. Startup Safety and Maintenance—A Study.

Ladson, S. 1987. Georgia Pacific Fined for Safety Breaches at Mill. *Greenville, S.C. News* (Thursday, April 2).

National Safety Council. 1974. *Accident Prevention Manual For Industrial Operations*, 1283.

———. 1984. At FMC Corporation—Achieving Safety Excellence is No Accident. *National Safety Council News* (October).

Schmidt, W. 1983. Safety Rule "Lock Out" Maintenance Accidents. *1983 Maintenance*. Maintenance Practices. Part E. Shop Layout, Stores Safety. Plant Engineering Library. Cahner's Publishing Co.

Teresko, J. 1981. The Safest Plant in the World. *Industry Week 10* (October 5): 45–47.

———. 1986. A Million Listening as Radio Copter Crashes. *Atlanta Journal* (Thursday, October 23).

PART THREE

PREDICTIVE MAINTENANCE: TOOLS AND TECHNIQUES

CHAPTER 10

Predictive Maintenance: An Overview

The sawmill superintendent was disappointed and frustrated. The week's cut at the headrig was 200 mbf less than target. Problems just seemed to plague the mill even after the previous weekend's inspection, repairs, and preventive maintenance activities. "The mill will run just like a sewing machine for several weeks, then, bam! You get hit hard!" he lamented.

The mill operator discovered that even the most comprehensive lubrication and preventive maintenance activities have limitations. Equipment reliability in a forest products operation depends on a maintenance program that can identify problems before they are readily discernible.

Failure Finding

Problems often develop before the human senses can detect the symptoms. The resulting failures begin either as wear-induced changes in the composition of the lubricating or hydraulic oil, imperceptible changes of heat or light, inaudible noise levels, and other symptoms that are virtually indetectable without the aid of special lengthy downtime.

Several years ago a West Coast paper mill described a recent near miss in its bi-monthly maintenance newsletter. A 55-inch-diameter press suction roll on its number two paper machine had developed a vibration that was inaudible to the machine tenders. A routine vibration analysis, conducted while the paper machine was running, pinpointed a developing problem; a defect was identified in the outer race of the front side bearing.

Further analysis indicated that a major failure could result; subsequently, the roll was removed and the bearing replaced during an already scheduled major shutdown. Timely identification saved a possible twenty-four hours of unscheduled downtime and $173,000. This incident occurred in the early 1980s; the cost would be even larger today with higher maintenance costs and higher paper prices. And there was an added benefit: The $14,000 bearing was only lightly damaged and was later refurbished and put back into service.

The vibration analysis technique is one of a number of predictive maintenance tools that are achieving ready acceptance in the mill. In fact, any method that entails periodic inspection or monitoring to detect and diagnose problems is, in a broad sense, a predictive maintenance tool. The correct tool is determined by the type of the equipment to be maintained, the importance to the manufacturing process, and the plant's maintenance competence and expertise.

The higher speeds required to compete for lower costs, and the increased sophistication and costliness of the initial investment, are prompting mill operators and maintenance professionals to seek out high-tech maintenance techniques. A Finnish automatic condition-monitoring device called Safe Control is one example.

This predictive maintenance system, designed specifically as an online paper machine monitoring device, is an example of what is available not only for paper machines but other conversion processes. The device, permanently mounted on the paper machine, audits the equipment functions and reports on the trends developing. The resulting system has four core functions:

1. Analysis of trends. This feature identifies changes in operating conditions and performance.
2. Detection and warning of impending failures.
3. Identification of the origin and nature of an impending failure.
4. Centralized and automatic lubrication, including the application of grease, oil, and the refilling of recirculating oil system.

Sophisticated sensors act as high-tech eyes and ears. Displacement transducers measure distance and change in distance, as in shaft whip. Thermocouples measure temperatures on components such as bearings or heat sinks. Accelerometers measure vibration levels; optical sensors generate a timing pulse. Each of these OY Safematic LTD systems such as Safe Control are custom designed for a specific application.

The newer condition-monitoring techniques provide advanced warning of machine failure. This advanced warning, combined with an accurate identification of faults, now allows the mill operator the opportunity to carry out the necessary repairs before failure occurs. In addition, spare parts can only be ordered as needed.

Secondary damage, when the failure of one component causes damage to interconnected parts, is less likely to occur with this advance warning. Many machine failures (such as the paper machine example cited earlier) can be avoided altogether by taking corrective action while the machine is running.

The Benefits

A well-established maintenance program that uses predictive techniques has at least four advantages over the more traditional approaches:

1. Failures and potential failures can be found early enough to avoid unscheduled downtime in most cases.
2. The predictive monitoring technique can often ascertain the precise nature of a machine fault.
3. Condition monitoring allows mills to track the development of a problem and make an accurate estimate of time remaining before repair is needed.
4. Frequently, the predictive process does not require a machine stoppage or dismantling of the machine to be effective.

A major benefit of predictive maintenance is quick results. Many programs experience dramatic improvements in machine condition levels and achieve significant avoidance of catastrophic failure. Cost reduction is equally dramatic.

Carol Nolden, senior editor of *Plant Engineering*, recently commented, "One rule of thumb states that condition-based maintenance results in average saving of 20 percent of direct maintenance costs plus twice that in increased production" (Nolden, 1987). The condition-based evaluations are usually more time efficient and allow maintenance personnel to make more effective use of their time.

The Tools Available

The more commonly used predictive maintenance tools and condition-monitoring devices can be categorized as illustrated in figure 10.1. The tools and techniques can be categorized as those which require specialized monitoring equipment or processes, or which utilize readily available instrumentation such as gauges and other commonly used measuring devices. Preventive techniques such as bearing induction heaters, laser shaft alignment, and computer modeling are related to but not part of the predictive or condition-monitoring techniques.

These condition-monitoring and predictive procedures can be further categorized into an additional two groups: (1) tools and techniques used

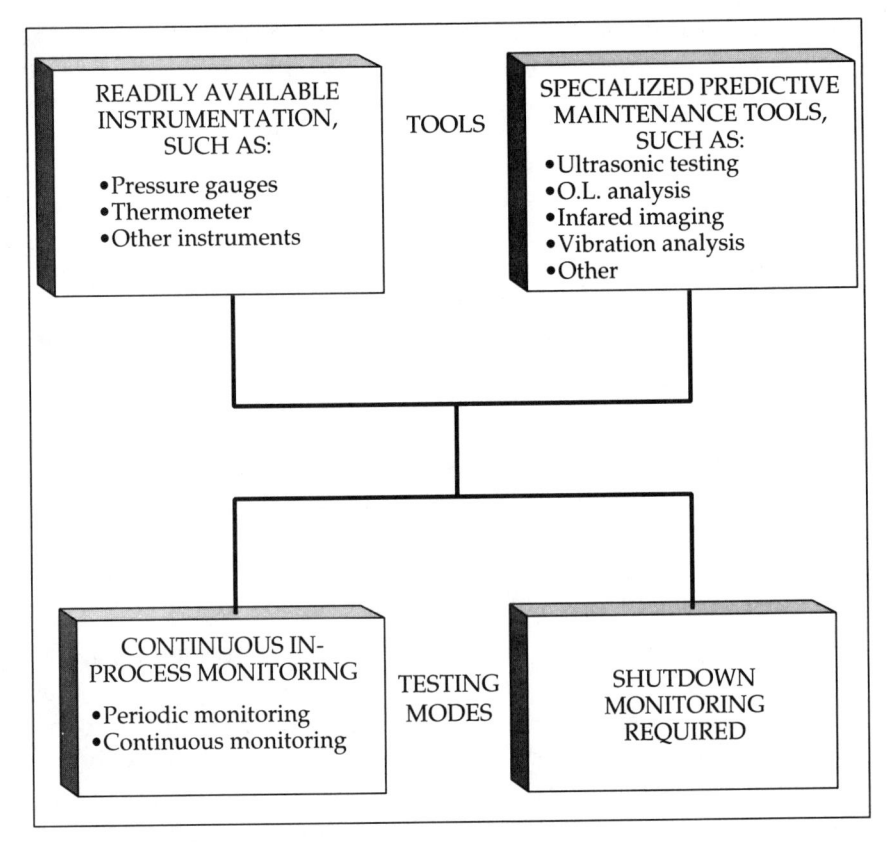

```
┌─────────────────────────────┬─────────────────────────────┐
│ READIY AVAILABLE            │ SPECIALIZED PREDICTIVE      │
│ INSTRUMENTATION,   TOOLS    │ MAINTENANCE TOOLS,          │
│ SUCH AS:                    │ SUCH AS:                    │
│ • Pressure gauges           │ • Ultrasonic testing        │
│ • Thermometer               │ • O.L. analysis             │
│ • Other instruments         │ • Infared imaging           │
│                             │ • Vibration analysis        │
│                             │ • Other                     │
└─────────────────────────────┴─────────────────────────────┘
```

Figure 10.1   **Tools and Testing Modes**

to periodically or continuously monitor machinery during operation; and (2) inspection or analysis techniques that require machinery downtime to implement. The thrust is to design devices that will do the latter rather than the former. Chapters 11 and 12 will provide detailed description of the use of each and the results achieved.

Implementation Steps

The following are essential steps to follow when installing an effective predictive maintenance program. Please review the flow chart in figure 10.2 to obtain an overview of how each fits as a part of the whole:

Step One: Review the performance of each machine or process and determine the number and type of machines and process systems that should be part of the program. Evaluate the criticality of each machine,

Predictive Maintenance: An Overview

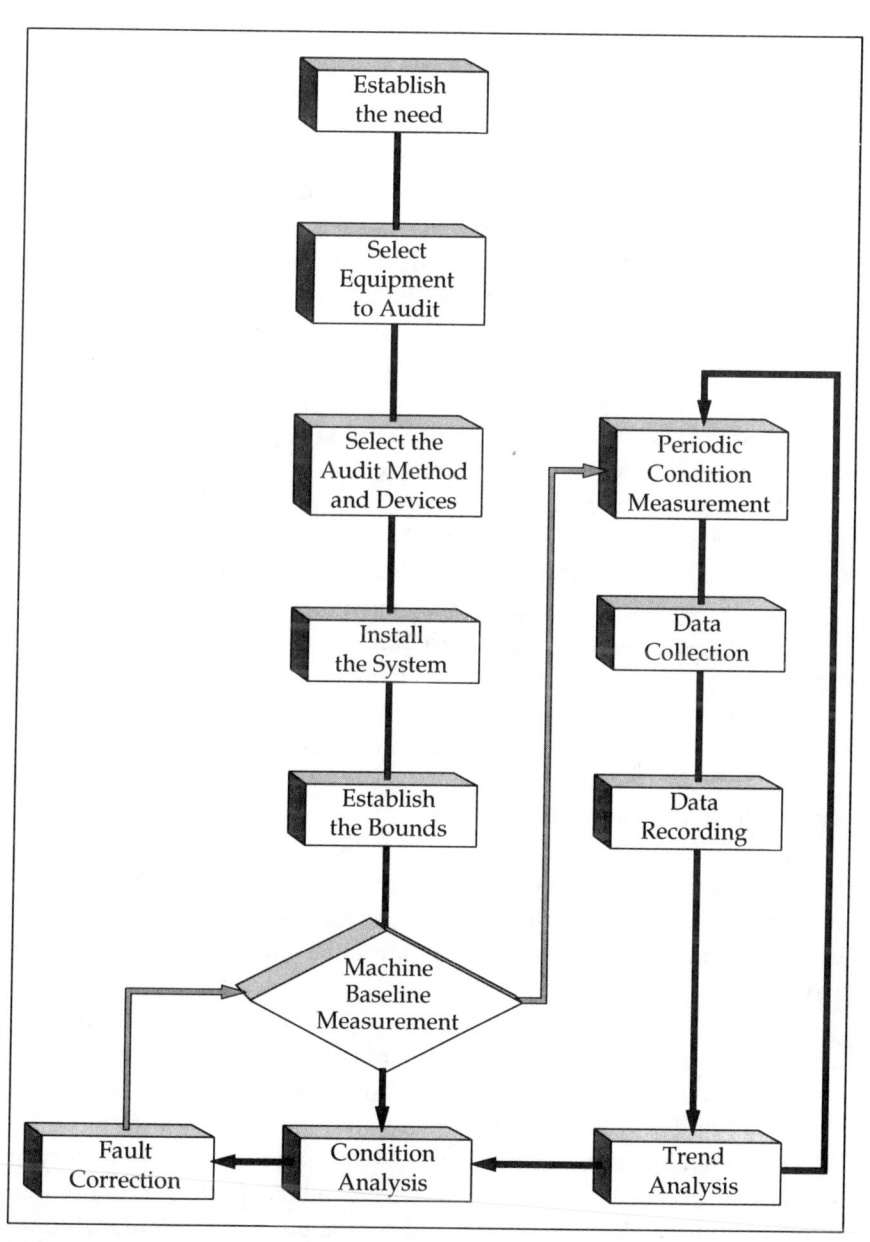

Figure 10.2 A Two-stage Screening Process
Source: Nolden, 1987

the type and extent of a possible failure, the frequency of the failure or problem, and the cost associated with each.

Step Two: Select a manageable number of machines for inclusion in a new program. A modest beginning with early and visible results is more likely to succeed than a more ambitious program. It makes sense to begin with a limited number of machines that will provide the greatest payback.

Step Three: Select the predictive maintenance tools and techniques. The following questions will guide that selection:

1. What parameters need to be audited? Parameters that best indicate machine condition and failure modes must be chosen.

2. How and when to monitor? Decisions must be made about how often to monitor and where on the equipment to take measurements.

3. What technology is to be chosen? The program should be built slowly and the simplest technology used until the personnel involved are able to master increasing levels of complexity.

4. What is the criticality of the machine or process? Does it warrant a permanent continuous online device? The predictive maintenance procedures should be weighed against the risk or cost avoidance expected.

Step Four: Install the equipment. Installation, training, and inspection schedules must be defined along with individual responsibilities. A structured means of communication needs to be in place to relay information about the equipment and the resulting program performance. The personnel responsible for the monitoring and diagnosis and those individuals who are planning and scheduling repair activities should have ready access to the developing information.

Step Five: Establish the standards and the bounds of those standards. Set the parameters that represent expected operating conditions for all points to be monitored. Layout monitoring routes and give each machine an identification number. Mark the points to be monitored on the respective machine.

Step Six: Take baseline measurements to establish the current condition of the machine or process. Compare the results to expected performance. (Actual performance will vary from machine to machine within like makes and sizes.) Expected performance criteria can be gotten from the vendor, an industry standard, or the historical performance history of the machine at the location. Investigate all suspected variances to accepted bounds, diagnose faults, and correct problems before including the machine or process in the program.

Monitoring and evaluation can begin once steps one through six have been initiated. Periodic monitoring usually entails taking measurements on a walk-about schedule; recording and charting the data then follows. The resulting information is evaluated to identify faults and trends that require corrective action. Figure 10.2 identifies the six steps to initiate a program; this figure also identifies the analysis steps that lead to problem correction.

These latter steps, combined with a comprehensive knowledge of the mill equipment and a knowledge of what is expected from a predictive maintenance program, can take most of the guesswork out of maintenance; it can also take out a lot of the cost. The next two chapters discuss specific details on many of the techniques and tools available.

References

Bos, M., T. B. Davis, and J. J. Redding. 1985. Key Steps to Establishing Sound Predictive Maintenance. *Plant Engineering* (December 12).

Dunn, R. 1987. Advanced Maintenance Technologies. *Plant Engineering* (June 18).

Hartley, W. 1986. Business and Technology News—Maintenance. Predictive Maintenance—The Next Step. *TAPPI Journal* (June): 15–16.

Kershaw, R. J. and B. Robertson. 1985. Condition-Based Maintenance Program Increases Production, Reduces Costs. *Paper Trade Journal* (February): 34–36.

Nolden, C. 1987. Predictive Maintenance. *Plant Engineering* (February): 38–41.

Timmerman, D. N. 1986. Checking the Condition of Gear Drives. Part 1. Diagnosing Temperature and Noise Problems. *Plant Engineering* (May 22).

CHAPTER 11

Vibration Monitoring and Analysis

Parts wear, foundations settle, shafts misalign, rotors become unbalanced, and clearances increase over time. Vibration usually accompanies these machine changes with a buildup of dynamic load on the bearings and other parts. The resulting dynamic energy of vibration is dissipated throughout the machine. Bit by bit the machine progresses toward a major breakdown as components wear and deform, with cause and effect reinforcing the process.

These telltale vibration and motion changes can be detected and measured in the early stages by specialized instruments and equally specialized measurement and analysis techniques. These tools and techniques will identify the subtle changes and relate each to the cause and effect.

An Overview

Routine preventive maintenance can only identify obvious signs of trouble, such as oil leaks, hot bearings, and sprockets out of alignment. Until now predicting when, why, and how the equipment will break down has been based on empirical data—for example, a bearing is replaced every six months because it has historically failed every eight months—or conjecture. The first is expensive; the last is even more so. Vibration monitoring and analysis can change all that.

Vibration monitoring and analysis techniques, developed by aerospace engineers back in the early 1960s, are widely accepted in a number of industries such as chemical and petroleum. The forest products industry has been a latecomer.

Moore International, a forest industry supplier, publicized the use of these techniques during the late 1970s. However, it has obtained the widest acceptance in the pulp and paper side of the business rather than wood products. This acceptance has only occurred over the last six to ten years.

The forest industries experience, along with the experiences of other industries, indicates that vibration monitoring and analysis techniques can extend the operating life of equipment by 10 percent to 20 percent. Maintenance man-hours productivity is increased, and spare parts replacement costs are reduced from 10 percent to 20 percent. The frequency and magnitude of unscheduled breakdowns has been reduced by 50 percent to 60 percent. These percentages are impressive; the results are even more impressive to the action-biased operator.

A number of well-publicized pilot programs have demonstrated excellent results. Here are some examples:

- Electrical motor rewind costs were reduced from $200,000 to $50,000 annually in a Weyerhaeuser paper mill. In addition, a Weyerhaeuser engine supplier increased the uptime on a heavily used machine 100 percent.
- Federal Paper Board reported a cumulative savings of "hundreds of thousands of dollars" using vibration monitoring techniques in the company's Augusta, Georgia, mill after three years into the formal program. This location is monitoring its rotating machinery components on a regular basis and keeping detailed records of each unit and the resulting vibration signatures.
- Four potentially costly problems were identified and corrected within months of introducing a vibration auditing program into Champion's plywood and lumber manufacturing complex at Camden, Texas. Major downtime was avoided and repairs made on a scheduled basis on the Boiler ID fan jack shaft, a bearing on the No. 1 compressor, the main drive bearing on the No. 3 veneer lathe, and an impending major malfunction on the No. 2 lathe MG set.

There are numerous applications in a mill or within a business. Each forest products business has its own process peculiar to that business. However there are numerous applications on support equipment, such as woodyards, by-products handling equipment, and boilers, which have applications almost too numerous to mention.

Equipment Systems and Components

There are various levels of sophistication in equipment systems and the components used within those systems. The level of sophistication may range from the pocket-sized vibration meter to the fully automated systems of the type described in chapter 10. Each of the percent systems contain some or all of the following system components; this includes transducers (sensors), meters, monitors, and analyzers.

Transducers (Sensors)

A vibration transducer converts the mechanical energy of vibration into an electrical signal somewhat like a human hand, although the transducer is less limited by temperature, accuracy, and repeatability. There are three transducer types: accelerometers, velocity pickups, and noncontact probes.

Accelerometer (see figure 11.1): A piezoelectric crystal is the heart of this transducer type. This crystal generates an electric charge when it is deformed, or when a mechanical force is applied. The crystal is mounted between the body of the accelerometer and a seismic mass. When vibration is transmitted the gravitational forces on the mass deform the crystal.

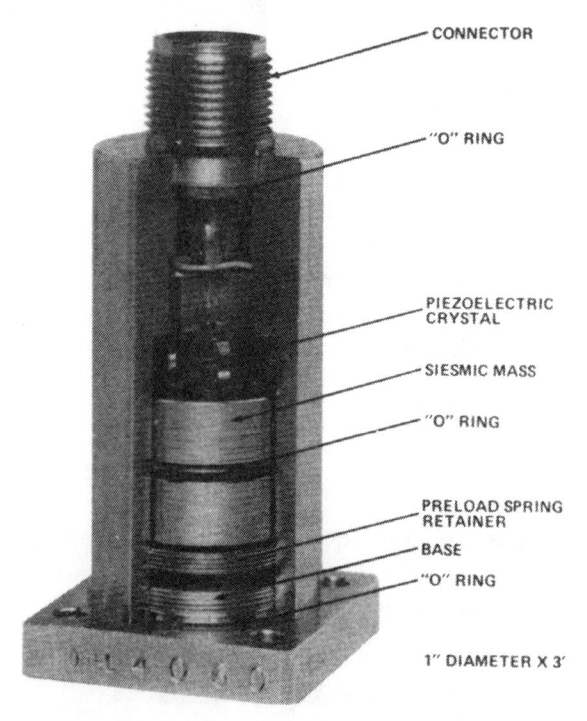

Figure 11.1   **A Typical Accelerometer.**
Source: Vitec, Inc., 1985.

Vibration Monitoring and Analysis 119

The crystal produces an electrical charge; the energy of this electrical charge is directly proportional to the acceleration value of the vibration. The advantages of the accelerometer sensor type are that it:

- tolerates temperature extremes up to 550° F.
- is easy to mount; typically smaller than other transducer types.
- has a wide frequency response range, often from 1 Hz to 5,000 Hz or more.
- is capable of measuring both the velocity and displacement value of the vibration.

This type has the following limitations:

- The signal generated is low, and charge amplifier assists are required on all cable runs longer than 100 feet.
- Filtering is often required to ignore unwanted vibration signal.

Velocity Pickups (see figure 11.2): The velocity pickup is so named because its output is directly proportional (within limits) to the velocity (speed) of vibration. The units of measurement used to indicate velocity are inches per second, similar to automobile speed measurements of miles per hour.

The principle is quite simple: A cylindrical coil is mounted to the case of the device. A permanent magnet is spring-suspended within the coil, and the assembled device is firmly secured to a machine. The case vibrates at the same frequency and magnitude as the machine. The spring-suspended magnet tends to stay stationary, and the relative difference in motion between the coil and magnet causes the magnet lines of force to be transmitted to the coil.

This function induces a voltage proportional to the velocity of vibration. Dampening is required in the pickup to prevent the magnet from vibrating more than the actual vibration.

The advantages of the velocity pickup sensor include:

- a sturdy, heavy-duty design, with a high output (200 mV/in/sec).
- temperature ratings from 400° F. to 500° F.
- sensors can be up to 1,000 feet away from the monitor.
- a simple mounting procedure, via ¼–28 unf tapped hole in the bottom of the transducer.

It also has the following limitations:

- The sensor is normally accurate ±5 in the frequency range of 20 Hz to 1,500 Hz, because the unit must overcome internal dampening

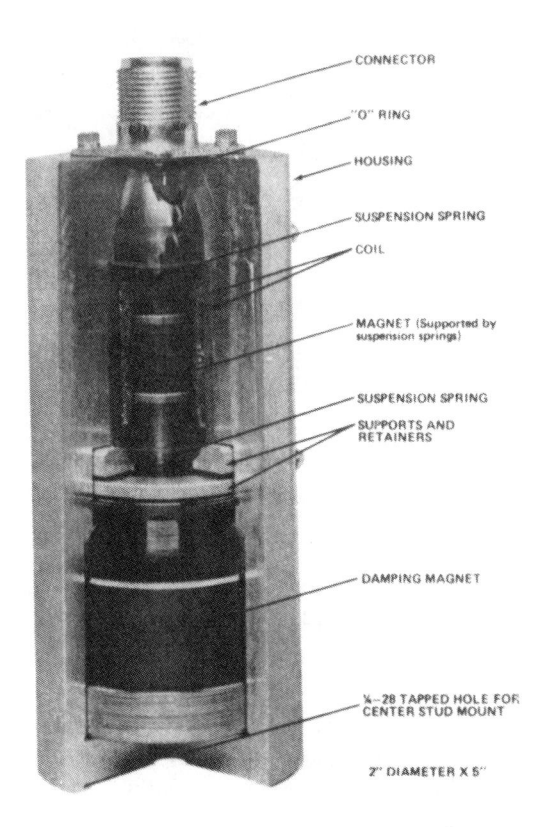

Figure 11.2   **A Typical Velocity Pump.**
Source: Vitec, Inc., 1985.

forces and is subject to dynamic force limitation.
- It is sometimes limited in the mounting position and typically should not be mounted.
- Velocity transducers are usually somewhat larger and more massive than accelerometers.

Noncontact Probe (see figure 11.3): A noncontact probe is a displacement-sensing device. It consists of three separate components: the probe, the driver, and probe-to-driver connectors.

The device is extremely accurate and the principle of operation is relatively simple. A magnetic energy field is generated around the probe tip as the driver produces a high frequency signal that is then transmitted into a coil in the probe.

Vibration Monitoring and Analysis

Figure 11.3 **A Typical Non-contact Probe System.**
Source: Vitec, Inc., 1985.

When a conductive material (shaft, etc.) is approached by the probe tip, eddy currents are produced on the surface of the material, and the power is absorbed which affects the field strength. The amount that the field strength is affected is proportional to the distance from the object to the probe tip. The closer the object, the more power is absorbed. The driver then measures the change in the field strength and converts it into a standard calibrated output. This output is normally 200 mV per mil (0.001") of air gap between probe and object. (Vitec, 1985, 12)

Noncontact probes have the following advantages:

- The device is very sensitive and very accurate (0.2 volt output change for a 0.001-inch vibration, or air-gap change).
- It accurately measures a wide range of vibration speeds. This feature ranges from the exact air gap of a nonvibrating object (zero Hz) to speeds up to 3,500 Hz (210,000 cpm).
- The driver can be located up to 1,500 feet from the probe.

It also has the following limitations:
- It is limited by temperature: the probe to 350° F., the driver to 200° F.
- Scratches, nicks, pits, or inclusions in the shaft being measured can impede accuracy. The magnetic properties of the machine component being sensed, the electrical currents passing through, or the electrical and mechanical runout can also impede accuracy.
- The installation is complicated by the need to chamfer or counter bore to a minimum of two times the probe tip diameter, because the energy developed at the probe tip is one-and-a-half to two times the probe diameter width.

Meters

Meters come in all sizes, shapes, and degrees of complexity. One may be as simple as a hand-held device or as complex as a computerized measurement tool. A meter simply quantifies measurements, which are then compared with the standards or established reference values for the machine or component being audited. A vibration meter measures the amount of vibration by displacement, velocity, acceleration, or a combination of each.

Displacement is the total measured movement of a component between extremes. This is a useful measurement at low speeds and specific frequencies. It is not the most accurate method for measuring over a variable speed range or a wide frequency range.

Velocity is best described as the "time rate of change of displacement." This method of measurement is useful for applications in which a machine requires a wide frequency range of monitoring or operates over a variable speed range. Vibration is described in terms of velocity of motion. The machine is then audited and compared to a predetermined velocity, a velocity that is damaging to a specific machine or application.

Acceleration, the time rate change of velocity, is a measurement of the vibration forces being applied to a machine at a given speed. Low speeds may produce significant deflections or displacements in the machine, while the same acceleration at high speeds may actually reduce the vibrations and its damaging effects.

Monitors

A vibration monitor tracks, regulates, and/or controls the operation of a machine. It has the features of a meter with some added functions, such as a relay closure at a specific set point. This makes it a more useful device when permanently installed on a machine such as a paper machine.

A vibration monitor senses the machine parameter, measures these parameters, and then takes action if the conditions fall outside the preset parameter. These features are frequently critical to safe low-cost operations.

Analyzers

An analyzer goes one step further than the meter or the monitor. It determines or assists in determining the cause by interpreting the vibration signature of a machine or component against a predetermined baseline. This interpretation can be achieved using a manual method or a computer-assisted interpretation. The resulting analysis provides direction to the operation in selecting one of three options: Continue operations as at present; schedule a shutdown or overhaul; or cease operations immediately.

The resulting analyses allow the operator to make the right decision at the right time.

Establishing Standards

Each machine will have critical points of wear or vibration. These points should be documented; subsequent measurements will reveal trends only if made under the same conditions. There are few recognized standards for evaluating acceptable vibration levels for bearings, shafts, and rotating equipment. The following are the two most recognized: International Organization for Standardization (ISO) Standards 2372 and 2373; and American Petroleum Institute (API) Standards 610, 612, 616, and 619.

These standards set out general guidelines for measuring and analyzing machine vibration. The ISO methodology, the more applicable of the two, prescribes the auditing of vibrations directly on rotating shafts to determine vibrational behavior change, kinetic load build-up, and radial clearances. The ISO standard is used for both operational monitoring and acceptance testing on a test stand. Although the ISO method excludes torsional or axial shaft vibrations, it is useful for selected measurements such as absolute and relative radial shaft vibrations.

These recognized standards have their limitations. Most problem diagnosis and maintenance decisions will be based on the development of baseline measurements for each machine. Ranges of acceptable performance are determined by mathematical calculations, the history of the particular machine type, or by trial and error.

The following are guidelines to use when measuring performance against the established standards:

- Machine Record Check: Determine what specific problems are occurring and how each is originating. A well-documented history will be a guide.

- Transducer Placement: Place the transducer (sensor) as close as possible to the expected problem source. Mount the device securely so that the resulting vibrations are transmitted accurately. Determine whether to mount in a vertical or horizontal plane; the choice will depend on which of the two axes is the most sensitive to the transducer.
- The Mechanics of Measurement: The simplest system uses a hand-held instrument connected by a short cable to a sensor. This device measures vibration amplitude over a specific, preselected wide-band frequency range.

A permanent monitoring system may include a large number of monitoring points with a multiplexer continuously stepping through the channels while dwelling for a preselected period before automatically moving to the next. Permanent systems require high operational reliability, long-term stability, and immunity to adverse environmental conditions.

The level of sophistication will depend on the needs for rapid response or early fault detection, the number of monitoring points, the frequency of measurement, and the degree of problem identification or analysis needed. Choose the monitoring system that is no more than can be safety- or cost-justified.

Vibration Prevention

Vibration can be prevented by proper installation and follow-up maintenance. Laser shaft alignment devices can be a major assist.

A laser shaft alignment system has two primary components: a laser transducer and a prism (see figure 11.4). The transducer, housing a laser diode, is attached to a secure point on one side of the shaft coupling. A collimated beam of infrared light is transmitted to a prism affixed to the opposite side of the shaft coupling.

The prism in turn reflects the beam back into the transducer, where it strikes a two-dimension position detector. The detector then transmits an electronic signal, which identifies the beam's deviation from the correct X and Y axis. Deviations are reported in increments of 1 micron (0.001/mm).

The electronic signal output can be displayed, recorded, and analyzed. Angular movement can be measured in both the vertical and horizontal planes. Currently, there are about one hundred or more of these laser optic shaft alignment systems in use in the forest products industry.

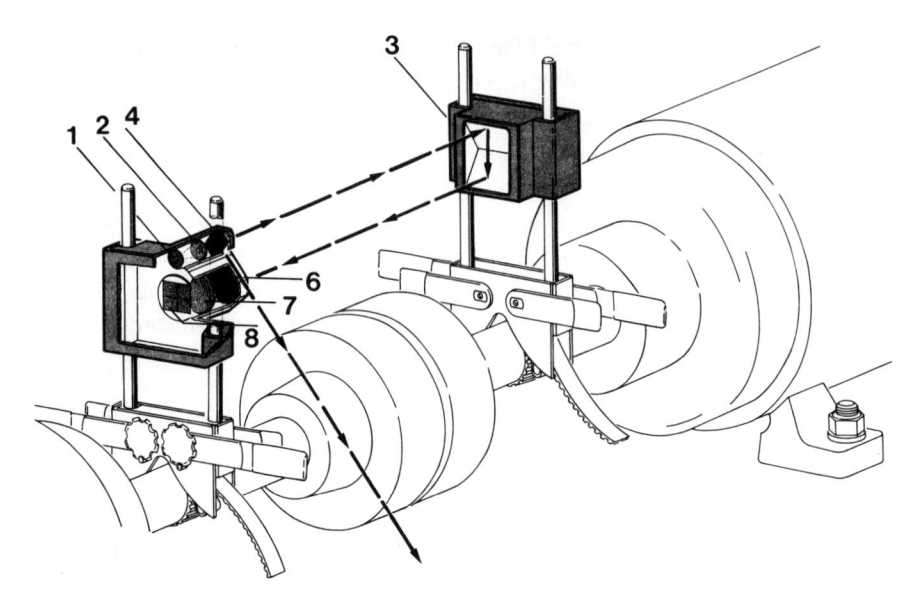

Figure 11.4 **Laser Shaft Alignment System.**
Source: Prüftechnik Dieter Bursch + Partner GmbH & Co., 1985.

A Look Ahead

Vibration monitoring and analysis techniques and the value of these techniques is just now gaining widespread acceptance. When T. Marshall Hahn (the dynamic growth-oriented Chairman and CEO of Georgia Pacific Corporation) observed a presentation of the benefits, he promptly instructed his plant operators to seek out and adopt this technique as part of a predictive maintenance program. This is a good example of what is happening generally in the industry.

These techniques and tools are becoming increasingly more sophisticated as the level of attention increases and the needs for such systems are defined. Vibration monitoring and analysis techniques are becoming a "maintenance must" for a mill.

References

International Organization for Standardization. 1983. *International Standard 7919/1*.
Katzel, J. 1987. Applying Predictive Maintenance. *Plant Engineering* (June 18).
Luming, H. 1986. Vibration Monitoring of Paper Machine Bearings. *TAPPI Journal* 69, no. 3 (March).

Machine-Health Monitoring. 1984. Naerum, Denmark: Bruel & Kjaer.
Spotting Problems with Predictive Analysis. 1979. *Wood & Wood Products* (June).
Springer, C. W. 1988. Don't Forget the Time Domain in Analyzing Bearings: A Case Study. *TAPPI Journal 71*, no. 8 (August).
Vinicki, J. 1987. Vibration Analysis in the Press Section. *TAPPI Journal 70*, no. 11 (November).
Vitec, Inc. 1985. *Vibration Primer.* Cleveland, OH: Vitec.
Yang, C. F. 1986. Vibration Monitoring Helps Mill Prevent Key Equipment Breakdowns. *Pulp & Paper* (March).
Zaharko, R. L. 1988. A History of Predictive Maintenance at James River's Vauna Mill, Clatskanie, Ore. *TAPPI Journal 71*, no. 3 (March).

CHAPTER 12

Infrared Imaging, Ultrasonic Testing, and Other Predictive Maintenance Techniques

Vibration monitoring and analysis is widely recognized as an effective predictive maintenance technique. But there are other useful techniques, both simple and complex. Each will alert the operator or maintenance person to a defective or failing situation that, if left uncorrected, will result in volume, quality, and opportunity losses.

Infrared Imaging

Infrared imaging finds and monitors thermal anomalies, or "hot spots," which need immediate attention. It relies on the use of sophisticated scanning devices that have one or more infrared detectors per unit. These components act in combination with electronic circuitry to produce an image, in much the same way as a video camera feeds an image onto a television screen.

But rather than using existing light, as is used to develop a video image, the infrared system uses an optical system that detects radiant energy. The radiant energy is focused, and a detector converts the focused energy pattern into an electrical signal. The signal is then amplified and simultaneously processed and converted to produce an image on a cathode ray tube (CRT).

The image, usually called a thermograph, is a detailed visual representation of the heat energy an object will radiate in proportion to the object's temperature and emissivity. The resulting thermograph can be studied concurrently, as the inspection takes place, or it can be recorded on videotape or photographed for later detailed analysis.

A failing component that cannot be detected with the human senses can be detected in 2.0 to 5.6 or 8.0 through 14.0 micron ranges of the electromagnetic spectrum. At normal temperatures most of this energy is in the infrared spectrum, and it can be readily detected by infrared scanning devices.

Weyerhaeuser's Dick Coffren describes this example of infrared scanning in the Hancock, Vermont, hardwood plywood plant: "On the second day, we scanned our 350-hp hammermill, found a hot roller bearing, pulled it down, and took up slack in it. Had we not found it in time, the bearing could have gone, and that would have damaged the shaft. The scan probably saved the hammermill" (Feit, 1986).

The observer can glean specific information by direct visual inspection of the thermograph, or the thermograph can be analyzed by computer to yield additional detailed information. Temperature traces along a line can be produced; thermal "contours" can be made using isothermal images; and readings can also be isolated at separate points and calculated and averaged for a defined area. Benefits are immediate, as the Weyerhaeuser example illustrates.

Infrared inspections are useful in the following situations:

- Electrical systems: A comprehensive survey, performed every six to twelve months, will locate thermal anomalies (abnormally high current levels or "hot spots") at bus and cable terminations, power distribution panels, motor control centers, splice connections, transformers, substations, and machine control panels.
- Mechanical systems: Motor bearings, steam traps, mechanical couplings, and boiler components (such as refractory linings) are mechanical systems that develop easily as detectable hot spots.
- Building systems: A building, particularly the roof and side walls, can be inspected for defects or energy losses. Infrared imaging can detect missing insulation, air infiltration, and moisture penetration. This is particularly true in low-slope roofing systems.

    Roof leaks can be located by identifying areas of moisture-laden insulation. The roof is usually surveyed after the sun has gone down; infrared scanning will detect wet insulation because it retains heat longer.

The uses for infrared imaging are many and varied. New, innovative approaches are continuously being developed for this predictive maintenance technique.

Ultrasonic Testing

Ultrasonic testing provides a fast, accurate diagnosis of structural flaws and wasteful problems, such as valves in a blowby mode, vacuum and pressure leaks, and faulty steam traps. Steam trap inspection is probably the most commonly used application of ultrasonic testing.

For example, the Cosmopolis pulp mill, a Weyerhaeuser facility, has instituted a regular system of biannual steam trap inspections. A field service worker, retained by the company from Ultrasonic Predictable Maintenance, checks steam traps by ultrasonics, or more conventional methods such as temperature variability monitoring, to identify malfunctioning units.

Weyerhaeuser reports reduced steam consumption of 20 percent and more at this and other similar operations. Ultrasonics pay off in even bigger ways on pressure vessels or other vessels that experience high degrees of stress and require periodic nondestructive testing. The Ultra Image III ultrasonic imaging system is an innovative device that takes the guesswork out of nondestructive testing.

It uses a technique known as "time-of-flight tip defraction." A transducer induces pulses of longitudinal or shear waves into the object being inspected. These are subsequently diffracted by the outer extremities of any defects encountered. The diffracted signals are detected by the transducer and displayed on a CRT.

The area scanned—a scan window varies in size from 2 inches by 4 inches to as large as 20 inches by 40 inches—allows the instrument to precisely locate the problem areas by allowing up to 20,000 data points per scan window. The inspection is further enhanced by obtaining three scans per area being examined; this feature is particularly important when examining weld joints and other suspected flaw locations. Three scans of the same area include a straight beam for thickness and corrosion profile, and two shear wave beams to detect and measure crack indications. The latter emits shear waves that cross the weld and run parallel to the weld. These shear waves not only detect cracks and flaws but also estimate the size of each.

Surface grinding on the face of each weld before inspection will detect surface flaws that are less than 1/32-inch deep. This extra sensitivity is obtained when the exterior surface of the object or vessel is ground smooth.

Ultrasonic signals, actually short-wave low-frequency sound, can readily detect flaws or impending failures even in the presence of a high ambient-noise level. A short-wave signal needs greater amplitude to travel the same distance as a low-frequency sound; therefore the ultrasonic components of a problem sound are loudest closest to the source. A contact inspection device, such as a stethoscope or metal rod, can act as a wave guide. A contact device connected to an amplifier or recorder device can locate and identify the signal-strength intensity.

Actual testing occurs in the two modes described; the faulty machine or system emits the sound or the sound is induced by the inspection device. The former requires a transducer or receiver to detect the sound; the latter uses a transmitter or transducer to create the sound and a receiver or transducer to process the resulting response.

Inspection and testing will sense the ultrasound waves produced by the operating machine, such as loose electrical connections and other openings in an electrical system that force the current to jump a gap. Other sound-emitting flaws are vacuum and pressure vessel leaks, gas leaks, valves in a blowby mode, and bearing failures. Bearing failures, a progressive process, will be detected long before the impending failure is detectable by other means.

Tank seams, digesters, deaerators, and heat exchanger shell inspections require the creation of an ultrasonic sound by the inspection device, as is the case with Ultra Image III. Other inspection devices place a transmitter within a container or structure and use a scanner to detect areas of ultrasonic penetration. This method is useful for preservice checks of tank seams, hatches, seals, caulking, gaskets, or building wall joints. A fairly accurate diagnosis of pending problems can occur before the system, structure, or device is placed into service. Overall, ultrasonic inspection and testing methods are relatively cheap, versatile, and effective.

Motor Failure Prevention

Predictive testing of electric motors has occurred for at least seven decades and more. An early pioneer, James G. Biddle Co., introduced the Megger insulation resistance tester about 1912. The Megohmmeter, a modified and upgraded descendent of the earliest Megger tester, still tests for integrity of electrical insulation. The test is cheap and simple, but the results are limited in scope and provide little insight in predicting future performance. Until recently, the megohmmeter test, combined with the low-resistance ohmmeter test and visual inspection, were the major ingredients of a predictive maintenance program.

The science and practice of predictive maintenance has grown in recent years. Periodic condition monitoring for electric motors should include high-frequency surge comparison testing and direct current (DC) high-potential testing as well as vibration monitoring. DC high-potential testing and high-frequency surge testing are two predictive maintenance techniques that will minimize, if not eliminate, the downtime caused by electric motor failures. These tests, a vehicle to make motor reliability more predictive, have a welcome place in the predictive maintenance program of a pulp mill, sawmill, or structural board mill.

The ease of testing and the need to minimize inservice motor failures has moved the predictive testing techniques from the motor manufacturer's factory onto the shop floor of the user. This factory-to-factory doubling up of reliability testing has allowed planned, orderly repair and replacement in the field.

Some test instruments are designed to perform both DC high-potential testing and high-frequency surge testing; each test is conducted at the load side of the motor controller. The motor controller is cleared and tagged for safety purposes, while the motor leads are left connected.

DC high-potential testing is a quantitative test that indicates the possibility of winding failures. Test voltage is increased in uniform increments up to a set limit. Leakage current is recorded on the test instrument microammeter. An erratic or disproportionate increase in linkage current indicates an eventual winding failure as additional voltage is applied or the motor ages in service.

High-frequency surge testing will detect open coils, reversed coils, and faulty insulation to ground. This test applies a pair of high-frequency, high-voltage pulses (surges) to the motor winding, which are then recorded as reflected pulse waveforms on the oscilloscope. The resulting pulses, a voltage of double the equipment voltage rating plus 1,000, are reflected onto the screen of the oscilloscope and are easily read by the operator (figure 12.1).

Good winding is characterized by an identical overlapping of two reflected traces as the test instrument imposes identical simultaneous high-voltage, high-frequency pulses on two phases of the motor winding. The other signature traces indicated in figure 12.1 indicate other characteristics that predict failure, such as a turn-to-turn short, phase-to-phase short, open coil, and ground. The sensitivity of this testing is such that even a one-turn winding short circuit can be detected.

These tests are reliable and accurate; the nondestructive nature of these tests, plus the predictive leadtime the results provide, allow for periodic testing on inservice importance. The most critical motors should be tested every six to eight weeks; the less critical twice a year.

Infrared Imaging, Ultrasonic Testing, and Other Predictive Maintenance Techniques   133

Good winding

Turn-to-turn short

Phase-to-phase short

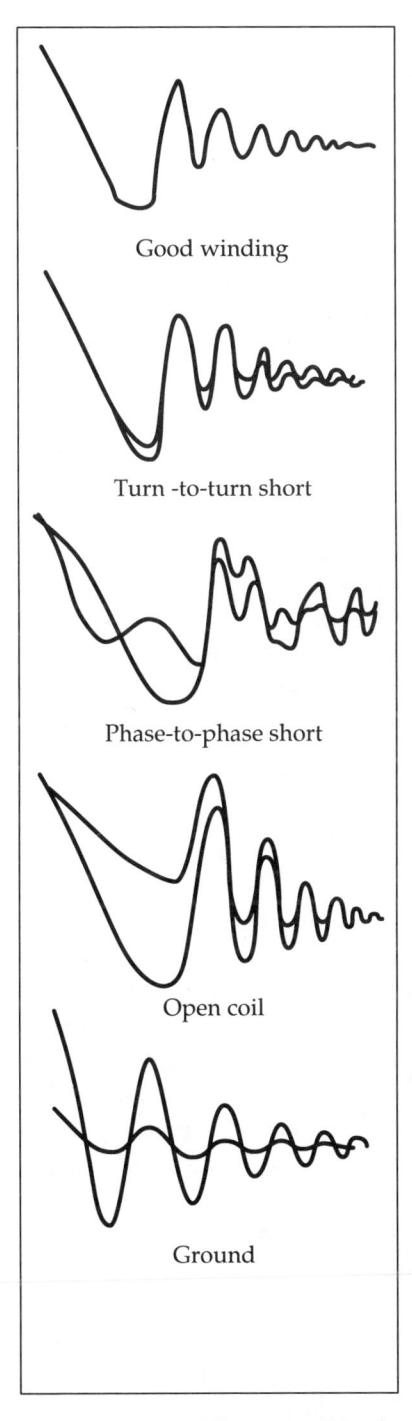

Open coil

Ground

Figure 12.1 Oscilloscope Display on Test Instrument.
Source: Kochenspargor, 1987, 187

Predictive testing of electric motors has an added benefit beyond less downtime. A vendor supplying motors is sensitized to quality demands, demands that reach right back to the factory floor. In addition, local motor repair services provided by suppliers will be upgraded as each becomes aware of the quality checks made by the customer.

Oil Sampling and Analysis

Oil sampling and the resulting laboratory analysis of these samples has become an important aid in predicting how and when such equipment as rolling stock and production systems will fail. Oil sampling is particularly suited for engine, transmission, or hydraulic system analysis.

Samples are taken at scheduled intervals to identify trends and detect abnormalities. Bimonthly sampling is about right for steam turbines, gears, and bearings, and hydraulic systems; diesel engines typically require monthly sampling or at 500 hours, whichever comes first. Sampling intervals for air compressors and natural gas engines are similar to the diesel engine. The actual length of time between samples will vary with the equipment type and the operating conditions.

A wide range of tests can be run on a sample. Each test will provide important clues to the operating condition of the machine. The decision to run a test will be based on a judgment call that considers cost, relative probability, and expected benefits. The machine's dependable operation, often critical, is also an important consideration. The following are eight of the most common tests:

- *Viscosity*: Viscosity, a measure of the flow characteristics of a liquid or semiliquid, is an important property of a lubricating oil. Excessively high viscosity may impede the flow of oil and the oil's ability to lubricate. If the viscosity is too low, the oil's film strength is impaired and its ability to prevent metal-to-metal contact is hampered. Test results will provide an index number, which is then compared to the benchmark for that application.
- *Contamination and Dilution*: Water, fuel, or coolant contamination will sharply reduce the effectiveness of a lubricant. The contaminants and diluents also indicate that something else is wrong in the total system.

    For example, fuel dilution, considered excessive when it tests out at 2.5 percent and more, may be a symptom of fuel system leaks, excessive idling or lugging, ignition problems, improper timing, or other combustion engine deficiencies.

- *Solids Content*: This can be a general test or a specific analysis such as the more specialized wear particle analysis described later in the chapter. Solids, measured as a percent of sample volume or weight, can cause excessive wear on lubricated parts.
- *Fuel Soot*: Fuel soot, minute particles of soft carbon or like materials, indicates the relative efficiency of fuel combustion.
- *Lacquer Deposits*: Most lubricants contain oxidation inhibitors. However, when these inhibitors break down or are not present, the lubricating oil thickens, creates a corrosive condition, or results in lacquer deposits as the lubricating oil ages with operating hours.
- *Total Acid Number (TAN)*: This is a measure of the amount of acid or acid-like material in the lubricating oil. The oil sample should be compared to the benchmark established for new oils that may or may not contain additives that influence the TAN number.
- *Nitration*: Combustion products, formed during operation, are highly acidic. Residual combustion products may be deposited on the internal surfaces, which in turn enhances oil oxidation.
- *Total Base Number (TBN)*: This is an objective measurement of the ability of a lubricating oil to neutralize acidity. Improper oil for the application operating too long between oil changes, overheating, and using high-sulfur fuel, will yield a low number. The higher the TBN, the greater the oil's neutralizing capability.

Wear Particle Analysis

Solids can cause excessive wear on lubricated parts; wear particle analysis defines where and why. Wear particle analysis characterizes the shape and composition of the solids and draws certain conclusions about the equipment being sampled. These conclusions are derived from the study of particle shapes, composition, sizes, and quantities.

Wear particle analysis occurs in two stages. The first establishes the benchmark by collecting particles and determining normal conditions and trends. The second stage, analysis, establishes the benchmark with which to compare future results. As a rule of thumb, when a machine is operating normally, the ratio of large particles (greater than 5 microns) to small particles should remain fairly constant after a break-in period, assuming that operating conditions do not vary widely.

Four abnormal wear types may show up in later analysis: rubbing, cutting, rolling, and sliding, and various combinations of each.

Rubbing wear can be a result of normal break-in of a wear surface. A unique layer forms at the surface; as long as this layer is stable, the surface wears normally and replacement or resurfacing can be predicted as a function of load, machine hours, and the engineered durability of the components. If the layer is removed faster than it is generated, the wear rate and the maximum particle size each increase. The dramatic increase in wear particles results in accelerated wear.

Cutting wear is characterized by one surface penetrating another. For example, misaligned or fractured hard surface produces an edge that cuts into a softer surface; or abrasive contaminants become embedded in a soft surface and cut an opposing surface. Increasing quantities of longer particles signal a potentially imminent component failure. If the wear particles are only a few microns long and a fraction of a micron wide, the cause is probably a contaminant.

Rolling fatigue is primarily associated with the rolling contact bearings and may produce three distinct particle types:

- *Spall particles*: These metallic particles are produced when a pit or spall opens up. An early indication of pending failures is an increase in the quantity of these particles.
- *Spherical particles*: These particles are usually detectable before any actual spalling occurs. Spherical particles are often generated by rolling fatigue.
- *Laminar particles*: These very thin particles are thought to be formed by the passage of a wear particle through a rolling contact. They frequently have holes in them. They may be generated throughout the life of a bearing, but the quantity increases at the onset of fatigue spalling.

Sliding wear is caused by excessive loads, speeds, or heat; it is typically a by-product of excessive loads and speeds in a gear train or system. Large particles break away from the wear surface, causing an increase in the wear rate. As additional stresses are applied to the surface, a second transition point is reached. The surface breaks down and catastrophic wear ensues. A failure is usually imminent.

Combined rolling and sliding wear results from the moving contact of surfaces in gear systems. The chunkier particles result from tensile stresses on the gear surface, causing the fatigue cracks to spread deeper into the gear tooth before pitting.

Scuffing of gears is caused by too high a load or speed. The excessive heat generated by this condition breaks down the lubricant film and causes adhesion of the mating gear teeth. As the wear surfaces become rougher the wear rate increases. Once started, scuffing usually affects each gear tooth, although the actual tooth damage will vary based on the variability of the metallic properties of the gear tooth to tooth.

The actual wear particle analysis sample may be processed on site or sent off site as an oil sample. The latter will diagnose the wear type and can even identify the equipment components that are failing. This takes the guesswork out of what to repair and when the task needs to be done. This predictability cuts repair costs and slashes downtime.

Computerized Modeling

The development of methods and technologies in support of maintenance has lagged behind efforts to improve and automate production. Too often the application of state-of-the-art maintenance technology is handicapped by maintenance methods that only seem to emerge as experience is gained in hands-on operation and maintenance. Computer modeling and the application of the techniques described earlier in this chapter can help the operator overcome that handicap.

Computer modeling is just emerging as a predictive maintenance technique. It is a means to determine or predetermine the maintainability of a mill or facility. The existing or proposed plant is modeled, the resulting model is coupled with a comprehensive database and a flexible manipulation. This capability will aid maintenance planning and provide predictability to the process. The model provides some or all of the following benefits:

- *Comparative analysis*: The model can be compared to existing systems and the experiences gained can be evaluated for application in the plant being modeled.
- *Maintenance simulation*: The model provides a means to simulate maintenance methods and to evaluate the merits of alternatives.
- *Data sharing*: Scheduling, job cost accounting, and performance monitoring can be easily shared with support personnel or operating personnel. Vendors and subcontractors can be alerted well ahead of the material and job requirements.

Computerized modeling has attracted the interest of the paper manufacturing portion of the industry. The automated and computerized nature of the papermaking process lends itself to modeling. This technique will become more widely used even in the solid wood business sector as the years go by.

References

Anliker, D. M. and S. A. Cilauro. 1988. Computer-Assisted Ultrasonic Detection and Measurement of Cracks in Pressure Vessels. *TAPPI Journal 71*, no. 3. (March).

Bos, M., T. B. Davis, and J. H. Redding. 1985. Key Steps to Establishing Sound Predictive Maintenance. *Plant Engineering* (December 12).

Feit, E. 1986. Infrared Inspection Saves Time and Money. *Forest Industries* (February).

Hartley, W. 1986. Predictive Maintenance—The Next Step. *TAPPI Journal 71*, no. 6. (June).

Kochensparger, J. 1987. Minimize Motor Failure Downtime. *Plant Engineering* (March 12).

LeFevre, R. 1987. Predictive Maintenance Surge Testing. *Plant Engineering* (December 17).

PART FOUR

BUDGETS AND COST CONTROLS

CHAPTER 13

The Economics of Maintenance

Downtime and the related costs of that downtime are often so newsworthy that the event spills over onto the headlines of a community newspaper. Such was the case with the following incident:

> [A] paper machine was extensively damaged when a chain snapped, causing a dryer felt to run into the back of a machine.
>
> John L. Lewis, mill facilitator, said repair crews worked around the clock to get the machine back on line after the Saturday night incident. Repair work was completed at 5:30 P.M. Wednesday, when the machine began rolling again.
>
> "Damage was extensive to the equipment, but at this time cost figures have not been completed," said Mr. Lewis. (Chmieiewski, 1987)

This newspaper account is a visible exception to what usually occurs in the forest products industry: We pay the bill, analyze the cause, chalk the breakdown up to bad luck, keep it to ourselves — and then hope it does not happen again. But attitudes may be changing as the traditional interrelationship between performance and maintenance economics is increasingly being challenged.

Changing Perceptions

The traditional manager focuses on costs and considers the obvious benefits of equipment uptime. When times are good parts and systems are replaced, new equipment is purchased, and an effort is made to upgrade the mill. The emphasis switches to cost avoidance when the next downturn occurs.

Maintenance man-hours and spending are both sharply reduced. Preventive and predictive maintenance activities begin to lag. The result is that a well-maintained mill may have a performance decline so subtle as to go unnoticed. With a little luck, this downward trend can go on for

141

months without costly failures. Unfortunately, luck and an operating mill are infrequent companions.

The manager's challenge is to understand the economic necessity of excellent maintenance performance and then track the indicators that identify the results of that performance as a means to keep the program on the track. The thought process is necessarily different than the traditional perception of maintenance as a cost.

Assessing the Cost

"You can't spend your way out of trouble," is a maintenance adage too often ignored. "New is often no better than the old" could be another. Each also runs counter to traditional thinking. A northern Florida sawmill is an example.

The mill was troubled; so was the manager. All the key performance indicators—overrun factors, production, and grade yield—were below standard. The initial answer was to improve maintenance; the long-range solution was to substitute technologically superior equipment at selected points in the process in place of outmoded models.

The manager replaced chains, gear-boxes, motors, and equipment parts. Outside contractors with in-house help performed miracles on weekends, but the key performance indicators demonstrated little improvement.

A rudimentary cost and tracking system did not tell the manager what he needed to know. Operator habits, lubrication results, maintenance skill levels, and a few recurring problems seemed to nag the mill. Repeat breakdowns, which often took up an inordinate amount of time and attention during the week, effectively masked the improvements that were being made.

A veteran plant manager later analyzed the situation:

> Newly installed parts and equipment often show dramatic early results, and these results are interpreted as a sign of improved performance. The reality is that the gains erode over time because the machine that was replaced was poorly maintained and wasn't doing the job properly; a new machine or component often suffers the same fate.
>
> The rule of thumb that if a machine's maintenance costs are X percent of the replacement cost then the operator should replace just doesn't hold water anymore. The decision to replace needs to be determined by analyzing many factors and information based on the history of the machine. You can't make the right decisions without good cost records unless the decision is so obvious or unless you are a gambler. Even if

records are good they may show a very skewed picture if maintenance productivity is low, the machinery is pushed constantly beyond design limits, or many other factors.

The Florida sawmill maintenance situation was eventually solved; but not before the manager was replaced and his approach was replaced by an emphasis on maintenance skill enhancement and tracking. This mill is typical: Pumping dollars into an operation is not always the answer. The cost of borrowed money is often too high. As another manager commented, "We can't go out and buy new stuff all the time, we must do better with what we have."

The Organization and Systems Investment

The ideal maintenance cost performance will only be achieved when an optimum balance of resources are used in a program.

"Ideally, effective maintenance will have the correct economic balance between maintenance costs and equipment performance. This happens only by the actions and decisions of effective people having adequate supportive resources (reporting systems and controls) tailored to the particular needs of a particular plant," cited an unpublished study.

The actual organization and systems needed will be based on the initial estimate of the cost-reducing potential over the short and long term. The organization and systems will be comprehensive enough to meet indicated needs, but no more complex than necessary. One South Carolina maintenance manager had an answer tailored to his situation:

> The actual lead in and operation of a preventive maintenance program is quite simple. To start a program, only two pieces of paper are necessary . . . go as far as you want from there, but only these two are essential. You need a 9 × 12 envelope with the name of the machine or equipment on it, and a written work order for all preventive and corrective maintenance performed.
>
> In the 9 × 12 envelope, you put the instruction book and parts list for the piece of equipment. Then each time a work order is written and completed, drop a copy in the envelope. From time to time examine it. Too many corrective orders indicate not enough preventive orders or not enough good ones. . . .
>
> Too few corrective orders may mean too many preventive orders. So you may wish to cut down just a little on the preventive orders to see what happens. The paperwork details can be placed in a card system. All that a computer can do for you, by the way, is hold the file and tell you when it is getting heavy.

Whether or not a manager will subscribe to this approach is not as important as the ingredients described. Proper and cost-effective maintenance requires a detailed knowledge of the machine or system. It also requires sufficient documentation that will highlight problems and opportunities. Work to be done needs to be classified and prioritized; the overall control system is carefully structured to provide visibility to the management process. This last feature, the "heavy envelope," is essential to the cost-control process.

The Heavy Envelope

A heavy envelope device can be structured into an almost endless variety of result-oriented systems. The heavy envelope evaluation can occur before or after the process. The objective is to construct a maintenance cost-control system that assures the operator that he or she is getting the biggest bang for the buck.

A computerized machine history or downtime report can be described as a heavy envelope. An excessive number of entries over time (frequency) for total causes, or a particular cause or fewer more costly entries (magnitude), can indicate that a maintenance program is failing to address the needs, the machine has inherent problems in capacity or design, or the mix of corrective versus preventive jobs is not correct. An analysis of what is being done and how it is being done is needed.

The resulting analysis will raise questions, and the search for answers may yield more than the problem sought. Other problems and opportunities will often be discovered along the way.

Another heavy envelope is the performance ratio. The ratio can be as simple as a downtime-to-uptime ratio expressed as a percentage, or it can be a financial ratio that evaluates the performance of the industry and the individual plant.

Timber Processing magazine, a trade publication, conducted an industry-wide survey by region during early 1987. The 265 respondents, all sawmill owners or operators, answered all or part of thirty-two questions. Two questions were of particular interest: (1) Please give estimated value of your present machines/systems inventory; and (2) please estimate your mill's annual maintenance/repair expenditures.

These respondents in aggregate represented industry production of 13,599 billion board feet of lumber products. The results represent an estimated $1,008 million in machines/systems and about $115 million in repair and maintenance.

The information gleaned from this survey cannot be considered comprehensive or totally accurate, but it does yield several revealing benchmarks. Table 13.1 is a summary of this study.

The South's ratio of repair and maintenance costs to the value of machines/systems was 12.6 percent. The West was lowest at 10.6 percent; the industry average was 11.2 percent. This information was then compared to the estimated actual for three Dimension lumber operations (table 13.2) for a recent annual time period. An order of magnitude comparison can be obtained, although the result is not a direct comparison.

Table 13.1 Sawmill Survey

Geographical Area	Estimated Average Value of Machines/System ($000)	Average Annual Maintenance/Repair Expenses ($000)	% Repair and Maintenance to Machine/System Values ($000)
South	4,301	542	12.6
North	2,135	262	12.3
West	4,159	441	10.6
Average	3,938	442	11.2

Source: Donnell, 1987

Mill A is a high-tech sawmill with a book value of $8,517 million and a replacement value of $11,290 million. The latter is based on the original cost indexed to the then current replacement value (Marshal Valuation Services) adjusted to the local index from the national average.

Mill B is a CNS mill playing maintenance catch-up on a number of deteriorating systems. Mill C is an older narrow-dimension mill with high ongoing maintenance costs, which have resulted from heavy use and little basic maintenance and upgrading in prior years.

These mills are below the benchmark illustrated in table 13.1, but the data does provide a basis for examining the heavy envelope. This broad examination then leads to a detailed maintenance analysis at each location. When the improvements were installed, each mill was measured at monthly, quarterly, and annual intervals to determine if the appropriate mix of repair-and-maintenance costs to results has been achieved. Cost and uptime performance increased in proportion to the management emphasis placed on the program.

The selection of appropriate ratios is almost endless. The following are important ingredients of a successful performance ratio:

- Each ratio requires a benchmark with which to measure variable performance.
- The performance indicator being measured and the benchmark being used should be the same in each repetitive audit.
- Ratios should be comprehensive enough to meet the indicated needs but no more complex than necessary.
- The resulting ratio should be easy to describe and explain. This is a prerequisite to ready acceptance by the user.

The Economics of Maintenance

Table 13.2 Individual Sawmill Survey

Mill	Mill Type	Current Fixed-asset Book Value ($000)	Current Fixed-asset Replacement Value ($000)	Annualized Repair and Maintenance Cost ($000)	% Repair and Maintenance to Book Value	% Repair and Maintenance to Replacement Value
A	Twin band breakdown	8,517	11,290	1,151	13.5	10.2
B	Chip n saw	4,275	8,810	1,429	33.4	16.2
C	Chip n saw	2,733	10,106	801	29.3	7.9

Source: Author's Study, 1986

- The method/mode of measurement should remain the same throughout the life cycle of the ratio being used.
- Each should be relatively easy to obtain, because the information gathering process and calculation has computer support.
- The ratios should be comprehensive enough to meet the indicated needs but no more complex than necessary.

Ratios are management tools that raise questions and provide clues to addressing and solving maintenance problems and high costs. They complement common-sense economics.

Economics as Common Sense

Several years ago Bob Dickson, plant engineer at Weyerhaeuser Wood Products at Springfield, Oregon, converted his machine shop into a profit center.

> We've always been viewed as a cost center in the past, . . . I think we'll have a more positive atmosphere in the shop if we operate as a profit center. Our clients will have a better basis for judging our value to them and our employees will have a better idea of where we stand." (*Weyerhaeuser Maintenance*, 1984, 5)

His cost standards, the basis for a heavy envelope, are gleaned from comparisons made with local outside vendors, much as a grocery store compares competitors' prices. Dickson and his crew obtained savings of about $100,000 during a cited quarter.

Other wood product people also understand the economics of maintenance, as indicated in the remark of a paper mill maintenance foreman:

"I'd rather have a $500 motor go to ruin than a $2,000 shut down. I try to look closely at the overall cost rather than a maintenance-specific expenditure."

How well a mill does in achieving peak performance and optimizing maintenance costs will depend on individual initiative and cost competency. The challenge is to provide the correct management tools and operating environment so that personal initiative combined with teamwork will yield superior results.

References

Allerton, L. J. 1980. Maintenance Management Means Measurement and Control. CPPA Maintenance Conference.

Chmieiewski, D. C. 1987. Champion Paper Machine Damaged. Watertown, NY *Daily Times* (December 4).

Donnell, R. 1987. Softwood Survey. *Timber Processing* (June).

Garrick, B. and H. F. Perla. 1979. *Changing Energy Use Futures.* Second International Conference on Energy Use Management. Los Angeles, CA. October 22–26. Vol. 4, 1648–1655.

Herbaty, F. 1983. *Cost-Effective Maintenance Management—Productivity Improvement and Downtime Reduction.* Park Ridge, NJ: Noyes Publications.

Karl, W. 1987. Meeting the Maintenance Challenge. *Pulp and Paper Journal* (November).

Lawson, M. A. 1986. Applying Work Measurement to Improve Maintenance Performance. *Plant Engineering* (April 10).

Nolden, C. 1986. Gaining Control Over Maintenance Costs. *Plant Engineering* (May 22).

———. 1987. Plant Maintenance Costs—How Do They Measure Up? *Plant Engineering* (July 23).

Westerkamp, T. A. 1985. How to Test Maintenance Productivity. *Plant Engineering* (September 12).

Weyerhaeuser Maintenance Journal. 1984. (July-August).

CHAPTER 14

Record Keeping and Cost Tracking

An old Chinese proverb states, "The palest ink is better than the best memory." A maintenance person could enhance this proverb by adding, "Complex equipment and many players make for many breakdowns without well-organized records and accurate information."

The Importance of Record Keeping

Unfortunately, record keeping and cost tracking are often neglected by the typical maintenance person. There are at least four reasons why this activity is so important.

1. Decision making: Comprehensive data and other facts are a prerequisite to informed decision making. It is difficult to plan if there is little historical information on which to base man-hour requirements, material usage, and other resource needs.
2. Planning for results: Proper man-hour utilization is the largest leverage point for lowering controllable costs; controlling material usage is the next largest. Maintenance information systems combined with specialized record-keeping and cost-tracking methods provide tools for effective planning.
3. Gathering resources: The most effective use of maintenance resources is achieved by planning work as far in advance as practical. Specialized training, parts and material ordering, and arranging for outside resources can be accomplished with ample lead time. In addition, maintenance materials can be shopped to provide the best value considering cost, quality, and service.
4. Establishing peak performance: Decision making and accountability can be moved downward in the organization proportionately

to the amount of information available to the participants actually doing the work. Comprehensive, timely, and accurate information allows simultaneous loose-tight organizational characteristics. That is a fancy way of saying that the work environment expects and encourages personal and group initiative within the framework of results-oriented controls.

Record-keeping and cost-tracking methods and procedures operate in tandem. In fact, the value of either is diminished greatly without the other.

Maintenance Record Keeping

Record-keeping methods range from simple to complex. The simplest system will have work orders, preventive maintenance (PM) checklists, and time cards; or it may use the envelope-stuffing system described in the previous chapter. The next step upward is the addition of the machine history file.

A comprehensive record-keeping system will have all of the items discussed below, and related items (such as downtime reports, mentioned earlier). Each of the nine record types listed here are representative of the parts of the whole; a well-functioning whole makes the maintenance task easier, swifter, and less costly. The aggregate of all nine record types forms the basic foundation for an effective cost-tracking system.

Written Work Requests

The work request can be the cornerstone of all other maintenance record and cost-tracking procedures. This record initiates the repair process and actually precedes the work order in many instances.

The actual document can be as simple as a pocket notepad or as complex as a multicopy formal form. The work request form is intended to document basic information about the needed repairs. It should answer the questions what, why, where, and state the expected end results and the priority of each.

Work Order

The work order (described fully in Chapter 5) is the foundation for record keeping, cost tracking, and budgeting, in addition to its use as a planning document.

The work order functions as an extension of the work request and is the next step in the record-keeping process. It documents the final word on what is to be done, when the task is to be initiated and completed, and what resources are to be used.

The work order also acts as an authorization to proceed and provides the basis for tracking man-hours and materials use. The necessary activities are then formalized to prevent the project from falling between the cracks. The resulting document is an excellent communication tool for coordinating the activities production of the maintenance workers.

Standing Work Order

The standing work order is an extension of the work order system. Its purpose is to set up repetitive maintenance needs so that each can be done on a timely basis. This system is most often used with rolling stock, chippers, digesters, and other heavily used equipment with work that is done periodically on a predictive or forecasted basis. The standing work order can be the basis for a formal predictive maintenance program.

Preventive Maintenance (PM) Checklist

A PM checklist is a machine-, system-, or site-specific checklist that provides a detailed listing of individual inspection items for any machine center or other assets requiring routine inspection. Small repairs or adjustments can be made on the spot; larger repairs are written up as a work request or work order when the inspection indicates the need.

Daily Individual Maintenance Report

This important planning document was fully described in chapter 5. It also functions as a tool for cost tracking and establishes needs for the budgeting process.

Time Card

The time card is a daily pay record for each individual maintenance worker. It allows tracking of man-hours against predetermined account numbers and work standards. Labor costs can then be allocated to an account number that represents a specific job and machine center.

Machine History File

This document, set up for each machine or system, is illustrated in figure 14.1. It is used to record all machine particulars, including the manufacturer's location and access, and that of the vendor or service person.

The front portion of the card identifies the specifics of the machine and its components. The back portion lists the repair and replacement history of the machine. Additional cards may be needed to fully document the repairs and rebuilds.

Repair and troubleshooting instructions, learned from hands-on experience, may also be included in the more comprehensive systems.

Master Drawing File

The master drawing file includes a complete updated set of drawings or blueprints for all components and systems in the mill. This includes all electrical, mechanical, steam and power, and other mainline or support systems. The master drawing file is especially valuable when planning major repairs or overhauls. In addition, the drawings enable workers to build in-house spares, and provide accurate details for vendor-supplied components.

Redlined Drawings

An accurate redlined drawing is essential for troubleshooting and repair. The maintenance person has ready access to a quick update on the machine or system should trouble occur. This feature is particularly important in larger facilities and multishift operations.

The drawings, used as worksheets, are used to "redline" in additions and modifications to the machine or system. The sequence of change, modification, and update, which occurs over time, provides the base information for updating the master drawing file.

Record Keeping and Cost Tracking 153

FRONT

HISTORY CARD

Mfg.	Address		Telephone	
Vendor	Address		Telephone	
Model	Style		Serial	
Catalog	Drawing		Floor Space	
Weight	Dimensions L ___ x W ___ x H ___			

MOTOR		MFG. SERIAL #	CO. SERIAL #
Type	H.P.		
Voltage	Amp.		
Cycle	R.P.M.		
Frame			

ACCESSORIES	DESCRIPTION	PROPERTY #

BACK

REPLACEMENT PARTS

DESCRIPTION	MFR.	SERIAL #	COST

P.O. # _____ Instal. Mtr Cost _____ Freight Cost _____ Date Purch. _____
Cost _____ Instal. Labor Cost _____ Other Cost _____ Date Instal _____

Remarks _____

DEPT.	LOCATION	DATE	DEPT.	LOCATION	DATE

Figure 14.1 **Machine or System Card**

Cost Tracking

Repair and maintenance costs are usually within the top four categories of controllable costs over which a manager has to cope. Only wood, labor, and sometimes supplies run higher. Repair and maintenance costs also seem to be much more management time intensive than the others.

The purpose of cost tracking is to obtain cost control while achieving the other intended benefits, such as improved quality and increased uptime. Ideally, the cost-tracking system should work as illustrated in figure 14.2.

Labor costs, stock issues, purchased materials, and other resources are identified as part of the work order input. The work order then identi-

```
┌─────────────┐ ┌─────────────┐ ┌─────────────┐ ┌─────────────┐
│ LABOR COST  │ │STOCK ISSUES │ │  PURCHASED  │ │ OTHER COSTS │
│  (From time │ │ (From store │ │  MATERIAL   │ │ •Contractors│
│    cards)   │ │ room issue  │ │(From P.O. or│ │ •Equipment  │
│             │ │   cards)    │ │ requisition)│ │   rental    │
└─────────────┘ └─────────────┘ └─────────────┘ └─────────────┘
```

         WORK ORDER SYSTEM (RECORD KEEPING)

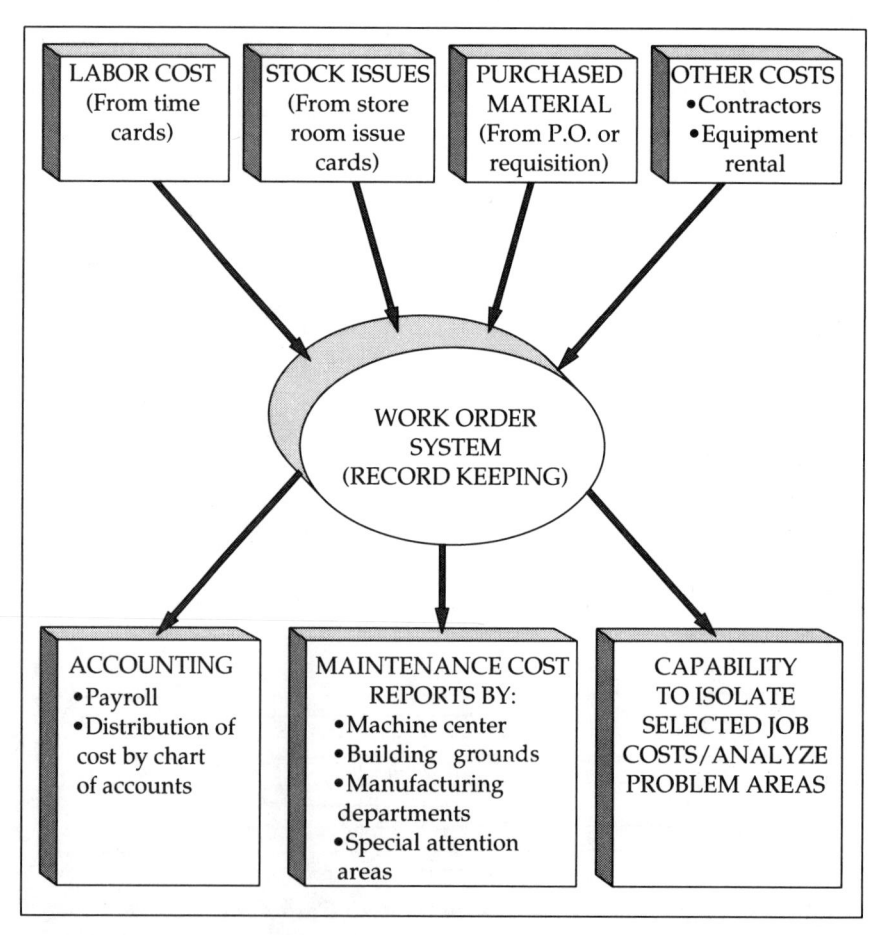

```
┌─────────────────┐ ┌──────────────────┐ ┌─────────────────┐
│   ACCOUNTING    │ │ MAINTENANCE COST │ │   CAPABILITY    │
│  •Payroll       │ │   REPORTS BY:    │ │   TO ISOLATE    │
│  •Distribution of│ │ •Machine center  │ │  SELECTED JOB   │
│  cost by chart  │ │ •Building grounds│ │ COSTS/ANALYZE   │
│  of accounts    │ │ •Manufacturing   │ │ PROBLEM AREAS   │
│                 │ │   departments    │ │                 │
│                 │ │ •Special attention│ │                 │
│                 │ │   areas          │ │                 │
└─────────────────┘ └──────────────────┘ └─────────────────┘
```

Figure 14.2   **Simplified Cost Accumulation/Tracking**

fies the expenditure of these resources and provides a mechanism for measuring cost effectiveness.

Three categories of benefits flow from this tracking system. Accounting has the total maintenance payroll bill identified and distributed by machine center or system; other costs are reported and are subsequently available to measure performance; and the manager and others now have the capability to isolate selected jobs and determine what future activities will yield lower costs and better methods. The result is an objective method for measuring job effectiveness.

Figure 14.3 provides an overview for one machine center, the planer in a western mill. This weekly control report communicates the actual repair and maintenance cost for this machine and support systems. It excludes the dry trimmer and sling sorter costs.

The report, issued a week at a time on Tuesday of the following week, identifies the actual out-of-pocket costs for maintaining the planer. The operating uptime and the quality of lumber product produced are not shown; these numbers are available elsewhere.

Figure 14.3 *Newburg Lumber Manufacturing Expense Recap*

Date: 08-26-88

Planer 7360

Cost Description	Account Number	Tactical Plan Current Week	Actual Current Week	Actual MTD	Tactical Plan MTD	Variance MTD (Over)/ Under
R & M Labor	50975	$ 380	$370	$1,295	$1,140	$(155)
R & M Outside	70037	160	0	325	480	155
R & M Materials	50989	590	610	1,785	1,770	(15)
		$1,130	$980	$3,405	$3,390	$(15)

Distribution:
J. Barnes
D. Jones
D. Willis

Each of the categories of costs shown can be further broken down by machine center or even components in some instances. The subsequent analysis can be as detailed or as broad as is necessary to achieve control of the costs and the process.

The results are provided on relatively brief time increments (weekly) and provide a manageable length of time to effect improved results before the month ends. Financial and performance results can then be uniformly higher as control is obtained, as subsequently indicated on the monthly and quarterly profit and loss statements.

A look at the experience of other industries illustrates what can be achieved in cost control in the forest products industry. For example, the Alumax plant in South Carolina, billed as the world's most efficient aluminum plant, uses a cost-tracking system not unlike the method described in this chapter. Maintenance costs, identified by cost or machine center, are listed by current period, year to date, and life to date. This report, issued at the end of each four week period during the year, identifies the high-cost machine centers during the period and what equipment or groups of equipment were responsible. Other reports provide more detailed interim information. Costs are continually tracked for labor and materials on each piece of equipment. This world class producer also has world class competitive costs. Maintenance record keeping and cost tracking has proved an underpinning for the overall effort.

References

Making Planned Maintenance Pay Off. 1984. *Plant Engineering* (August 9).
Westerkamp, T. A. 1985. How to Test Maintenance Productivity. *Plant Engineering* (October 10).

CHAPTER 15

Budgeting and Forecasting

Maintenance budgeting and forecasting is a megabuck process. Annual budgets can range from about $500,000 annually in a well-maintained Chip-N-Saw sawmill to that and more monthly in a large paper mill complex. What these repair and maintenance expenditures accomplish is often even more important than the amount.

Spent wisely, the dollar amount can be a bargain; spent without planning on break-it/fix-it maintenance can mean that these expenditures are little more than a stopgap measure to prevent downtime and further losses.

Management Decision Making

How can the manager spend these dollars wisely? How does he or she know what is being purchased for the money? And is the spending predictable? The answers to these commonly asked questions are not easy, but there is an answer for each. Three organizational attributes are essential for providing answers:

- A maintenance management structure that is designed, staffed, trained, organized, and motivated to achieve peak results.
- A record-keeping and cost-tracking system that provides timely, accurate, and visible facts upon demand.
- A formalized system of budgeting and forecasting that provides a zero-based perspective with the input of the operating line and staff.

An effective organization will get results; a record-keeping and cost-tracking system will measure those results. Maintenance budgeting and forecasting provides the framework for forward planning and results-oriented decision making. The process is not much different than budgeting and planning for production.

"Budgeting and forecasting can be applied in the maintenance function just as easily as it can in the production function, only it's applied a little bit differently," commented a plant engineer in a Pacific Northwest multiplant complex. The "little bit differently" may not be all that much different when establishing "should-be costs."

Should-be Costs

Establishing "should-be costs" starts with a plan. The maintenance planning process was described in chapter 5. Budgeting and forecasting is merely an extension of the planning and scheduling process. Short-range plans and schedules are extended a year or more and called a budget.

A forecast, defined as an anticipation of the future, uses the present as a base. The tendency is to use historical costs, add an assumed inflation figure, and then project the cost. But there are better, more accurate methods, which will provide a new dimension: the questioning attitude. The questioning attitude is a hallmark of the zero-based budgeting process.

Simplify, rearrange, combine, and *eliminate* are questioning words that can work magic on a zero-based budget or forecast. Each word frames a question with a fresh perspective.

Simplify

The zeal to automate has often resulted in equipment installations that can dazzle the observer but do little more than transfer costs. For example, an additional maintenance person, supported by related maintenance expenses, often has replaced a semiskilled operator and the relatively lower cost of a more manual operation.

Rearrange

An operation had several supplies and materials stores scattered around the plant site. Each department would obtain parts from one of several sources. The combination of over-ordering, the acquisition of vast amounts of unused stock, and the lack of accountability resulted in waste and high costs.

The mill subsequently hired a professional purchasing manager who began to sort and rearrange the tasks and procedures of the purchasing function. Specialized parts were stored near the appropriate use center and common parts were issued from a central storeroom. The result? Spare parts availability was increased, downtime was reduced, and resupply costs fell 20 percent and more.

Combine

Expanding the individual maintenance person's skills from a single craft, such as a millwright, pipe fitter, or electrician, into a well-trained combination of several skills—multicraft—results in fewer millwrights doing more in fewer hours with less downtime. One mill used a strategy of training and attrition to reduce a maintenance department head count from forty-four to thirty-two in a southern pine plywood plant. The added costs of training, recruiting, and contract bargaining were more than offset by the cost savings in job count and mill efficiency.

Eliminate

One western wood products company operated for decades with a full machine shop. The shop, fully staffed with skilled machinists, was capable of major rebuilds and equipment fabrication. This operation was something more than the usual plant shop, which can do little more than size sprockets and mill keyways.

During a zero-based budgeting session, where each line item was being challenged, a participant asked, "What would happen if we curtailed the machine shop? Could we get by? What would the real costs be?"

The tough-minded answer was, "We could get by all right with a little more advance planning and a closer relationship with an adjacent commercial machine shop." The result? Nearly $300,000 dollars slashed from the first year's maintenance costs with no decrease in service to the mills.

The Linkage Between Statistics and Cost

Frequently a mill will have developed reports that provide copious statistical detail at the operating level and equally copious detail at the accounting level. Computer-assisted data-gathering devices at the process machine centers and the almost universal acceptance of the personal computer as a data manipulating tool has led to the widespread development of new tailormade reports.

These reports in aggregate often provide little assistance in understanding the cause-and-effect relationship between maintenance statistics and the bottom line. Frequently, the conversion factors will even be different; it is almost like two groups are working separately.

The problem can go further than the linkage between the machine and the bottom line. Understanding what is going on at the machine is even a problem.

Frank Herbaty, a well-known maintenance management consultant, comments,

> 100% of all the accounting and computer systems I was involved in during my experience as a maintenance and fleet management consultant provided no useful information to the maintenance or fleet manager. The message from this experience is simple: Accounting and computer systems designed to provide management information to the maintenance manager must be designed by him or others under his strong technical supervision. He is the man who is charged with the responsibility of managing maintenance, and he was hired as the top expert on maintenance in the plant and, therefore, only he knows better than anyone else, what he needs to properly manage his department. (Herbaty, 1983, 250–251)

Frank makes an important point; the maintenance manager needs to know what is going on. How else can he effectively run his department and aid in the budgeting and forecasting process? The maintenance manager needs to know his costs.

There is a real need to tie the process of maintenance cost accounting and financial reporting into a common framework of understanding. Figure 15.1 illustrates the linkage between the statement and the machine center for maintenance budgeting and forecasting.

Labor costs, stock issues, purchased materials, outside services, and other resources are identified by machine center. The documentation provided by the machine history and work order reports are an important assist. The identified costs then feed into the cost center financials and on to the annual budget or the monthly, quarterly, or annual profit and loss statement.

All or nearly all of the statistical and cost reports should provide the following:

- A linkage between the budget or current financials and the machine center statistical reports.
- A compromise between the needs of the financial reporting and the needs of the operating and maintenance personnel.

Once established, the linkage between the financials and the statistical reports needs to be preserved. This fact-gathering and cost-accounting process sounds complicated; but in practice it is not. The overall objective is to provide a bottom-line understanding of maintenance costs.

Budgeting and Forecasting 161

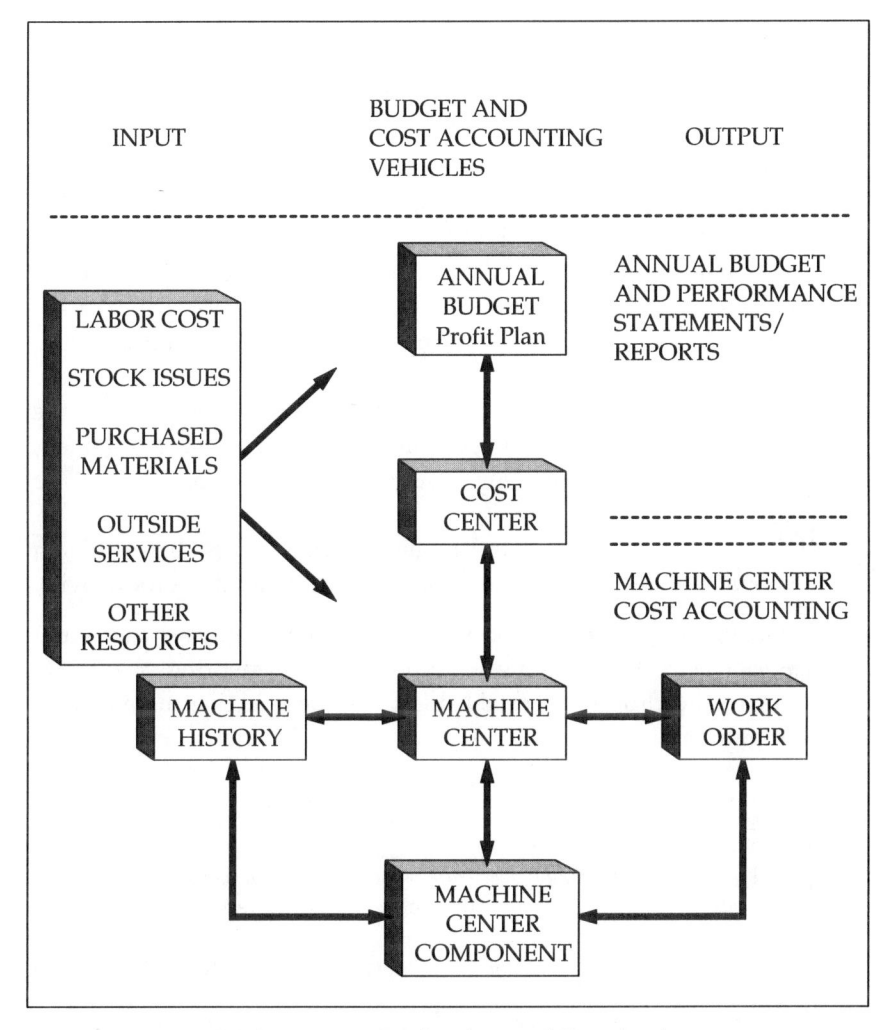

Figure 15.1 Maintenance Budgeting and Forecasting

Budgeting and Forecasting Tips

There are no easy methods to obtain a lean and cost effective estimate of future performance; but there are a number of useful tips learned from years of trial, error, and experience. The following are a few:

- Work with the accounting department to design a summary profit and loss statement in which repair and maintenance is visible on

the summary sheet; repair and maintenance then become easy to track to the department and the machine within that department.
- Initiate profit and loss-related interim cost reports (daily, weekly, and month to date) so costs are controlled in increments leading up to the monthly statement.
- Budget major repair and maintenance separately from the ongoing repair and maintenance budget. Major repair and maintenance, defined as one-time high-cost projects that will provide benefits for a year and more, can be visibly controlled so that large expenses are expected in a certain accounting period and are subsequently budgeted for that period.
- Push the budgeting and forecasting process as far down in the organization as possible. Additional insights will be gained; accountability for achieving results will be a by-product of the process.
- Use work measurement techniques whenever possible to obtain "should-be" benchmarks for measuring maintenance productivity.

The budgeting forecast process can be intimidating for the maintenance manager. But counting the dollars and measuring results are important to the process of establishing a value-effective maintenance program in the mill.

References

Arnold, T. L. 1980. *A Better Way to Use Work Sampling to Measure Maintenance Labor Productivity*. TAPPI Engineering Conference, Book III. September 7–11, 1980, Washington, D.C.

Herbaty, F. 1983. *Cost-Effective Maintenance Management*. Park Ridge, NJ: Noyes Publications.

Heyel, C. 1979. *The VNR Concise Guide to Industrial Management*. New York: Van Nostrand Reinhold.

CHAPTER 16

Rolling Stock Maintenance Scheduling and Cost Control

The idle string of loaded log trucks was visible well before the paper mill came into sight. The drivers were clustered in knots telling war stories, spitting, and passing the time. Oversized bib overalls, unbuttoned on the sides and cut high-water, allowed for air circulation on a hot, muggy Gulf Coast day.

The circulating air was about all that was moving that afternoon. Two log loaders, each costing about $300,000 new, were out of service at the repair shop. Several mechanics were at work.

The paper mill, with a cited replacement value of nearly $750 million, continued to operate in the background. The tree-length Loblolly pine pulpwood inventory was low after several weeks of sustained rain.

It wasn't a fluke that these massive log loaders were out of service and the mill nearly out of wood. It also wasn't a fluke that an overloaded green tray sorter and storage chains brought a Chip-N-Saw mill to a halt in an adjacent state about the same time because of maintenance downtime on its forklifts. Unfortunately, neither the paper mill nor sawmill has an adequate rolling stock maintenance program.

An effective rolling stock maintenance program has several common categories of activities: the groundwork is laid for the maintenance activity, the repair job is accomplished in the most effective fashion, and the results are reported and recorded.

Laying the Groundwork

The first step in laying the groundwork is to prepare a master list of all company-owned rolling stock. List each piece by type and the department assigned. This information should include:

- A permanent vehicle-assigned equipment number; this assignment extends throughout the life of the unit at the designated plant site.
- The year of manufacture and date purchased by the company.
- The vehicle model, serial number, and description.
- The condition of each unit—excellent, fair, poor—and any other special designation.

This information then becomes the core information for the equipment history file prepared for each vehicle. The Equipment History file card, illustrated in chapter 14, is also used for rolling stock record keeping, with a few minor revisions. It can be prepared manually or stored on a computer disk. This information is also useful for preparing an equipment replacement schedule.

Figure 16.1 illustrates an equipment replacement schedule for a structural board plant. Not all of the equipment is shown. What is shown is a listing by unit number, assigned department, model, type, year purchased, and condition of the equipment. The replacement year is also identified along with the recommended replacement vehicle, where appropriate.

The term "trickle down" is used to denote vehicles that will be replaced by higher-use vehicles. For example, pickup trucks previously used in log procurement can continue to be used for years as welding trucks, where engine time is low but exterior abuse may be high.

The actual replacement decision is based on many factors. The weight given to a particular factor will depend on the operating hours; the severity of use; and the economic durability of brand, type, and model. The resulting replacement schedule then provides a guide for the rotation and replacement of each unit. This guide, in turn, provides an insight for determining the economic necessity of major repairs, such as engine or transmission replacement. The replacement schedule is updated annually as part of the maintenance operating budget and capital plan.

Getting the Job Done

Properly maintaining a rolling stock fleet requires a combination of preventive and predictive maintenance activities. There are three specific categories: a routine mobile equipment checklist, a maintenance and service schedule, and an oil sampling program. A cost-conscious operator will use all three.

The vehicle operator completes the checklist card (illustrated in chapter 9, figure 9.4) prior to the start of the shift or before the vehicle is

MOBILE EQUIPMENT REPLACEMENT SCHEDULE

DATE 4-4-83   Pg. 2

LOCATION Corrigan, Texas

UNIT #	DEPARTMENT	MODEL	TYPE	YEAR PURCH.	CONDITION	84	85	86	87	88	REPLACE WITH
80134	Shipping	S80E	Hyster	1980	Good				36.2		Same
80212	Finishing	S80E	Hyster	1978	Good				36.2		Same
80213	Shipping	S80E	Hyster	1978	Good				36.2		Same
80534	Finishing	S60B	Hyster	1972	Poor I	22.8					Hyster S80E
04707	Maint-Welder	3/4 Ton	Ford	1976		(Trickle Down)					
04725	Maint-Welder	3/4 Ton	Ford	1976		(Trickle Down)					
44532	Maint-Mach. Shop	3/4 Ton	Ford	1976		(Trickle Down)					
44762	Prod. Supt.	1/2 Ton	Ford	1978	Poor II	9.9					Equivalent
82518	Maint-Winch	2 Ton	Chevy	1964		(Trickle Down)					
82524	Clean up	2 Ton	G.M.C.	1978	Fair	(Trickle Down)					
82589	Storeroom	1 Ton	Chevy	1980	Fair						Equivalent
83044	Clean up	White Freight Liner		1969	Poor '83	Do Not Replace					
84511	Plant Mgr.	1/2 Ton	Ford	1979	Poor II	9.9					Equivalent
85013	Truck Shop	1/2 Ton	Ford	1976	Good	(Trickle Down)					

Figure 16.1   Mobile Equipment Replacement Schedule

used. This will help the operator complete a step-by-step inspection of the vehicle.

The vehicle operator then turns the checklist into his or her supervisor or designate for verification and data recording. Any minor service needs are taken care of on the spot. Other repairs, if not urgent or unsafe, are noted on the checklist card and scheduled by the mobile mechanic or millwright.

The checklist card prompts the mobile equipment operator to note the following:

- unit number
- oil, water, and fuel levels
- safety and fire protection equipment
- the condition of tires, wheels, lights, horn, back-up alarm, and electrical components
- brakes and steering check
- any other comment on the operating condition and safety of the machine

The checklist cards are maintained in the respective vehicle equipment file with a thirty-day retention schedule. This time interval allows time for repair and follow-up while using the checklist card as backup.

The maintenance and service schedule is identified for each vehicle utilizing vendor recommendations and mill experience. A scheduling board (see figure 16.2) is used to visibly display the scheduled repair and service needs at a glance. Information posted on the board includes:

- unit number
- next service date and hour/mileage reading
- type of repairs or service required
- status of the parts required
- last oil sample date
- mechanic assigned to the repair/service

The service schedule recognizes that peak performing equipment requires periodic servicing performed on a regularly scheduled basis. This periodic maintenance program can reduce machine operating costs, increase the equipment's life, boost material-handling productivity and efficiency, and improve the mill's bottom line. An indispensable part of this effort is the oil sampling program.

Oil sampling is the periodic testing of a unit's operating fluids (engine oil, transmission, hydraulic) by an outside resource (the tests are more fully described in chapter 12).

Rolling Stock Maintenance Scheduling and Cost Control 167

Equipment No. Description	Next Service Date	Type of Service Required	Parts Status	Last Oil Sample Date	Mechanic Assigned

Mobile Equipment Maintenance Schedule Board

Figure 16.2 Mobile Equipment Maintenance Schedule Board

Mobile Equipment Repair/Cost form

SHOP USE ONLY	Delete
Job 620388	
1 6	7
Loc	
8 11	
Date	
12 / / 17	
Unit	
18 22	
Dept	
23 26	
Out Hr	
27 30	

Service Code	Parts Cost	Labor Hours	Fuel Gallons	Labor Cost	Total Cost
31 □ 32 □ 33 □ 36	37 42	43 45	46 48		
31 □ 32 □ 33 □ 36	37 42	43 45	46 48		
31 □ 32 □ 33 □ 36	37 42	43 45	46 48		
31 □ 32 □ 33 □ 36	37 42	43 45	46 48		
31 □ 32 □ 33 □ 36	37 42	43 45	46 48		

Location _____ Unit No. _____ Foreman _____ Date _____ Time _____ AM/PM

Instructions _____

Work Performed _____

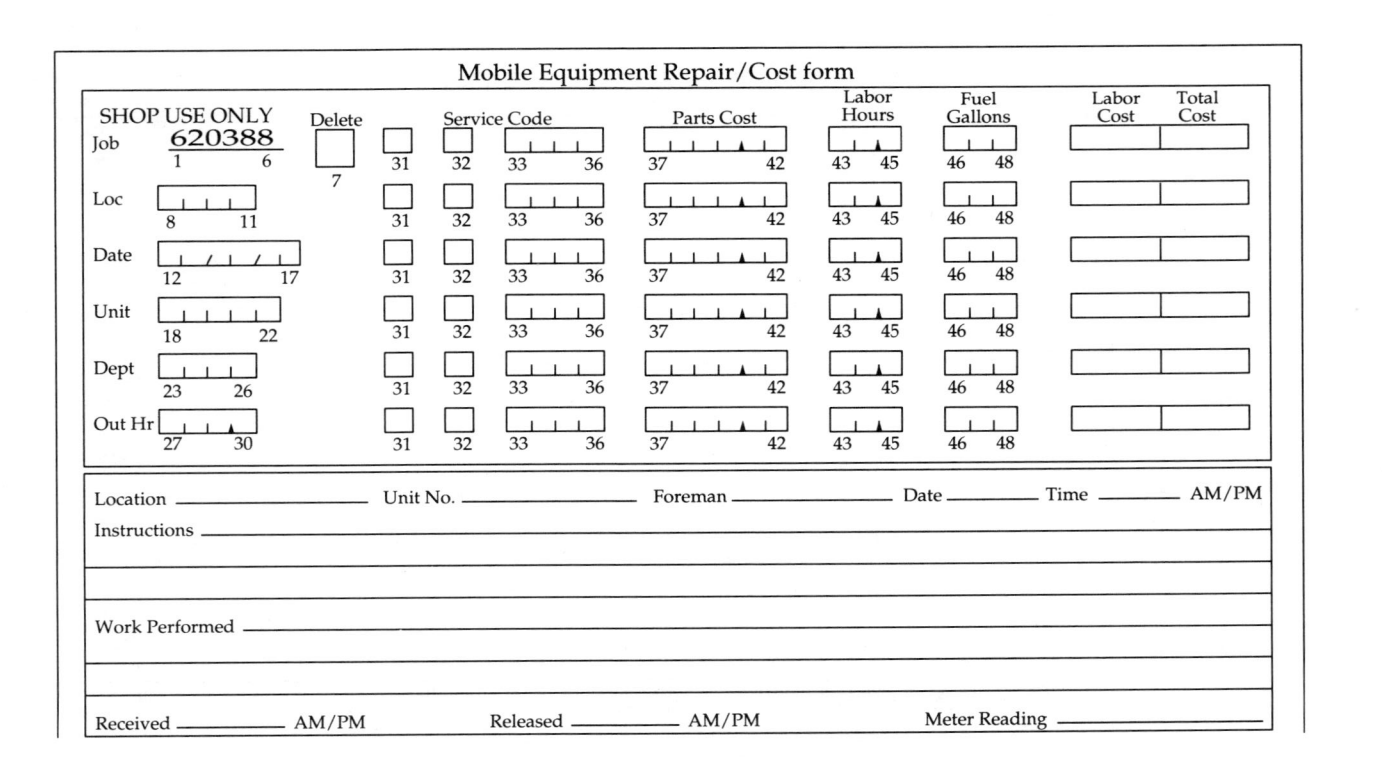

Received _____ AM/PM   Released _____ AM/PM   Meter Reading _____

Quantity	Iden. No.	PARTS Description	COST Unit Cost	Total	Date	LABOR Mech.	Actual Time	Flat Rate

Block 31 Use numerical character only.
Block 32 Use alpha character only as follows: A Alter M Manuf R Reg
C Craft O Oper V Vndr

1
1. SEND TO M.E.C.
2. SHOP
3. SHOP
4. ORIGINATOR

Figure 16.3 Mobile Equipment Repair/Cost Form

This sampling is designed to detect signs of excessive internal vehicle wear that may be evident in the unit's engine, transmission, and hydraulic components. The resulting assay, or test, will yield telltale clues that provide early warning of service and repair needs.

Mobile Equipment Reporting and Cost Tracking

A systematic method of recording, reporting, and maintaining mobile equipment records is a good idea. Figure 16.3 is an example of an input form used to manually record the repair or service event. The information can be entered directly into the computer or from the manual input form and then into the computer. The mobile equipment input form is a numerically sequenced form that is used to record and categorize all repairs performed on an individual mobile unit.

The example shown is an actual example of a mechanic solving a problem. The input data includes date (Sept. 19, 1988), labor cost ($32.04), total cost ($35.90), the description of work being performed, and other pertinent information. The resulting record is a control that will assist in repairing this machine, and others in the future.

Management reports are available as input information is accumulated. Figure 16.4 is a simple report used to identify the monthly repair and maintenance bill by unit. The actual format or report architecture can

Figure 16.4 *Mobile Equipment Monthly Repair and Cost Report*

GROVETAR PLYWOOD

Unit #	Description	Department	Parts Cost	Labor Cost	Total Cost
00235	C10C10 80 ½ TON PICKUP	MAINT	101.20	72.71	173.91
06115	L-555 BUCKET LOADER	PLY GEN CLEANUP	116.76	356.87	473.63
45659	½ TON PICKUP (1981)	MOBILE	11.44	59.49	70.93
45/64	82 ½ TON PICKUP	MAINTENANCE	0.00	6.61	6.61
5502	SHOP CLEAN-UP TIME	MOBILE	1.00	13.22	14.22
5506	WELDING MACHINE	MAINTENANCE	5.77	26.44	32.21
5536	WELDING MACHINE	MAINTENANCE	6.37	13.22	19.59
5540	LOG GRAPPLE LOADER	VATS	23.97	105.76	129.73
80014	S70E FORKLIFT	PLANT	1.10	13.22	14.32
80079	S-80E BCS FORKLIFT	FIN/SHPG	10.05	26.44	36.49
80116	S80-BCS FORKLIFT	DRYER	353.91	204.91	558.82*
80117	S-80BCS FORKLIFT	DRYERS	337.07	399.21	736.28*
80118	S-80E FORKLIFT	GREENEND	141.84	158.73	300.57
80119	S-80E FORKLIFT	GLUE/PRESS	310.28	158.69	468.97
80163	S80E FORKLIFT	FIN/SHPG	326.56	257.79	584.35*
80164	S80E FORKLIFT	FIN/SHPG	706.14	389.49	1095.63*
80176	S80E FORKLIFT	FIN/SHPG	100.47	152.05	252.52
80177	S80E FORKLIFT	FIN/SHPG	216.20	211.52	427.72
80455	H100E 10000LB FORKLIFT	STUDMILL	27.47	132.20	159.67
80584	S70E FORKLIFT	PLANT	50.37	185.08	235.45
80585	S70E FORKLIFT	PLANT	28.49	106.37	134.86
82514	77 LT800 TRUCK	WOODYARD	164.28	924.20	1088.48*
83074	LT 8000 14YD DUMP TRUCK	BOILER	24.63	132.20	156.83
85035	85 ¾ TON PICKUP	MILL SERVICE	0.00	19.83	19.83
86019	722 BOBCAT	WOODYARD	192.62	264.40	457.02
86020	D-4E DOZER	CHIP AREA	0.00	19.83	19.83
86042	930 LOADER	PROCESSOR	69.18	297.45	366.63
86055	966D LOADER	WOODYARD	412.61	290.84	703.45*
86124	OMEGA 18 TON	MOBILE MAINT	620.76	901.90	1522.66*
86146	930 LOADER	STUDMILL	154.69	305.67	460.36
86263	450 DOZER	BOILER	12.69	19.83	32.52
86264	LOG STACKER	WOODYARD	6.10	59.49	65.59
86265	LOG STACKER	WOODYARD	642.21	489.14	1131.35*
86308	930 LOADER	BOILER	846.98	290.84	1137.82*
86494	930 LOADER	WOODYARD	281.70	667.61	949.31*
89538	280 SWEEPER	PLY GEN CLEANUP	11.53	52.88	64.41
89541	BASKET LIFT	ELECT MAINT	103.64	224.74	328.38
*** Total ***			6420.08	8010.87	14430.95

* Total cost of units w/$500+ per week repair = $9,507.00

be a full report or an exception report. The latter flags out only the items requiring attention. It can summarize the data and apply performance ratios such as cost per operating hour, cost per unit of production, and more.

Preparing and acting upon the management reports is an effective way to improve mobile equipment uptime and reduce costs. The resulting information combined with up-to-date service manuals and input of knowledgeable vendor representatives can improve uptime and lower costs. That's the mission of an effective mobile equipment program.

References

Berge, K. H. 1976. Maintaining Fork Lift Trucks. *Plant Engineering* (April 1).

Erhart, L. 1985. Raising Productivity with Periodic Maintenance. *The Logger and Lumberman* (October).

Griffin, G. 1985. Survey Examines Logging Shop, Service Truck Trends. *Forest Industries* (August).

PART FIVE

MAINTENANCE SUPPORT SYSTEMS

CHAPTER 17

Energy Conservation

There is a correlation between the quality of the maintenance effort and the energy efficiency of the plant. Energy wasters such as air leaks, inefficient electrical systems, drive and transmission units in poor repair, and inadequate lubrication are just a few of the many. The task of a total maintenance (TM) program is something more than the generally accepted role of maintenance, that of production enhancement and mill preservation. The broader definition includes the activities associated with obtaining more out of the mill with less. Energy cost reduction is central to that task.

"The most effective, ongoing device available for energy conservation is good, technical manpower," stated a corporate energy policy manager (Horovitz, 1981, 45). That "device" is the maintenance person.

The Maintenance Person

The maintenance person has the skills, knowledge, and scope of activity to observe, question, and correct energy-wasting systems or procedures. This veteran maintenance manager recognizes the importance of the individual worker:

> In our industry, controlling or reducing energy costs will not be mainly achieved through technology advances or capital improvement and modernization, though to be sure, these will play a significant role as a means to an end.
>
> The real key lies in the heightened awareness of the large potential for no cost/low cost improvements in energy efficiency and reduced energy usage through maintenance initiative, imagination, and the attention to the dull but vital details of routine maintenance. We must find the flavor in what is flavorless.

The maintenance person has a unique opportunity to spot energy-cost reduction opportunities, and then do something about them. The example set by the manager will set a pace for the energy conservation effort.

Yes, There Really Is a Free Lunch

"Turn it off when it is not in use" is a free lunch. Ordinary effort is translated into substantial cost savings. A Mississippi plywood plant manager is one such example. The lights were off in his office during business hours. As we walked through the doorway, he flipped the wall switch on. Then he remained behind long enough to turn off the switch as we left.

"What's that all about?" I asked. His atypical habit might be a clue to something more.

"What's that? Oh, the light. I just want to set an example for our energy conservation program."

We toured the mill. The illumination was just right throughout the plant. Motors, conveyors, and rolling stock were shut off when not in use, and used to capacity when in service. A timer jogged the green veneer waste conveyor ahead every few minutes. One waste veneer chipper was being used instead of the usual two. And the differences didn't stop there.

Motors were sized correctly for the job; the bearings, chains, and other drive components demonstrated evidence of timely and regular lubrication. Bright green ultra-high molecular weight (UHMW)-low-friction wearstrips lined the conveyors. The greenend was quiet enough between shifts to allow an ordinary conversation; there were no airleaks to be heard. This tour brought new meaning to the following energy conservation story:

> In any case, experts advise, investment in energy-saving equipment should be the very last conservation step a manufacturer takes. And many have got it backwards. The temptation for a quick fix lures many executives into buying newfangled gadgets even before they've checked the major source of energy waste: improper operation and poor maintenance of machinery. (Horovitz, 1981, 43 and 45)

A Department of Energy supervisor was quoted in the same article as saying, "Most people do the frivolous stuff first. . . . then pay for it later" (Horovitz, 1981, 45).

Here are a few examples of energy wasters:

- unnecessary or incorrect lighting
- a low power factor

- oversized or energy-inefficient electric motors
- loose or faulty electrical connections
- machines left running, such as fans, blowers, hogs, chippers, and conveyors
- compressed-air system leaks
- improper lubrication
- steam, air, and water hoses not properly shut off
- faulty steam traps
- uninsulated deaerator tanks

Repairing and correcting each of these deficiencies—and there are others—will increase the overall energy efficiency of the plant. Time and a few materials is all that is needed. When taken in aggregate, they represent a "free lunch."

Why Use Two When One Will Do?

Several years ago, while visiting an engineering office in northern Italy, I was shown blueprints of a proposed eastern European wood products complex. As we examined the prints someone asked, "What is the planned capacity of this mill?"

I quickly converted the engineers' response from cubic meters to board measure and thousand 3/8ths.

"Well, that mill may have about 40 percent more equipment than it needs for the planned volume," I countered.

"But you Americans don't understand. There is not the incentive to operate as efficiently as you do in North America. We are designing to suit their needs."

There is a tendency to be a smug American and think that a modern forest products plant is run as efficiently as possible in North America. Too often, however, that simply is not the case. Redundancy and overcapacity is also built into our mills to prevent downtime and to insure that volume norms will be met. The redundant equipment is justified on the basis of necessity even when an upgraded maintenance program would prevent the need. Let's look at a Mississippi plywood plant that is an excellent example of what can be done.

This mill, originally built with two green veneer chippers and related conveyor systems, had increased green end production about 40 percent over the original design capacity and yet had retired one of two green veneer chippers and some other equipment. How could the mill do this?

One reason is that improved maintenance and operating practices, plus timely introduction of state-of-the-art innovations, had increased the usable veneer from the log while reducing scrap veneer. The result was a lower electrical bill and reduced production and maintenance man-hours. The out-of-pocket cost per thousand 3/8th of green veneer was substantially lower.

Extra digesters in a paper mill and extra planers in a lumber operation are all examples of overcapacity and extra energy costs built into a mill because of inadequate maintenance and less than optimum operating practices. A maintenance program and its participants can sharply reduce energy costs by systematically upgrading the operation of each piece of needed equipment and retiring others. The results on the operating statement will be dramatic.

Newfangled Gadgets and Methods

Newfangled gadgets and methods are what a mill operator installs subsequent to or in conjunction with the easy stuff mentioned earlier. Tangible savings can be obtained in a variety of ways, but at a price. The price is usually disproportionately low when compared to the benefits obtained. Compressed-air systems are an example of how gadgets and methods can pay big dividends.

Compressed-air Systems

The presence or absence of air leaks can be detected when the mill is down between shifts and on weekends. The task is more difficult in a four-shift paper or board plant, but the task of identifying air leaks can be done. And air leaks are expensive. Table 17.1 is an example of what the costs might be with electrical costs of $0.05/kilowatt hour.

The size of the single air leak or an aggregate of air leaks is identified in the left-hand column. The air loss (cfm) is identified in the next column with the respective annual costs shown to the right. Four-digit excess costs can be achieved easily with neglected maintenance, with five-digit losses not far behind.

The following are a combination of further conservation practices, new methods, and gadgets that can improve the resulting energy costs.

Eliminate the Need   Some applications of compressed air are unnecessary; eliminate those first off. Blowing or cleaning of debris is one, using a steady stream of compressed air as a coolant is another. The number of unsuitable applications is limited to the creativity of a mill person. Use

Energy Conservation

Table 17.1 *Compressed-air Leakage Costs*

Hole Size (inches)	CFM at 100 psi	Cost/Year
1/32	1.11	$ 55
1/16	4.20	210
1/8	16.80	840
1/4	67.50	3,375
1/2	270.00	13,500

Note: These costs assume a twenty-four-hour daily operation of the compressor and electricity costs of $0.05 per kilowatt hour.

Source: Baldwin, 1984, 218

this creativity as an advantage to figure out other less costly ways to get the job done.

Reduce the Usage Turn off each compressor during lunch, breaks, and between shifts; purchase a small "pony" compressor to maintain the minimum required line pressure. This may only be possible with an otherwise efficient compressed-air system. Use a timer within the compressor electrical circuits to activate the start and stop functions.

Relocate the Air Compressor Air compressors operate most efficiently when located in a relatively dry and cool location. Air intakes, located outside on the shady side of the building, will provide cooler air with lower costs.

Table 17.2 identifies a range of air intake temperatures along with the intake volume required to deliver 1,000 cubic feet of free air at 70° F. The percent available savings or increased horsepower required is identified using 70° F. as a base. The cooler the air the greater the horsepower savings available.

Many compressors are situated next to an exterior wall and have a short pipe situated between the intake manifold and the air filter. Simply extend the pipe through the exterior wall and then reinstall the filter.

Find the Leaks and Fix Them Promptly Leaks occur at valve packings, quick disconnects, regulator handles, blow-off nozzles, pipe connections, and areas of vibration. The solution is simple: Fix each as it occurs and prevent further occurrence when possible.

In addition, search for and repair compressed-air control valves that have failed internal seals. This bypassing of compressed air is a more subtle form of leakage.

Table 17.2 *Air Intake Temperature versus Compressor Horsepower (hp) Requirements*

Temperature of Air Intake, °F.	Intake Volume Required to Deliver 1,000 cu ft of Free Air at 70° F.	% hp Saving or Increase Relative to 70° F. Intake
30	925	7.5 Saving
40	943	5.7 Saving
50	962	3.8 Saving
60	981	1.9 Saving
70	1,000	0.0
80	1,020	1.9 Increase
90	1,040	3.8 Increase
100	1,060	5.7 Increase
110	1,080	7.6 Increase
120	1,100	9.5 Increase

Install a Variable Frequency Drive Install a variable air-compressor drive; the Georgia Pacific plant in Toledo, Oregon, has achieved a 20 percent savings in power use for compressing mill air and a 33 percent reduction in mill air pressure variations. An Emerson variable frequency drive with manual switching gear permits the automatic speed control of either of two 1,000 hp compressors. The air compressor speed of each is controlled within a variable range, the speed can be turned down approximately 50 percent if dictated by the needs of the mill. Each turn down translates into cost savings.

Minimize the Air Pressure Use regulators on the air compressor to maintain pressure only at levels required to get the job done. Size the compressor and motor to the tasks required. Compressors frequently operate at pressures higher than needed. Modest amounts of energy can be saved and wear on equipment reduced when operated at lower pressures (see table 17.3).

These costs, accumulated daily based on a nine-hour operation, can vary with the compressor horsepower rating and the pressure pumped through the line. For example, a 25 hp compressor will cost $80 per day at 10 psi; a 15 hp compressor will cost $48 per day for the same air pressure. A 25 hp compressor operating at 25 psi when only 10 psi is needed will cost $200 per day rather than $80.

These costs or savings add up rapidly over time.

Table 17.3 *Annual Energy Dollars Saved by Reducing Operating Air Pressures*

Compressor Horsepower	Pressure Difference						
	5 psi	10 psi	15 psi	20 psi	25 psi	30 psi	35 psi
5	$ 8	$ 16	$ 24	$ 32	$ 40	$ 48	$ 56
10	16	32	48	64	80	96	112
15	24	48	72	96	120	144	168
25	40	80	120	160	200	240	280
50	80	160	240	320	400	480	560
75	120	240	360	480	600	720	840
100	160	320	480	640	800	960	1,120
150	240	480	720	960	1,200	1,440	1,680

Note: These costs assume a nine-hour daily operation of the compressor and electricity costs of $0.05 per kilowatt hour.
Source: Frederick T. Kurpiel, Clark E. McDonald, 1987. *Energy Strategies for Increasing Productivity*, 38.

Electrical-powered Production Systems

The all-electric mill was considered a boon to the industry a generation or so ago. Now it is the norm, with other forms of power taking a back seat. But improperly designed, operated, or maintained systems can sometimes turn the boon into a bane, at least until the inefficiencies are corrected. The following are a few of many that will lead to greater energy efficiency.

Power Factor The power factor of an electrical device (motor, resistance heater, lighting and so on) is the ratio of the actual or working power used to the apparent power delivered to the consumer by the power company. The power factor is expressed as a percentage, and is usually less than or equal to 100 percent.

For example, a device using 2,000 kw at a given instant, operating at a power factor of 100 percent, would require 278 amps in a 3-phase 4,160-volt, 60-Hz feeder to that power system. If the power factor were low, say 85 percent, 327 amps would be required to supply the same 2,000 kw load.

A low power factor creates additional costs because of the following:

- Many utilities charge a penalty for a power factor below a predetermined value. Some give a credit for a high factor.
- A low power factor necessitates that transformers, generators, and

power cables must be overloaded or oversized. Voltage drops and power losses are greater than necessary.
- A low power factor limits the capability to add additional electrical equipment on an existing power supply configuration.

A lower power factor can be corrected by determining the extent of the problem, and then taking corrective action. An electrical contractor, the power company, and the mill's maintenance and engineering personnel can work together to determine the nature and extent of the problem. Corrective measures are then taken. The corrective measures can be summarized as follows:

- Capacitors: A properly sized capacitor installation can restore a lower power factor to near 100 percent or at least in the high 90 percent range. Capacitors can be installed as banks or as separate units within the system. They can be stationary or be switched on when needed. The capacitor can be situated within the power grid or system prior to the mill hookup or within the mill's electrical system.
- Synchronous motors: These are sometimes used to correct a low power factor. Large motors of this type have a capacitor-type effect on the electrical distribution network.

The benefits are immediate: Power bills go down and there is less wear on the electrical equipment.

High-efficiency Motors

Correct sizing is the initial consideration when selecting a motor for a job.

> When the theoretical motor horsepower required for a given application is calculated, the resulting number usually falls between two standard motor sizes, so the larger value is selected to ensure that sufficient power will be available. However, accepted design practice also calls for a 15% safety/design calculation contingency factor. For example, an actual 4.8-hp mechanical load becomes a 5.5-hp motor requirement after the contingency factor multiplier is applied. A 7.5-hp motor is therefore selected, resulting in a motor that is 36% larger than the actual horsepower requirements of the load with contingency factor applied. (Greenwald, 1988, 84)

This initial oversizing can then be compounded if the motor goes out and is then replaced with the next larger size, a 10-hp motor, as an emergency replacement. Unfortunately, the oversized replacement may never be changed back again.

The mill operator should ascertain that each motor is correctly sized and then locate a suitable replacement in the event of need. A mill audit may discover a number of incorrectly sized motors; these should be changed out on a scheduled basis. Energy-efficient motors are another way to cut the energy bill.

"Energy efficient" has almost become a generic term; but describing an electric motor as energy efficient is quite specific. Energy-efficient motors are designed and built with more steel, steel with improved electromagnetic properties, thinner steel laminations in the stator and rotor core, improved rotor slot design, increased wire volume in the stator, and smaller, more efficient fans. These increased and improved materials combined with the higher comparative manufacturing costs will result in a premium price, high enough to make the purchasing decision more difficult.

A number of companies and organizations, such as the Bonneville Power Administration (BPA), BC Hydro, and General Electric, have developed complex yet understandable computer programs that calculate paybacks, return on investments, and other more detailed financial data. The best approach is to find a computer program that fits the needs of the decision maker, and then fit together a purchasing policy for a wide range of motor sizes and types prior to the need. Figure 17.1, a graph prepared by Carroll, Hatch and Associates for the Bonneville Power Administration (BPA), is an example of one such effort. The vertical axis represents the operating hours per year for a specific horsepower size. The horizontal axis provides the payback time stated in years.

For example, a 5-hp motor operating in a paper mill with operating hours in excess of 7,000 hours per year would have a payback time of less than a year. The larger motors have a progressively longer payback period.

Robert Mitchell, Jr., a marketing development specialist for General Electric, stated, "In a typical paper mill involving a mix of motors ranging from 7½ to 125 hp and containing 200 motors, savings could range as high as $60,000/year with a life-cycle savings of over $500,000 in 10 years" (Mitchell, Jr., 63).

The choice is more difficult on a cost or maintenance basis in the larger horsepower motors. These motors, built to progressively more demanding specifications as the horsepower rating increases, will stretch out the payback period. The return becomes harder to justify based on anticipated savings alone. The repair/rewind of older conventional motors is usually much cheaper and continues to be the favored alternative.

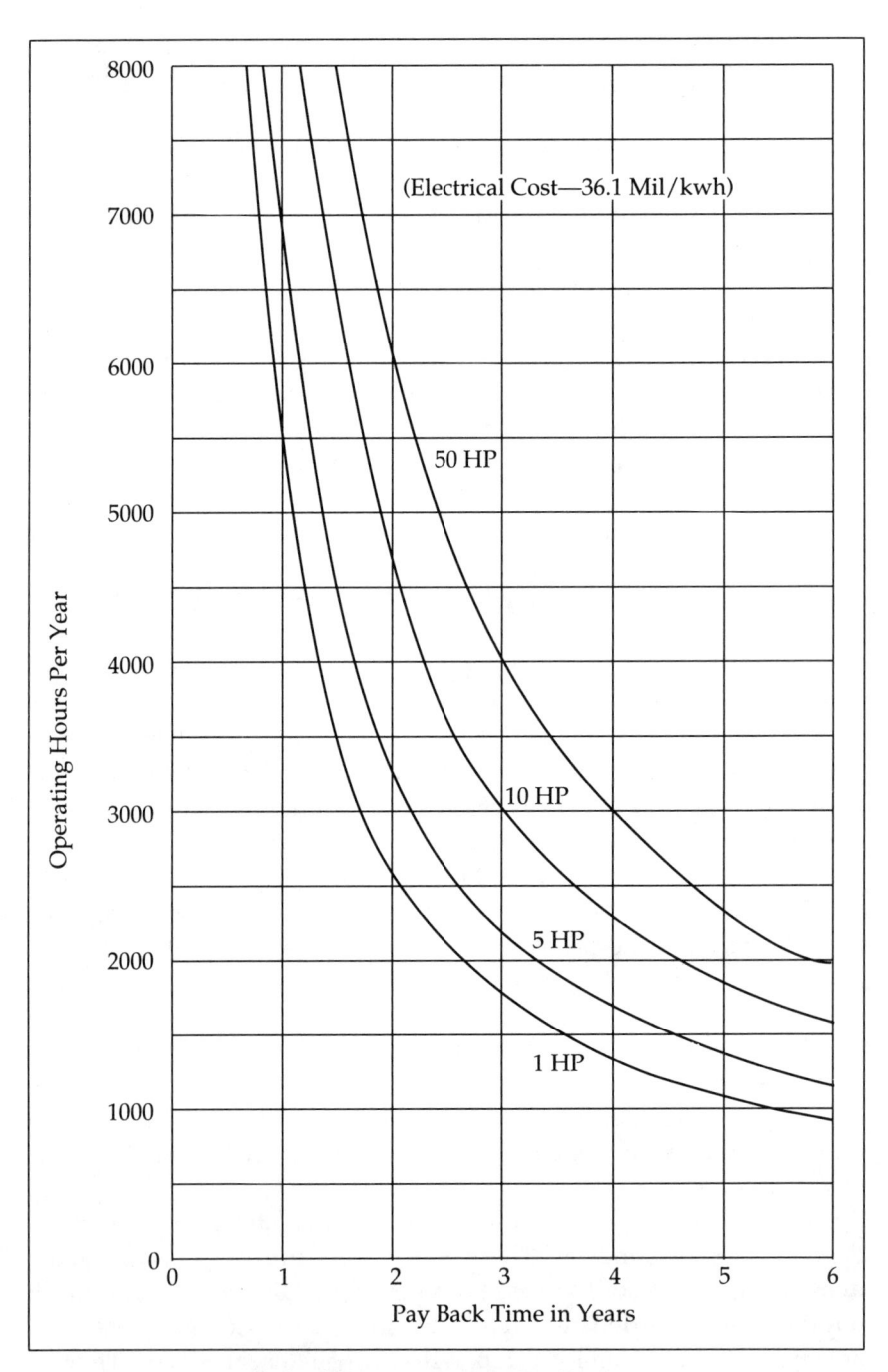

Figure 17.1 **High-efficiency Motors Payback versus Operating Time**
Source: Bloch, 1988

Load Reduction Obvious energy savings come as a result of the correct motor selection and power factor. Additional savings will come with a thoughtful evaluation of the downstream systems, and the load these systems and the individual components place on the electrical network.

Mismatched power transmission belts, misaligned sprockets and sheaves, rubbing belt guards, overtensioned belt drives, inadequately lubricated bearings, and poorly designed conveyors are only a few of the many important considerations that, when corrected, can shed the load on the electrical network. Well-designed conveyor systems are one such example of what can be done.

The conventional design of material-handling conveyors has used steel-link chain combined with a shaped steel conveyor trough to transport everything from logs to by-products within the mill site. Most of the conveyance systems in use today follow this design concept. There is an energy-efficient alternative.

The substitution of ultra-high molecular weight (UHMW) wear plate in place of the more conventional abrasive resistant (AR) plate is rapidly gaining acceptance. Wear plate, a lining for the bottom and sides of a conveyor trough, forms the sliding/wearing surface the chain and material contacts as it slides along from entry point to exit.

UHMW has many benefits; the reduction of wear on steel is significant. The reduced coefficient of friction results in reduced loading; this reduced loading can be translated into lower horsepower requirements and longer motor life.

Load reduction efforts combined with other maintenance-related energy conservation efforts can provide an ever sharper competitive edge for the forest products producer. These activities are well within the scope of a TM effort.

References

Baldwin, R. F. 1984. *Operations Management in the Forest Products Industry*. San Francisco: Miller Freeman.

Bloch, H. P. 1983. *Practical Machinery Management for Process Plants Volume 2: Machinery Failure Analysis and Troubleshooting*. Houston, TX: Gulf Publishing Company.

―――. 1988. Bonneville Power Administration Tech Brief: Electrical Energy Reduction in a Mill Air Compressor (March).

―――. 1981. California Dry Kiln Club Minutes: Technical Session (Winter).

―――. 1980. *Getting the Most from Your Electrical Power System*. Barrington, IL: Technical Publishing.

Greenwald, E. K. 1988. The Hidden Costs of Oversizing Motors. *Plant Engineering* (July 21).

Helvogt, E., Jr. 1975. *Electrical Power Management*. Plywood Research Foundation. Tacoma, WA (July).

Horovitz, B. 1981. Cutting Your Energy Costs. *Industry Week* (February 23).

Kurpiel, F. and C. McDonald. 1987. Energy Strategies for Increasing Productivity. Hardwood Plywood Manufacturers Association & American Plywood Association.

Mitchell, R., Jr. Evaluation of Energy-Efficient Motors. A Technical Report to the Industry.

Pacente, J. E. 1981. Power Factor Controllers Increase Operating Efficiency of A.C. Motors. *Pulp & Paper* (June).

Price, S. G. 1973. *A Guide to Monitoring and Controlling Utility Costs*. Washington, DC: BNA Books.

Thumann, A. 1977. *Plant Engineers and Managers Guide to Energy Conservation*. New York: Van Nostrand Reinhold.

Westergaard, B. 1983. The Evolving Sawmill—Power Transmission. *Logging & Sawmilling Journal* (July).

CHAPTER 18

The Role of the Engineer

The role of the engineer is twofold; design and install projects, and obtain the most from these projects and the other existing facilities. Each role is demanding, and the results of each will in large measure determine the competitiveness and maintainability of the mill over time.

The Engineer as a Problem Solver

The engineer is a resource person for the operator and the maintenance person. He or she is often delegated the problem-solving task.

Problems come in all sizes and shapes. Some are readily apparent and the solutions are easy to find. Others require extensive analytical work both off site and on site. On-site analysis is called "handrail sitting."

Handrail sitting is an art rather than a science. It is an effective way for an engineer to identify telltale symptoms and to diagnose problems. It is a technique that bridges the gap between the engineers' craft and mill operations. It is also an extension of the maintenance problem-solving techniques as described in chapter 8.

The participant selects an unobstructed yet safe observation point at the site. It will take a minute or two of uninterrupted observation before the observer is able to target his or her thoughts and observations and begins to focus on the task at hand.

One engineer, troubleshooting a papermill maintenance problem, describes the results of his colleague's handrail-sitting session:

"His findings absolutely boggled our minds, because he found a worn flexible coupling of less than $10 value that connected the master tach generator to the press. Someone had bumped the flimsy bracket that the tach sits on, throwing it out of alignment, which then wore the coupling, causing the irregular voltage output." The irregular voltage output was responsible for random, but frequent, sheet breaks.

Another engineer discussed his handrail-sitting sessions and concluded, "It provides an opportunity to keep in touch with what is going on. I solve problems, identify improvement opportunities, and enjoy being away from the distraction of the phone and office routine. It turns out to be my most productive thinking time."

Handrail sitting is just one way to assist the maintenance and production effort. The resulting maintenance problem solving and idea gathering positions the engineer to work more effectively with the maintenance manager and capital project participants. He or she becomes a direct participant in improving the competitiveness and maintainability of the mill.

The Engineer as a Project Designer and Manager

Proper project design, management, and installation are important to a maintenance program. A well-designed and properly installed project will minimize maintenance and subsequently require fewer modifications. The engineer's initial focus is on the raw material.

Decisions must be made in an uncertain environment; the task is to take as much of the uncertainty out of the operating environment as possible. The failure to do the homework necessary to precisely establish what raw material is available in both the short term and long term at what cost is probably the most frequent reason for project failure. The potential for failure is increasing as converting machines become even more raw-material specific and diameter sensitive.

The engineer will team up with the forester to determine what timber or fiber is available over both the short and long term. The raw-material base should be established prior to the implementation of a project. The wood available by year should be identified for at least the duration of the payback period and preferably over the life of the project.

An operator seeking raw material from a number of competitive sources will use data prepared from others, such as Forest Service FS2400 (U.S. Forest Service timber sales) reports and other readily available industry sources. This intelligence will be supplemented with site-specific information developed by the mill's forester or outside consultants. The engineer and the forester pull the information together in a format that will be useful in designing and evaluating the project.

A forest inventory is frequently required. The forest inventory can be based on land-based sampling methods such as strip cruise or the line-plot system of cruising. Satellite photos can be used to achieve the same results over a wider area within a shorter time span. Digitizing these aerial photos further enhances and details the database.

The compilation of stand and stock tables will summarize the resulting data. These tables will identify total volume; more important, the volume is identified by species and diameter class. A difficult task comes next: An evaluation is made of each real and potential competitor and how each will compete and draw on the available raw material sources.

Trade sources, competitor profiles, and other public inquiries will yield substantial information. Sometimes the premature announcement of the intent to expand or build a greenfield project will smoke out the competition and determine who is doing what.

The resulting information is not as precise as usually desired. However, decisions based on the best available information will benefit from the effort. The resulting information, integrated into the growth and depletion projects by year, then forms the underpinning of the project.

Project Design

The most visible project activities are the actual installation and startup. These activities are like the tip of an iceberg, very visible but only a small part of the total. The bulk of project activities will be invisible to the casual observer, but the success of the project often depends on the unseen. The unseen is defined as the homework that anticipates and plans events.

The easy projects are those that install well-tested equipment. The project designer must document installation needs such as foundation plans, tie-ins with other equipment, and air, water, and electrical hookups. Potential training and startup needs must be detailed and the resources identified. Project costs are relatively easy to identify; actual cost history is usually readily available. The designer should closely observe the successes and the problems developing from earlier installations.

The tough projects feature untested conceptual ideas that break new ground or require specific tailoring to a particular mill. Often these project types are the ones that determine the current state of the art and frequently provide a decided competitive edge. But there are pitfalls to avoid.

Breaking new ground requires a carefully tailored project definition. A broad conceptual idea initiates the process. This idea is segmented into manageable parts prior to a detailed scoping. The detailed scoping should benefit from the input of the stakeholders, technical personnel, and the workers who will make the resulting project work. Checkpoints further clarify details and ascertain that acceptance is gained as the project proceeds.

Rough sketches give way to line drawings; the resulting line drawings eventually become detailed prints as the engineer and his or her "customers" critique the ideas and the engineered representation of those ideas. The scope definition should answer the questions:

- What is the overall framework of the project?
- What are we trying to do? Will it work the way we think it will work? Why or why not?
- What is being done to minimize maintenance?
- What will the benefits be? How will they develop and what will the value be?
- What will be the expenditures of time and money? What are the musts, need to haves, and wants? Which are to be included?
- What input from outside the project group is needed to successfully accomplish the project? Who do we have or who is available to initiate and implement this project?
- What are the management controls? How will each work to track project spending and implementation?
- How can we prevent unwelcome surprises (cost and performance)? How will we report the successes that have been achieved?

Each of these questions will stimulate answers that will result in a tighter, more focused project scope.

The Steps to Complete Engineering

The eleven-step process to complete engineering is outlined in figure 18.1. The computer is used in two key areas: modeling the project in the expected operating and business environment, and designing the project components. Modeling the project is the initial activity.

First the engineer establishes the flow of log, furnish, or semifinished goods through each conversion point. He or she then calculates the quantities using fixed and variable flows; the incoming log or nonlog wood components are calculated based on average, mode, and range of volumes.

The mathematical (simulation) model should model the raw material and the downstream process flow as closely as possible. Repetitive runs are made until the software is debugged. The model is then run repetitively over a range of raw material and product options. These reiterations test the capacity and versatility of the manufacturing process.

Figure 18.1 *Steps to Complete Engineering*

1. Establish a process flow chart.
2. Calculate flow quantities by conversion point and transportation method.
3. Identify log profile:
    - average
    - range
    - mode
4. Construct mathematical (simulation) model:
    - set up
    - debug
    - run
5. Document the operating procedure.
6. Prepare conceptual engineered solutions (alternatives).
7. Determine feasibility of each solution.
8. Test solutions in simulation.
9. Refine solutions and select best fit.
10. Critique the project drawings.
11. Refine drawings until acceptance is gained.

The user then documents the operating procedures and parameters needed to obtain a specific answer. The model determines the capability of each alternative and test for feasibility. The user then refines the solutions and selects the best fit. The next step is detailed engineering.

The detailed engineering begins with simple line drawings and concludes with the completion of certified construction drawings. Timely critiques are scheduled and carried out with the project group; this group includes representatives from manufacturing and maintenance plus other specialized services. Computer assisted design (CAD) can accelerate the process in at least two ways.

First, CAD drawings are easier and faster to prepare. The software architecture is structured to screen out errors and to provide instant replay. Second, the stakeholders are able to participate and interact with the developing drawings. It is not uncommon for the stakeholders to gather around the terminal and provide input as the engineer or draftsman interacts with the computer. This feature is particularly important when the engineer is dealing with critical issues where hands-on production and maintenance input is essential for the success of the project.

Newer, more participative organizations will welcome suggestions and critiques as each drawing is prepared. Acceptance of each drawing is obtained when the project objectives are integrated onto the drawings and a consensus is reached by the stakeholders. This consensus includes the participation of all stakeholders, including the engineer who is responsible for the installation and startup of the project.

The Engineer's Task: An Overview

The engineer bridges the gap between the conceptual idea and the successful operation of the resulting project. His or her input is invaluable at each step in the process. It is particularly valuable in designing away from maintenance.

Recognizing maintenance considerations and troubleshooting are integral parts of the engineer's overall task. The mill will benefit greatly when the role of the engineer is closely matched to the needs of maintenance and operations.

CHAPTER 19

Total Lubrication

A lubrication program is the lifeblood of a total maintenance (TM) program. A sound program is individually tailored to provide the necessary management control over results for each mill. The results of a well-thought-out program can be impressive.

This chief planner for a southern paper mill knows from experience that "A direct result of a good lubrication program is a gradual increase in production. Properly selected and correctly applied, modern lubricants provide adequate protection against friction for longer periods of time. As a result, consumption and costs are lowered and equipment breakdowns are eventually reduced to the barest minimum" (Carson, 1983, Part C, 2).

The need for such a program continues and is becoming more urgent as machine loading, speeds, and tasks become ever more demanding.

The Lubricant

Lubricants are many and varied; they come in a multiplicity of types and materials. The lubricant properties will range from something as simple as a light water mist to something as solid as a metal substance. The traditional substances, the oils and greases, will be somewhere in between. Oils and greases are the primary focus of this chapter.

Industrial lubricants common to the forest products plant are generally made of base oils and additives. The number of industrial applications for a lubricant is almost endless. The ingredients and the resulting formulation may be as selective and precise as a medical prescription.

The base oils and the appropriate additives must be used within the proper proportions to meet the needs prescribed by the situation and the needs defined by the equipment manufacturer. Additives improve performance and the life of the lubricant. The pour point can be modified; the temperature range over which satisfactory viscosity is maintained can be increased. And additives can do much, much more.

Additives prevent varnish and sludge deposit formation, reduce friction wear, inhibit foam formation, and control oxidation and its harmful effects. Precise formulations will achieve these benefits or meet other exacting needs. Do-it-yourself formulations can be a problem.

These inexact formulations, a maintenance worker's home brew, may be intended to make the lubricant do a better job. However, the resulting formulation often is not compatible with the manufacturer's recommended lubricant and its ingredients. These additives may upset the balance of the formula and actually reduce the effectiveness of the lubricant. Do-it-yourself formulations are an unacceptable risk.

Physical specifications such as color, flash point, and gravity allow oil companies to manufacture lubricants to exacting standards. The purpose is to reduce friction, heat, and wear when introduced as a film between solid moving surfaces. In many applications an oil lubricant must also flush away dirt and wear particles and transport them to the machine's filters. Oil also dissipates heat; both oil and grease lubricants may help seal bearings to prevent the entry of contaminants. In some situations the sole purpose of a lubricant will be to lessen or prevent friction or the difficulty caused by corrosion in separating two static components.

Choosing a Lubricant

Forest products manufacturing operations contain a great diversity of machinery. This machinery must operate under varied and difficult conditions, including extremes of pressure, temperature, and speed. A wide variety of machine parts must be lubricated in different ways.

Open and enclosed gear types, and differing chain types, hydraulic, and pneumatic systems are all found in the mills. Differing sizes and types of plain and antifriction bearings are part of larger production systems. Each is lubricated by a variety of methods ranging from the inefficient oil can or grease gun to the most modern centralized lubrication system. The lubricants face contamination everywhere, especially from water and steam, which is used or is present through much of the log- or wood-converting process. A lubricant must meet specific requirements of the particular equipment to be a correct choice.

All this makes the selection of the correct lubricants more difficult. Manufacturer's recommendations should be closely followed, and the advice of the oil company's field engineers can also be helpful in developing a lubrication program.

Pay particular attention to the specifications and performance designations situated within the operator's manual. Decals on the equipment and other information available from the original equipment manufacturer or dealer is also helpful. There are also a number of valuable supplemental sources of information and recommendations.

Mill personnel or the supplier may have time-tested recommendations based on like equipment in like applications. Various product vendors, and outside resource information such as the several Miller Freeman trade periodicals, including *World Wood* and *Forest Industries*, provide state-of-the-art ideas. The monthly *TAPPI* magazine is also a valuable aid to the papermaking maintenance person; *Plant Engineering* magazine provides excellent examples and recommendations. Tables, lubrication guides, articles written by industry professionals, and technical publications are all part of the vast information pool available to the mill operator and maintenance professional.

Table 19.1 is an example. This table is a recent *Plant Engineering* chart of interchangeable lubricants. This chart, the fifth update since the original 1968 chart, contains information on more than one hundred suppliers. It can be an invaluable reference tool when used thoughtfully.

The maintenance person can easily identify equivalent lubricant products and sources. Twenty-four lubrication types are listed; each as a *Plant Engineering* magazine designation. The ISO viscosity grade is listed, along with a brief description of the lubricant type and the viscosity, SUS at 100° F.

Each of the manufacturers are listed with a comparable lubrication type. Comparable lubrication types are identified on the same line horizontally along with the *Plant Engineering* comparable type designation. Many of the lubricant manufacturers produce each of the twenty-four listed types, some produce only a select few. Some manufacturers are specific; their markets are defined by geographic or market limitations.

Table 19.1 benefits the user in many ways. For example, this table can serve as a guide for consolidating lubricant stocks; it gives the customer a greater opportunity to shop for lower cost or greater value; and the inventory of lubricants can be controlled more effectively. In addition, the chance of the maintenance person using the wrong product is diminished and fewer personnel are involved in the requisitioning and purchasing decisions.

Table 19.1 does have its limitations, however. It only represents the then-current technology. Lubricants and particularly site-specific lubricants are being developed and improved on at an exponential pace. A paper machine lubrication oil, Teresstic N, is one such example.

This lubricant, an Exxon product, is used primarily on self-aligning spherical roller bearings and plain bearings in the dryer section of a paper

Total Lubrication

Table 19.1 Chart of Interchangeable Lubricants

Plant Engineering Designation	ISO Viscosity Grade	Lubricant Type	Viscosity, SUS at 100°F	Advance Engineering	Amalie Refining Co. (Division of Witco Chemical Corp.)
PE-150-A	32	Light Inhibited Hydraulic & Gen. Purpose	135–165	S/1065 Sterling R&O 32	AMA Oil R&O 100 AW
PE-215-A	46	Med. Inhibited Hydraulic & Gen. Purpose	194–236	S/1067 Sterling R&O 46	AMA Oil R&O 200 AW
PE-315-A	68	Med.-Heavy Inhibited Hyd. & Gen. Purpose	284–346	S/1069 Sterling R&O 68	AMA Oil R&O 300 AW
PE-700-A	150	Heavy Inhibited Hydraulic & Gen. Purpose	630–770	S/1071 Sterling R&O 150	AMA Oil R&O 800 AW
PE-150-HP	32	High-Pressure (Anti-Wear) Hydraulic Oil	135–165	S/1064 Sterling R&O AW LP 32	AMA Oil R&O 100 AW
PE-215-HP	46	High-Pressure (Anti-Wear) Hydraulic Oil	194–236	S/1066 Sterling R&O AW LP 46	AMA Oil R&O 200 AW
PE-315-HP	68	High-Pressure (Anti-Wear) Hydraulic Oil	284–346	S/1068 Sterling R&O AW LP 68	AMA Oil R&O 300 AW
PE-FRH-1	—	Fire-Resistant Hyd. Fluid/Synthetic		NR	NR
PE-FRH-2	—	Fire-Resistant Hyd. Fluid/Water-Glycol		NR	NR
PE-FRH-3	—	Fire-Resistant Hyd. Fluid/Water-Oil Emulsion		NR	NR
PE-32-B	2	Very Light Spindle Oil (Over 6000 rpm)	29–35	S/1026 Sterling Spindle 2	NR
PE-60-B	10	Light Spindle Oil (3600–6000 rpm)	54–66	S/1027 Sterling Spindle 10	NR
PE-105-B	22	Spindle Oil (Up to 3600 rpm)	95–115	S/1063 Sterling Spindle 22	NR
PE-150-C	32	Light Way Oil	135–165	NR	Bar & Chain Oil
PE-315-C	68	Medium Way Oil	284–346	S/1060 Waylube 68	NR
PE-1000-C	220	Heavy Way Oil	900–1100	S/1062 Waylube 220	NR
PE-700-D	150	Light Gear Oil	630–770	S/1086 Gear Lube EP 150	800 MT Lube
PE-1000-D	220	Medium Gear Oil	900–1100	S/1087 Gear Lube EP 220	SMG 90
PE-2150-D	460	Heavy Gear Oil	1935–2365	S/1089 Gear Lube EP 460	SMG 140
PE-315-E	68	Light Extreme-Pressure Gear Oil	283–347	S/1084 Gear Lube EP 68	NR
PE-1500-E	320	Heavy Extreme-Pressure Gear Oil	1350–1650	S/1088 Gear Lube EP 320	Tri-Vis Plus
PE-OG-G	—	Cling-Type Gear Shield (Open Gears)		Clingshield 220	NR
PE-GPG-2	—	Gen. Purpose E.P. Lithium-Base Grease	NLGI2	NR	All Purpose/Moly
PE-MG-2	—	Molybdenum Disulfide E.P. Grease		NR	All Purpose/Moly

NR = No recommendation
1. Does not contain tackiness additives normally found in way lubricants. Formulated to perform as combination hydraulic oil and way lubricant.
2. To be used where grades 90, 125, and 140 are recommended.
3. Not lithium base, but equals or exceeds application requirements.
4. Falls outside specified viscosity range, but meets application requirements.
5. Not moly grease, but exceeds application requirements.
6. Straight phosphate ester fluids available in four viscosity grades.
7. Available in range of viscosities.
8. Various ISO grades.
9. Synthetic lubricants.
10. All products formulated from polyalkylene glycol base stocks.
11. Anhydrous product, but water soluble.

Source: Marinello, 1983

Table 19.1 Chart of Interchangeable Lubricants (continued)

Plant Engineering Designation	ISO Viscosity Grade	Lubricant Type	Viscosity, SUS at 100°F	American Industrial Research Corp.	American Industries, Inc.
PE-150-A	32	Light Inhibited Hydraulic & Gen. Purpose	135–165	NR	253 #10 R&O Hyd. Oil
PE-215-A	46	Med. Inhibited Hydraulic & Gen. Purpose	194–236	NR	253 #15 R&O Hyd. Oil
PE-315-A	68	Med.-Heavy Inhibited Hyd. & Gen. Purpose	284–346	NR	253 #20 R&O Hyd. Oil
PE-700-A	150	Heavy Inhibited Hydraulic & Gen. Purpose	630–770	NR	253 #30 R&O Hyd. Oil
PE-150-HP	32	High-Pressure (Anti-Wear) Hydraulic Oil	135–165	NR	255 #10 AW Hyd. Oil
PE-215-HP	46	High-Pressure (Anti-Wear) Hydraulic Oil	194–236	NR	255 #15 AW Hyd. Oil
PE-315-HP	68	High-Pressure (Anti-Wear) Hydraulic Oil	284–346	NR	255 #20 AW Hyd. Oil
PE-FRH-1	—	Fire-Resistant Hyd. Fluid/Synthetic		NR	NR
PE-FRH-2	—	Fire-Resistant Hyd. Fluid/Water-Glycol		NR	NR
PE-FRH-3	—	Fire-Resistant Hyd. Fluid/Water-Oil Emulsion		NR	254 FR Hyd. Oil
PE-32-B	2	Very Light Spindle Oil (Over 6000 rpm)	29–35	NR	NR
PE-60-B	10	Light Spindle Oil (3600–6000 rpm)	54–66	Rexlube Spindle Oil Light	273 Spindle Oil #1
PE-105-B	22	Spindle Oil (Up to 3600 rpm)	95–115	NR	273 Spindle Oil #2
PE-150-C	32	Light Way Oil	135–165	NR	516 Way Lube #10
PE-315-C	68	Medium Way Oil	284–346	Rexlube #20	516 Way Lube #20
PE-1000-C	220	Heavy Way Oil	900–1100	Rexlube #90	516 Way Lube #50
PE-700-D	150	Light Gear Oil	630–770	Rexlube #30	322 Ind. GO #40
PE-1000-D	220	Medium Gear Oil	900–1100	Rexlube #95	322 Ind. GO #90
PE-2150-D	460	Heavy Gear Oil	1935–2365	Rexlube #145	322 Ind. GO #140
PE-315-E	68	Light Extreme-Pressure Gear Oil	283–347	Rexlube #20	325 BIG 7 80W90
PE-1500-E	320	Heavy Extreme-Pressure Gear Oil	1350–1650	Rexlube #140	325 BIG 7 85W140
PE-OG-G	—	Cling-Type Gear Shield (Open Gears)		Rexlube OGH	336 Open Gear W/Tacky
PE-GPG-2	—	Gen. Purpose E.P. Lithium-Base Grease	NLGI2	Rexlube #2	556 MP Bearing Grease
PE-MG-2	—	Molybdenum Disulfide E.P. Grease		Rexlube #2	557 A-33 Moly Grease

Plant Engineering Designation	ISO Viscosity Grade	Lubricant Type	Viscosity, SUS at 100°F	The American Lubricants Co. (Alubco)	American Lubricants, Inc.
PE-150-A	32	Light Inhibited Hydraulic & Gen. Purpose	135–165	Moly Hyd. Oil #32	160 Hyd. Oil (R&O)
PE-215-A	46	Med. Inhibited Hydraulic & Gen. Purpose	194–236	Moly Hyd. Oil #46	200 Hyd. Oil (R&O)
PE-315-A	68	Med.-Heavy Inhibited Hyd. & Gen. Purpose	284–346	Moly Hyd. Oil #68	300 Hyd. Oil (R&O)
PE-700-A	150	Heavy Inhibited Hydraulic & Gen. Purpose	630–770	Moly Hyd. Oil #150	650 Hyd. Oil (R&O)
PE-150-HP	32	High-Pressure (Anti-Wear) Hydraulic Oil	135–165	Moly Hyd. Oil #32	160 AW Hyd. Oil
PE-215-HP	46	High-Pressure (Anti-Wear) Hydraulic Oil	194–236	Moly Hyd. Oil #46	200 AW Hyd. Oil
PE-315-HP	68	High-Pressure (Anti-Wear) Hydraulic Oil	284–346	Moly Hyd. Oil #68	300 AW Hyd. Oil
PE-FRH-1	—	Fire-Resistant Hyd. Fluid/Synthetic		NR	NR
PE-FRH-2	—	Fire-Resistant Hyd. Fluid/Water-Glycol		NR	NR
PE-FRH-3	—	Fire-Resistant Hyd. Fluid/Water-Oil Emulsion		NR	NR
PE-32-B	2	Very Light Spindle Oil (Over 6000 rpm)	29–35	NR	Spindle Oil 60
PE-60-B	10	Light Spindle Oil (3600–6000 rpm)	54–66	NR	Spindle Oil 100
PE-105-B	22	Spindle Oil (Up to 3600 rpm)	95–115	Moly Spindle Oil #22	
PE-150-C	32	Light Way Oil	135–165	Moly Special Way Lube #32	NR
PE-315-C	68	Medium Way Oil	284–346	Moly Special Way Lube #68	Medium Way Lube
PE-1000-C	220	Heavy Way Oil	900–1100	Moly Special Way Lube #220	Heavy Way Lube
PE-700-D	150	Light Gear Oil	630–770	Moly Ultra-Tec Gear Lube 80W90	Gear Oil Light
PE-1000-D	220	Medium Gear Oil	900–1100	Moly Ultra-Tec Gear Lube 90	Gear Oil Medium
PE-2150-D	460	Heavy Gear Oil	1935–2365	Moly Ultra-Tec Gear Lube 140	Gear Oil Heavy
PE-315-E	68	Light Extreme-Pressure Gear Oil	283–347	Moly Ultra-Tec Gear Lube 80	EP 300 Gear Oil
PE-1500-E	320	Heavy Extreme-Pressure Gear Oil	1350–1650	Moly Ultra-Tec Gear Lube 85W140	EP 1500 Gear Oil
PE-OG-G	—	Cling-Type Gear Shield (Open Gears)		Bison 88	Super Gear Shield
PE-GPG-2	—	Gen. Purpose E.P. Lithium-Base Grease	NLGI2	Improved Molyshield	#2 EP Lith Grease
PE-MG-2	—	Molybdenum Disulfide E.P. Grease		Moly Deluxe #2	MOS$_2$ Grease

NR = No recommendation
1. Does not contain tackiness additives normally found in way lubricants. Formulated to perform as combination hydraulic oil and way lubricant.
2. To be used where grades 90, 125, and 140 are recommended.
3. Not lithium base, but equals or exceeds application requirements.
4. Falls outside specified viscosity range, but meets application requirements.
5. Not moly grease, but exceeds application requirements.
6. Straight phosphate ester fluids available in four viscosity grades.
7. Available in range of viscosities.
8. Various ISO grades.
9. Synthetic lubricants.
10. All products formulated from polyalkylene glycol base stocks.
11. Anhydrous product, but water soluble.

Table 19.1 Chart of Interchangeable Lubricants (continued)

Plant Engineering Designation	ISO Viscosity Grade	Lubricant Type	Viscosity, SUS at 100°F	American Oil & Supply Co.	American Petroleum and Chemical Corp.
PE-150-A	32	Light Inhibited Hydraulic & Gen. Purpose	135–165	PQ 32	Module-Lube 303 Oil
PE-215-A	46	Med. Inhibited Hydraulic & Gen. Purpose	194–236	PQ 46	Module-Lube 304 Oil
PE-315-A	68	Med.-Heavy Inhibited Hyd. & Gen. Purpose	284–346	PQ 68	Module-Lube 305 Oil
PE-700-A	150	Heavy Inhibited Hydraulic & Gen. Purpose	630–770	PQ 150	Module-Lube SD-40 Oil
PE-150-HP	32	High-Pressure (Anti-Wear) Hydraulic Oil	135–165	PQ 32	Module-Lube 303 Oil
PE-215-HP	46	High-Pressure (Anti-Wear) Hydraulic Oil	194–236	PQ 46	Module-Lube 304 Oil
PE-315-HP	68	High-Pressure (Anti-Wear) Hydraulic Oil	284–346	PQ 68	Module-Lube 305 Oil
PE-FRH-1	—	Fire-Resistant Hyd. Fluid/Synthetic		NR	PPC Phosphate Ester
PE-FRH-2	—	Fire-Resistant Hyd. Fluid/Water-Glycol		NR	PPC Water Ester
PE-FRH-3	—	Fire-Resistant Hyd. Fluid/Water-Oil Emulsion		NR	NR
PE-32-B	2	Very Light Spindle Oil (Over 6000 rpm)	29–35	NR	Module-Lube 290 Oil
PE-60-B	10	Light Spindle Oil (3600–6000 rpm)	54–66	PQ Spindle Oil 5	Module-Lube 301 Oil
PE-105-B	22	Spindle Oil (Up to 3600 rpm)	95–115	PQ Spindle Oil 10	Module-Lube 302 Oil
PE-150-C	32	Light Way Oil	135–165	NR	Module-Lube SD-10
PE-315-C	68	Medium Way Oil	284–346	PQ L 30	Module-Lube Way Oil 47
PE-1000-C	220	Heavy Way Oil	900–1100	PQ L 90	Module-Lube Way Oil 50
PE-700-D	150	Light Gear Oil	630–770	PQ AGMA 4EP	Module-Lube SD-40 Oil
PE-1000-D	220	Medium Gear Oil	900–1100	PQ AGMA 5EP	Module-Lube SD-50 Oil
PE-2150-D	460	Heavy Gear Oil	1935–2365	PQ AGMA 7EP	Module-Lube AG-200 Oil
PE-315-E	68	Light Extreme-Pressure Gear Oil	283–347	PQ AGMA 2EP	Module-Lube SD-20
PE-1500-E	320	Heavy Extreme-Pressure Gear Oil	1350–1650	PQ AGMA 6EP	Module-Lube 123 Gear Oil
PE-OG-G	—	Cling-Type Gear Shield (Open Gears)		PQ Open Gear DSL	Module-Lube Open Gear Grease
PE-GPG-2	—	Gen. Purpose E.P. Lithium-Base Grease	NLGI2	PQ C 4005-2	Module-Lube 7 Plus Grease
PE-MG-2	—	Molybdenum Disulfide E.P. Grease		PQ C 4001-F	Module-Lube BRB 77 Grease

Total Lubrication

Plant Engineering Designation	ISO Viscosity Grade	Lubricant Type	Viscosity, SUS at 100°F	Amoco Oil Co.	Anderson Oil & Chemical Co.
PE-150-A	32	Light Inhibited Hydraulic & Gen. Purpose	135–165	American Ind. Oil #32	Winsor Hyd. Oil 43
PE-215-A	46	Med. Inhibited Hydraulic & Gen. Purpose	194–236	American Ind. Oil #46	Winsor Hyd. Oil 45
PE-315-A	68	Med.-Heavy Inhibited Hyd. & Gen. Purpose	284–346	American Ind. Oil #68	Winsor Hyd. Oil 52
PE-700-A	150	Heavy Inhibited Hydraulic & Gen. Purpose	630–770	American Ind. Oil #150	NR
PE-150-HP	32	High-Pressure (Anti-Wear) Hydraulic Oil	135–165	Rykon Oil #32 or Amoco AW 32	Winsor Hyd. Oil 43 AW
PE-215-HP	46	High-Pressure (Anti-Wear) Hydraulic Oil	194–236	Rykon Oil #46 or Amoco AW 46	Winsor Hyd. Oil 45 AW
PE-315-HP	68	High-Pressure (Anti-Wear) Hydraulic Oil	284–346	Rykon Oil #68 or Amoco AW 68	Winsor Hyd. Oil 52 AW
PE-FRH-1	—	Fire-Resistant Hyd. Fluid/Synthetic		Amoco FR Fluid PE	Starlit EM
PE-FRH-2	—	Fire-Resistant Hyd. Fluid/Water-Glycol		Amoco FR Fluid WG	NR
PE-FRH-3	—	Fire-Resistant Hyd. Fluid/Water-Oil Emulsion		Amoco FR Fluid WO	NR
PE-32-B	2	Very Light Spindle Oil (Over 6000 rpm)	29–35	Amoco Spindle Oil "A"	NR
PE-60-B	10	Light Spindle Oil (3600–6000 rpm)	54–66	Amoco Spindle Oil "A"	Winsor Hi-Speed Spindle Oil
PE-105-B	22	Spindle Oil (Up to 3600 rpm)	95–115	Amoco Spindle Oil "C"	Winsor Spindle Oil 4
PE-150-C	32	Light Way Oil	135–165	Waytac Oil #32	NR
PE-315-C	68	Medium Way Oil	284–346	Waytac Oil #68	Winsor Way Oil L
PE-1000-C	220	Heavy Way Oil	900–1100	Waytac Oil #220	NR
PE-700-D	150	Light Gear Oil	630–770	American Ind. Oil #150	Winsor Gear Oil 80
PE-1000-D	220	Medium Gear Oil	900–1100	American Ind. Oil #220	Winsor Gear Oil 90
PE-2150-D	460	Heavy Gear Oil	1935–2365	American Ind. Oil #460	Winsor Gear Oil 140
PE-315-E	68	Light Extreme-Pressure Gear Oil	283–347	Permagear or Amogear EP 68	NR
PE-1500-E	320	Heavy Extreme-Pressure Gear Oil	1350–1650	Permagear or Amogear EP 320	Hodson Metalcoil 4111
PE-OG-G	—	Cling-Type Gear Shield (Open Gears)		Amoco Compound #9	Hodson Metalcoil A 185
PE-GPG-2	—	Gen. Purpose E.P. Lithium-Base Grease	NLGI2	Amolith Grease #2 EP	NR
PE-MG-2	—	Molybdenum Disulfide E.P. Grease		Amoco Super Chassis Grease	Hodson Nomelt 2254

NR = No recommendation
1. Does not contain tackiness additives normally found in way lubricants. Formulated to perform as combination hydraulic oil and way lubricant.
2. To be used where grades 90, 125, and 140 are recommended.
3. Not lithium base, but equals or exceeds application requirements.
4. Falls outside specified viscosity range, but meets application requirements.
5. Not moly grease, but exceeds application requirements.
6. Straight phosphate ester fluids available in four viscosity grades.
7. Available in range of viscosities.
8. Various ISO grades.
9. Synthetic lubricants.
10. All products formulated from polyalkylene glycol base stocks.
11. Anhydrous product, but water soluble.

Table 19.1 Chart of Interchangeable Lubricants (continued)

Plant Engineering Designation	ISO Viscosity Grade	Lubricant Type	Viscosity, SUS at 100°F	Arco Petroleum Products Co.	Ashland Oil, Inc. Valvoline Oil Co.
PE-150-A	32	Light Inhibited Hydraulic & Gen. Purpose	135–165	Duro 32	ETC (R&O) #15
PE-215-A	46	Med. Inhibited Hydraulic & Gen. Purpose	194–236	Duro 46	ETC (R&O) #20
PE-315-A	68	Med.-Heavy Inhibited Hyd. & Gen. Purpose	284–346	Duro 68	ETC (R&O) #30
PE-700-A	150	Heavy Inhibited Hydraulic & Gen. Purpose	630–770	Duro 117 or 150	ETC (R&O) #70
PE-150-HP	32	High-Pressure (Anti-Wear) Hydraulic Oil	135–165	Duro AW 32	AW Oil #15
PE-215-HP	46	High-Pressure (Anti-Wear) Hydraulic Oil	194–236	Duro AW 46	AW Oil #20
PE-315-HP	68	High-Pressure (Anti-Wear) Hydraulic Oil	284–346	Duro AW 68	AW Oil #30
PE-FRH-1	—	Fire-Resistant Hyd. Fluid/Synthetic		NR	NR
PE-FRH-2	—	Fire-Resistant Hyd. Fluid/Water-Glycol		NR	NR
PE-FRH-3	—	Fire-Resistant Hyd. Fluid/Water-Oil Emulsion		Duro FR-HD	NR
PE-32-B	2	Very Light Spindle Oil (Over 6000 rpm)	29–35	NR	NR
PE-60-B	10	Light Spindle Oil (3600–6000 rpm)	54–66	Diamond 7	NR
PE-105-B	22	Spindle Oil (Up to 3600 rpm)	95–115	Diamond 20	ETC (R&O) #10
PE-150-C	32	Light Way Oil	135–165	Truslide 32	Waylube CHW-15
PE-315-C	68	Medium Way Oil	284–346	Truslide 68	Waylube W-30
PE-1000-C	220	Heavy Way Oil	900–1100	Truslide 220	Waylube W-100
PE-700-D	150	Light Gear Oil	630–770	Duro 117 or 150	ETC (R&O) 70
PE-1000-D	220	Medium Gear Oil	900–1100	Duro 220	ETC (R&O) 100
PE-2150-D	460	Heavy Gear Oil	1935–2365	Rubilene 460	ETC (R&O) 200
PE-315-E	68	Light Extreme-Pressure Gear Oil	283–347	Pennant NL 68	NR
PE-1500-E	320	Heavy Extreme-Pressure Gear Oil	1350–1650	Pennant NL 320	NR
PE-OG-G	—	Cling-Type Gear Shield (Open Gears)		Jet Lubricant TM	NR
PE-GPG-2	—	Gen. Purpose E.P. Lithium-Base Grease	NLGI2	Litholine HEP 2	Multi-lube Lithium EP Grease
PE-MG-2	—	Molybdenum Disulfide E.P. Grease		EP Moly D Grease #2	Special Moly EP Grease

Total Lubrication

Plant Engineering Designation	ISO Viscosity Grade	Lubricant Type	Viscosity, SUS at 100°F	Autoline Lubricants Inc.	Baum's Castorine Co., Inc.
PE-150-A	32	Light Inhibited Hydraulic & Gen. Purpose	135–165	Terrapin 32 R&O	Tena-Film #150-TH Oil
PE-215-A	46	Med. Inhibited Hydraulic & Gen. Purpose	194–236	Terrapin 46 R&O	Tena-Film #300-LTH Oil
PE-315-A	68	Med.-Heavy Inhibited Hyd. & Gen. Purpose	284–346	Terrapin 68 R&O	Tena-Film #300-MTH Oil
PE-700-A	150	Heavy Inhibited Hydraulic & Gen. Purpose	630–770	Terrapin 150 R&O	Tena-Film #400-TH Oil
PE-150-HP	32	High-Pressure (Anti-Wear) Hydraulic Oil	135–165	Terrapin 32 AW/Super Blue 32 AW	Tena-Film #150-TH Oil
PE-215-HP	46	High-Pressure (Anti-Wear) Hydraulic Oil	194–236	Terrapin 46 AW/Super Blue 46 AW	Tena-Film #300-LTH Oil
PE-315-HP	68	High-Pressure (Anti-Wear) Hydraulic Oil	284–346	Terrapin 68 AW/Super Blue 68 AW	Tena-Film #300-MTH Oil
PE-FRH-1	—	Fire-Resistant Hyd. Fluid/Synthetic		NR	NR
PE-FRH-2	—	Fire-Resistant Hyd. Fluid/Water-Glycol		NR	NR
PE-FRH-3	—	Fire-Resistant Hyd. Fluid/Water-Oil Emulsion		NR	NR
PE-32-B	2	Very Light Spindle Oil (Over 6000 rpm)	29–35	Spindle Oil 2	NR
PE-60-B	10	Light Spindle Oil (3600–6000 rpm)	54–66	Spindle Oil 10	NR
PE-105-B	22	Spindle Oil (Up to 3600 rpm)	95–115	Spindle Oil 22	Tena-Film #100-TH Oil
PE-150-C	32	Light Way Oil	135–165	Way Lube 32	Tena-Film #EP-150-ST Oil
PE-315-C	68	Medium Way Oil	284–346	Way Lube 68	Tena-Film #EP-300-ST Oil
PE-1000-C	220	Heavy Way Oil	900–1100	Way Lube 220	Tena-Film #EP-1000-ST Oil
PE-700-D	150	Light Gear Oil	630–770	Terrapin 150 AW	Tena-Film #400-TH Oil
PE-1000-D	220	Medium Gear Oil	900–1100	Terrapin 220 AW/MP 80W-90	Tena-Film #500-TH Oil
PE-2150-D	460	Heavy Gear Oil	1935–2365	Terrapin 460 AW/MP 85W-140	Tena-Film #2500-TH Oil
PE-315-E	68	Light Extreme-Pressure Gear Oil	283–347	Industrial EP Gear 68	Tena-Film #EP-300-ST Oil
PE-1500-E	320	Heavy Extreme-Pressure Gear Oil	1350–1650	Industrial EP Gear 320	Tena-Film #EP-1400 Oil
PE-OG-G	—	Cling-Type Gear Shield (Open Gears)		Syncote Open Gear	Tena-Film Moly OG Comp. #0-8470
PE-GPG-2	—	Gen. Purpose E.P. Lithium-Base Grease	NLGI2	Lithium EP #2	Tena-Film Grease #2 EP
PE-MG-2	—	Molybdenum Disulfide E.P. Grease		Moly Lith EP #2	Tena-Film Moly Compound #0-23

NR = No recommendation
1. Does not contain tackiness additives normally found in way lubricants. Formulated to perform as combination hydraulic oil and way lubricant.
2. To be used where grades 90, 125, and 140 are recommended.
3. Not lithium base, but equals or exceeds application requirements.
4. Falls outside specified viscosity range, but meets application requirements.
5. Not moly grease, but exceeds application requirements.
6. Straight phosphate ester fluids available in four viscosity grades.
7. Available in range of viscosities.
8. Various ISO grades.
9. Synthetic lubricants.
10. All products formulated from polyalkylene glycol base stocks.
11. Anhydrous product, but water soluble.

Table 19.1 Chart of Interchangeable Lubricants (continued)

Plant Engineering Designation	ISO Viscosity Grade	Lubricant Type	Viscosity, SUS at 100°F	Bel-Ray Co., Inc.	Benz Oil Co., Inc.
PE-150-A	32	Light Inhibited Hydraulic & Gen. Purpose	135–165	Bel-Ray AW Lube #0	Petralube 32
PE-215-A	46	Med. Inhibited Hydraulic & Gen. Purpose	194–236	Bel-Ray AW Lube #1	Petralube 46
PE-315-A	68	Med.-Heavy Inhibited Hyd. & Gen. Purpose	284–346	Bel-Ray AW Lube #2	Petralube 68
PE-700-A	150	Heavy Inhibited Hydraulic & Gen. Purpose	630–770	Bel-Ray AW Lube #4	Petralube 150
PE-150-HP	32	High-Pressure (Anti-Wear) Hydraulic Oil	135–165	Raylene AW Hyd. Fluid #0	Petraulic 32
PE-215-HP	46	High-Pressure (Anti-Wear) Hydraulic Oil	194–236	Raylene AW Hyd. Fluid #1	Petraulic 46
PE-315-HP	68	High-Pressure (Anti-Wear) Hydraulic Oil	284–346	Raylene AW Hyd. Fluid #2	Petraulic 68
PE-FRH-1	—	Fire-Resistant Hyd. Fluid/Synthetic		Bel-Ray "No Flame" Hyd. Fluid S	NR
PE-FRH-2	—	Fire-Resistant Hyd. Fluid/Water-Glycol		NR	Petraulic Sur-Safe FR-AW
PE-FRH-3	—	Fire-Resistant Hyd. Fluid/Water-Oil Emulsion		Bel-Ray "No Flame" Hyd. Fluid IE	NR
PE-32-B	2	Very Light Spindle Oil (Over 6000 rpm)	29–35	Raylene EP Spindle Oil Light	NR
PE-60-B	10	Light Spindle Oil (3600–6000 rpm)	54–66	Raylene EP Spindle Oil Med.	Petraspeed 600
PE-105-B	22	Spindle Oil (Up to 3600 rpm)	95–115	Raylene EP Spindle Oil Heavy	Petraspeed 1000
PE-150-C	32	Light Way Oil	135–165	Raylene EP Lube #1	NR
PE-315-C	68	Medium Way Oil	284–346	Raylene EP Lube #2	Petac 68
PE-1000-C	220	Heavy Way Oil	900–1100	Raylene EP Lube #5	Petac 220
PE-700-D	150	Light Gear Oil	630–770	Raylene EP Lube #3	Petraulic 150
PE-1000-D	220	Medium Gear Oil	900–1100	Raylene EP Lube #5	Petraulic 220
PE-2150-D	460	Heavy Gear Oil	1935–2365	Raylene EP Lube #7	Petraulic 460
PE-315-E	68	Light Extreme-Pressure Gear Oil	283–347	Bel-Ray 100 Gear Oil #50	Gearol 68
PE-1500-E	320	Heavy Extreme-Pressure Gear Oil	1350–1650	Bel-Ray 100 Gear Oil #90	Gearol 320
PE-OG-G	—	Cling-Type Gear Shield (Open Gears)		Bel-Ray ALO Open Gear Lube #1	Pinion Lube 1500
PE-GPG-2	—	Gen. Purpose E.P. Lithium-Base Grease	NLGI2	Termalene EP Grease #2	Multi-Service EP #2
PE-MG-2	—	Molybdenum Disulfide E.P. Grease		Molylube 126 EP Grease #2	Moly Alumaplex EP #2

Plant Engineering Designation	ISO Viscosity Grade	Lubricant Type	Viscosity, SUS at 100°F	BP Oil Inc.	Brooks Technology Co.
PE-150-A	32	Light Inhibited Hydraulic & Gen. Purpose	135–165	Energol HLP 32	Versalene 600
PE-215-A	46	Med. Inhibited Hydraulic & Gen. Purpose	194–236	Energol HLP 46	Versalene 610
PE-315-A	68	Med.-Heavy Inhibited Hyd. & Gen. Purpose	284–346	Energol HLP 68	Versalene 620
PE-700-A	150	Heavy Inhibited Hydraulic & Gen. Purpose	630–770	Energol HLP 150	Versalene 630
PE-150-HP	32	High-Pressure (Anti-Wear) Hydraulic Oil	135–165	Energol HLP 32	Versalene 600
PE-215-HP	46	High-Pressure (Anti-Wear) Hydraulic Oil	194–236	Energol HLP 46	Versalene 610
PE-315-HP	68	High-Pressure (Anti-Wear) Hydraulic Oil	284–346	Energol HLP 68	Versalene 620
PE-FRH-1	—	Fire-Resistant Hyd. Fluid/Synthetic		NR	NR
PE-FRH-2	—	Fire-Resistant Hyd. Fluid/Water-Glycol		NR	NR
PE-FRH-3	—	Fire-Resistant Hyd. Fluid/Water-Oil Emulsion		NR	Versalene 650
PE-32-B	2	Very Light Spindle Oil (Over 6000 rpm)	29–35	Energol HLP 2	NR
PE-60-B	10	Light Spindle Oil (3600–6000 rpm)	54–66	Energol HLP 10	NR
PE-105-B	22	Spindle Oil (Up to 3600 rpm)	95–115	Energol HLP 22	NR
PE-150-C	32	Light Way Oil	135–165	Energol HP 32[1]	NR
PE-315-C	68	Medium Way Oil	284–346	Energol HP 68-C	NR
PE-1000-C	220	Heavy Way Oil	900–1100	Energol HP 220-C	Slide & Way
PE-700-D	150	Light Gear Oil	630–770	Energol HLP 150	Lifeguard 55
PE-1000-D	220	Medium Gear Oil	900–1100	Energol HLP 220	Lifeguard 70
PE-2150-D	460	Heavy Gear Oil	1935–2365	Energol HLP 460	Lifeguard 110
PE-315-E	68	Light Extreme-Pressure Gear Oil	283–347	Gearep 80	Lifeguard 40
PE-1500-E	320	Heavy Extreme-Pressure Gear Oil	1350–1650	Gearep 80W-140[2]	Lifeguard 90
PE-OG-G	—	Cling-Type Gear Shield (Open Gears)		Gearep OG	Klingfast 85
PE-GPG-2	—	Gen. Purpose E.P. Lithium-Base Grease	NLGI2	Bearing Gard-2	Plexalene 726[3]
PE-MG-2	—	Molybdenum Disulfide E.P. Grease		Bearing Gard-2	Plexalene 725-MO

NR = No recommendation
1. Does not contain tackiness additives normally found in way lubricants. Formulated to perform as combination hydraulic oil and way lubricant.
2. To be used where grades 90, 125, and 140 are recommended.
3. Not lithium base, but equals or exceeds application requirements.
4. Falls outside specified viscosity range, but meets application requirements.
5. Not moly grease, but exceeds application requirements.
6. Straight phosphate ester fluids available in four viscosity grades.
7. Available in range of viscosities.
8. Various ISO grades.
9. Synthetic lubricants.
10. All products formulated from polyalkylene glycol base stocks.
11. Anhydrous product, but water soluble.

Table 19.1 Chart of Interchangeable Lubricants (continued)

Plant Engineering Designation	ISO Viscosity Grade	Lubricant Type	Viscosity, SUS at 100°F	Cambridge Technical Center	Cato Oil & Grease Co.
PE-150-A	32	Light Inhibited Hydraulic & Gen. Purpose	135–165	Moly Hyd. 150	Pawnee R&O Ind. Oil A.5
PE-215-A	46	Med. Inhibited Hydraulic & Gen. Purpose	194–236	Moly Hyd. 225	Pawnee R&O Ind. Oil B
PE-315-A	68	Med.-Heavy Inhibited Hyd. & Gen. Purpose	284–346	Moly Hyd. 315	Pawnee R&O Ind. Oil C
PE-700-A	150	Heavy Inhibited Hydraulic & Gen. Purpose	630–770	Moly Hyd. 700	Pawnee R&O Ind. Oil E.5
PE-150-HP	32	High-Pressure (Anti-Wear) Hydraulic Oil	135–165	Moly Hyd. AW 150	Mystik AW/AL Hyd. Oil 10
PE-215-HP	46	High-Pressure (Anti-Wear) Hydraulic Oil	194–236	Moly Hyd. AW 225	Mystik AW/AL Hyd. Oil 10
PE-315-HP	68	High-Pressure (Anti-Wear) Hydraulic Oil	284–346	Moly Hyd. AW 315	Mystik AW/AL Hyd. Oil 20
PE-FRH-1	—	Fire-Resistant Hyd. Fluid/Synthetic		Saf-T-Lube S	NR
PE-FRH-2	—	Fire-Resistant Hyd. Fluid/Water-Glycol		Sil-A-Col 200	NR
PE-FRH-3	—	Fire-Resistant Hyd. Fluid/Water-Oil Emulsion		Saf-T-Lube FR	NR
PE-32-B	2	Very Light Spindle Oil (Over 6000 rpm)	29–35	#3 Moly Spindle	Twin Disc Torque Convertor Fluid
PE-60-B	10	Light Spindle Oil (3600–6000 rpm)	54–66	#60 Moly Spindle	Mystik Hyd. Jack Oil R&O
PE-105-B	22	Spindle Oil (Up to 3600 rpm)	95–115	#1 Moly Spindle	Pawnee R&O Ind. Oil A
PE-150-C	32	Light Way Oil	135–165	Moly-Way #15	Mystik AW/AL Hyd. Oil 10[1]
PE-315-C	68	Medium Way Oil	284–346	Moly-Way #3	Mystik Anti-Leak Ind. Oil
PE-1000-C	220	Heavy Way Oil	900–1100	Moly-Way #9	Mystik JT-7 80/90
PE-700-D	150	Light Gear Oil	630–770	Moly-Gear 750	Pawnee R&O Ind. Oil E.5
PE-1000-D	220	Medium Gear Oil	900–1100	Moly-Gear 990	Pawnee R&O Ind. Oil F
PE-2150-D	460	Heavy Gear Oil	1935–2365	Moly-Gear 2250	Pawnee R&O Ind. Oil H
PE-315-E	68	Light Extreme-Pressure Gear Oil	283–347	Moly-Gear EP 325	Cato Ind. EP Gear ISO 68
PE-1500-E	320	Heavy Extreme-Pressure Gear Oil	1350–1650	Moly-Gear EP 1500	Cato Ind. EP Gear ISO 320
PE-OG-G	—	Cling-Type Gear Shield (Open Gears)		Moly Open Gear #1000	Ca-Gear 1
PE-GPG-2	—	Gen. Purpose E.P. Lithium-Base Grease	NLGI2	#2 WL Grease	Mystik JT-6 Hi-Temp
PE-MG-2	—	Molybdenum Disulfide E.P. Grease		#2 ML Grease	Moly Lithflex CX All Season

Total Lubrication

Plant Engineering Designation	ISO Viscosity Grade	Lubricant Type	Viscosity, SUS at 100°F	Century Hulburt Inc.	Certified Laboratories
PE-150-A	32	Light Inhibited Hydraulic & Gen. Purpose	135–165	Huldraulic 150	HOC 32 or Multoil 5W-20
PE-215-A	46	Med. Inhibited Hydraulic & Gen. Purpose	194–236	Huldraulic 215	HOC 46 or Multoil 5W-20
PE-315-A	68	Med.-Heavy Inhibited Hyd. & Gen. Purpose	284–346	Huldraulic 315	HOC 68
PE-700-A	150	Heavy Inhibited Hydraulic & Gen. Purpose	630–770	Huldraulic 700	HOC 150
PE-150-HP	32	High-Pressure (Anti-Wear) Hydraulic Oil	135–165	Huldraulic 150	HOC 32 or HITOP 10W-30
PE-215-HP	46	High-Pressure (Anti-Wear) Hydraulic Oil	194–236	Huldraulic 215	HOC 46 or HITOP 10W-30
PE-315-HP	68	High-Pressure (Anti-Wear) Hydraulic Oil	284–346	Huldraulic 315	HOC 68 or HITOP 10W-30
PE-FRH-1	—	Fire-Resistant Hyd. Fluid/Synthetic		NR	NR
PE-FRH-2	—	Fire-Resistant Hyd. Fluid/Water-Glycol		NR	NR
PE-FRH-3	—	Fire-Resistant Hyd. Fluid/Water-Oil Emulsion		Hulsafe 600	NR
PE-32-B	2	Very Light Spindle Oil (Over 6000 rpm)	29–35	NR	NR
PE-60-B	10	Light Spindle Oil (3600–6000 rpm)	54–66	NR	SOC 10
PE-105-B	22	Spindle Oil (Up to 3600 rpm)	95–115	NR	SOC 22
PE-150-C	32	Light Way Oil	135–165	NR	NR
PE-315-C	68	Medium Way Oil	284–346	NR	WLC 68
PE-1000-C	220	Heavy Way Oil	900–1100	NR	WLC 220
PE-700-D	150	Light Gear Oil	630–770	Hulbest 70	HOC 150
PE-1000-D	220	Medium Gear Oil	900–1100	#32 Gear Oil	HOC 220
PE-2150-D	460	Heavy Gear Oil	1935–2365	#33 Gear Oil	Certop 85W-140
PE-315-E	68	Light Extreme-Pressure Gear Oil	283–347	Hulbest 50	NR
PE-1500-E	320	Heavy Extreme-Pressure Gear Oil	1350–1650	#31 Gear Oil	Phenomen-ol 80W-140
PE-OG-G	—	Cling-Type Gear Shield (Open Gears)		#28 Gear Oil	NR
PE-GPG-2	—	Gen. Purpose E.P. Lithium-Base Grease	NLGI2	Replex GP-EP	CCL-24 EP2
PE-MG-2	—	Molybdenum Disulfide E.P. Grease		Hullith EP-2 Moly	Premalube EP2 or CCL-500 EP2

NR = No recommendation
1. Does not contain tackiness additives normally found in way lubricants. Formulated to perform as combination hydraulic oil and way lubricant.
2. To be used where grades 90, 125, and 140 are recommended.
3. Not lithium base, but equals or exceeds application requirements.
4. Falls outside specified viscosity range, but meets application requirements.
5. Not moly grease, but exceeds application requirements.
6. Straight phosphate ester fluids available in four viscosity grades.
7. Available in range of viscosities.
8. Various ISO grades.
9. Synthetic lubricants.
10. All products formulated from polyalkylene glycol base stocks.
11. Anhydrous product, but water soluble.

Table 19.1 Chart of Interchangeable Lubricants (continued)

Plant Engineering Designation	ISO Viscosity Grade	Lubricant Type	Viscosity, SUS at 100°F	Champlin Petroleum Co.	Chemtool, Inc.
PE-150-A	32	Light Inhibited Hydraulic & Gen. Purpose	135–165	Hydrol R&O 150	Hydro #15
PE-215-A	46	Med. Inhibited Hydraulic & Gen. Purpose	194–236	Hydrol R&O 215	Hydro #25
PE-315-A	68	Med.-Heavy Inhibited Hyd. & Gen. Purpose	284–346	Hydrol R&O 315	Hydro #3
PE-700-A	150	Heavy Inhibited Hydraulic & Gen. Purpose	630–770	Hydrol R&O 700	Hydro #7
PE-150-HP	32	High-Pressure (Anti-Wear) Hydraulic Oil	135–165	Hydrol AW 150	Hydro AW #15
PE-215-HP	46	High-Pressure (Anti-Wear) Hydraulic Oil	194–236	Hydrol AW 215	Hydro AW #225
PE-315-HP	68	High-Pressure (Anti-Wear) Hydraulic Oil	284–346	Hydrol AW 315	Hydro AW #315
PE-FRH-1	—	Fire-Resistant Hyd. Fluid/Synthetic		NR	Syn. Hyd. Fluid (SHF)
PE-FRH-2	—	Fire-Resistant Hyd. Fluid/Water-Glycol		NR	Chemtool #900
PE-FRH-3	—	Fire-Resistant Hyd. Fluid/Water-Oil Emulsion		NR	Emulsion Hyd. Fluid (EHF)
PE-32-B	2	Very Light Spindle Oil (Over 6000 rpm)	29–35	NR	#30 Spindle Oil
PE-60-B	10	Light Spindle Oil (3600–6000 rpm)	54–66	NR	#60 Spindle Oil
PE-105-B	22	Spindle Oil (Up to 3600 rpm)	95–115	Varitol A	#100 Spindle Oil
PE-150-C	32	Light Way Oil	135–165	Hydrol AW 150/Varitol A[1]	#15 Way Lube
PE-315-C	68	Medium Way Oil	284–346	Hydrol AW 215/Varitol B[1]	#3 Way Lube
PE-1000-C	220	Heavy Way Oil	900–1100	NR	#9 Way Lube
PE-700-D	150	Light Gear Oil	630–770	Hydrol R&O 700/GL Plus 80W-90	#750 Gear Oil
PE-1000-D	220	Medium Gear Oil	900–1100	Hydrol R&O 1000	#990 Gear Oil
PE-2150-D	460	Heavy Gear Oil	1935–2365	GL Plus 85W-140	#2250 Gear Oil
PE-315-E	68	Light Extreme-Pressure Gear Oil	283–347	Champlin Gear Oil 6650	EP 325 Gear Oil
PE-1500-E	320	Heavy Extreme-Pressure Gear Oil	1350–1650	NR	EP 1500 Gear Oil
PE-OG-G	—	Cling-Type Gear Shield (Open Gears)		NR	Open Gear #1000
PE-GPG-2	—	Gen. Purpose E.P. Lithium-Base Grease	NLGI2	Pyrolex[3]	White MP Lithium
PE-MG-2	—	Molybdenum Disulfide E.P. Grease		Deluxe With Moly	Moly Lithium Grease

Total Lubrication

Plant Engineering Designation	ISO Viscosity Grade	Lubricant Type	Viscosity, SUS at 100°F	Chevron U.S.A., Inc.	Cities Service Co.
PE-150-A	32	Light Inhibited Hydraulic & Gen. Purpose	135–165	GST Oil 32	Citgo Pacemaker 32
PE-215-A	46	Med. Inhibited Hydraulic & Gen. Purpose	194–236	GST Oil 46	Citgo Pacemaker 46
PE-315-A	68	Med.-Heavy Inhibited Hyd. & Gen. Purpose	284–346	GST Oil 68	Citgo Pacemaker 68
PE-700-A	150	Heavy Inhibited Hydraulic & Gen. Purpose	630–770	AW Machine Oil 150	Citgo Pacemaker 150
PE-150-HP	32	High-Pressure (Anti-Wear) Hydraulic Oil	135–165	AW Hyd. Oil 32	Citgo Pacemaker XD-32 or AW Hyd. Oil 32
PE-215-HP	46	High-Pressure (Anti-Wear) Hydraulic Oil	194–236	AW Hyd. Oil 46	Citgo Pacemaker XD-46 or AW Hyd. Oil 46
PE-315-HP	68	High-Pressure (Anti-Wear) Hydraulic Oil	284–346	AW Hyd. Oil 68	Citgo Pacemaker XD-68 or AW Hyd. Oil 68
PE-FRH-1	—	Fire-Resistant Hyd. Fluid/Synthetic		NR	NR
PE-FRH-2	—	Fire-Resistant Hyd. Fluid/Water-Glycol		NR	Citgo Glycol FR-40XD
PE-FRH-3	—	Fire-Resistant Hyd. Fluid/Water-Oil Emulsion		FR Fluid D	Citgo Invert FR Fluid
PE-32-B	2	Very Light Spindle Oil (Over 6000 rpm)	29–35	NR	NR
PE-60-B	10	Light Spindle Oil (3600–6000 rpm)	54–66	AW Machine Oil 10	NR
PE-105-B	22	Spindle Oil (Up to 3600 rpm)	95–115	AW Machine Oil 22	NR
PE-150-C	32	Light Way Oil	135–165	NR	NR
PE-315-C	68	Medium Way Oil	284–346	Vistac Oil 68X	Citgo SlideRite 68
PE-1000-C	220	Heavy Way Oil	900–1100	Vistac Oil 220X	Citgo Sliderite 220
PE-700-D	150	Light Gear Oil	630–770	AW Machine Oil 150	Citgo Pacemaker 150
PE-1000-D	220	Medium Gear Oil	900–1100	AW Machine Oil 220	Citgo Extra Duty Circ. Oil 220
PE-2150-D	460	Heavy Gear Oil	1935–2365	NL Gear Compound 460	Citgo Extra Duty Circ. Oil 320
PE-315-E	68	Light Extreme-Pressure Gear Oil	283–347	NL Gear Compound 68	Citgo EP Compound 68
PE-1500-E	320	Heavy Extreme-Pressure Gear Oil	1350–1650	NL Gear Compound 320	Citgo EP Compound 320
PE-OG-G	—	Cling-Type Gear Shield (Open Gears)		Pinion Grease MS2	NR
PE-GPG-2	—	Gen. Purpose E.P. Lithium-Base Grease	NLGI2	Polyurea EP Grease 2	Citgo Prem. Lithium EP Grease #2
PE-MG-2	—	Molybdenum Disulfide E.P. Grease		Moly Grease 2	Citgo Extra Range Grease

NR = No recommendation
1. Does not contain tackiness additives normally found in way lubricants. Formulated to perform as combination hydraulic oil and way lubricant.
2. To be used where grades 90, 125, and 140 are recommended.
3. Not lithium base, but equals or exceeds application requirements.
4. Falls outside specified viscosity range, but meets application requirements.
5. Not moly grease, but exceeds application requirements.
6. Straight phosphate ester fluids available in four viscosity grades.
7. Available in range of viscosities.
8. Various ISO grades.
9. Synthetic lubricants.
10. All products formulated from polyalkylene glycol base stocks.
11. Anhydrous product, but water soluble.

Table 19.1 Chart of Interchangeable Lubricants (continued)

Plant Engineering Designation	ISO Viscosity Grade	Lubricant Type	Viscosity, SUS at 100°F	Cling Surface Co., Inc.	Conoco Inc.
PE-150-A	32	Light Inhibited Hydraulic & Gen. Purpose	135–165	HYO Oil 10	Dectol R&O Oil 32
PE-215-A	46	Med. Inhibited Hydraulic & Gen. Purpose	194–236	HYO Oil 20	Dectol R&O Oil 46
PE-315-A	68	Med.-Heavy Inhibited Hyd. & Gen. Purpose	284–346	NR	Dectol R&O Oil 68
PE-700-A	150	Heavy Inhibited Hydraulic & Gen. Purpose	630–770	NR	Dectol R&O Oil 150
PE-150-HP	32	High-Pressure (Anti-Wear) Hydraulic Oil	135–165	AW Oil 10	Super Hyd. Oil 32
PE-215-HP	46	High-Pressure (Anti-Wear) Hydraulic Oil	194–236	AW Oil 20	Super Hyd. Oil 46
PE-315-HP	68	High-Pressure (Anti-Wear) Hydraulic Oil	284–346	NR	Super Hyd. Oil 68
PE-FRH-1	—	Fire-Resistant Hyd. Fluid/Synthetic		NR	NR
PE-FRH-2	—	Fire-Resistant Hyd. Fluid/Water-Glycol		NR	FC Fluid
PE-FRH-3	—	Fire-Resistant Hyd. Fluid/Water-Oil Emulsion		NR	FR Fluid
PE-32-B	2	Very Light Spindle Oil (Over 6000 rpm)	29–35	NR	TD Torque Fluid[4]
PE-60-B	10	Light Spindle Oil (3600–6000 rpm)	54–66	NR	GP Spindle Oil 7[4]
PE-105-B	22	Spindle Oil (Up to 3600 rpm)	95–115	NR	Super Hyd. Oil 22
PE-150-C	32	Light Way Oil	135–165	NR	Dectol R&O Oil 32[1]
PE-315-C	68	Medium Way Oil	284–346	NR	HD Way Lube 31
PE-1000-C	220	Heavy Way Oil	900–1100	NR	HD Way Lube 92
PE-700-D	150	Light Gear Oil	630–770	NR	Dectol R&O Oil 150
PE-1000-D	220	Medium Gear Oil	900–1100	NR	Dectol R&O Oil 220
PE-2150-D	460	Heavy Gear Oil	1935–2365	NR	Dectol R&O Oil 460
PE-315-E	68	Light Extreme-Pressure Gear Oil	283–347	APG 80	Gear Oil 68
PE-1500-E	320	Heavy Extreme-Pressure Gear Oil	1350–1650	AGG 90	Gear Oil 320
PE-OG-G	—	Cling-Type Gear Shield (Open Gears)		NR	Cogrease L Lube
PE-GPG-2	—	Gen. Purpose E.P. Lithium-Base Grease	NLGI2	Lithium #2 EP	EP Conolith Grease 2
PE-MG-2	—	Molybdenum Disulfide E.P. Grease		NR	Super Lube M Grease

Total Lubrication

Plant Engineering Designation	ISO Viscosity Grade	Lubricant Type	Viscosity, SUS at 100°F	Convoy Oil Corp.	Cook's Industrial Lubricants, Inc.
PE-150-A	32	Light Inhibited Hydraulic & Gen. Purpose	135-165	Con HY 618	Albavis 8
PE-215-A	46	Med. Inhibited Hydraulic & Gen. Purpose	194-236	Con HY 128	Albavis 10
PE-315-A	68	Med.-Heavy Inhibited Hyd. & Gen. Purpose	284-346	Con HY 138	Albavis 20
PE-700-A	150	Heavy Inhibited Hydraulic & Gen. Purpose	630-770	Con HY 178	Albavis 40
PE-150-HP	32	High-Pressure (Anti-Wear) Hydraulic Oil	135-165	Con HY 618	Albavis 8 Hyd. Oil
PE-215-HP	46	High-Pressure (Anti-Wear) Hydraulic Oil	194-236	Con HY 128	Albavis 10 Hyd. Oil
PE-315-HP	68	High-Pressure (Anti-Wear) Hydraulic Oil	284-346	Con HY 138	Albavis 20 Hyd. Oil
PE-FRH-1	—	Fire-Resistant Hyd. Fluid/Synthetic		Syn Con FR Fluid	NR
PE-FRH-2	—	Fire-Resistant Hyd. Fluid/Water-Glycol		Convoy FR Fluid WG	NR
PE-FRH-3	—	Fire-Resistant Hyd. Fluid/Water-Oil Emulsion		Convoy FR Fluid WO	NR
PE-32-B	2	Very Light Spindle Oil (Over 6000 rpm)	29-35	Spinfree XL	NR
PE-60-B	10	Light Spindle Oil (3600-6000 rpm)	54-66	Spinfree L	Spindle Oil 70
PE-105-B	22	Spindle Oil (Up to 3600 rpm)	95-115	Spinfree M	Spindle Oil 115
PE-150-C	32	Light Way Oil	135-165	Waylube 160	Way Lube 8
PE-315-C	68	Medium Way Oil	284-346	Waylube 310	Way Lube 20
PE-1000-C	220	Heavy Way Oil	900-1100	Waylube 1000	Way Lube 50
PE-700-D	150	Light Gear Oil	630-770	Conep 1080	EP Gear Lube 80
PE-1000-D	220	Medium Gear Oil	900-1100	Conep 1090	EP Gear Lube 90
PE-2150-D	460	Heavy Gear Oil	1935-2365	Conep 140	EP Gear Lube 140
PE-315-E	68	Light Extreme-Pressure Gear Oil	283-347	Contrans Light	EP Gear Lube 55
PE-1500-E	320	Heavy Extreme-Pressure Gear Oil	1350-1650	Contrans Heavy	EP Gear Lube 110
PE-OG-G	—	Cling-Type Gear Shield (Open Gears)		Conshield II	Open Gear Compound
PE-GPG-2	—	Gen. Purpose E.P. Lithium-Base Grease	NLGI2	Convoy Litho EP-2	Universal Pressure Grease
PE-MG-2	—	Molybdenum Disulfide E.P. Grease		Convoy Moly EP-2	NR

NR = No recommendation
1. Does not contain tackiness additives normally found in way lubricants. Formulated to perform as combination hydraulic oil and way lubricant.
2. To be used where grades 90, 125, and 140 are recommended.
3. Not lithium base, but equals or exceeds application requirements.
4. Falls outside specified viscosity range, but meets application requirements.
5. Not moly grease, but exceeds application requirements.
6. Straight phosphate ester fluids available in four viscosity grades.
7. Available in range of viscosities.
8. Various ISO grades.
9. Synthetic lubricants.
10. All products formulated from polyalkylene glycol base stocks.
11. Anhydrous product, but water soluble.

Table 19.1 Chart of Interchangeable Lubricants (continued)

Plant Engineering Designation	ISO Viscosity Grade	Lubricant Type	Viscosity, SUS at 100°F	Darmex Industrial Corp.	Davis-Howland Oil Corp.
PE-150-A	32	Light Inhibited Hydraulic & Gen. Purpose	135–165	Hyd. 100	Convis OC 150
PE-215-A	46	Med. Inhibited Hydraulic & Gen. Purpose	194–236	Hyd. 100/200	Convis OC 200
PE-315-A	68	Med.-Heavy Inhibited Hyd. & Gen. Purpose	284–346	Hyd. 100/200	Convis OC 300
PE-700-A	150	Heavy Inhibited Hydraulic & Gen. Purpose	630–770	Hyd. 100/200	DSL 48
PE-150-HP	32	High-Pressure (Anti-Wear) Hydraulic Oil	135–165	Hyd. 100	DSL 44
PE-215-HP	46	High-Pressure (Anti-Wear) Hydraulic Oil	194–236	Hyd. 100/200	DSL 45
PE-315-HP	68	High-Pressure (Anti-Wear) Hydraulic Oil	284–346	Hyd. 100/200	DSL 46
PE-FRH-1	—	Fire-Resistant Hyd. Fluid/Synthetic		Darmex NF 50	DSL Syn-Draulic
PE-FRH-2	—	Fire-Resistant Hyd. Fluid/Water-Glycol		FR 150 GW	DSL FR-200
PE-FRH-3	—	Fire-Resistant Hyd. Fluid/Water-Oil Emulsion		FR 100 IE	DSL Hydro-Draulic
PE-32-B	2	Very Light Spindle Oil (Over 6000 rpm)	29–35	SPO L	Conspin 3
PE-60-B	10	Light Spindle Oil (3600–6000 rpm)	54–66	SPO M	Conspin 6
PE-105-B	22	Spindle Oil (Up to 3600 rpm)	95–115	SPO H	Conspin 10
PE-150-C	32	Light Way Oil	135–165	Darmex 10	Way Oil 75
PE-315-C	68	Medium Way Oil	284–346	Darmex 1050	Way Oil 80
PE-1000-C	220	Heavy Way Oil	900–1100	Darmex 9140 NM	Way Oil 90
PE-700-D	150	Light Gear Oil	630–770	Darmex 50	Convis OC 750
PE-1000-D	220	Medium Gear Oil	900–1100	Darmex 9140	Convis OC 1000
PE-2150-D	460	Heavy Gear Oil	1935–2365	Darmex 140	DH 167
PE-315-E	68	Light Extreme-Pressure Gear Oil	283–347	Darmex GO 1050	Compound 1
PE-1500-E	320	Heavy Extreme-Pressure Gear Oil	1350–1650	Darmex 9140	Compound 4
PE-OG-G	—	Cling-Type Gear Shield (Open Gears)		Darmex 421	Open Gear #2
PE-GPG-2	—	Gen. Purpose E.P. Lithium-Base Grease	NLGI2	Darmex 123	AP Lithium EP #2
PE-MG-2	—	Molybdenum Disulfide E.P. Grease		Darmex 123 M	Poly-Moly

Total Lubrication 213

Plant Engineering Designation	ISO Viscosity Grade	Lubricant Type	Viscosity, SUS at 100°F	Delta Resins & Refractories	Dryden Oil Co., Inc.
PE-150-A	32	Light Inhibited Hydraulic & Gen. Purpose	135-165	Deltalene Lite Hyd. Oil #930	Paradene 32 R&O
PE-215-A	46	Med. Inhibited Hydraulic & Gen. Purpose	194-236	Deltalene Med. Hyd. Oil #931	Paradene 46 R&O
PE-315-A	68	Med.-Heavy Inhibited Hyd. & Gen. Purpose	284-346	Deltalene Med-Hvy. Hyd. Oil #932	Paradene 68 R&O
PE-700-A	150	Heavy Inhibited Hydraulic & Gen. Purpose	630-770	Deltalene Heavy Hyd. Oil #934	Paradene 150 R&O
PE-150-HP	32	High-Pressure (Anti-Wear) Hydraulic Oil	135-165	Deltalene Lite Hyd. Oil #930	Paradene 32 AW/Blue Hyd. Light
PE-215-HP	46	High-Pressure (Anti-Wear) Hydraulic Oil	194-236	Deltalene Med. Hyd. Oil #931	Paradene 46 AW/Blue Hyd. 10
PE-315-HP	68	High-Pressure (Anti-Wear) Hydraulic Oil	284-346	Deltalene Med-Hvy. Hyd. Oil #932	Paradene 68 AW/Blue Hyd. 20
PE-FRH-1	—	Fire-Resistant Hyd. Fluid/Synthetic		NR	NR
PE-FRH-2	—	Fire-Resistant Hyd. Fluid/Water-Glycol		NR	NR
PE-FRH-3	—	Fire-Resistant Hyd. Fluid/Water-Oil Emulsion		NR	NR
PE-32-B	2	Very Light Spindle Oil (Over 6000 rpm)	29-35	NR	Spindle Oil 2
PE-60-B	10	Light Spindle Oil (3600-6000 rpm)	54-66	Delta Light Spindle Oil #52B	Spindle Oil 10
PE-105-B	22	Spindle Oil (Up to 3600 rpm)	95-115	NR	Spindle Oil 22
PE-150-C	32	Light Way Oil	135-165	NR	Way Lube 32
PE-315-C	68	Medium Way Oil	284-346	NR	Way Lube 80
PE-1000-C	220	Heavy Way Oil	900-1100	NR	Way Lube 90
PE-700-D	150	Light Gear Oil	630-770	NR	Paradene 150 W
PE-1000-D	220	Medium Gear Oil	900-1100	NR	Paradene 220 W/APC 80W90
PE-2150-D	460	Heavy Gear Oil	1935-2365	Delta IF-5 Gear Compound #257E	Paradene 460 W/APC 85W140
PE-315-E	68	Light Extreme-Pressure Gear Oil	283-347	NR	EP Gear Lube #2
PE-1500-E	320	Heavy Extreme-Pressure Gear Oil	1350-1650	NR	EP Gear Lube #6/ESGL 80W140
PE-OG-G	—	Cling-Type Gear Shield (Open Gears)		NR	NR
PE-GPG-2	—	Gen. Purpose E.P. Lithium-Base Grease	NLGI2	Delta Lithium Grease 2 #242	Lithium EP #2
PE-MG-2	—	Molybdenum Disulfide E.P. Grease		NR	Moly EP #2

NR = No recommendation
1. Does not contain tackiness additives normally found in way lubricants. Formulated to perform as combination hydraulic oil and way lubricant.
2. To be used where grades 90, 125, and 140 are recommended.
3. Not lithium base, but equals or exceeds application requirements.
4. Falls outside specified viscosity range, but meets application requirements.
5. Not moly grease, but exceeds application requirements.
6. Straight phosphate ester fluids available in four viscosity grades.
7. Available in range of viscosities.
8. Various ISO grades.
9. Synthetic lubricants.
10. All products formulated from polyalkylene glycol base stocks.
11. Anhydrous product, but water soluble.

Table 19.1 Chart of Interchangeable Lubricants (continued)

Plant Engineering Designation	ISO Viscosity Grade	Lubricant Type	Viscosity, SUS at 100°F	Du Bois Chemicals	R. W. Eaken, Inc.
PE-150-A	32	Light Inhibited Hydraulic & Gen. Purpose	135–165	MPO-10	Fluidvis 32
PE-215-A	46	Med. Inhibited Hydraulic & Gen. Purpose	194–236	MPO-20	Fluidvis 46
PE-315-A	68	Med.-Heavy Inhibited Hyd. & Gen. Purpose	284–346	MPO-20	Fluidvis 68
PE-700-A	150	Heavy Inhibited Hydraulic & Gen. Purpose	630–770	EGO-80.90 or MPO-30	Fluidvis 150
PE-150-HP	32	High-Pressure (Anti-Wear) Hydraulic Oil	135–165	MPO-10	Premco 32
PE-215-HP	46	High-Pressure (Anti-Wear) Hydraulic Oil	194–236	MPO-20	Premco 46
PE-315-HP	68	High-Pressure (Anti-Wear) Hydraulic Oil	284–346	MPO-20	Premco 68
PE-FRH-1	—	Fire-Resistant Hyd. Fluid/Synthetic		NR	NR
PE-FRH-2	—	Fire-Resistant Hyd. Fluid/Water-Glycol		NR	NR
PE-FRH-3	—	Fire-Resistant Hyd. Fluid/Water-Oil Emulsion		Pyro-Safe	NR
PE-32-B	2	Very Light Spindle Oil (Over 6000 rpm)	29–35	NR	NR
PE-60-B	10	Light Spindle Oil (3600–6000 rpm)	54–66	NR	Eaken Spindle Oil
PE-105-B	22	Spindle Oil (Up to 3600 rpm)	95–115	MPO-10	Premco 22
PE-150-C	32	Light Way Oil	135–165	MPO-10	Wayall 60
PE-315-C	68	Medium Way Oil	284–346	MPO-20	Wayall 70
PE-1000-C	220	Heavy Way Oil	900–1100	EGO-80.90	Wayall 90
PE-700-D	150	Light Gear Oil	630–770	EGO 80.90 or MPO-30	Fluidvis 150
PE-1000-D	220	Medium Gear Oil	900–1100	EGO 80.90	Fluidvis 220
PE-2150-D	460	Heavy Gear Oil	1935–2365	EGO 90.140	Fluidvis 460
PE-315-E	68	Light Extreme-Pressure Gear Oil	283–347	MPO-20	Gear-X 2EP
PE-1500-E	320	Heavy Extreme-Pressure Gear Oil	1350–1650	EGO-90.140	Gear-X 6EP
PE-OG-G	—	Cling-Type Gear Shield (Open Gears)		OGG-H	NR
PE-GPG-2	—	Gen. Purpose E.P. Lithium-Base Grease	NLGI2	TPG	NR
PE-MG-2	—	Molybdenum Disulfide E.P. Grease		MPG-2[5]	NR

Plant Engineering Designation	ISO Viscosity Grade	Lubricant Type	Viscosity, SUS at 100°F	E/M Lubricants, Inc.	Exxon Co., U.S.A.
PE-150-A	32	Light Inhibited Hydraulic & Gen. Purpose	135–165	K 15032	Teresstic 32 or 33
PE-215-A	46	Med. Inhibited Hydraulic & Gen. Purpose	194–236	NR	Teresstic 46
PE-315-A	68	Med.-Heavy Inhibited Hyd. & Gen. Purpose	284–346	K 15068	Teresstic 68
PE-700-A	150	Heavy Inhibited Hydraulic & Gen. Purpose	630–770	NR	Teresstic 150
PE-150-HP	32	High-Pressure (Anti-Wear) Hydraulic Oil	135–165	K 15032	Nuto H 32
PE-215-HP	46	High-Pressure (Anti-Wear) Hydraulic Oil	194–236	NR	Nuto H 46
PE-315-HP	68	High-Pressure (Anti-Wear) Hydraulic Oil	284–346	K 15068	Nuto H 68
PE-FRH-1	—	Fire-Resistant Hyd. Fluid/Synthetic		NR	NR
PE-FRH-2	—	Fire-Resistant Hyd. Fluid/Water-Glycol		NR	NR
PE-FRH-3	—	Fire-Resistant Hyd. Fluid/Water-Oil Emulsion		NR	3110 FR Hyd. Fluid
PE-32-B	2	Very Light Spindle Oil (Over 6000 rpm)	29–35	NR	NR
PE-60-B	10	Light Spindle Oil (3600–6000 rpm)	54–66	NR	Spinesstic 10
PE-105-B	22	Spindle Oil (Up to 3600 rpm)	95–115	K 150324	Spinesstic 22
PE-150-C	32	Light Way Oil	135–165	K 15032	NR
PE-315-C	68	Medium Way Oil	284–346	K 15068	Febis K 68
PE-1000-C	220	Heavy Way Oil	900–1100	K 400-90	Febis K 220
PE-700-D	150	Light Gear Oil	630–770	K 460 85W140	Teresstic 150
PE-1000-D	220	Medium Gear Oil	900–1100	K 400 90	Teresstic 220
PE-2150-D	460	Heavy Gear Oil	1935–2365	K 400 140	Teresstic 460 or Cylesstic TK 460
PE-315-E	68	Light Extreme-Pressure Gear Oil	283–347	NR	Spartan EP 68
PE-1500-E	320	Heavy Extreme-Pressure Gear Oil	1350–1650	K 400 90	Spartan EP 320
PE-OG-G	—	Cling-Type Gear Shield (Open Gears)		K 333	Surett N80k
PE-GPG-2	—	Gen. Purpose E.P. Lithium-Base Grease	NLGI2	K 100[3]	Lidok EP 2
PE-MG-2	—	Molybdenum Disulfide E.P. Grease		K 558	Beacon O2

NR = No recommendation
1. Does not contain tackiness additives normally found in way lubricants. Formulated to perform as combination hydraulic oil and way lubricant.
2. To be used where grades 90, 125, and 140 are recommended.
3. Not lithium base, but equals or exceeds application requirements.
4. Falls outside specified viscosity range, but meets application requirements.
5. Not moly grease, but exceeds application requirements.
6. Straight phosphate ester fluids available in four viscosity grades.
7. Available in range of viscosities.
8. Various ISO grades.
9. Synthetic lubricants.
10. All products formulated from polyalkylene glycol base stocks.
11. Anhydrous product, but water soluble.

Table 19.1 Chart of Interchangeable Lubricants (continued)

Plant Engineering Designation	ISO Viscosity Grade	Lubricant Type	Viscosity, SUS at 100°F	Farbest Corp. Allube Products	Filmite Oil Corp.
PE-150-A	32	Light Inhibited Hydraulic & Gen. Purpose	135–165	Hydra-Shield 150	Industrial 150
PE-215-A	46	Med. Inhibited Hydraulic & Gen. Purpose	194–236	Hydra-Shield 200	Industrial 200
PE-315-A	68	Med.-Heavy Inhibited Hyd. & Gen. Purpose	284–346	Hydra-Shield 300	Industrial 300
PE-700-A	150	Heavy Inhibited Hydraulic & Gen. Purpose	630–770	Hydra-Shield 800	Industrial 750
PE-150-HP	32	High-Pressure (Anti-Wear) Hydraulic Oil	135–165	Hydra-Shield 150	Industrial 150
PE-215-HP	46	High-Pressure (Anti-Wear) Hydraulic Oil	194–236	Hydra-Shield 200	Industrial 200
PE-315-HP	68	High-Pressure (Anti-Wear) Hydraulic Oil	284–346	Hydra-Shield 300	Industrial 300
PE-FRH-1	—	Fire-Resistant Hyd. Fluid/Synthetic		NR	NR
PE-FRH-2	—	Fire-Resistant Hyd. Fluid/Water-Glycol		NR	NR
PE-FRH-3	—	Fire-Resistant Hyd. Fluid/Water-Oil Emulsion		Hydra-Shield FR-40	NR
PE-32-B	2	Very Light Spindle Oil (Over 6000 rpm)	29–35	NR	NR
PE-60-B	10	Light Spindle Oil (3600–6000 rpm)	54–66	Lubri-Shield 60	Industrial 50
PE-105-B	22	Spindle Oil (Up to 3600 rpm)	95–115	Lubri-Shield 100	Industrial 100
PE-150-C	32	Light Way Oil	135–165	Lubri-Shield #1	Way Lube 1
PE-315-C	68	Medium Way Oil	284–346	Lubri-Shield #2	Way Lube 3
PE-1000-C	220	Heavy Way Oil	900–1100	Lubri-Shield #4	Way Lube 9
PE-700-D	150	Light Gear Oil	630–770	Lubri-Shield #3	Gear Film 70
PE-1000-D	220	Medium Gear Oil	900–1100	Lubri-Shield #4	Gear Film 90
PE-2150-D	460	Heavy Gear Oil	1935–2365	Lubri-Shield #5	Gear Film 140
PE-315-E	68	Light Extreme-Pressure Gear Oil	283–347	Lubri-Shield #2	Gear Film 50
PE-1500-E	320	Heavy Extreme-Pressure Gear Oil	1350–1650	Lubri-Shield EP 90 I.G.O.	Gear Film 110
PE-OG-G	—	Cling-Type Gear Shield (Open Gears)		Lubri-Shield OGL Hvy.	Lubriplate Gear Shield
PE-GPG-2	—	Gen. Purpose E.P. Lithium-Base Grease	NLGI2	Lubri-Shield HTL-2HD	Lubriplate 1200-2
PE-MG-2	—	Molybdenum Disulfide E.P. Grease		Moly-Shield 2HDM	Lubriplate MO-Lith 2

Total Lubrication

Plant Engineering Designation	ISO Viscosity Grade	Lubricant Type	Viscosity, SUS at 100°F	Gard Corp.	Georgia-Carolina Oil Co.
PE-150-A	32	Light Inhibited Hydraulic & Gen. Purpose	135–165	HydraGard R&O 32	G-C Turbine Oil Light
PE-215-A	46	Med. Inhibited Hydraulic & Gen. Purpose	194–236	HydraGard R&O 46	G-C Turbine Oil 15
PE-315-A	68	Med.-Heavy Inhibited Hyd. & Gen. Purpose	284–346	HydraGard R&O 68	G-C Turbine Oil Medium
PE-700-A	150	Heavy Inhibited Hydraulic & Gen. Purpose	630–770	HydraGard R&O 150	G-C Turbine Oil Extra Heavy 40
PE-150-HP	32	High-Pressure (Anti-Wear) Hydraulic Oil	135–165	HydraGard AW 32	G-C Safety-Press AW Light
PE-215-HP	46	High-Pressure (Anti-Wear) Hydraulic Oil	194–236	HydraGard AW 46	G-C Safety-Press AW 15
PE-315-HP	68	High-Pressure (Anti-Wear) Hydraulic Oil	284–346	HydraGard AW 68	G-C Safety-Press AW Medium
PE-FRH-1	—	Fire-Resistant Hyd. Fluid/Synthetic		SafeGard FR Fluid SF	NR
PE-FRH-2	—	Fire-Resistant Hyd. Fluid/Water-Glycol		SafeGard FR Fluid WG	NR
PE-FRH-3	—	Fire-Resistant Hyd. Fluid/Water-Oil Emulsion		SafeGard FR Fluid WO	NR
PE-32-B	2	Very Light Spindle Oil (Over 6000 rpm)	29–35	SpinGard 2	NR
PE-60-B	10	Light Spindle Oil (3600–6000 rpm)	54–66	SpinGard 10	G-C White Star Spindle Oil 60
PE-105-B	22	Spindle Oil (Up to 3600 rpm)	95–115	SpinGard 22	G-C White Star Spindle Oil 100
PE-150-C	32	Light Way Oil	135–165	Gardway 32	G-C Way Oil Light
PE-315-C	68	Medium Way Oil	284–346	Gardway 68	G-C Way Oil Medium
PE-1000-C	220	Heavy Way Oil	900–1100	Gardway 220	G-C Way Oil 90
PE-700-D	150	Light Gear Oil	630–770	Gardgear 150	G-C Trans Lube 55
PE-1000-D	220	Medium Gear Oil	900–1100	Gardgear 220	G-C Trans Lube 90
PE-2150-D	460	Heavy Gear Oil	1935–2365	Gardgear 460	G-C Trans Lube 140
PE-315-E	68	Light Extreme-Pressure Gear Oil	283–347	Gardgear EP 68	G-C EP Gear Lube 45
PE-1500-E	320	Heavy Extreme-Pressure Gear Oil	1350–1650	Gardgear EP 320	G-C EP Gear Lube 90
PE-OG-G	—	Cling-Type Gear Shield (Open Gears)		Gardtac 220	G-C Fluid Open Gear Lube 50
PE-GPG-2	—	Gen. Purpose E.P. Lithium-Base Grease	NLGI2	Gard MP Lithium #2	G-C Ben Boy 55-B
PE-MG-2	—	Molybdenum Disulfide E.P. Grease		Gardmoly HiTemp EP	G-C Ben Boy Moly 5

NR = No recommendation
1. Does not contain tackiness additives normally found in way lubricants. Formulated to perform as combination hydraulic oil and way lubricant.
2. To be used where grades 90, 125, and 140 are recommended.
3. Not lithium base, but equals or exceeds application requirements.
4. Falls outside specified viscosity range, but meets application requirements.
5. Not moly grease, but exceeds application requirements.
6. Straight phosphate ester fluids available in four viscosity grades.
7. Available in range of viscosities.
8. Various ISO grades.
9. Synthetic lubricants.
10. All products formulated from polyalkylene glycol base stocks.
11. Anhydrous product, but water soluble.

Table 19.1 *Chart of Interchangeable Lubricants (continued)*

Plant Engineering Designation	ISO Viscosity Grade	Lubricant Type	Viscosity, SUS at 100°F	Getty Refining & Marketing Co. Eastern Region	Getty Refining & Marketing Co. Central Region
PE-150-A	32	Light Inhibited Hydraulic & Gen. Purpose	135–165	Aturbrio 50	Skelvis INH-150
PE-215-A	46	Med. Inhibited Hydraulic & Gen. Purpose	194–236	Aturbrio 58	Skelvis INH-10
PE-315-A	68	Med.-Heavy Inhibited Hyd. & Gen. Purpose	284–346	Aturbrio 60	Skelvis INH-20
PE-700-A	150	Heavy Inhibited Hydraulic & Gen. Purpose	630–770	Aturbrio 71	Skelvis INH-40
PE-150-HP	32	High-Pressure (Anti-Wear) Hydraulic Oil	135–165	Aturbrio AW 51	Skelvis MP 150
PE-215-HP	46	High-Pressure (Anti-Wear) Hydraulic Oil	194–236	Aturbrio AW 59	Skelvis MP 10
PE-315-HP	68	High-Pressure (Anti-Wear) Hydraulic Oil	284–346	Aturbrio AW 61	Skelvis MP 20
PE-FRH-1	—	Fire-Resistant Hyd. Fluid/Synthetic		NR	NR
PE-FRH-2	—	Fire-Resistant Hyd. Fluid/Water-Glycol		NR	NR
PE-FRH-3	—	Fire-Resistant Hyd. Fluid/Water-Oil Emulsion		NR	NR
PE-32-B	2	Very Light Spindle Oil (Over 6000 rpm)	29–35	NR	NR
PE-60-B	10	Light Spindle Oil (3600–6000 rpm)	54–66	NR	Skelux
PE-105-B	22	Spindle Oil (Up to 3600 rpm)	95–115	Alweave 12	Skelvis 100
PE-150-C	32	Light Way Oil	135–165	Aturbrio 53	Skelvis 150
PE-315-C	68	Medium Way Oil	284–346	Aturbrio 61	Skelvis 20
PE-1000-C	220	Heavy Way Oil	900–1100	Aturbrio 77	Skelvis 50
PE-700-D	150	Light Gear Oil	630–770	Aturbrio 71	Skelvis MP 40
PE-1000-D	220	Medium Gear Oil	900–1100	Apreslube 80	GP Gear 90
PE-2150-D	460	Heavy Gear Oil	1935–2365	Apreslube 90	GP Gear 140
PE-315-E	68	Light Extreme-Pressure Gear Oil	283–347	NR	GP Gear 80
PE-1500-E	320	Heavy Extreme-Pressure Gear Oil	1350–1650	Apreslube 86	NR
PE-OG-G	—	Cling-Type Gear Shield (Open Gears)		NR	NR
PE-GPG-2	—	Gen. Purpose E.P. Lithium-Base Grease	NLGI2	Alithex MP #2	Getty MPEP #2
PE-MG-2	—	Molybdenum Disulfide E.P. Grease		Moly EP	Molly EP

Total Lubrication

Plant Engineering Designation	ISO Viscosity Grade	Lubricant Type	Viscosity, SUS at 100°F	Getty Refining & Marketing Co. Western Region	Graphite Products Corp.
PE-150-A	32	Light Inhibited Hydraulic & Gen. Purpose	135–165	150 AW Hyd.	NR
PE-215-A	46	Med. Inhibited Hydraulic & Gen. Purpose	194–236	10 AW Hyd.	NR
PE-315-A	68	Med.-Heavy Inhibited Hyd. & Gen. Purpose	284–346	20 AW Hyd.	NR
PE-700-A	150	Heavy Inhibited Hydraulic & Gen. Purpose	630–770	NR	NR
PE-150-HP	32	High-Pressure (Anti-Wear) Hydraulic Oil	135–165	150 AW Hyd.	NR
PE-215-HP	46	High-Pressure (Anti-Wear) Hydraulic Oil	194–236	10 AW Hyd.	NR
PE-315-HP	68	High-Pressure (Anti-Wear) Hydraulic Oil	284–346	20 AW Hyd.	NR
PE-FRH-1	—	Fire-Resistant Hyd. Fluid/Synthetic		NR	NR
PE-FRH-2	—	Fire-Resistant Hyd. Fluid/Water-Glycol		NR	NR
PE-FRH-3	—	Fire-Resistant Hyd. Fluid/Water-Oil Emulsion		NR	NR
PE-32-B	2	Very Light Spindle Oil (Over 6000 rpm)	29–35	NR	GP-SO-#40
PE-60-B	10	Light Spindle Oil (3600–6000 rpm)	54–66	NR	GP-SO-#70
PE-105-B	22	Spindle Oil (Up to 3600 rpm)	95–115	NR	GP-SO-#100
PE-150-C	32	Light Way Oil	135–165	NR	GP-MWO-305
PE-315-C	68	Medium Way Oil	284–346	NR	GP-MWO-1000
PE-1000-C	220	Heavy Way Oil	900–1100	NR	GP-MWO-1200
PE-700-D	150	Light Gear Oil	630–770	AW Hyd. 40	SS-MGO-#80
PE-1000-D	220	Medium Gear Oil	900–1100	EP Gear 90	SS-MGO-#90
PE-2150-D	460	Heavy Gear Oil	1935–2365	EP Gear 140	SS-MGO-#140
PE-315-E	68	Light Extreme-Pressure Gear Oil	283–347	NR	SS-MGO-80/90
PE-1500-E	320	Heavy Extreme-Pressure Gear Oil	1350–1650	NR	NR
PE-OG-G	—	Cling-Type Gear Shield (Open Gears)		NR	GP-OG (MED)
PE-GPG-2	—	Gen. Purpose E.P. Lithium-Base Grease	NLGI2	Getty MPEP #2	GP 33
PE-MG-2	—	Molybdenum Disulfide E.P. Grease		Molly EP	GP 3

NR = No recommendation
1. Does not contain tackiness additives normally found in way lubricants. Formulated to perform as combination hydraulic oil and way lubricant.
2. To be used where grades 90, 125, and 140 are recommended.
3. Not lithium base, but equals or exceeds application requirements.
4. Falls outside specified viscosity range, but meets application requirements.
5. Not moly grease, but exceeds application requirements.
6. Straight phosphate ester fluids available in four viscosity grades.
7. Available in range of viscosities.
8. Various ISO grades.
9. Synthetic lubricants.
10. All products formulated from polyalkylene glycol base stocks.
11. Anhydrous product, but water soluble.

Table 19.1 Chart of Interchangeable Lubricants (continued)

Plant Engineering Designation	ISO Viscosity Grade	Lubricant Type	Viscosity, SUS at 100°F	Gulf Oil Corp.	E. F. Houghton & Co.
PE-150-A	32	Light Inhibited Hydraulic & Gen. Purpose	135–165	Harmony 32	Hydro-Drive HP-150
PE-215-A	46	Med. Inhibited Hydraulic & Gen. Purpose	194–236	Harmony 46	Hydro-Drive HP-200
PE-315-A	68	Med.-Heavy Inhibited Hyd. & Gen. Purpose	284–346	Harmony 68	Hydro-Drive HP-300
PE-700-A	150	Heavy Inhibited Hydraulic & Gen. Purpose	630–770	Harmony 150	Hydro-Drive HP-750
PE-150-HP	32	High-Pressure (Anti-Wear) Hydraulic Oil	135–165	Harmony 32 AW	Hydro-Drive HP-150
PE-215-HP	46	High-Pressure (Anti-Wear) Hydraulic Oil	194–236	Harmony 46 AW	Hydro-Drive HP-200
PE-315-HP	68	High-Pressure (Anti-Wear) Hydraulic Oil	284–346	Harmony 68 AW	Hydro-Drive HP-300
PE-FRH-1	—	Fire-Resistant Hyd. Fluid/Synthetic		[6]	Houghto-Safe 1000 Series[7]
PE-FRH-2	—	Fire-Resistant Hyd. Fluid/Water-Glycol		FR Fluid G-200	Houghto-Safe 620
PE-FRH-3	—	Fire-Resistant Hyd. Fluid/Water-Oil Emulsion		FR Fluid	Houghto-Safe 5000 Series
PE-32-B	2	Very Light Spindle Oil (Over 6000 rpm)	29–35	NR	NR
PE-60-B	10	Light Spindle Oil (3600–6000 rpm)	54–66	Gulfspin 10	NR
PE-105-B	22	Spindle Oil (Up to 3600 rpm)	95–115	Gulfspin 22	NR
PE-150-C	32	Light Way Oil	135–165	Harmony 32 AW	Hydro-Drive HP-150
PE-315-C	68	Medium Way Oil	284–346	Gulfway 68	NR
PE-1000-C	220	Heavy Way Oil	900–1100	Gulfway 220	Sta-Put 370[3]
PE-700-D	150	Light Gear Oil	630–770	Harmony 150 or 150D	NR
PE-1000-D	220	Medium Gear Oil	900–1100	Harmony 220	MP Gear Oil 90
PE-2150-D	460	Heavy Gear Oil	1935–2365	Harmony 460	NR
PE-315-E	68	Light Extreme-Pressure Gear Oil	283–347	EP Lube HD68	NR
PE-1500-E	320	Heavy Extreme-Pressure Gear Oil	1350–1650	EP Lube HD320	NR
PE-OG-G	—	Cling-Type Gear Shield (Open Gears)		Premium Lubcote EP	Tenac-M
PE-GPG-2	—	Gen. Purpose E.P. Lithium-Base Grease	NLGI2	Gulfcrown Grease EP #2	Cosmolube #2
PE-MG-2	—	Molybdenum Disulfide E.P. Grease		Gulflex Moly	Hi-Temp 2409[5]

Total Lubrication

Plant Engineering Designation	ISO Viscosity Grade	Lubricant Type	Viscosity, SUS at 100°F	Imperial Oil & Grease Co.	International Refining & Manufacturing Co.
PE-150-A	32	Light Inhibited Hydraulic & Gen. Purpose	135–165	Molub-Alloy 601	IRMCO HL-14
PE-215-A	46	Med. Inhibited Hydraulic & Gen. Purpose	194–236	Molub-Alloy 602	IRMCO HL-20
PE-315-A	68	Med.-Heavy Inhibited Hyd. & Gen. Purpose	284–346	Molub-Alloy 603	IRMCO HL-30
PE-700-A	150	Heavy Inhibited Hydraulic & Gen. Purpose	630–770	Molub-Alloy 606	IRMCO HL-69
PE-150-HP	32	High-Pressure (Anti-Wear) Hydraulic Oil	135–165	Tribol 771	IRMCO HL-15
PE-215-HP	46	High-Pressure (Anti-Wear) Hydraulic Oil	194–236	Tribol 772	IRMCO HL-21
PE-315-HP	68	High-Pressure (Anti-Wear) Hydraulic Oil	284–346	Tribol 773	IRMCO HL-31
PE-FRH-1	—	Fire-Resistant Hyd. Fluid/Synthetic		NR	NR
PE-FRH-2	—	Fire-Resistant Hyd. Fluid/Water-Glycol		NR	NR
PE-FRH-3	—	Fire-Resistant Hyd. Fluid/Water-Oil Emulsion		Tribol 587	NR
PE-32-B	2	Very Light Spindle Oil (Over 6000 rpm)	29–35	NR	NR
PE-60-B	10	Light Spindle Oil (3600–6000 rpm)	54–66	NR	IRMCO S-6
PE-105-B	22	Spindle Oil (Up to 3600 rpm)	95–115	NR	IRMCO S-10
PE-150-C	32	Light Way Oil	135–165	Molub-Alloy MWO 10	IRMCO W-15
PE-315-C	68	Medium Way Oil	284–346	Molub-Alloy MWO 20	IRMCO W-31
PE-1000-C	220	Heavy Way Oil	900–1100	Molub-Alloy MWO 40	IRMCO W-100
PE-700-D	150	Light Gear Oil	630–770	Molub-Alloy 30	IRMCO HL-70
PE-1000-D	220	Medium Gear Oil	900–1100	Molub-Alloy 40	IRMCO HL-125[4]
PE-2150-D	460	Heavy Gear Oil	1935–2365	Molub-Alloy 494	IRMCO HL-215
PE-315-E	68	Light Extreme-Pressure Gear Oil	283–347	Molub-Alloy 804	IRMCO G2EP
PE-1500-E	320	Heavy Extreme-Pressure Gear Oil	1350–1650	Molub-Alloy 690	IRMCO G6EP
PE-OG-G	—	Cling-Type Gear Shield (Open Gears)		Molub-Alloy 882 EP-H	NR
PE-GPG-2	—	Gen. Purpose E.P. Lithium-Base Grease	NLGI2	Molub-Alloy 777-2	IRMCO MP-2
PE-MG-2	—	Molybdenum Disulfide E.P. Grease		Molub-Alloy 777-2	IRMCO Moly-Temp

NR = No recommendation
1. Does not contain tackiness additives normally found in way lubricants. Formulated to perform as combination hydraulic oil and way lubricant.
2. To be used where grades 90, 125, and 140 are recommended.
3. Not lithium base, but equals or exceeds application requirements.
4. Falls outside specified viscosity range, but meets application requirements.
5. Not moly grease, but exceeds application requirements.
6. Straight phosphate ester fluids available in four viscosity grades.
7. Available in range of viscosities.
8. Various ISO grades.
9. Synthetic lubricants.
10. All products formulated from polyalkylene glycol base stocks.
11. Anhydrous product, but water soluble.

Table 19.1 Chart of Interchangeable Lubricants (continued)

Plant Engineering Designation	ISO Viscosity Grade	Lubricant Type	Viscosity, SUS at 100°F	Inter-State Oil Co., Inc.	Jet Lube, Inc.
PE-150-A	32	Light Inhibited Hydraulic & Gen. Purpose	135–165	Resistal EP H-150	NR
PE-215-A	46	Med. Inhibited Hydraulic & Gen. Purpose	194–236	Resistal EP H-215	NR
PE-315-A	68	Med.-Heavy Inhibited Hyd. & Gen. Purpose	284–346	Resistal EP H-315	NR
PE-700-A	150	Heavy Inhibited Hydraulic & Gen. Purpose	630–770	Resistal EP H-700	NR
PE-150-HP	32	High-Pressure (Anti-Wear) Hydraulic Oil	135–165	Resistal EP H-150	NR
PE-215-HP	46	High-Pressure (Anti-Wear) Hydraulic Oil	194–236	Resistal EP H-215	NR
PE-315-HP	68	High-Pressure (Anti-Wear) Hydraulic Oil	284–346	Resistal EP H-315	NR
PE-FRH-1	—	Fire-Resistant Hyd. Fluid/Synthetic		NR	NR
PE-FRH-2	—	Fire-Resistant Hyd. Fluid/Water-Glycol		NR	NR
PE-FRH-3	—	Fire-Resistant Hyd. Fluid/Water-Oil Emulsion		NR	NR
PE-32-B	2	Very Light Spindle Oil (Over 6000 rpm)	29–35	Spindle Oil S-32	NR
PE-60-B	10	Light Spindle Oil (3600–6000 rpm)	54–66	Spindle Oil S-60	NR
PE-105-B	22	Spindle Oil (Up to 3600 rpm)	95–115	Spindle Oil S-105	NR
PE-150-C	32	Light Way Oil	135–165	Way-Hyd. Lube W-150	NR
PE-315-C	68	Medium Way Oil	284–346	Way-Hyd. Lube W-315	NR
PE-1000-C	220	Heavy Way Oil	900–1100	Way-Hyd. Lube W-1000	NR
PE-700-D	150	Light Gear Oil	630–770	Ind. Oil H-700	NR
PE-1000-D	220	Medium Gear Oil	900–1100	Ind. Oil H-1000	NR
PE-2150-D	460	Heavy Gear Oil	1935–2365	Ind. Oil H-2150	NR
PE-315-E	68	Light Extreme-Pressure Gear Oil	283–347	Ind. EP Oil 315	NR
PE-1500-E	320	Heavy Extreme-Pressure Gear Oil	1350–1650	Ind. EP Oil 1500	NR
PE-OG-G	—	Cling-Type Gear Shield (Open Gears)		1-S Outside Cog & Gear	Gear Guard WLD OG-M OG-H
PE-GPG-2	—	Gen. Purpose E.P. Lithium-Base Grease	NLGI2	1-S Preferred MP Grease	CB-2 & 202
PE-MG-2	—	Molybdenum Disulfide E.P. Grease		1-S Moly EP Grease	202 & AP-5 (NLGI-00,0,1,2,3)

Total Lubrication

Plant Engineering Designation	ISO Viscosity Grade	Lubricant Type	Viscosity, SUS at 100°F	Kendall Refining Co. (Division of Witco Chemical Corp.)	Kent Oil Co. (Moly NRG)
PE-150-A	32	Light Inhibited Hydraulic & Gen. Purpose	135–165	Kenoil R&O AW-32	Moly Special Duty #10
PE-215-A	46	Med. Inhibited Hydraulic & Gen. Purpose	194–236	Kenoil R&O AW-46	Moly Special Duty #15
PE-315-A	68	Med.-Heavy Inhibited Hyd. & Gen. Purpose	284–346	Kenoil R&O AW-68	Moly Special Duty #20
PE-700-A	150	Heavy Inhibited Hydraulic & Gen. Purpose	630–770	Ken-Tran 080	Moly Special Duty #40
PE-150-HP	32	High-Pressure (Anti-Wear) Hydraulic Oil	135–165	Kenoil R&O AW-32	Moly Hydro-Servoil #303
PE-215-HP	46	High-Pressure (Anti-Wear) Hydraulic Oil	194–236	Kenoil R&O AW-46	Moly Hydro-Servoil #304
PE-315-HP	68	High-Pressure (Anti-Wear) Hydraulic Oil	284–346	Kenoil R&O AW-68	Moly Hydro-Servoil #305
PE-FRH-1	—	Fire-Resistant Hyd. Fluid/Synthetic		NR	NR
PE-FRH-2	—	Fire-Resistant Hyd. Fluid/Water-Glycol		NR	NR
PE-FRH-3	—	Fire-Resistant Hyd. Fluid/Water-Oil Emulsion		NR	FR Fluid-Invert Emulsion
PE-32-B	2	Very Light Spindle Oil (Over 6000 rpm)	29–35	NR	Moly Spindle Oil Extra Light
PE-60-B	10	Light Spindle Oil (3600–6000 rpm)	54–66	NR	Moly Spindle Oil Light
PE-105-B	22	Spindle Oil (Up to 3600 rpm)	95–115	Kenoil 040	Moly Spindle Oil Medium
PE-150-C	32	Light Way Oil	135–165	Kenoil 945 EP	Moly Way Oil #10
PE-315-C	68	Medium Way Oil	284–346	NR	Moly Way Oil #20
PE-1000-C	220	Heavy Way Oil	900–1100	Kenoil 985 EP	Moly Way Oil #50
PE-700-D	150	Light Gear Oil	630–770	Ken-Tran 080	Moly Gear Oil #89
PE-1000-D	220	Medium Gear Oil	900–1100	All Oil Gear Lube 85W-90	Moly Gear Oil 90 or 89
PE-2150-D	460	Heavy Gear Oil	1935–2365	All Oil Gear Lube 140	Moly Gear Oil 140 or 123
PE-315-E	68	Light Extreme-Pressure Gear Oil	283–347	NR	Moly Gear Oil RM 300
PE-1500-E	320	Heavy Extreme-Pressure Gear Oil	1350–1650	Three Star Gear Lube	Moly Gear Oil #123
PE-OG-G	—	Cling-Type Gear Shield (Open Gears)		SR 12X	Moly Open Gear Medium
PE-GPG-2	—	Gen. Purpose E.P. Lithium-Base Grease	NLGI2	L-426	GP-2 or 7 Plus 2
PE-MG-2	—	Molybdenum Disulfide E.P. Grease		L-424	7 Plus 2

NR = No recommendation
1. Does not contain tackiness additives normally found in way lubricants. Formulated to perform as combination hydraulic oil and way lubricant.
2. To be used where grades 90, 125, and 140 are recommended.
3. Not lithium base, but equals or exceeds application requirements.
4. Falls outside specified viscosity range, but meets application requirements.
5. Not moly grease, but exceeds application requirements.
6. Straight phosphate ester fluids available in four viscosity grades.
7. Available in range of viscosities.
8. Various ISO grades.
9. Synthetic lubricants.
10. All products formulated from polyalkylene glycol base stocks.
11. Anhydrous product, but water soluble.

Table 19.1 Chart of Interchangeable Lubricants (continued)

Plant Engineering Designation	ISO Viscosity Grade	Lubricant Type	Viscosity, SUS at 100°F	Keystone Div. Pennwalt Corp.	Leahy-Wolf Co.
PE-150-A	32	Light Inhibited Hydraulic & Gen. Purpose	135–165	KLC-6	Gold Seal Hydrol W
PE-215-A	46	Med. Inhibited Hydraulic & Gen. Purpose	194–236	KLC-5	Gold Seal Hydrol W-H
PE-315-A	68	Med.-Heavy Inhibited Hyd. & Gen. Purpose	284–346	KLC-4A	Gold Seal Hydrol S
PE-700-A	150	Heavy Inhibited Hydraulic & Gen. Purpose	630–770	KLC-3	Gold Seal Hydrol 400
PE-150-HP	32	High-Pressure (Anti-Wear) Hydraulic Oil	135–165	KLC-6	Hydrol Master WHD
PE-215-HP	46	High-Pressure (Anti-Wear) Hydraulic Oil	194–236	KLC-5	Hydrol Master WHHD
PE-315-HP	68	High-Pressure (Anti-Wear) Hydraulic Oil	284–346	KLC-4A	Hydrol Master SHD
PE-FRH-1	—	Fire-Resistant Hyd. Fluid/Synthetic		NR	Hydrol Master FR-S
PE-FRH-2	—	Fire-Resistant Hyd. Fluid/Water-Glycol		NR	Hydrol Master FR-G
PE-FRH-3	—	Fire-Resistant Hyd. Fluid/Water-Oil Emulsion		NR	Hydrol Master FR-FWE
PE-32-B	2	Very Light Spindle Oil (Over 6000 rpm)	29–35	NR	NR
PE-60-B	10	Light Spindle Oil (3600–6000 rpm)	54–66	NR	Lubemaster MAA
PE-105-B	22	Spindle Oil (Up to 3600 rpm)	95–115	Spindle Oil #4	Lubemaster MA
PE-150-C	32	Light Way Oil	135–165	NR	Tac Master EP 1000
PE-315-C	68	Medium Way Oil	284–346	GP-20	Tac Master EP 2000
PE-1000-C	220	Heavy Way Oil	900–1100	GP-30	Tac Master EP 5000
PE-700-D	150	Light Gear Oil	630–770	KLC-3	Gold Seal Hydrol 400
PE-1000-D	220	Medium Gear Oil	900–1100	1790	Gold Seal Hydrol 500
PE-2150-D	460	Heavy Gear Oil	1935–2365	1791	Gold Seal Hydrol 700
PE-315-E	68	Light Extreme-Pressure Gear Oil	283–347	NR	Industrial EP 2000
PE-1500-E	320	Heavy Extreme-Pressure Gear Oil	1350–1650	WG-1	Industrial EP 6000
PE-OG-G	—	Cling-Type Gear Shield (Open Gears)		426	Metallic Gear Cote
PE-GPG-2	—	Gen. Purpose E.P. Lithium-Base Grease	NLGI2	81 EP LT	Lith Master 200
PE-MG-2	—	Molybdenum Disulfide E.P. Grease		NR	Lith Moly Master 200

Plant Engineering Designation	ISO Viscosity Grade	Lubricant Type	Viscosity, SUS at 100°F	LubraSystems	Lubrication Analysis, Inc.
PE-150-A	32	Light Inhibited Hydraulic & Gen. Purpose	135–165	SHO 32 or 1GM 5W-20	Hyd. Oil 150
PE-215-A	46	Med. Inhibited Hydraulic & Gen. Purpose	194–236	SHO 46 or 1GM 5W-20	Hyd. Oil 250
PE-315-A	68	Med.-Heavy Inhibited Hyd. & Gen. Purpose	284–346	SHO 68	Hyd. Oil 300
PE-700-A	150	Heavy Inhibited Hydraulic & Gen. Purpose	630–770	SHO 150	Hyd. Oil 700
PE-150-HP	32	High-Pressure (Anti-Wear) Hydraulic Oil	135–165	SHO 32 or MHO 10W-30	Hyd. Oil AW 150
PE-215-HP	46	High-Pressure (Anti-Wear) Hydraulic Oil	194–236	SHO 46 or MHO 10W-30	Hyd. Oil AW 250
PE-315-HP	68	High-Pressure (Anti-Wear) Hydraulic Oil	284–346	SHO 68 or MHO 10W-30	Hyd. Oil AW 300
PE-FRH-1	—	Fire-Resistant Hyd. Fluid/Synthetic		NR	NR
PE-FRH-2	—	Fire-Resistant Hyd. Fluid/Water-Glycol		NR	FR-Oil #3
PE-FRH-3	—	Fire-Resistant Hyd. Fluid/Water-Oil Emulsion		NR	NR
PE-32-B	2	Very Light Spindle Oil (Over 6000 rpm)	29–35	NR	Spindle Oil 32
PE-60-B	10	Light Spindle Oil (3600–6000 rpm)	54–66	SPL 10	Spindle Oil 60
PE-105-B	22	Spindle Oil (Up to 3600 rpm)	95–115	SPL 22	Spindle Oil 100
PE-150-C	32	Light Way Oil	135–165	NR	Way Oil 150
PE-315-C	68	Medium Way Oil	284–346	WAL 68	Way Oil 300
PE-1000-C	220	Heavy Way Oil	900–1100	WAL 220	Way Oil 1000
PE-700-D	150	Light Gear Oil	630–770	SHO 150	Gear Oil 700
PE-1000-D	220	Medium Gear Oil	900–1100	SHO 220	Gear Oil 900
PE-2150-D	460	Heavy Gear Oil	1935–2365	MIG 85W-140	Gear Oil 140
PE-315-E	68	Light Extreme-Pressure Gear Oil	283–347	NR	Gear Oil EP 300
PE-1500-E	320	Heavy Extreme-Pressure Gear Oil	1350–1650	1GO 80W-140	Gear Oil EP 1300
PE-OG-G	—	Cling-Type Gear Shield (Open Gears)		AOG	Spray Gear Lube
PE-GPG-2	—	Gen. Purpose E.P. Lithium-Base Grease	NLGI2	MML EP2	#2 Grease
PE-MG-2	—	Molybdenum Disulfide E.P. Grease		PCL EP2 or HTL EP2	#2 Moly Grease

NR = No recommendation
1. Does not contain tackiness additives normally found in way lubricants. Formulated to perform as combination hydraulic oil and way lubricant.
2. To be used where grades 90, 125, and 140 are recommended.
3. Not lithium base, but equals or exceeds application requirements.
4. Falls outside specified viscosity range, but meets application requirements.
5. Not moly grease, but exceeds application requirements.
6. Straight phosphate ester fluids available in four viscosity grades.
7. Available in range of viscosities.
8. Various ISO grades.
9. Synthetic lubricants.
10. All products formulated from polyalkylene glycol base stocks.
11. Anhydrous product, but water soluble.

Table 19.1 Chart of Interchangeable Lubricants (continued)

Plant Engineering Designation	ISO Viscosity Grade	Lubricant Type	Viscosity, SUS at 100°F	Lubriplate Div. Fiske Brothers Refining Co.	Luscon Industries Corp.
PE-150-A	32	Light Inhibited Hydraulic & Gen. Purpose	135–165	HO-0	Hydralube 32
PE-215-A	46	Med. Inhibited Hydraulic & Gen. Purpose	194–236	HO-1	Hydralube 46
PE-315-A	68	Med.-Heavy Inhibited Hyd. & Gen. Purpose	284–346	HO-2	Hydralube 68
PE-700-A	150	Heavy Inhibited Hydraulic & Gen. Purpose	630–770	HO-3	Hydralube 150
PE-150-HP	32	High-Pressure (Anti-Wear) Hydraulic Oil	135–165	HO-0	Hydralube XD32 or 32AW
PE-215-HP	46	High-Pressure (Anti-Wear) Hydraulic Oil	194–236	HO-1	Hydralube XD46 or 46AW
PE-315-HP	68	High-Pressure (Anti-Wear) Hydraulic Oil	284–346	HO-2	Hydralube XD68 or 68AW
PE-FRH-1	—	Fire-Resistant Hyd. Fluid/Synthetic		NR	Unisafe SF
PE-FRH-2	—	Fire-Resistant Hyd. Fluid/Water-Glycol		NR	Unisafe 40XD
PE-FRH-3	—	Fire-Resistant Hyd. Fluid/Water-Oil Emulsion		NR	Unisafe WO
PE-32-B	2	Very Light Spindle Oil (Over 6000 rpm)	29–35	NR	ISOSOLV 30
PE-60-B	10	Light Spindle Oil (3600–6000 rpm)	54–66	No. 0	Hydralube T-10
PE-105-B	22	Spindle Oil (Up to 3600 rpm)	95–115	No. 1	Hydralube T-22
PE-150-C	32	Light Way Oil	135–165	No. 1	Waylube 32
PE-315-C	68	Medium Way Oil	284–346	No. 3-V	Waylube 68
PE-1000-C	220	Heavy Way Oil	900–1100	No. 4	Waylube 220
PE-700-D	150	Light Gear Oil	630–770	APG 80	Hydralube 150
PE-1000-D	220	Medium Gear Oil	900–1100	APG 90	Hydralube 220
PE-2150-D	460	Heavy Gear Oil	1935–2365	APG 140	Hydralube 460
PE-315-E	68	Light Extreme-Pressure Gear Oil	283–347	APG 80	EP Compound 68
PE-1500-E	320	Heavy Extreme-Pressure Gear Oil	1350–1650	APG 140	EP Compound 320
PE-OG-G	—	Cling-Type Gear Shield (Open Gears)		Gear Shield	ALGO M-90
PE-GPG-2	—	Gen. Purpose E.P. Lithium-Base Grease	NLGI2	No. 630-2	Lithium Grease #2
PE-MG-2	—	Molybdenum Disulfide E.P. Grease		Mo-Lith No. 2	Moly Grease #2

Total Lubrication

Plant Engineering Designation	ISO Viscosity Grade	Lubricant Type	Viscosity, SUS at 100°F	Mainpro, Inc.	Mantek
PE-150-A	32	Light Inhibited Hydraulic & Gen. Purpose	135–165	Ultra Shield 5000-10	MHY 32
PE-215-A	46	Med. Inhibited Hydraulic & Gen. Purpose	194–236	NR	MHY 46
PE-315-A	68	Med.-Heavy Inhibited Hyd. & Gen. Purpose	284–346	Ultra Shield 5000-20	MHY 68
PE-700-A	150	Heavy Inhibited Hydraulic & Gen. Purpose	630–770	Ultra Shield 5000-30	MHY 150
PE-150-HP	32	High-Pressure (Anti-Wear) Hydraulic Oil	135–165	Ultra Shield 5000-10	MHY 32
PE-215-HP	46	High-Pressure (Anti-Wear) Hydraulic Oil	194–236	NR	MHY 46
PE-315-HP	68	High-Pressure (Anti-Wear) Hydraulic Oil	284–346	Ultra Shield 5000-20	MHY 68
PE-FRH-1	—	Fire-Resistant Hyd. Fluid/Synthetic		NR	NR
PE-FRH-2	—	Fire-Resistant Hyd. Fluid/Water-Glycol		NR	NR
PE-FRH-3	—	Fire-Resistant Hyd. Fluid/Water-Oil Emulsion		NR	NR
PE-32-B	2	Very Light Spindle Oil (Over 6000 rpm)	29–35	NR	NR
PE-60-B	10	Light Spindle Oil (3600–6000 rpm)	54–66	NR	MSP 10
PE-105-B	22	Spindle Oil (Up to 3600 rpm)	95–115	NR	MSP 22
PE-150-C	32	Light Way Oil	135–165	US EP Pneumatic 10	NR
PE-315-C	68	Medium Way Oil	284–346	US EP Pneumatic 20	MWL 68
PE-1000-C	220	Heavy Way Oil	900–1100	US EP Pneumatic 40	MWL 220
PE-700-D	150	Light Gear Oil	630–770	TK-65 80/90	MHY 150
PE-1000-D	220	Medium Gear Oil	900–1100	TK-65 85W/140	MHY 220
PE-2150-D	460	Heavy Gear Oil	1935–2365	TK-65 140	Manco MP 85W-140
PE-315-E	68	Light Extreme-Pressure Gear Oil	283–347	TK-100 20	NR
PE-1500-E	320	Heavy Extreme-Pressure Gear Oil	1350–1650	TK-100 85W/140	Acclaim 80W-140
PE-OG-G	—	Cling-Type Gear Shield (Open Gears)		TK-100 140	NR
PE-GPG-2	—	Gen. Purpose E.P. Lithium-Base Grease	NLGI2	Pro Lube 600	Staunch EP2
PE-MG-2	—	Molybdenum Disulfide E.P. Grease		Pro Lube 800	Manco Moly EP2 or Elite EP2

NR = No recommendation
1. Does not contain tackiness additives normally found in way lubricants. Formulated to perform as combination hydraulic oil and way lubricant.
2. To be used where grades 90, 125, and 140 are recommended.
3. Not lithium base, but equals or exceeds application requirements.
4. Falls outside specified viscosity range, but meets application requirements.
5. Not moly grease, but exceeds application requirements.
6. Straight phosphate ester fluids available in four viscosity grades.
7. Available in range of viscosities.
8. Various ISO grades.
9. Synthetic lubricants.
10. All products formulated from polyalkylene glycol base stocks.
11. Anhydrous product, but water soluble.

Table 19.1 Chart of Interchangeable Lubricants (continued)

Plant Engineering Designation	ISO Viscosity Grade	Lubricant Type	Viscosity, SUS at 100°F	A. Margolis & Sons Corp.	McCollister & Co. (United Petroleum Corp.)
PE-150-A	32	Light Inhibited Hydraulic & Gen. Purpose	135–165	Silogram TIP 100-15-7	Univis R&O 32
PE-215-A	46	Med. Inhibited Hydraulic & Gen. Purpose	194–236	Silogram TIP 100-20-7	Univis R&O 46
PE-315-A	68	Med.-Heavy Inhibited Hyd. & Gen. Purpose	284–346	Silogram TIP 100-30-7	Univis R&O 68
PE-700-A	150	Heavy Inhibited Hydraulic & Gen. Purpose	630–770	Silogram MP 707	Univis R&O 150
PE-150-HP	32	High-Pressure (Anti-Wear) Hydraulic Oil	135–165	Silogram TIP 100-15-7	Univis Hyd. AW 32
PE-215-HP	46	High-Pressure (Anti-Wear) Hydraulic Oil	194–236	Silogram TIP 100-20-7	Univis Hyd. AW 46
PE-315-HP	68	High-Pressure (Anti-Wear) Hydraulic Oil	284–346	Silogram TIP 100-30-7	Univis Hyd. AW 68
PE-FRH-1	—	Fire-Resistant Hyd. Fluid/Synthetic		NR	NR
PE-FRH-2	—	Fire-Resistant Hyd. Fluid/Water-Glycol		Silogram FR Fluid 200	NR
PE-FRH-3	—	Fire-Resistant Hyd. Fluid/Water-Oil Emulsion		Silogram FR Emulsion Fluid	NR
PE-32-B	2	Very Light Spindle Oil (Over 6000 rpm)	29–35	Silogram LVS 35	NR
PE-60-B	10	Light Spindle Oil (3600–6000 rpm)	54–66	Silogram LVS 60	NR
PE-105-B	22	Spindle Oil (Up to 3600 rpm)	95–115	Silogram LVS 100	NR
PE-150-C	32	Light Way Oil	135–165	Silogram MP 157	Way Oil 32
PE-315-C	68	Medium Way Oil	284–346	Silogram MP 307	Way Oil 68
PE-1000-C	220	Heavy Way Oil	900–1100	Silogram MP 907	Way Oil 220
PE-700-D	150	Light Gear Oil	630–770	Silogram MP 707	Univis AW 150
PE-1000-D	220	Medium Gear Oil	900–1100	Silogram MP 907	Univis AW 220
PE-2150-D	460	Heavy Gear Oil	1935–2365	Silogram EP Gear 140	Univis AW 460
PE-315-E	68	Light Extreme-Pressure Gear Oil	283–347	Silogram EP Gear 80	EP 68 Gear Comp
PE-1500-E	320	Heavy Extreme-Pressure Gear Oil	1350–1650	Silogram EP Gear 90	EP 320 Gear Comp
PE-OG-G	—	Cling-Type Gear Shield (Open Gears)		Silogram Moly Cling	NR
PE-GPG-2	—	Gen. Purpose E.P. Lithium-Base Grease	NLGI2	Silogram Centralized EP 2	MP Lithium
PE-MG-2	—	Molybdenum Disulfide E.P. Grease		Silogram HD MO-Lith	Moly Poly Lithium Complex

Total Lubrication 229

Plant Engineering Designation	ISO Viscosity Grade	Lubricant Type	Viscosity, SUS at 100°F	McGean-Rohco, Inc. Rohco Div.	Metal Lubricants Co.
PE-150-A	32	Light Inhibited Hydraulic & Gen. Purpose	135–165	McEase AW/AL Polymer Oil 10	Meltran AW 405
PE-215-A	46	Med. Inhibited Hydraulic & Gen. Purpose	194–236	McEase AW/AL Polymer Oil 10	Meltran AW 410
PE-315-A	68	Med.–Heavy Inhibited Hyd. & Gen. Purpose	284–346	McEase AW/AL Polymer Oil 20	Meltran AW 420
PE-700-A	150	Heavy Inhibited Hydraulic & Gen. Purpose	630–770	McEase 75W/90 Polymer Oil	Meltran AW 440
PE-150-HP	32	High-Pressure (Anti-Wear) Hydraulic Oil	135–165	McEase AW/AL Polymer Oil 10	Meltran AW 405
PE-215-HP	46	High-Pressure (Anti-Wear) Hydraulic Oil	194–236	McEase AW/AL Polymer Oil 20	Meltran AW 410
PE-315-HP	68	High-Pressure (Anti-Wear) Hydraulic Oil	284–346	McEase AW/AL Polymer Oil 30	Meltran AW 420
PE-FRH-1	—	Fire-Resistant Hyd. Fluid/Synthetic		NR	NR
PE-FRH-2	—	Fire-Resistant Hyd. Fluid/Water-Glycol		NR	Melsyn FR 200
PE-FRH-3	—	Fire-Resistant Hyd. Fluid/Water-Oil Emulsion		NR	NR
PE-32-B	2	Very Light Spindle Oil (Over 6000 rpm)	29–35	McEase AW/AL Polymer Oil 10	NR
PE-60-B	10	Light Spindle Oil (3600–6000 rpm)	54–66	McEase AW/AL Polymer Oil 10	Melspin 5
PE-105-B	22	Spindle Oil (Up to 3600 rpm)	95–115	McEase AW/AL Polymer Oil 10	Melspin 3
PE-150-C	32	Light Way Oil	135–165	McEase AW/AL Polymer Oil 10	Meltac WL-221
PE-315-C	68	Medium Way Oil	284–346	McEase AW/AL Polymer Oil 20	Meltac WL-222
PE-1000-C	220	Heavy Way Oil	900–1100	McEase 75W/90 Polymer Oil	Meltac WL-224
PE-700-D	150	Light Gear Oil	630–770	McEase 75W/90 Polymer Gear Oil	Meltran AW 440
PE-1000-D	220	Medium Gear Oil	900–1100	McEase 80W/140 Polymer Gear Oil	Meltran AW 450
PE-2150-D	460	Heavy Gear Oil	1935–2365	NR	Meltran AW 480
PE-315-E	68	Light Extreme-Pressure Gear Oil	283–347	McEase AW/AL Polymer Oil 30	Melcolube 101-CP
PE-1500-E	320	Heavy Extreme-Pressure Gear Oil	1350–1650	McEase 80W/140 Polymer Oil	Melcolube 105-CP
PE-OG-G	—	Cling-Type Gear Shield (Open Gears)		NR	NR
PE-GPG-2	—	Gen. Purpose E.P. Lithium-Base Grease	NLGI2	McEase MLC-2	Melco PM-2
PE-MG-2	—	Molybdenum Disulfide E.P. Grease		NR	Melcomoly 1433

NR = No recommendation
1. Does not contain tackiness additives normally found in way lubricants. Formulated to perform as combination hydraulic oil and way lubricant.
2. To be used where grades 90, 125, and 140 are recommended.
3. Not lithium base, but equals or exceeds application requirements.
4. Falls outside specified viscosity range, but meets application requirements.
5. Not moly grease, but exceeds application requirements.
6. Straight phosphate ester fluids available in four viscosity grades.
7. Available in range of viscosities.
8. Various ISO grades.
9. Synthetic lubricants.
10. All products formulated from polyalkylene glycol base stocks.
11. Anhydrous product, but water soluble.

Table 19.1 Chart of Interchangeable Lubricants (continued)

Plant Engineering Designation	ISO Viscosity Grade	Lubricant Type	Viscosity, SUS at 100°F	Metalworking Lubricants Co.	Mobil Oil Corp.
PE-150-A	32	Light Inhibited Hydraulic & Gen. Purpose	135–165	Metlube H-100	Mobil DTE Oil Light
PE-215-A	46	Med. Inhibited Hydraulic & Gen. Purpose	194–236	Metlube H-200	Mobil DTE Oil Med.
PE-315-A	68	Med.-Heavy Inhibited Hyd. & Gen. Purpose	284–346	Metlube H-300	Mobil DTE Oil Med-Hvy.
PE-700-A	150	Heavy Inhibited Hydraulic & Gen. Purpose	630–770	Metlube H-700	Mobil DTE Oil Extra Heavy
PE-150-HP	32	High-Pressure (Anti-Wear) Hydraulic Oil	135–165	Metlube H-150AW	Mobil DTE 24
PE-215-HP	46	High-Pressure (Anti-Wear) Hydraulic Oil	194–236	Metlube H-200AW	Mobil DTE 25
PE-315-HP	68	High-Pressure (Anti-Wear) Hydraulic Oil	284–346	Metlube H-300AW	Mobil DTE 26
PE-FRH-1	—	Fire-Resistant Hyd. Fluid/Synthetic		Metsafe FR 310	Mobil Pyrogard 53
PE-FRH-2	—	Fire-Resistant Hyd. Fluid/Water-Glycol		Metsafe FR 200	Nyvac FR 200 Fluid
PE-FRH-3	—	Fire-Resistant Hyd. Fluid/Water-Oil Emulsion		Metsafe IFR	Mobil Pyrogard D
PE-32-B	2	Very Light Spindle Oil (Over 6000 rpm)	29–35	99C21	Mobil Velocite Oil #3
PE-60-B	10	Light Spindle Oil (3600–6000 rpm)	54–66	Metlube MS	Mobil Velocite Oil #6
PE-105-B	22	Spindle Oil (Up to 3600 rpm)	95–115	Metway 100	Mobil Velocite Oil #10
PE-150-C	32	Light Way Oil	135–165	Lubernet 150	Mobil Vactra Oil #1
PE-315-C	68	Medium Way Oil	284–346	Lubernet 4868A	Mobil Vactra Oil #2
PE-1000-C	220	Heavy Way Oil	900–1100	Lubernet 4868B	Mobil Vactra Oil #4
PE-700-D	150	Light Gear Oil	630–770	Lubernet 4622D	Mobil DTE Oil Extra Heavy
PE-1000-D	220	Medium Gear Oil	900–1100	Lubernet 4622A	Mobil DTE Oil BB
PE-2150-D	460	Heavy Gear Oil	1935–2365	Lubernet 4622B	Mobil DTE Oil HH
PE-315-E	68	Light Extreme-Pressure Gear Oil	283–347	Lubernet 2EP	Mobilgear 626
PE-1500-E	320	Heavy Extreme-Pressure Gear Oil	1350–1650	Lubernet 1500	Mobilgear 632
PE-OG-G	—	Cling-Type Gear Shield (Open Gears)		NR	Mobiltac A
PE-GPG-2	—	Gen. Purpose E.P. Lithium-Base Grease	NLGI2	Lubernet M1C21	Mobilux EP2
PE-MG-2	—	Molybdenum Disulfide E.P. Grease		NR	NR

Total Lubrication

Plant Engineering Designation	ISO Viscosity Grade	Lubricant Type	Viscosity, SUS at 100°F	Moroil Corp.	National Chemsearch
PE-150-A	32	Light Inhibited Hydraulic & Gen. Purpose	135-165	R&O 100	HLN-32 or Soludize 5W-20
PE-215-A	46	Med. Inhibited Hydraulic & Gen. Purpose	194-236	R&O 200	HLN-46 or Soludize 5W-20
PE-315-A	68	Med.-Heavy Inhibited Hyd. & Gen. Purpose	284-346	R&O 300	HLN-68
PE-700-A	150	Heavy Inhibited Hydraulic & Gen. Purpose	630-770	R&O 750	HLN-150
PE-150-HP	32	High-Pressure (Anti-Wear) Hydraulic Oil	135-165	AW/AL 100	HLN-32 or Enerlex 10W-30
PE-215-HP	46	High-Pressure (Anti-Wear) Hydraulic Oil	194-236	AW/AL 200	HLN-46 or Enerlex 10W-30
PE-315-HP	68	High-Pressure (Anti-Wear) Hydraulic Oil	284-346	AW/AL 300	HLN-68 or Enerlex 10W-30
PE-FRH-1	—	Fire-Resistant Hyd. Fluid/Synthetic		SNF[8]	NR
PE-FRH-2	—	Fire-Resistant Hyd. Fluid/Water-Glycol		NFH[6]	NR
PE-FRH-3	—	Fire-Resistant Hyd. Fluid/Water-Oil Emulsion		NR	NR
PE-32-B	2	Very Light Spindle Oil (Over 6000 rpm)	29-35	NR	NR
PE-60-B	10	Light Spindle Oil (3600-6000 rpm)	54-66	Spindle Oil 10	SLN 10
PE-105-B	22	Spindle Oil (Up to 3600 rpm)	95-115	Spindle Oil 22	SLN 22
PE-150-C	32	Light Way Oil	135-165	Way Oil 32	NR
PE-315-C	68	Medium Way Oil	284-346	Way Oil 68	WLN 68
PE-1000-C	220	Heavy Way Oil	900-1100	Way Oil 220	WLN 220
PE-700-D	150	Light Gear Oil	630-770	Indlube 5-150	HLN 150
PE-1000-D	220	Medium Gear Oil	900-1100	Indlube 5-220	HLN 220
PE-2150-D	460	Heavy Gear Oil	1935-2365	Indlube 5-460	Gearco 85W/140
PE-315-E	68	Light Extreme-Pressure Gear Oil	283-347	Indlube 10-68	NR
PE-1500-E	320	Heavy Extreme-Pressure Gear Oil	1350-1650	Indlube 10-320	Effi-cient 80W-140
PE-OG-G	—	Cling-Type Gear Shield (Open Gears)		NR	GEX
PE-GPG-2	—	Gen. Purpose E.P. Lithium-Base Grease	NLGI2	NR	Lube Plus EP2 or Chem-A-Lube NL 660 EP2
PE-MG-2	—	Molybdenum Disulfide E.P. Grease		NR	Lube Shield EP2

NR = No recommendation
1. Does not contain tackiness additives normally found in way lubricants. Formulated to perform as combination hydraulic oil and way lubricant.
2. To be used where grades 90, 125, and 140 are recommended.
3. Not lithium base, but equals or exceeds application requirements.
4. Falls outside specified viscosity range, but meets application requirements.
5. Not moly grease, but exceeds application requirements.
6. Straight phosphate ester fluids available in four viscosity grades.
7. Available in range of viscosities.
8. Various ISO grades.
9. Synthetic lubricants.
10. All products formulated from polyalkylene glycol base stocks.
11. Anhydrous product, but water soluble.

Table 19.1 Chart of Interchangeable Lubricants (continued)

Plant Engineering Designation	ISO Viscosity Grade	Lubricant Type	Viscosity, SUS at 100°F	Niagara Lubricant Co., Inc.	NonFluid Oil Corp.
PE-150-A	32	Light Inhibited Hydraulic & Gen. Purpose	135–165	Nia Vis R&O 32	1183
PE-215-A	46	Med. Inhibited Hydraulic & Gen. Purpose	194–236	Nia Vis R&O 46	1184
PE-315-A	68	Med.-Heavy Inhibited Hyd. & Gen. Purpose	284–346	Nia Vis R&O 68	1185
PE-700-A	150	Heavy Inhibited Hydraulic & Gen. Purpose	630–770	Nia Vis R&O 150	NR
PE-150-HP	32	High-Pressure (Anti-Wear) Hydraulic Oil	135–165	Nia Vis R&O AW 32	1183
PE-215-HP	46	High-Pressure (Anti-Wear) Hydraulic Oil	194–236	Nia Vis R&O AW 46	1184
PE-315-HP	68	High-Pressure (Anti-Wear) Hydraulic Oil	284–346	Nia Vis R&O AW 68	1185
PE-FRH-1	—	Fire-Resistant Hyd. Fluid/Synthetic		NR	FRHF #68 CI
PE-FRH-2	—	Fire-Resistant Hyd. Fluid/Water-Glycol		Nilco Hydrolube 446	NR
PE-FRH-3	—	Fire-Resistant Hyd. Fluid/Water-Oil Emulsion		NR	NR
PE-32-B	2	Very Light Spindle Oil (Over 6000 rpm)	29–35	NR	NR
PE-60-B	10	Light Spindle Oil (3600–6000 rpm)	54–66	Spindol 10	300 HSSO
PE-105-B	22	Spindle Oil (Up to 3600 rpm)	95–115	Spindol 22	SP Oil #30
PE-150-C	32	Light Way Oil	135–165	Niagara Waylube 32	NR
PE-315-C	68	Medium Way Oil	284–346	Niagara Waylube 68	NR
PE-1000-C	220	Heavy Way Oil	900–1100	Niagara Waylube 220	NR
PE-700-D	150	Light Gear Oil	630–770	Aragain 150	Gear Pro #4
PE-1000-D	220	Medium Gear Oil	900–1100	Aragain 220	Gear Pro #5
PE-2150-D	460	Heavy Gear Oil	1935–2365	Aragain 460	Gear Pro #7
PE-315-E	68	Light Extreme-Pressure Gear Oil	283–347	Aragain EP 68	Gear Pro #2/EP
PE-1500-E	320	Heavy Extreme-Pressure Gear Oil	1350–1650	Aragain EP 320	Gear Pro #6/EP
PE-OG-G	—	Cling-Type Gear Shield (Open Gears)		Gear Shield Spec. X9277	B-576/MS
PE-GPG-2	—	Gen. Purpose E.P. Lithium-Base Grease	NLGI2	Tri-Gard EP #2	G-60/EPV
PE-MG-2	—	Molybdenum Disulfide E.P. Grease		EP Poly Moly #2	Chem-Plex 2/MS

Total Lubrication

Plant Engineering Designation	ISO Viscosity Grade	Lubricant Type	Viscosity, SUS at 100°F	North American Chemical of Texas	The Ore-Lube Corp.
PE-150-A	32	Light Inhibited Hydraulic & Gen. Purpose	135–165	Power Lube 815	00230
PE-215-A	46	Med. Inhibited Hydraulic & Gen. Purpose	194–236	Power Lube 802	00230
PE-315-A	68	Med.-Heavy Inhibited Hyd. & Gen. Purpose	284–346	Power Lube 803	00230
PE-700-A	150	Heavy Inhibited Hydraulic & Gen. Purpose	630–770	Power Lube 807	00230-40
PE-150-HP	32	High-Pressure (Anti-Wear) Hydraulic Oil	135–165	Power Lube 8	00230
PE-215-HP	46	High-Pressure (Anti-Wear) Hydraulic Oil	194–236	Power Lube 8	00230
PE-315-HP	68	High-Pressure (Anti-Wear) Hydraulic Oil	284–346	Power Lube 803	00230
PE-FRH-1	—	Fire-Resistant Hyd. Fluid/Synthetic		Fluid Power FR-200	00141
PE-FRH-2	—	Fire-Resistant Hyd. Fluid/Water-Glycol		Fluid Power GHF-20	00265
PE-FRH-3	—	Fire-Resistant Hyd. Fluid/Water-Oil Emulsion		Fluid Power 1810	NR
PE-32-B	2	Very Light Spindle Oil (Over 6000 rpm)	29–35	Precision 1924	00227
PE-60-B	10	Light Spindle Oil (3600–6000 rpm)	54–66	Precision 1925	00106
PE-105-B	22	Spindle Oil (Up to 3600 rpm)	95–115	Precision 1926	00107
PE-150-C	32	Light Way Oil	135–165	Lube Way 15	00171
PE-315-C	68	Medium Way Oil	284–346	Lube Way 30	00300
PE-1000-C	220	Heavy Way Oil	900–1100	Lube Way 90	00301
PE-700-D	150	Light Gear Oil	630–770	Gear Guard 60	00214
PE-1000-D	220	Medium Gear Oil	900–1100	Gear Guard 90	00173
PE-2150-D	460	Heavy Gear Oil	1935–2365	Gear Guard 200	00292
PE-315-E	68	Light Extreme-Pressure Gear Oil	283–347	Gear Guard 30	00214
PE-1500-E	320	Heavy Extreme-Pressure Gear Oil	1350–1650	Gear Guard 130	00292
PE-OG-G	—	Cling-Type Gear Shield (Open Gears)		Gear Cling	10164
PE-GPG-2	—	Gen. Purpose E.P. Lithium-Base Grease	NLGI2	Omegaline 2L	10260[3]
PE-MG-2	—	Molybdenum Disulfide E.P. Grease		Omegaline 2L-M	10260

NR = No recommendation
1. Does not contain tackiness additives normally found in way lubricants. Formulated to perform as combination hydraulic oil and way lubricant.
2. To be used where grades 90, 125, and 140 are recommended.
3. Not lithium base, but equals or exceeds application requirements.
4. Falls outside specified viscosity range, but meets application requirements.
5. Not moly grease, but exceeds application requirements.
6. Straight phosphate ester fluids available in four viscosity grades.
7. Available in range of viscosities.
8. Various ISO grades.
9. Synthetic lubricants.
10. All products formulated from polyalkylene glycol base stocks.
11. Anhydrous product, but water soluble.

Table 19.1 Chart of Interchangeable Lubricants *(continued)*

Plant Engineering Designation	ISO Viscosity Grade	Lubricant Type	Viscosity, SUS at 100°F	Pacer Lubricants, Inc.	Parr Inc.
PE-150-A	32	Light Inhibited Hydraulic & Gen. Purpose	135–165	Thermal T 32 (150)	NR
PE-215-A	46	Med. Inhibited Hydraulic & Gen. Purpose	194–236	Thermal T 46 (215)	Hydroil EP 82X
PE-315-A	68	Med.-Heavy Inhibited Hyd. & Gen. Purpose	284–346	Thermal T 68 (315)	Hydroil EP 83
PE-700-A	150	Heavy Inhibited Hydraulic & Gen. Purpose	630–770	Thermal T 150 (700)	Hydroil EP 85
PE-150-HP	32	High-Pressure (Anti-Wear) Hydraulic Oil	135–165	Power V 32 (150)	Hydroil AW 32
PE-215-HP	46	High-Pressure (Anti-Wear) Hydraulic Oil	194–236	Power V 46 (215)	Hydroil AW 46
PE-315-HP	68	High-Pressure (Anti-Wear) Hydraulic Oil	284–346	Power V 68 (315)	Hydroil AW 68
PE-FRH-1	—	Fire-Resistant Hyd. Fluid/Synthetic		NR	NR
PE-FRH-2	—	Fire-Resistant Hyd. Fluid/Water-Glycol		NR	NR
PE-FRH-3	—	Fire-Resistant Hyd. Fluid/Water-Oil Emulsion		NR	NR
PE-32-B	2	Very Light Spindle Oil (Over 6000 rpm)	29–35	NR	NR
PE-60-B	10	Light Spindle Oil (3600–6000 rpm)	54–66	Spindle Oil 70	NR
PE-105-B	22	Spindle Oil (Up to 3600 rpm)	95–115	Spindle Oil 100	NR
PE-150-C	32	Light Way Oil	135–165	Tru-Slide 150	NR
PE-315-C	68	Medium Way Oil	284–346	Tru-Slide 300	Way Lubricant #75
PE-1000-C	220	Heavy Way Oil	900–1100	Tru-Slide 1000	882 Gear Lube SAE 90
PE-700-D	150	Light Gear Oil	630–770	Goltex AGMA 4EP	NR
PE-1000-D	220	Medium Gear Oil	900–1100	Goltex AGMA 5EP	882 Gear Lube SAE 90
PE-2150-D	460	Heavy Gear Oil	1935–2365	Goltex AGMA 7EP	882 Gear Lube SAE 140
PE-315-E	68	Light Extreme-Pressure Gear Oil	283–347	Golden G Gearoyl AGMA 2EP	NR
PE-1500-E	320	Heavy Extreme-Pressure Gear Oil	1350–1650	Golden G Gearoyl AGMA 6EP	882 Gear Lube 90 or 140
PE-OG-G	—	Cling-Type Gear Shield (Open Gears)		NR	Plastigear X
PE-GPG-2	—	Gen. Purpose E.P. Lithium-Base Grease	NLGI2	Synfilm LCX	Litholube EPMP #2
PE-MG-2	—	Molybdenum Disulfide E.P. Grease		Lith-O-Mol	Green Gold Moly #2

234   MANAGING MILL MAINTENANCE

Plant Engineering Designation	ISO Viscosity Grade	Lubricant Type	Viscosity, SUS at 100°F	Pennzoil Products Co.	Phillips Petroleum Co.
PE-150-A	32	Light Inhibited Hydraulic & Gen. Purpose	135–165	AW 32 Hyd. Oil/Penreco Oil 32	Magnus Oil 32
PE-215-A	46	Med. Inhibited Hydraulic & Gen. Purpose	194–236	AW 46 Hyd. Oil/Penreco Oil 46	Magnus Oil 46
PE-315-A	68	Med.-Heavy Inhibited Hyd. & Gen. Purpose	284–346	AW 68 Hyd. Oil/Penreco Oil 68	Magnus Oil 68
PE-700-A	150	Heavy Inhibited Hydraulic & Gen. Purpose	630–770	AW 150 Hyd. Oil/Penreco Oil 150	Magnus Oil 150
PE-150-HP	32	High-Pressure (Anti-Wear) Hydraulic Oil	135–165	AW 32 Hyd. Oil/Penreco Oil 32	Magnus A Oil 32
PE-215-HP	46	High-Pressure (Anti-Wear) Hydraulic Oil	194–236	AW 46 Hyd. Oil/Penreco Oil 46	Magnus A Oil 46
PE-315-HP	68	High-Pressure (Anti-Wear) Hydraulic Oil	284–346	AW 68 Hyd. Oil/Penreco Oil 68	Magnus A Oil 68
PE-FRH-1	—	Fire-Resistant Hyd. Fluid/Synthetic		NR	NR
PE-FRH-2	—	Fire-Resistant Hyd. Fluid/Water-Glycol		NR	NR
PE-FRH-3	—	Fire-Resistant Hyd. Fluid/Water-Oil Emulsion		Maxmul Hyd. Fluid FR	NR
PE-32-B	2	Very Light Spindle Oil (Over 6000 rpm)	29–35	NR	NR
PE-60-B	10	Light Spindle Oil (3600–6000 rpm)	54–66	NR	NR
PE-105-B	22	Spindle Oil (Up to 3600 rpm)	95–115	AW 22 Hyd. Oil/Penreco Oil 22	Magnus Oil 32
PE-150-C	32	Light Way Oil	135–165	NR	NR
PE-315-C	68	Medium Way Oil	284–346	Tableways Lube Medium	NR
PE-1000-C	220	Heavy Way Oil	900–1100	Tableways Lube Heavy	NR
PE-700-D	150	Light Gear Oil	630–770	AW 150 Hyd. Oil/Penreco Oil 150	Magnus Oil 150
PE-1000-D	220	Medium Gear Oil	900–1100	AW 220 Hyd. Oil/Penreco Oil 220	Magnus Oil 220
PE-2150-D	460	Heavy Gear Oil	1935–2365	AW 460 Hyd. Oil/Penreco Oil 460	Hector Oil 460 (2000S)
PE-315-E	68	Light Extreme-Pressure Gear Oil	283–347	Maxol EP Gear Oil 68	Philube AP GO 80W
PE-1500-E	320	Heavy Extreme-Pressure Gear Oil	1350–1650	Maxol EP Gear Oil 320	Philube AP GO 85W-90
PE-OG-G	—	Cling-Type Gear Shield (Open Gears)		NR	Philstik D-1 Grease
PE-GPG-2	—	Gen. Purpose E.P. Lithium-Base Grease	NLGI2	707L Lube/Pennlith EP 712 Lube/MP 705 Lube	Philube EP-2
PE-MG-2	—	Molybdenum Disulfide E.P. Grease		Molysulfide 704 Lube/TTM 302 Lube	Philube MW-Grease

NR = No recommendation
1. Does not contain tackiness additives normally found in way lubricants. Formulated to perform as combination hydraulic oil and way lubricant.
2. To be used where grades 90, 125, and 140 are recommended.
3. Not lithium base, but equals or exceeds application requirements.
4. Falls outside specified viscosity range, but meets application requirements.
5. Not moly grease, but exceeds application requirements.
6. Straight phosphate ester fluids available in four viscosity grades.
7. Available in range of viscosities.
8. Various ISO grades.
9. Synthetic lubricants.
10. All products formulated from polyalkylene glycol base stocks.
11. Anhydrous product, but water soluble.

Table 19.1 Chart of Interchangeable Lubricants (continued)

Plant Engineering Designation	ISO Viscosity Grade	Lubricant Type	Viscosity, SUS at 100°F	Pillsbury Chemical & Oil Inc.	Rock Valley Oil & Chemical Co., Inc.
PE-150-A	32	Light Inhibited Hydraulic & Gen. Purpose	135–165	Power Lube 815	Trojan 150
PE-215-A	46	Med. Inhibited Hydraulic & Gen. Purpose	194–236	Power Lube 802	Trojan 200
PE-315-A	68	Med.-Heavy Inhibited Hyd. & Gen. Purpose	284–346	Power Lube 803	Trojan 300
PE-700-A	150	Heavy Inhibited Hydraulic & Gen. Purpose	630–770	Power Lube 807	Trojan 750
PE-150-HP	32	High-Pressure (Anti-Wear) Hydraulic Oil	135–165	Power Lube 815	Trojan 160-AW
PE-215-HP	46	High-Pressure (Anti-Wear) Hydraulic Oil	194–236	Power Lube 802	Trojan 210-AW
PE-315-HP	68	High-Pressure (Anti-Wear) Hydraulic Oil	284–346	Power Lube 803	Trojan 315-AW
PE-FRH-1	—	Fire-Resistant Hyd. Fluid/Synthetic		Fluid Power FR-200	NR
PE-FRH-2	—	Fire-Resistant Hyd. Fluid/Water-Glycol		Fluid Power GHF-20	FR Hyd. Fluid WG-200
PE-FRH-3	—	Fire-Resistant Hyd. Fluid/Water-Oil Emulsion		Fluid Power 1810	NR
PE-32-B	2	Very Light Spindle Oil (Over 6000 rpm)	29–35	Precision 1924	Rockspin 40
PE-60-B	10	Light Spindle Oil (3600–6000 rpm)	54–66	Precision 1925	Rockspin 60
PE-105-B	22	Spindle Oil (Up to 3600 rpm)	95–115	Precision 1926	Rockspin 100
PE-150-C	32	Light Way Oil	135–165	Lube Way 15	Rockway 150-S
PE-315-C	68	Medium Way Oil	284–346	Lube Way 30	Rockway 300-S
PE-1000-C	220	Heavy Way Oil	900–1100	Lube Way 90	Rockway 1000-S
PE-700-D	150	Light Gear Oil	630–770	Gear Guard 60	Trojan 750
PE-1000-D	220	Medium Gear Oil	900–1100	Gear Guard 90	Trojan 1000
PE-2150-D	460	Heavy Gear Oil	1935–2365	Gear Guard 200	Trojan 2000
PE-315-E	68	Light Extreme-Pressure Gear Oil	283–347	Gear Guard 30	EP Gear Lube S-300
PE-1500-E	320	Heavy Extreme-Pressure Gear Oil	1350–1650	Gear Guard 130	EP Gear Lube S-1600
PE-OG-G	—	Cling-Type Gear Shield (Open Gears)		Gear Cling	Royal Dripless 1000
PE-GPG-2	—	Gen. Purpose E.P. Lithium-Base Grease	NLGI2	Omegaline 2L	Premium Lithium 2
PE-MG-2	—	Molybdenum Disulfide E.P. Grease		Omegaline 2L-M	Premium Moly-Lith

Total Lubrication

Plant Engineering Designation	ISO Viscosity Grade	Lubricant Type	Viscosity, SUS at 100°F	Henry E. Sanson & Sons, Inc.	Schaeffer Manufacturing Co.
PE-150-A	32	Light Inhibited Hydraulic & Gen. Purpose	135–165	No-Gum Hyd. Oil Light	#112 Micron Moly HTC SAE 10
PE-215-A	46	Med. Inhibited Hydraulic & Gen. Purpose	194–236	No-Gum Hyd. Oil #10	#112 Micron Moly HTC SAE 10
PE-315-A	68	Med.-Heavy Inhibited Hyd. & Gen. Purpose	284–346	No-Gum Hyd. Oil #20	#112 Micron Moly HTC SAE 20
PE-700-A	150	Heavy Inhibited Hydraulic & Gen. Purpose	630–770	No-Gum Hyd. Oil #40	#112 Micron Moly HTC SAE 40
PE-150-HP	32	High-Pressure (Anti-Wear) Hydraulic Oil	135–165	AW Hyd. Oil 150	#112 Micron Moly HTC SAE 10
PE-215-HP	46	High-Pressure (Anti-Wear) Hydraulic Oil	194–236	AW Hyd. Oil 215	#112 Micron Moly HTC SAE 10
PE-315-HP	68	High-Pressure (Anti-Wear) Hydraulic Oil	284–346	AW Hyd. Oil 315	#112 Micron Moly HTC SAE 20
PE-FRH-1	—	Fire-Resistant Hyd. Fluid/Synthetic		Hydra-Safe PE Series[7]	NR
PE-FRH-2	—	Fire-Resistant Hyd. Fluid/Water-Glycol		Hydra-Safe Standard Glycol Series[7]	NR
PE-FRH-3	—	Fire-Resistant Hyd. Fluid/Water-Oil Emulsion		Hydra-Mul Premium Emulsion Series[7]	NR
PE-32-B	2	Very Light Spindle Oil (Over 6000 rpm)	29–35	NR	NR
PE-60-B	10	Light Spindle Oil (3600–6000 rpm)	54–66	No-Gum Spindle Oil VL	NR
PE-105-B	22	Spindle Oil (Up to 3600 rpm)	95–115	No-Gum Spindle Oil #9	#119 White Ind. Machine Oil 5
PE-150-C	32	Light Way Oil	135–165	No-Gum Hyd. Way Lube 150	#203 EP Ind. Machine Oil 10
PE-315-C	68	Medium Way Oil	284–346	No-Drip Way Lube #297	#203 EP Ind. Machine Oil 20
PE-1000-C	220	Heavy Way Oil	900–1100	No-Drip Way Lube Heavy	#203 EP Ind. Machine Oil 50
PE-700-D	150	Light Gear Oil	630–770	No-Gum Hyd. Oil #40	#209 Moly Univ. Gear Lube 80W-90
PE-1000-D	220	Medium Gear Oil	900–1100	No-Gum Lube Oil 550-P	#209 Moly Univ. Gear Lube 80W-90
PE-2150-D	460	Heavy Gear Oil	1935–2365	No-Gum Gear Oil #2100	#209 Moly Univ. Gear Lube 140
PE-315-E	68	Light Extreme-Pressure Gear Oil	283–347	No-Gum EP Gear Oil #315	#209 Moly Univ. Gear Lube 80W-90
PE-1500-E	320	Heavy Extreme-Pressure Gear Oil	1350–1650	No-Gum Lube Oil #1500-V	#209 Moly Univ. Gear Lube 80W-90
PE-OG-G	—	Cling-Type Gear Shield (Open Gears)		No-Drip TM	#200 Moly Silver Streak or #224
PE-GPG-2	—	Gen. Purpose E.P. Lithium-Base Grease	NLGI2	Syndralube #2	#221 Moly Ultra 800 EP #2
PE-MG-2	—	Molybdenum Disulfide E.P. Grease		Syndralube #2M	#221 Moly Ultra 800 or #260 or #248

NR = No recommendation
1. Does not contain tackiness additives normally found in way lubricants. Formulated to perform as combination hydraulic oil and way lubricant.
2. To be used where grades 90, 125, and 140 are recommended.
3. Not lithium base, but equals or exceeds application requirements.
4. Falls outside specified viscosity range, but meets application requirements.
5. Not moly grease, but exceeds application requirements.
6. Straight phosphate ester fluids available in four viscosity grades.
7. Available in range of viscosities.
8. Various ISO grades.
9. Synthetic lubricants.
10. All products formulated from polyalkylene glycol base stocks.
11. Anhydrous product, but water soluble.

Table 19.1 Chart of Interchangeable Lubricants (continued)

Plant Engineering Designation	ISO Viscosity Grade	Lubricant Type	Viscosity, SUS at 100°F	Seaboard Industries, Inc.	Sentinel Lubricants Corp.
PE-150-A	32	Light Inhibited Hydraulic & Gen. Purpose	135–165	Superior R&O 32	S-10 Hyd. Oil
PE-215-A	46	Med. Inhibited Hydraulic & Gen. Purpose	194–236	Superior R&O 46	S-10/20 Hyd. Oil
PE-315-A	68	Med.-Heavy Inhibited Hyd. & Gen. Purpose	284–346	Superior R&O 68	S-10/20 Hyd. Oil
PE-700-A	150	Heavy Inhibited Hydraulic & Gen. Purpose	630–770	Superior R&O 150	S-10/50 M.P. Oil
PE-150-HP	32	High-Pressure (Anti-Wear) Hydraulic Oil	135–165	Superior A/W Hyd. 32	S-10 Hyd. Oil
PE-215-HP	46	High-Pressure (Anti-Wear) Hydraulic Oil	194–236	Superior A/W Hyd. 46	S-10/20 Hyd. Oil
PE-315-HP	68	High-Pressure (Anti-Wear) Hydraulic Oil	284–346	Superior A/W Hyd. 68	S-10/20 Hyd. Oil
PE-FRH-1	—	Fire-Resistant Hyd. Fluid/Synthetic		NR	N.F. 65
PE-FRH-2	—	Fire-Resistant Hyd. Fluid/Water-Glycol		NR	N.F. 650
PE-FRH-3	—	Fire-Resistant Hyd. Fluid/Water-Oil Emulsion		NR	N.F. 750
PE-32-B	2	Very Light Spindle Oil (Over 6000 rpm)	29–35	NR	SPO "L"
PE-60-B	10	Light Spindle Oil (3600–6000 rpm)	54–66	Superior Spindle 10	SPO LM
PE-105-B	22	Spindle Oil (Up to 3600 rpm)	95–115	Superior Spindle 22	SPO M
PE-150-C	32	Light Way Oil	135–165	Superior Waylube 32	S-10
PE-315-C	68	Medium Way Oil	284–346	Superior Waylube 68	S-10/50
PE-1000-C	220	Heavy Way Oil	900–1100	Superior Waylube 220	S-50
PE-700-D	150	Light Gear Oil	630–770	Superior EP Compound 150	S-75/80
PE-1000-D	220	Medium Gear Oil	900–1100	Superior EP Compound 220	S-90/140
PE-2150-D	460	Heavy Gear Oil	1935–2365	Superior EP Compound 460	S-140
PE-315-E	68	Light Extreme-Pressure Gear Oil	283–347	Superior EP Compound 68	S-75/80 EP
PE-1500-E	320	Heavy Extreme-Pressure Gear Oil	1350–1650	Superior EP Compound 320	90/140 EP
PE-OG-G	—	Cling-Type Gear Shield (Open Gears)		NR	SOG
PE-GPG-2	—	Gen. Purpose E.P. Lithium-Base Grease	NLGI2	Superior EP Grease B-2	S1 123
PE-MG-2	—	Molybdenum Disulfide E.P. Grease		Superior Moly Bento Lube	SLM-2

Total Lubrication

Plant Engineering Designation	ISO Viscosity Grade	Lubricant Type	Viscosity, SUS at 100°F	Shell Oil Co.	Siegel Oil Co.
PE-150-A	32	Light Inhibited Hydraulic & Gen. Purpose	135–165	Turbo 32	Titon Hyd. Oil #15
PE-215-A	46	Med. Inhibited Hydraulic & Gen. Purpose	194–236	Turbo 46	Titon Hyd. Oil #21
PE-315-A	68	Med.-Heavy Inhibited Hyd. & Gen. Purpose	284–346	Turbo 68	Titon Hyd. Oil #31
PE-700-A	150	Heavy Inhibited Hydraulic & Gen. Purpose	630–770	Turbo 150	Titon Hyd. Oil #51
PE-150-HP	32	High-Pressure (Anti-Wear) Hydraulic Oil	135–165	Tellus 32	Titon AW Hyd. Oil #15
PE-215-HP	46	High-Pressure (Anti-Wear) Hydraulic Oil	194–236	Tellus 46	Titon AW Hyd. Oil #21
PE-315-HP	68	High-Pressure (Anti-Wear) Hydraulic Oil	284–346	Tellus 68	Titon AW Hyd. Oil #31
PE-FRH-1	—	Fire-Resistant Hyd. Fluid/Synthetic		NR	NR
PE-FRH-2	—	Fire-Resistant Hyd. Fluid/Water-Glycol		NR	NR
PE-FRH-3	—	Fire-Resistant Hyd. Fluid/Water-Oil Emulsion		NR	NR
PE-32-B	2	Very Light Spindle Oil (Over 6000 rpm)	29–35	NR	NR
PE-60-B	10	Light Spindle Oil (3600–6000 rpm)	54–66	Tellus 10	NR
PE-105-B	22	Spindle Oil (Up to 3600 rpm)	95–115	Tellus 22	Titon AW Hyd. Oil #15
PE-150-C	32	Light Way Oil	135–165	NR	NR
PE-315-C	68	Medium Way Oil	284–346	Tonna 68	NR
PE-1000-C	220	Heavy Way Oil	900–1100	Tonna 220	NR
PE-700-D	150	Light Gear Oil	630–770	Turbo 150	Titon MP Gear Lube #80
PE-1000-D	220	Medium Gear Oil	900–1100	Turbo 220	Titon MP Gear Lube #90
PE-2150-D	460	Heavy Gear Oil	1935–2365	Turbo 460	Titon MP Gear Lube #140
PE-315-E	68	Light Extreme-Pressure Gear Oil	283–347	Omala 68	Titon MP Gear Lube #80
PE-1500-E	320	Heavy Extreme-Pressure Gear Oil	1350–1650	Omala 320	Titon MP Gear Lube #140
PE-OG-G	—	Cling-Type Gear Shield (Open Gears)		Omala H	NR
PE-GPG-2	—	Gen. Purpose E.P. Lithium-Base Grease	NLGI2	Alvania EP 2	Titon Plex EP #2
PE-MG-2	—	Molybdenum Disulfide E.P. Grease		Super Duty	Titon HD Moly Grease

NR = No recommendation
1. Does not contain tackiness additives normally found in way lubricants. Formulated to perform as combination hydraulic oil and way lubricant.
2. To be used where grades 90, 125, and 140 are recommended.
3. Not lithium base, but equals or exceeds application requirements.
4. Falls outside specified viscosity range, but meets application requirements.
5. Not moly grease, but exceeds application requirements.
6. Straight phosphate ester fluids available in four viscosity grades.
7. Available in range of viscosities.
8. Various ISO grades.
9. Synthetic lubricants.
10. All products formulated from polyalkylene glycol base stocks.
11. Anhydrous product, but water soluble.

Table 19.1 Chart of Interchangeable Lubricants (continued)

Plant Engineering Designation	ISO Viscosity Grade	Lubricant Type	Viscosity, SUS at 100°F	Southwestern Petroleum Corp.	Sta-Lube, Inc.
PE-150-A	32	Light Inhibited Hydraulic & Gen. Purpose	135–165	Swepco Ind. Oil 702-1	Sta-Lube GPO 32
PE-215-A	46	Med. Inhibited Hydraulic & Gen. Purpose	194–236	Swepco Ind. Oil 702-1	Sta-Lube GPO 46
PE-315-A	68	Med.-Heavy Inhibited Hyd. & Gen. Purpose	284–346	Swepco Ind. Oil 702-2	Sta-Lube GPO 68
PE-700-A	150	Heavy Inhibited Hydraulic & Gen. Purpose	630–770	Swepco Ind. Oil 702-4	Sta-Lube GPO 150
PE-150-HP	32	High-Pressure (Anti-Wear) Hydraulic Oil	135–165	Swepco AW Hyd. Oil 704-10	Premium Clear 201
PE-215-HP	46	High-Pressure (Anti-Wear) Hydraulic Oil	194–236	Swepco AW Hyd. Oil 704-10	Premium Clear 202
PE-315-HP	68	High-Pressure (Anti-Wear) Hydraulic Oil	284–346	Swepco AW Hyd. Oil 704-20	Premium Clear 203
PE-FRH-1	—	Fire-Resistant Hyd. Fluid/Synthetic		NR	NR
PE-FRH-2	—	Fire-Resistant Hyd. Fluid/Water-Glycol		NR	NR
PE-FRH-3	—	Fire-Resistant Hyd. Fluid/Water-Oil Emulsion		Swepco FR Hyd. Oil 718	NR
PE-32-B	2	Very Light Spindle Oil (Over 6000 rpm)	29–35	NR	Moly Shur Spindle Oil X-Light
PE-60-B	10	Light Spindle Oil (3600–6000 rpm)	54–66	NR	NR
PE-105-B	22	Spindle Oil (Up to 3600 rpm)	95–115	NR	Moly Shur Spindle Oil Medium
PE-150-C	32	Light Way Oil	135–165	NR	Moly Shur RDW 150
PE-315-C	68	Medium Way Oil	284–346	Swepco Gear Lube 201-80/90	Moly Shur RDW 315
PE-1000-C	220	Heavy Way Oil	900–1100	Swepco Gear Lube 201/90	Moly Shur RDW 1000
PE-700-D	150	Light Gear Oil	630–770	Swepco Gear Lube 201-80/90	Clear Shur GO 150
PE-1000-D	220	Medium Gear Oil	900–1100	Swepco Gear Lube 201-90	Clear Shur GO 220
PE-2150-D	460	Heavy Gear Oil	1935–2365	Swepco Gear Lube 201-140	Clear Shur GO 460
PE-315-E	68	Light Extreme-Pressure Gear Oil	283–347	Swepco Gear Lube 201-80/90	Moly Shur 2EP 80W
PE-1500-E	320	Heavy Extreme-Pressure Gear Oil	1350–1650	Swepco Gear Lube 201-90	Moly Shur 6EP 940
PE-OG-G	—	Cling-Type Gear Shield (Open Gears)		Swepco Outside Gear Lube 604	Moly Shur 383 EP OG
PE-GPG-2	—	Gen. Purpose E.P. Lithium-Base Grease	NLGI2	NR	Clear Shur MPEP #2
PE-MG-2	—	Molybdenum Disulfide E.P. Grease		Swepco Moly Grease 101	Moly Shur BRB #2

Total Lubrication

Plant Engineering Designation	ISO Viscosity Grade	Lubricant Type	Viscosity, SUS at 100°F	Standard Oil Co. (Ohio) Boron Oil Co.	Stewart-Warner Corp.
PE-150-A	32	Light Inhibited Hydraulic & Gen. Purpose	135–165	Energol HL 32	Ind. Oil #"O"
PE-215-A	46	Med. Inhibited Hydraulic & Gen. Purpose	194–236	Energol HL 46	Ind. Oil #1
PE-315-A	68	Med.-Heavy Inhibited Hyd. & Gen. Purpose	284–346	Energol HL 68	Ind. Oil #2
PE-700-A	150	Heavy Inhibited Hydraulic & Gen. Purpose	630–770	Energol HLP 150	Ind. Hyd. Oil #3
PE-150-HP	32	High-Pressure (Anti-Wear) Hydraulic Oil	135–165	Energol HLP 32	HD Hyd. Oil #"O"
PE-215-HP	46	High-Pressure (Anti-Wear) Hydraulic Oil	194–236	Energol HLP 46	HD Hyd. Oil #1
PE-315-HP	68	High-Pressure (Anti-Wear) Hydraulic Oil	284–346	Energol HLP 68	HD Hyd. Oil #2
PE-FRH-1	—	Fire-Resistant Hyd. Fluid/Synthetic		NR	NR
PE-FRH-2	—	Fire-Resistant Hyd. Fluid/Water-Glycol		NR	NR
PE-FRH-3	—	Fire-Resistant Hyd. Fluid/Water-Oil Emulsion		NR	NR
PE-32-B	2	Very Light Spindle Oil (Over 6000 rpm)	29–35	Energol HLP 2	NR
PE-60-B	10	Light Spindle Oil (3600–6000 rpm)	54–66	Energol HLP 10	Spindle Oil "A"
PE-105-B	22	Spindle Oil (Up to 3600 rpm)	95–115	Energol HLP 22	Spindle Oil "A"
PE-150-C	32	Light Way Oil	135–165	Energol HLP 32[1]	NR
PE-315-C	68	Medium Way Oil	284–346	Energol HP-68-C	NR
PE-1000-C	220	Heavy Way Oil	900–1100	Energol HP-220-C	NR
PE-700-D	150	Light Gear Oil	630–770	Energol HLP 150	HD Hyd. Oil #4
PE-1000-D	220	Medium Gear Oil	900–1100	Energol HLP 220	HD Gear Oil #5
PE-2150-D	460	Heavy Gear Oil	1935–2365	Energol HLP 460	HD Gear Oil #7
PE-315-E	68	Light Extreme-Pressure Gear Oil	283–347	Gearep 80	NR
PE-1500-E	320	Heavy Extreme-Pressure Gear Oil	1350–1650	Gearep 80W-140[2]	HD Gear Oil #7
PE-OG-G	—	Cling-Type Gear Shield (Open Gears)		Gearep OG	Gear Coating "C"
PE-GPG-2	—	Gen. Purpose E.P. Lithium-Base Grease	NLGI2	Bearing Gard-2	MP Lithium
PE-MG-2	—	Molybdenum Disulfide E.P. Grease		Bearing Gard-2	NR

NR = No recommendation

1. Does not contain tackiness additives normally found in way lubricants. Formulated to perform as combination hydraulic oil and way lubricant.
2. To be used where grades 90, 125, and 140 are recommended.
3. Not lithium base, but equals or exceeds application requirements.
4. Falls outside specified viscosity range, but meets application requirements.
5. Not moly grease, but exceeds application requirements.
6. Straight phosphate ester fluids available in four viscosity grades.
7. Available in range of viscosities.
8. Various ISO grades.
9. Synthetic lubricants.
10. All products formulated from polyalkylene glycol base stocks.
11. Anhydrous product, but water soluble.

Table 19.1 Chart of Interchangeable Lubricants (continued)

Plant Engineering Designation	ISO Viscosity Grade	Lubricant Type	Viscosity, SUS at 100°F	D. A. Stuart Oil Co. of America	Sun Refining & Marketing Co.
PE-150-A	32	Light Inhibited Hydraulic & Gen. Purpose	135–165	Dasco PS-15 Hyd. Oil	Sunvis 916
PE-215-A	46	Med. Inhibited Hydraulic & Gen. Purpose	194–236	Dasco PS-20 Hyd. Oil	Sunvis 921
PE-315-A	68	Med.-Heavy Inhibited Hyd. & Gen. Purpose	284–346	Dasco PS-30 Hyd. Oil	Sunvis 931
PE-700-A	150	Heavy Inhibited Hydraulic & Gen. Purpose	630–770	Dasco PS-70 Hyd. Oil	Sunvis 975
PE-150-HP	32	High-Pressure (Anti-Wear) Hydraulic Oil	135–165	Dasco PS-15 Hyd. Oil	Sunvis 706, 816WR
PE-215-HP	46	High-Pressure (Anti-Wear) Hydraulic Oil	194–236	Dasco PS-20 Hyd. Oil	Sunvis 747, 821WR
PE-315-HP	68	High-Pressure (Anti-Wear) Hydraulic Oil	284–346	Dasco PS-30 Hyd. Oil	Sunvis 754, 831WR
PE-FRH-1	—	Fire-Resistant Hyd. Fluid/Synthetic		Dasco FR 420 Hyd. Fluid	NR
PE-FRH-2	—	Fire-Resistant Hyd. Fluid/Water-Glycol		Dasco FR 201 Hyd. Fluid	NR
PE-FRH-3	—	Fire-Resistant Hyd. Fluid/Water-Oil Emulsion		Dasco IFR Hyd. Fluid	Sunsafe 450
PE-32-B	2	Very Light Spindle Oil (Over 6000 rpm)	29–35	Dasco 1473	NR
PE-60-B	10	Light Spindle Oil (3600–6000 rpm)	54–66	NR	Solnus 55
PE-105-B	22	Spindle Oil (Up to 3600 rpm)	95–115	Astral 0045	Sunvis 911
PE-150-C	32	Light Way Oil	135–165	NR	Lubeway 1706
PE-315-C	68	Medium Way Oil	284–346	Sturaco 7140 Way Lube	Sun Way Lube 1180
PE-1000-C	220	Heavy Way Oil	900–1100	Sturaco 7164 Way Lube	Sun Way Lube 1190
PE-700-D	150	Light Gear Oil	630–770	Sturaco 7134	Sunvis 975, 775
PE-1000-D	220	Medium Gear Oil	900–1100	Sturaco 7135	Sunvis 999, 790
PE-2150-D	460	Heavy Gear Oil	1935–2365	Sturaco 7137	Sunvis 9112
PE-315-E	68	Light Extreme-Pressure Gear Oil	283–347	Sturaco 7132	Sunep 1050
PE-1500-E	320	Heavy Extreme-Pressure Gear Oil	1350–1650	Sturaco 7136	Sunep 1090
PE-OG-G	—	Cling-Type Gear Shield (Open Gears)		Sturaco 7105	Sunep Compound 250 SP
PE-GPG-2	—	Gen. Purpose E.P. Lithium-Base Grease	NLGI2	NR	Sun Prestige 742 EP
PE-MG-2	—	Molybdenum Disulfide E.P. Grease		NR	Sunaplex 882 EPM

Total Lubrication

Plant Engineering Designation	ISO Viscosity Grade	Lubricant Type	Viscosity, SUS at 100°F	Superior Industrial Lubricants	Synthetic Oil Corp. of America
PE-150-A	32	Light Inhibited Hydraulic & Gen. Purpose	135–165	#13-32 Hyd. R&O 32	SOC Hyd. 135.3
PE-215-A	46	Med. Inhibited Hydraulic & Gen. Purpose	194–236	#13-46 Hyd. R&O 46	NR
PE-315-A	68	Med.-Heavy Inhibited Hyd. & Gen. Purpose	284–346	#13-68 Hyd. R&O 68	NR
PE-700-A	150	Heavy Inhibited Hydraulic & Gen. Purpose	630–770	#13-150 Hyd. R&O 150	NR
PE-150-HP	32	High-Pressure (Anti-Wear) Hydraulic Oil	135–165	#14-32 Hyd. R&O AW 32	SOC Hyd. 135.3
PE-215-HP	46	High-Pressure (Anti-Wear) Hydraulic Oil	194–236	#14-46 Hyd. R&O AW 46	NR
PE-315-HP	68	High-Pressure (Anti-Wear) Hydraulic Oil	284–346	#14-68 Hyd. R&O AW 68	NR
PE-FRH-1	—	Fire-Resistant Hyd. Fluid/Synthetic		#80-61 FR Synthetic Fluid	SOC Hyd. 135.3
PE-FRH-2	—	Fire-Resistant Hyd. Fluid/Water-Glycol		#80-60 FR 40 XD Fluid	NR
PE-FRH-3	—	Fire-Resistant Hyd. Fluid/Water-Oil Emulsion		#80-62 Invert FR Fluid	NR
PE-32-B	2	Very Light Spindle Oil (Over 6000 rpm)	29–35	#80-50-2 Super Spin 2	SOC Artic 30
PE-60-B	10	Light Spindle Oil (3600–6000 rpm)	54–66	#80-50 Super Spin 10	NR
PE-105-B	22	Spindle Oil (Up to 3600 rpm)	95–115	#80-52 Super Spin 22	NR
PE-150-C	32	Light Way Oil	135–165	#8-150 Slide-A-Way 32	SOC Longhaul I 135.3
PE-315-C	68	Medium Way Oil	284–346	#8-320 Slide-A-Way 68	SOC Longhaul II 285.0
PE-1000-C	220	Heavy Way Oil	900–1100	#8-460 Slide-A-Way 220	SOC Longhaul III 901.0
PE-700-D	150	Light Gear Oil	630–770	#9001 Mineral Gear Oil Light	SOC GO 90
PE-1000-D	220	Medium Gear Oil	900–1100	#9002 Mineral Gear Oil Medium	SOC GO 140
PE-2150-D	460	Heavy Gear Oil	1935–2365	#9003 Mineral Gear Oil Heavy	SOC GO 160
PE-315-E	68	Light Extreme-Pressure Gear Oil	283–347	#9-68 HD Gear Oil 68	SOC GO 90
PE-1500-E	320	Heavy Extreme-Pressure Gear Oil	1350–1650	#9-320 HD Gear Oil 320	SOC GO 140
PE-OG-G	—	Cling-Type Gear Shield (Open Gears)		#8-001 Super HD Bar, Chain, Cable Lube	SOC Chain Drive
PE-GPG-2	—	Gen. Purpose E.P. Lithium-Base Grease	NLGI2	#8-012 EP Lithium 2 Grease	SOC Grease I
PE-MG-2	—	Molybdenum Disulfide E.P. Grease		#8-011 Moly Lith EP #2 Grease	SOC Grease II

NR = No recommendation
1. Does not contain tackiness additives normally found in way lubricants. Formulated to perform as combination hydraulic oil and way lubricant.
2. To be used where grades 90, 125, and 140 are recommended.
3. Not lithium base, but equals or exceeds application requirements.
4. Falls outside specified viscosity range, but meets application requirements.
5. Not moly grease, but exceeds application requirements.
6. Straight phosphate ester fluids available in four viscosity grades.
7. Available in range of viscosities.
8. Various ISO grades.
9. Synthetic lubricants.
10. All products formulated from polyalkylene glycol base stocks.
11. Anhydrous product, but water soluble.

Table 19.1 Chart of Interchangeable Lubricants (continued)

Plant Engineering Designation	ISO Viscosity Grade	Lubricant Type	Viscosity, SUS at 100°F	Tech-Lube Corp.	Texaco Inc.
PE-150-A	32	Light Inhibited Hydraulic & Gen. Purpose	135–165	Off Leak 10 LT	Regal Oil R&O 32
PE-215-A	46	Med. Inhibited Hydraulic & Gen. Purpose	194–236	Off Leak 10	Regal Oil R&O 46
PE-315-A	68	Med.-Heavy Inhibited Hyd. & Gen. Purpose	284–346	Off Leak 20	Regal Oil R&O 68
PE-700-A	150	Heavy Inhibited Hydraulic & Gen. Purpose	630–770	Off Leak 10/50	Regal Oil R&O 150
PE-150-HP	32	High-Pressure (Anti-Wear) Hydraulic Oil	135–165	TH 10 LT	Rando Oil HD 32
PE-215-HP	46	High-Pressure (Anti-Wear) Hydraulic Oil	194–236	TH 10	Rando Oil HD 46
PE-315-HP	68	High-Pressure (Anti-Wear) Hydraulic Oil	284–346	TH 20	Rando Oil HD 68
PE-FRH-1	—	Fire-Resistant Hyd. Fluid/Synthetic		TH PH	Safetytex 46
PE-FRH-2	—	Fire-Resistant Hyd. Fluid/Water-Glycol		TH 150 WS	Hyd. Safety Fluid 46
PE-FRH-3	—	Fire-Resistant Hyd. Fluid/Water-Oil Emulsion		THW	FR Hydrafluid 82
PE-32-B	2	Very Light Spindle Oil (Over 6000 rpm)	29–35	TSO 5	NR
PE-60-B	10	Light Spindle Oil (3600–6000 rpm)	54–66	TSO 10	Spindura Oil 10
PE-105-B	22	Spindle Oil (Up to 3600 rpm)	95–115	TSO	Spindura Oil 32
PE-150-C	32	Light Way Oil	135–165	T 10 LT	Rando Oil 32[1]
PE-315-C	68	Medium Way Oil	284–346	T 20	Way Lube 68
PE-1000-C	220	Heavy Way Oil	900–1100	T 90	Way Lube 220
PE-700-D	150	Light Gear Oil	630–770	T 75/80	Regal Oil R&O 150
PE-1000-D	220	Medium Gear Oil	900–1100	T 90	Regal Oil R&O 220
PE-2150-D	460	Heavy Gear Oil	1935–2365	T 140	Regal Oil 390
PE-315-E	68	Light Extreme-Pressure Gear Oil	283–347	T 20 EP	Meropa 68
PE-1500-E	320	Heavy Extreme-Pressure Gear Oil	1350–1650	T 90/140 EP	Meropa 320
PE-OG-G	—	Cling-Type Gear Shield (Open Gears)		TG OG	Crater 2X Fluid
PE-GPG-2	—	Gen. Purpose E.P. Lithium-Base Grease	NLGI2	TG Lithium EP2	Multifak EP 2
PE-MG-2	—	Molybdenum Disulfide E.P. Grease		TG M2	Molytex EP 2

Total Lubrication

Plant Engineering Designation	ISO Viscosity Grade	Lubricant Type	Viscosity, SUS at 100°F	Texas Refinery Corp.	Tower Oil & Technology Co.
PE-150-A	32	Light Inhibited Hydraulic & Gen. Purpose	135–165	TRC Hyd. Oil SAE 10	Hydroil CC
PE-215-A	46	Med. Inhibited Hydraulic & Gen. Purpose	194–236	TRC Hyd. Oil SAE 10	Hydroil D
PE-315-A	68	Med.-Heavy Inhibited Hyd. & Gen. Purpose	284–346	TRC Hyd. Oil SAE 20	Hydroil EE
PE-700-A	150	Heavy Inhibited Hydraulic & Gen. Purpose	630–770	TRC Hyd. Oil SAE 30	Hydroil F
PE-150-HP	32	High-Pressure (Anti-Wear) Hydraulic Oil	135–165	TRC Hyd. Oil SAE 10	Hydroil AW-3
PE-215-HP	46	High-Pressure (Anti-Wear) Hydraulic Oil	194–236	TRC Hyd. Oil SAE 10	Hydroil AW-4
PE-315-HP	68	High-Pressure (Anti-Wear) Hydraulic Oil	284–346	TRC Hyd. Oil SAE 20	Hydroil AW-5
PE-FRH-1	—	Fire-Resistant Hyd. Fluid/Synthetic		NR	NR
PE-FRH-2	—	Fire-Resistant Hyd. Fluid/Water-Glycol		NR	FR Fluid 40
PE-FRH-3	—	Fire-Resistant Hyd. Fluid/Water-Oil Emulsion		NR	Safoil #22
PE-32-B	2	Very Light Spindle Oil (Over 6000 rpm)	29–35	NR	Durol AA
PE-60-B	10	Light Spindle Oil (3600–6000 rpm)	54–66	NR	Durol A
PE-105-B	22	Spindle Oil (Up to 3600 rpm)	95–115	TRC Spindle Oil SAE 5	Durol B
PE-150-C	32	Light Way Oil	135–165	TRC Rock Drill Oil 10	#15 Way & Gear Lube
PE-315-C	68	Medium Way Oil	284–346	TRC #890 Vari Purpose 75	#47 Way Lube
PE-1000-C	220	Heavy Way Oil	900–1100	TRC #890 Vari Purpose 80/90	#95 Way & Gear Lube
PE-700-D	150	Light Gear Oil	630–770	TRC #790 Sure Univ. Gear Lube 80	Express Gear Lube F
PE-1000-D	220	Medium Gear Oil	900–1100	TRC #790 Sure Univ. Gear Lube 90	Express Gear Lube GH
PE-2150-D	460	Heavy Gear Oil	1935–2365	TRC #790 Sure Univ. Gear Lube 140	Express Gear Lube J
PE-315-E	68	Light Extreme-Pressure Gear Oil	283–347	TRC #890 Vari Purpose 75	Express Gear Lube EF
PE-1500-E	320	Heavy Extreme-Pressure Gear Oil	1350–1650	TRC #890 Vari Purpose 80/90	Express Gear Lube GH
PE-OG-G	—	Cling-Type Gear Shield (Open Gears)		TRC Takilube	Kotall
PE-GPG-2	—	Gen. Purpose E.P. Lithium-Base Grease	NLGI2	TRC Molyplate	Grezall R
PE-MG-2	—	Molybdenum Disulfide E.P. Grease		TRC Moly EP	Grezall ME-1

NR = No recommendation
1. Does not contain tackiness additives normally found in way lubricants. Formulated to perform as combination hydraulic oil and way lubricant.
2. To be used where grades 90, 125, and 140 are recommended.
3. Not lithium base, but equals or exceeds application requirements.
4. Falls outside specified viscosity range, but meets application requirements.
5. Not moly grease, but exceeds application requirements.
6. Straight phosphate ester fluids available in four viscosity grades.
7. Available in range of viscosities.
8. Various ISO grades.
9. Synthetic lubricants.
10. All products formulated from polyalkylene glycol base stocks.
11. Anhydrous product, but water soluble.

Table 19.1 Chart of Interchangeable Lubricants *(continued)*

Plant Engineering Designation	ISO Viscosity Grade	Lubricant Type	Viscosity, SUS at 100°F	Tri-State Industrial Lubricants, Inc.	Ultrachem Inc.[9]
PE-150-A	32	Light Inhibited Hydraulic & Gen. Purpose	135–165	Hydro-Flo #15	Chemlube 207
PE-215-A	46	Med. Inhibited Hydraulic & Gen. Purpose	194–236	Hydro-Flo #2	Chemlube 217
PE-315-A	68	Med.-Heavy Inhibited Hyd. & Gen. Purpose	284–346	Hydro-Flo #3	Chemlube 217
PE-700-A	150	Heavy Inhibited Hydraulic & Gen. Purpose	630–770	Hydro-Flo #65	Chemlube 751
PE-150-HP	32	High-Pressure (Anti-Wear) Hydraulic Oil	135–165	Hydro-Flo AW-15	NR
PE-215-HP	46	High-Pressure (Anti-Wear) Hydraulic Oil	194–236	Hydro-Flo AW-2	Chemlube 217
PE-315-HP	68	High-Pressure (Anti-Wear) Hydraulic Oil	284–346	Hydro-Flo AW-3	Chemlube 217
PE-FRH-1	—	Fire-Resistant Hyd. Fluid/Synthetic		NR	NR
PE-FRH-2	—	Fire-Resistant Hyd. Fluid/Water-Glycol		Flo Kool AFH-AW	NR
PE-FRH-3	—	Fire-Resistant Hyd. Fluid/Water-Oil Emulsion		NR	NR
PE-32-B	2	Very Light Spindle Oil (Over 6000 rpm)	29–35	#30 Spindle	NR
PE-60-B	10	Light Spindle Oil (3600–6000 rpm)	54–66	#60 Spindle	NR
PE-105-B	22	Spindle Oil (Up to 3600 rpm)	95–115	#1 Spindle	Chemspin 22
PE-150-C	32	Light Way Oil	135–165	Sta-Lube #15	NR
PE-315-C	68	Medium Way Oil	284–346	Sta-Lube #3	NR
PE-1000-C	220	Heavy Way Oil	900–1100	Sta-Lube #9	NR
PE-700-D	150	Light Gear Oil	630–770	Gearmate #65	Chemlube 85W-90
PE-1000-D	220	Medium Gear Oil	900–1100	Gearmate #9	Chemlube 140
PE-2150-D	460	Heavy Gear Oil	1935–2365	Gearmate #2100	Chemlube 250
PE-315-E	68	Light Extreme-Pressure Gear Oil	283–347	Gearmate EP #3	NR
PE-1500-E	320	Heavy Extreme-Pressure Gear Oil	1350–1650	Gearmate EP #1600	Chemlube 250
PE-OG-G	—	Cling-Type Gear Shield (Open Gears)		Sta-Lube EP #9	Vischem 373
PE-GPG-2	—	Gen. Purpose E.P. Lithium-Base Grease	NLGI2	GL-85	Vischem 352
PE-MG-2	—	Molybdenum Disulfide E.P. Grease		GL-88	Vischem 350M

246 MANAGING MILL MAINTENANCE

Plant Engineering Designation	ISO Viscosity Grade	Lubricant Type	Viscosity, SUS at 100°F	Union Carbide Corp.[9,10]	Union Oil Co. of California Eastern Region
PE-150-A	32	Light Inhibited Hydraulic & Gen. Purpose	135–165	Ucon LB-135XY-26	Unax RX 32
PE-215-A	46	Med. Inhibited Hydraulic & Gen. Purpose	194–236	Ucon LB-170XY-26	Unax RX 46
PE-315-A	68	Med.-Heavy Inhibited Hyd. & Gen. Purpose	284–346	Ucon LB-300XY-26	Unax RX 68
PE-700-A	150	Heavy Inhibited Hydraulic & Gen. Purpose	630–770	Ucon LB-650XY-26	Unax RX 150
PE-150-HP	32	High-Pressure (Anti-Wear) Hydraulic Oil	135–165	Ucon Hyd. Fluid AW32/WS-34[11]	Unax AW 32
PE-215-HP	46	High-Pressure (Anti-Wear) Hydraulic Oil	194–236	Ucon Hyd. Fluid AW46	Unax AW 46
PE-315-HP	68	High-Pressure (Anti-Wear) Hydraulic Oil	284–346	Ucon Hyd. Fluid AW68	Unax AW 68
PE-FRH-1	—	Fire-Resistant Hyd. Fluid/Synthetic		NR	NR
PE-FRH-2	—	Fire-Resistant Hyd. Fluid/Water-Glycol		Ucon Hydrolube CC-7467	NR
PE-FRH-3	—	Fire-Resistant Hyd. Fluid/Water-Oil Emulsion		NR	FR Fluid
PE-32-B	2	Very Light Spindle Oil (Over 6000 rpm)	29–35	NR	NR
PE-60-B	10	Light Spindle Oil (3600–6000 rpm)	54–66	NR	NR
PE-105-B	22	Spindle Oil (Up to 3600 rpm)	95–115	NR	Unax 22
PE-150-C	32	Light Way Oil	135–165	NR	NR
PE-315-C	68	Medium Way Oil	284–346	NR	Way Oil HD 68
PE-1000-C	220	Heavy Way Oil	900–1100	NR	Way Oil HD 220
PE-700-D	150	Light Gear Oil	630–770	Ucon Gear Lube 150	Unax 150
PE-1000-D	220	Medium Gear Oil	900–1100	Ucon Gear Lube 220	Unax 220
PE-2150-D	460	Heavy Gear Oil	1935–2365	Ucon LB-1800XH-1	Unax 460
PE-315-E	68	Light Extreme-Pressure Gear Oil	283–347	Ucon Gear Lube 68 EP	Extra Duty NL 2 EP
PE-1500-E	320	Heavy Extreme-Pressure Gear Oil	1350–1650	Ucon Gear Lube 220 EP	Extra Duty NL 6 EP
PE-OG-G	—	Cling-Type Gear Shield (Open Gears)		NR	Gearite Heavy
PE-GPG-2	—	Gen. Purpose E.P. Lithium-Base Grease	NLGI2	NR	Unoba EP #2
PE-MG-2	—	Molybdenum Disulfide E.P. Grease		NR	Unoba Moly HD #2

NR = No recommendation

1. Does not contain tackiness additives normally found in way lubricants. Formulated to perform as combination hydraulic oil and way lubricant.
2. To be used where grades 90, 125, and 140 are recommended.
3. Not lithium base, but equals or exceeds application requirements.
4. Falls outside specified viscosity range, but meets application requirements.
5. Not moly grease, but exceeds application requirements.
6. Straight phosphate ester fluids available in four viscosity grades.
7. Available in range of viscosities.
8. Various ISO grades.
9. Synthetic lubricants.
10. All products formulated from polyalkylene glycol base stocks.
11. Anhydrous product, but water soluble.

MANAGING MILL MAINTENANCE

Table 19.1 Chart of Interchangeable Lubricants *(continued)*

Plant Engineering Designation	ISO Viscosity Grade	Lubricant Type	Viscosity, SUS at 100°F	Union Oil Co. of California Western Region	United Refining Co.
PE-150-A	32	Light Inhibited Hydraulic & Gen. Purpose	135–165	Turbine Oil 32	Emblem R&O 150
PE-215-A	46	Med. Inhibited Hydraulic & Gen. Purpose	194–236	Turbine Oil 46	Emblem R&O 200
PE-315-A	68	Med.-Heavy Inhibited Hyd. & Gen. Purpose	284–346	Turbine Oil 68	Emblem R&O 300
PE-700-A	150	Heavy Inhibited Hydraulic & Gen. Purpose	630–770	Turbine Oil 150	Emblem R&O 650
PE-150-HP	32	High-Pressure (Anti-Wear) Hydraulic Oil	135–165	Unax AW 32	Emblem AW-160
PE-215-HP	46	High-Pressure (Anti-Wear) Hydraulic Oil	194–236	Unax AW 46	Emblem AW-200
PE-315-HP	68	High-Pressure (Anti-Wear) Hydraulic Oil	284–346	Unax AW 68	Emblem AW-300
PE-FRH-1	—	Fire-Resistant Hyd. Fluid/Synthetic		NR	NR
PE-FRH-2	—	Fire-Resistant Hyd. Fluid/Water-Glycol		NR	NR
PE-FRH-3	—	Fire-Resistant Hyd. Fluid/Water-Oil Emulsion		FR Fluid	NR
PE-32-B	2	Very Light Spindle Oil (Over 6000 rpm)	29–35	NR	NR
PE-60-B	10	Light Spindle Oil (3600–6000 rpm)	54–66	NR	Emblem R&O 55
PE-105-B	22	Spindle Oil (Up to 3600 rpm)	95–115	Turbine Oil 22	Emblem R&O 100
PE-150-C	32	Light Way Oil	135–165	Way Oil HD 32	Emblem Powerway 150
PE-315-C	68	Medium Way Oil	284–346	Way Oil HD 68	Emblem Powerway 350
PE-1000-C	220	Heavy Way Oil	900–1100	Way Oil HD 220	Emblem Powerway 900
PE-700-D	150	Light Gear Oil	630–770	Unax 150	United Premium 40
PE-1000-D	220	Medium Gear Oil	900–1100	Unax 220	Emblem Mineral Gear 90
PE-2150-D	460	Heavy Gear Oil	1935–2365	Unax 460	Emblem Mineral Gear 140
PE-315-E	68	Light Extreme-Pressure Gear Oil	283–347	Extra Duty NL 2 EP	Emblem APG 80
PE-1500-E	320	Heavy Extreme-Pressure Gear Oil	1350–1650	Extra Duty NL 6 EP	Emblem APG 95
PE-OG-G	—	Cling-Type Gear Shield (Open Gears)		Gearite Heavy	Emblem Open Gear
PE-GPG-2	—	Gen. Purpose E.P. Lithium-Base Grease	NLGI2	Unoba EP #2	Emolube 302 EP
PE-MG-2	—	Molybdenum Disulfide E.P. Grease		Unoba Moly HD #2	Emolube 292

Total Lubrication

Plant Engineering Designation	ISO Viscosity Grade	Lubricant Type	Viscosity, SUS at 100°F	U.S. Industrial Lubricants	Viscosity Oil Co.
PE-150-A	32	Light Inhibited Hydraulic & Gen. Purpose	135–165	Polymer 141	PTO 32 AZ
PE-215-A	46	Med. Inhibited Hydraulic & Gen. Purpose	194–236	Polymer 141	PTO 46 AZ
PE-315-A	68	Med.-Heavy Inhibited Hyd. & Gen. Purpose	284–346	Polymer 141	PTO 68 AZ
PE-700-A	150	Heavy Inhibited Hydraulic & Gen. Purpose	630–770	Polymer 142	PTO 150 AZ
PE-150-HP	32	High-Pressure (Anti-Wear) Hydraulic Oil	135–165	Polymer 141	PTO 32 AZ
PE-215-HP	46	High-Pressure (Anti-Wear) Hydraulic Oil	194–236	Polymer 141	PTO 46 AZ
PE-315-HP	68	High-Pressure (Anti-Wear) Hydraulic Oil	284–346	Polymer 141	PTO 68 AZ
PE-FRH-1	—	Fire-Resistant Hyd. Fluid/Synthetic		FR-2	NR
PE-FRH-2	—	Fire-Resistant Hyd. Fluid/Water-Glycol		WGF 200/300	NR
PE-FRH-3	—	Fire-Resistant Hyd. Fluid/Water-Oil Emulsion		FR-WO	NR
PE-32-B	2	Very Light Spindle Oil (Over 6000 rpm)	29–35	Polymer 140	Vertex 40
PE-60-B	10	Light Spindle Oil (3600–6000 rpm)	54–66	Polymer 140	S-6
PE-105-B	22	Spindle Oil (Up to 3600 rpm)	95–115	Polymer 140	S-10
PE-150-C	32	Light Way Oil	135–165	Polymer 141	Visway 1
PE-315-C	68	Medium Way Oil	284–346	Polymer 142	Visway 2
PE-1000-C	220	Heavy Way Oil	900–1100	USL-90	Visway 4
PE-700-D	150	Light Gear Oil	630–770	USL-80	PTO 150 AZ
PE-1000-D	220	Medium Gear Oil	900–1100	USL-90	PTO 220 AZ
PE-2150-D	460	Heavy Gear Oil	1935–2365	USL-140	PTO 460
PE-315-E	68	Light Extreme-Pressure Gear Oil	283–347	USL-30	Rex 2 EP
PE-1500-E	320	Heavy Extreme-Pressure Gear Oil	1350–1650	USL-90/140	Rex 6 EP
PE-OG-G	—	Cling-Type Gear Shield (Open Gears)		Cling-Tac	Outside Gear Lube
PE-GPG-2	—	Gen. Purpose E.P. Lithium-Base Grease	NLGI2	Poly-Temp	EP Lith #2
PE-MG-2	—	Molybdenum Disulfide E.P. Grease		Moly X-D	HD Moly #2

NR = No recommendation
1. Does not contain tackiness additives normally found in way lubricants. Formulated to perform as combination hydraulic oil and way lubricant.
2. To be used where grades 90, 125, and 140 are recommended.
3. Not lithium base, but equals or exceeds application requirements.
4. Falls outside specified viscosity range, but meets application requirements.
5. Not moly grease, but exceeds application requirements.
6. Straight phosphate ester fluids available in four viscosity grades.
7. Available in range of viscosities.
8. Various ISO grades.
9. Synthetic lubricants.
10. All products formulated from polyalkylene glycol base stocks.
11. Anhydrous product, but water soluble.

Table 19.1 Chart of Interchangeable Lubricants (continued)

Plant Engineering Designation	ISO Viscosity Grade	Lubricant Type	Viscosity, SUS at 100°F	Wallover Oil Co.	West Penn Oil Co., Inc.
PE-150-A	32	Light Inhibited Hydraulic & Gen. Purpose	135–165	Woco Turbine & Hyd. Oil 150	W/P HBM-150
PE-215-A	46	Med. Inhibited Hydraulic & Gen. Purpose	194–236	Woco Turbine & Hyd. Oil 200	W/P HBM-200
PE-315-A	68	Med.-Heavy Inhibited Hyd. & Gen. Purpose	284–346	Woco Turbine & Hyd. Oil 300	W/P HBM-300
PE-700-A	150	Heavy Inhibited Hydraulic & Gen. Purpose	630–770	Woco Turbine & Hyd. Oil 700	W/P HBM-650
PE-150-HP	32	High-Pressure (Anti-Wear) Hydraulic Oil	135–165	Woco Hyd. Oil AW-150	W/P AWH-150
PE-215-HP	46	High-Pressure (Anti-Wear) Hydraulic Oil	194–236	Woco Hyd. Oil AW-200	W/P AWH-200
PE-315-HP	68	High-Pressure (Anti-Wear) Hydraulic Oil	284–346	Woco Hyd. Oil AW-300	W/P AWH-300
PE-FRH-1	—	Fire-Resistant Hyd. Fluid/Synthetic		NR	NR
PE-FRH-2	—	Fire-Resistant Hyd. Fluid/Water-Glycol		NR	NR
PE-FRH-3	—	Fire-Resistant Hyd. Fluid/Water-Oil Emulsion		NR	NR
PE-32-B	2	Very Light Spindle Oil (Over 6000 rpm)	29–35	Wocospin 35	W/P Westspin #3
PE-60-B	10	Light Spindle Oil (3600–6000 rpm)	54–66	Wocospin 57	W/P Westspin #6
PE-105-B	22	Spindle Oil (Up to 3600 rpm)	95–115	Wocospin 100	W/P Westspin #10
PE-150-C	32	Light Way Oil	135–165	Woco AWT-150	W/P Pennway Light
PE-315-C	68	Medium Way Oil	284–346	Woco AWT-300	W/P Pennway Med.
PE-1000-C	220	Heavy Way Oil	900–1100	Woco AWT-1000	W/P Pennway Heavy
PE-700-D	150	Light Gear Oil	630–770	Woco Regular Gear Oil 70	W/P Mineral Gear Light
PE-1000-D	220	Medium Gear Oil	900–1100	Woco Regular Gear Oil 90	W/P Mineral Gear Med.
PE-2150-D	460	Heavy Gear Oil	1935–2365	Woco Regular Gear Oil 130	W/P Mineral Gear Heavy
PE-315-E	68	Light Extreme-Pressure Gear Oil	283–347	Woco EP Gear Oil 50	W/P APG 80
PE-1500-E	320	Heavy Extreme-Pressure Gear Oil	1350–1650	Woco EP Gear Oil 105	W/P APG 96
PE-OG-G	—	Cling-Type Gear Shield (Open Gears)		NR	W/P OGS
PE-GPG-2	—	Gen. Purpose E.P. Lithium-Base Grease	NLGI2	Woco EP Lithium Grease #2	W/P Lith #2 EP
PE-MG-2	—	Molybdenum Disulfide E.P. Grease		Woco Moly-Lith Grease #2	W/P Moly Lith #2 EP

Total Lubrication

Plant Engineering Designation	ISO Viscosity Grade	Lubricant Type	Viscosity, SUS at 100°F	The White & Bagley Co.	White & Bagley of Michigan, Inc.
PE-150-A	32	Light Inhibited Hydraulic & Gen. Purpose	135–165	W&B Super Hyd. Oil 150	Penn-Mar Super Hyd. Oil 150
PE-215-A	46	Med. Inhibited Hydraulic & Gen. Purpose	194–236	W&B Super Hyd. Oil 225	Penn-Mar Super Hyd. Oil 225
PE-315-A	68	Med.-Heavy Inhibited Hyd. & Gen. Purpose	284–346	W&B Super Hyd. Oil 300	Penn-Mar Super Hyd. Oil 300
PE-700-A	150	Heavy Inhibited Hyd. & Gen. Purpose	630–770	W&B Super Hyd. Oil 600	Penn-Mar Super Hyd. Oil 600
PE-150-HP	32	High-Pressure (Anti-Wear) Hydraulic Oil	135–165	W&B Super Hyd. Oil 150	Penn-Mar Super Hyd. Oil 150
PE-215-HP	46	High-Pressure (Anti-Wear) Hydraulic Oil	194–236	W&B Super Hyd. Oil 225	Penn-Mar Super Hyd. Oil 225
PE-315-HP	68	High-Pressure (Anti-Wear) Hydraulic Oil	284–346	W&B Super Hyd. Oil 300	Penn-Mar Super Hyd. Oil 300
PE-FRH-1	—	Fire-Resistant Hyd. Fluid/Synthetic		NR	NR
PE-FRH-2	—	Fire-Resistant Hyd. Fluid/Water-Glycol		NR	NR
PE-FRH-3	—	Fire-Resistant Hyd. Fluid/Water-Oil Emulsion		NR	NR
PE-32-B	2	Very Light Spindle Oil (Over 6000 rpm)	29–35	W&B Precision Spindle Oil 45	Penn-Mar R&O Spindle Oil 45
PE-60-B	10	Light Spindle Oil (3600–6000 rpm)	54–66	W&B Universal Spindle Oil 60	Penn-Mar R&O Spindle Oil 60
PE-105-B	22	Spindle Oil (Up to 3600 rpm)	95–115	W&B Universal Spindle Oil 100	Penn-Mar R&O Spindle Oil 100
PE-150-C	32	Light Way Oil	135–165	W&B Light Hyd. & Way Lube	Penn-Mar Light Hyd. & Way Lube
PE-315-C	68	Medium Way Oil	284–346	W&B Med. Way Lube	Penn-Mar Med. Way Lube
PE-1000-C	220	Heavy Way Oil	900–1100	W&B Heavy Way Lube	Penn-Mar Heavy Way Lube
PE-700-D	150	Light Gear Oil	630–770	W&B Hyaline Oil H	Penn-Mar EP Gear Oil #2
PE-1000-D	220	Medium Gear Oil	900–1100	W&B Hyaline Oil J	Dari-Lube K
PE-2150-D	460	Heavy Gear Oil	1935–2365	W&B Hyaline Oil L	Penn-Mar EP Gear Oil #4
PE-315-E	68	Light Extreme-Pressure Gear Oil	283–347	W&B EP Gear Oil SAE 80-W	Penn-Mar EP Gear Oil #1
PE-1500-E	320	Heavy Extreme-Pressure Gear Oil	1350–1650	W&B EP Gear Oil SAE 90	Penn-Mar EP Gear Oil #3
PE-OG-G	—	Cling-Type Gear Shield (Open Gears)		Oilzum Open Gear Lub	Penn-Mar Open Gear Shield 800
PE-GPC-2	—	Gen. Purpose E.P. Lithium-Base Grease	NLGI2	Oilzum Multi-Purpose Lube	Penn-Mar Kote Z-1120-2
PE-MG-2	—	Molybdenum Disulfide E.P. Grease		Olizum Moly Lube	Penn-Mar Kote Z-1420-2

NR = No recommendation
1. Does not contain tackiness additives normally found in way lubricants. Formulated to perform as combination hydraulic oil and way lubricant.
2. To be used where grades 90, 125, and 140 are recommended.
3. Not lithium base, but equals or exceeds application requirements.
4. Falls outside specified viscosity range, but meets application requirements.
5. Not moly grease, but exceeds application requirements.
6. Straight phosphate ester fluids available in four viscosity grades.
7. Available in range of viscosities.
8. Various ISO grades.
9. Synthetic lubricants.
10. All products formulated from polyalkylene glycol base stocks.
11. Anhydrous product, but water soluble.

Table 19.1 Chart of Interchangeable Lubricants (continued)

Plant Engineering Designation	ISO Viscosity Grade	Lubricant Type	Viscosity, SUS at 100°F	Arthur C. Withrow Co.	Wylie Lubricants CW Petroleum and Chemical, Inc.
PE-150-A	32	Light Inhibited Hydraulic & Gen. Purpose	135–165	S Light Lube Oil	Turbinol 32
PE-215-A	46	Med. Inhibited Hydraulic & Gen. Purpose	194–236	S Med. Lube Oil	Turbinol 46
PE-315-A	68	Med.-Heavy Inhibited Hyd. & Gen. Purpose	284–346	S Med-Hvy. Lube Oil	Turbinol 68
PE-700-A	150	Heavy Inhibited Hydraulic & Gen. Purpose	630–770	S Extra Heavy Lube Oil	Turbinol 150
PE-150-HP	32	High-Pressure (Anti-Wear) Hydraulic Oil	135–165	H Light AW Hyd. Oil	Turbinol-AW 32
PE-215-HP	46	High-Pressure (Anti-Wear) Hydraulic Oil	194–236	H Med. AW Hyd. Oil	Turbinol-AW 46
PE-315-HP	68	High-Pressure (Anti-Wear) Hydraulic Oil	284–346	H Med-Hvy. AW Hyd. Oil	Turbinol-AW 68
PE-FRH-1	—	Fire-Resistant Hyd. Fluid/Synthetic		NR	Turbinol-FR Fluid
PE-FRH-2	—	Fire-Resistant Hyd. Fluid/Water-Glycol		Withrow 841 Safety Hyd. Fluid	Turbinol-FR-G Fluid
PE-FRH-3	—	Fire-Resistant Hyd. Fluid/Water-Oil Emulsion		NR	Turbinol-FR-E Fluid
PE-32-B	2	Very Light Spindle Oil (Over 6000 rpm)	29–35		NR
PE-60-B	10	Light Spindle Oil (3600–6000 rpm)	54–66	H-60 AW Hyd. Oil	Turbinol-S 10
PE-105-B	22	Spindle Oil (Up to 3600 rpm)	95–115	H Light AW Hyd. Oil	Turbinol-S 22
PE-150-C	32	Light Way Oil	135–165	Withrow 625-150 Way Oil	Turbinol-Way 32
PE-315-C	68	Medium Way Oil	284–346	Withrow 625-300 Way Oil	Turbinol-Way 68
PE-1000-C	220	Heavy Way Oil	900–1100	Withrow 625-900 Way Oil	Turbinol-Way 220
PE-700-D	150	Light Gear Oil	630–770	Withrow EP-4 Gear Oil	Turbinol-Gear 150
PE-1000-D	220	Medium Gear Oil	900–1100	Withrow EP-5 Gear Oil	Turbinol-Gear 220
PE-2150-D	460	Heavy Gear Oil	1935–2365	AP Gear Oil SAE 140	Turbinol-Gear 460
PE-315-E	68	Light Extreme-Pressure Gear Oil	283–347	NR	Turbinol-Gear EP 68
PE-1500-E	320	Heavy Extreme-Pressure Gear Oil	1350–1650	AP Gear Oil SAE 90	Turbinol-Gear EP 320
PE-OG-G	—	Cling-Type Gear Shield (Open Gears)		NR	Turbinol Open Gear G
PE-GPG-2	—	Gen. Purpose E.P. Lithium-Base Grease	NLGI2	Lithium EP #2 Grease	Turbinol EP 2 Grease
PE-MG-2	—	Molybdenum Disulfide E.P. Grease		Moly-Dee Multi-Purpose Grease	Turbinol SD Grease

Total Lubrication 253

Plant Engineering Designation	ISO Viscosity Grade	Lubricant Type	Viscosity, SUS at 100°F	O. F. Zurn Co.
PE-150-A	32	Light Inhibited Hydraulic & Gen. Purpose	135–165	Zurnpreem 15A
PE-215-A	46	Med. Inhibited Hydraulic & Gen. Purpose	194–236	Zurnpreem 21A
PE-315-A	68	Med.-Heavy Inhibited Hyd. & Gen. Purpose	284–346	Zurnpreem 30A
PE-700-A	150	Heavy Inhibited Hydraulic & Gen. Purpose	630–770	Zurnpreem 70A
PE-150-HP	32	High-Pressure (Anti-Wear) Hydraulic Oil	135–165	Zurnpreem 15A
PE-215-HP	46	High-Pressure (Anti-Wear) Hydraulic Oil	194–236	Zurnpreem 21A
PE-315-HP	68	High-Pressure (Anti-Wear) Hydraulic Oil	284–346	Zurnpreem 30A
PE-FRH-1	—	Fire-Resistant Hyd. Fluid/Synthetic		NR
PE-FRH-2	—	Fire-Resistant Hyd. Fluid/Water-Glycol		NR
PE-FRH-3	—	Fire-Resistant Hyd. Fluid/Water-Oil Emulsion		NR
PE-32-B	2	Very Light Spindle Oil (Over 6000 rpm)	29–35	Zurnpreem 3A
PE-60-B	10	Light Spindle Oil (3600–6000 rpm)	54–66	Zurnpreem 6A
PE-105-B	22	Spindle Oil (Up to 3600 rpm)	95–115	Zurnpreem 10A
PE-150-C	32	Light Way Oil	135–165	Zurn Waylube 15
PE-315-C	68	Medium Way Oil	284–346	Zurn Waylube 80
PE-1000-C	220	Heavy Way Oil	900–1100	Zurn Waylube 90
PE-700-D	150	Light Gear Oil	630–770	Zurnpreem 70A
PE-1000-D	220	Medium Gear Oil	900–1100	Zurnpreem 95A
PE-2150-D	460	Heavy Gear Oil	1935–2365	Zurnpreem 140A
PE-315-E	68	Light Extreme-Pressure Gear Oil	283–347	Zurn EP Lube 68
PE-1500-E	320	Heavy Extreme-Pressure Gear Oil	1350–1650	Zurn EP Lube 320
PE-OG-G	—	Cling-Type Gear Shield (Open Gears)		Zurn Open Gear Lube
PE-GPG-2	—	Gen. Purpose E.P. Lithium-Base Grease	NLGI2	Zurn MD #2 EP Grease
PE-MG-2	—	Molybdenum Disulfide E.P. Grease		Zurn MD #2-Moly Grease

NR = No recommendation
1. Does not contain tackiness additives normally found in way lubricants. Formulated to perform as combination hydraulic oil and way lubricant.
2. To be used where grades 90, 125, and 140 are recommended.
3. Not lithium base, but equals or exceeds application requirements.
4. Falls outside specified viscosity range, but meets application requirements.
5. Not moly grease, but exceeds application requirements.
6. Straight phosphate ester fluids available in four viscosity grades.
7. Available in range of viscosities.
8. Various ISO grades.
9. Synthetic lubricants.
10. All products formulated from polyalkylene glycol base stocks.
11. Anhydrous product, but water soluble.

machine. Additives inhibit oxidation, provide detergency, protect against rust and corrosion, inhibit foam, and ensure both static and dynamic demulsibility. Demulsibility, the ability to shed water, is an important property when the paper machine and its lubricant are constantly exposed to water and steam. Teresstic N also has antiwear additives to protect bearings that operate under high speeds and loads.

This paper machine lubrication oil is available in three viscosity grades: ISO 150, 220, and 320. The latter, Teresstic N 320, was designed for bearing applications where oil temperature can exceed 200° F. on up to 400° F. The higher viscosity assures that the lubricant film will be adequate at the higher temperatures.

Viscosity is one of the most important properties of a lubricant, and it is widely used as a prime selection criteria. Heavier oils and greases are more resistant to flow; they also provide thicker lubrication films. The resistance to flow, the thickness of the film, and the stability at a given temperature (the latter a prime feature of Teresstic N), are important selection criteria. Although most mills have used ISO 150 or 220, the trend is swinging toward the higher-viscosity oils because of the needs identified with the higher machine speeds and oil temperatures.

The viscosity designation is identified in several ways. The American Society for Testing and Materials (ASTM) and the American Society of Lubrication Engineers (ASLE) have established a standard viscosity scale as identified in table 19.2. This scale, based on Saybolt Universal Seconds (SUS) at 100° F. is a comparison of the various viscosity ratings that are commonly used.

The common viscosity classification system, based on International Standards Organization (ISO) viscosity grade numbers ("Industrial Liquid Lubricants–ISO Viscosity Classification," ISO Standard 3448), is described in "Standard Recommended Practice for Viscosity Systems for Industrial Fluid Lubricants," ASTM D242275. It is applicable to fluids such as lubricants that range in kinematic viscosity from 2 cSt to 1,500 cSt at 40° C.

Viscosity is an important criteria for selection, but it does not indicate the quality or performance of the lubricant. The data supplied to the authors of table 19.1 and 19.2 merely identify what products fall within the lubricant designation. Questions about the performance of a recommended subsituation should be answered by the lubricant producers or the supplier of the component or equipment.

In addition to an appropriate viscosity, a premium lubricant will have most, if not all, of the following properties:

Table 19.2 Commonly Used Industrial Lubricant Viscosity Ratings

Plant Engineering Magazine's Designation[1]	ISO Viscosity Grade	AGMA[2] Grade No. (approx.)	SAE[3] Viscosity No. (approx.)	SAE Gear Lubricant No. (approx.)	Viscosity, SUS at 210 °F. (approx.)
32	2	–	–	–	–
60	10	–	–	–	–
105	22	–	–	–	–
150	32	–	10W	75W	40
215	46	1	10	–	43
315	68	2	20	80W	50
465	100	3	30	–	60
700	150	4	40	85W	75
1,000	220	5	50	90	95
1,500	320	6	60	–	110
2,150	460	7	70	140	130
3,150	680	8	–	–	140

[1] Numbers correspond to viscosity ratings (SUS at 100F. + 10 percent) based on ASTM and ASLE recommendations.
[2] American Gear Manufacturers Association.
[3] Society of Automotive Engineers, Inc.
Source: Marinello, 1983

- *Oxidation stability* The lubricant resists the formation of system deposits, varnishes, and corrosive by-products that result in the breakdown of the lubricating film.
- *Rust protection* This feature is particularly important where the equipment is exposed to high humidity and wet conditions. It is an essential property of a woodyard or papermill application.
- *Demulsibility* This is a key lubricant property within a wet-end of a paper mill, where significant amounts of water are constantly present. The capability for a lubricant to shed water is a must.
- *Detergency* This property will prevent deposits such as carbon build up in bearing housings.
- *Antiwear protection* This is the supplemental antiwear protection that enhances the antiwear properties the oil or grease base provides.
- *Foam resistance* An additive will prevent the mixing of the lubricant with air. This prevents foaming and possibly an overflow situation.
- *Filterability* Oils are routinely filtered to remove abrasive contaminants, and some filtration systems can filter down to 6 microns.

The ability of an oil to be filtered at a required level is an important property. This is particularly important if an oil can be successfully filtered at a wide range of temperatures, particularly cold startup temperatures.

The cited properties, each with a varying level of importance depending on the application, are important. Several examples have been cited for oils; the greases are no less important. A grease-lubricated bearing needs to be properly coated to insure adequate lubrication and corrosion resistance. All roller bearings require a fairly soft grease that is evenly distributed to prevent metal-to-metal contact between components. The rolling elements and raceways must be properly lubricated; the cages are equally important.

The supply of lubricant must be uninterrupted; in the case of oil lubrication where a cooling feature is required, the correct flow must be continuous and unimpeded. There are telltale signs of how well this is occurring:

> A normal supply of lubricant to a bearing operating at medium to high speed generates a rise in temperature accompanied by a whistling sound. Too much lubricant produces a sharp temperature rise caused by churning in all but very-low-speed bearings. Abnormally high temperatures in a bearing can destroy a lubricant's effectiveness.
>
> Inadequate lubrication in a bearing causes damage that is hard to distinguish from primary fatigue failure. Unless detected early, spalling destroys the evidence of inadequate lubrication. (Guyer, 1988, 54)

This chapter has focused on the lubricating process for moving surfaces. No less important is the selection for the static surface application. A special class of lubricant called "antiseize" is often used to ensure quick and easy disassembly and reassembly of machinery.

> Traditional oil-base lubricants have two weaknesses when used in static joints. First, they vaporize even at moderate temperatures, leaving dry metal that can seize or corrode. Second, they squeeze out of metal-to-metal contact points, allowing cold welding to occur.
>
> Antiseize lubricants have ingredients that make them effective where common greases and oils fail. They are combinations of oil-base and solid lubricants that produce hybrid lubricants uniquely suited for static joints. Solid lubricants withstand heat and heavy loads. They remain between the metal surfaces; heavy loads will not squeeze them out, and heat will not vaporize them out of the joint. (Schaefer, 1987, 54)

Antiseize lubricants function in three ways: Joints are lubricated to provide smooth assembly and consistent torque/tension relationships;

Total Lubrication   257

corrosion and cold welding is prevented; and the joints separate cleanly and easily when necessary. The lubricants themselves are a mix of oil-base materials and solid lubricants such as copper, nickel, graphite, and molybdenum disulfide. The latter two are naturally flaked materials that orient themselves between contacting surfaces. The actual formulations are many and varied; the end use will dictate the best one to use. The specifications for each is usually available from the larger mill supply firms.

How to Use Lubricants

The first step in establishing an effective lubrication program is to understand what substances are available and what each can do. The next step is to implement a lubrication program. This activity starts with a lubrication survey.

The maintenance supervisor asks a lubrication engineer to visit the plant site and audit the needs of the mill. This individual, usually available on loan from a lubricant supplier, will audit the equipment and systems and determine what is needed, how much, at what frequency, and how the lubricant is to be delivered to the point of need. The recommendations are listed in chronological order along with the specific lubricant to be used, and the frequency of the lubrication. The resulting document is the basis for the activities that follow.

The top maintenance supervisor assumes overall responsibility for the implementation and ongoing effectiveness of the program. He or she then assigns specific responsibility to each participant, and delegates equally specific assignments to an individual for each machine or system. Machine operators are given job-specific lubrication assignments as appropriate; full-time oilers are identified and trained to implement the program.

"A sound lubrication program is based on: standardization of products used; pinpointing of responsibility; and establishment of uniform procedures. In fact, the essence of a good program can be stated as the four Rs of lubrication: right lubrication, right place, right time, right quantity" (Garretson, 1983, 29).

The four Rs sound easy enough to implement; but the actual implementation takes a dedication that only comes with the belief that a mill's maintenance program will never be any better than the quality of the overall lubrication program. Quality only comes after a comprehensive audit of the mill and an equally comprehensive assignment of responsibilities.

"When responsibility for oiling and greasing is spelled out to the last fitting, the company is assured that lubrication work is being done when it is needed. Costs of such work can be pinpointed and trouble areas can be spotted" (Barnes, 1983, 5).

Newer systems will take the tedium out of the lubrication task by utilizing automated systems. A centralized system can be as simple as a greasepot with a multiplicity of lines fanning outward from the reservoir to the individual fittings; or it can be as comprehensive as a computerized central system that functions with little or no human intervention. The newer or constantly updated mills will have a combination of the two plus other variations of these systems.

Automated lubrication systems have many advantages and one apparent disadvantage. The advantages include lubricant waste prevention, labor reduction, and the overriding assurance that the right lubricant is being fed into the right place at the right time in the right quantity.

The apparent disadvantage is the separation of the worker from the machine; the close personal audit of the machine functions that happens during manual lubrication is invaluable. These inspections should be integrated into a preventive or productive maintenance routine.

Training: The Key

Mills that retain a manual program should focus on training and upgrading. A Champion International maintenance professional describes one such recent program:

> A three-day intensive training schedule was set up and conducted with the help of Mobil engineers. Two days were set aside for classroom training on the basics of lubrication—what lubricants are, how they work, and other points—and on the particular lubrication requirements of paper machines and associated systems. The third day was devoted to in-plant training on the paper machines.
>
> A one-day training program was also given to maintenance supervisors to acquaint them with proper lubrication practices. (Akhavein, 1985, 13)

This training program has several key features:

- Supervisors were trained along with the oilers (lubrication inspectors).
- Training was conducted in a timely fashion.
- Training was handled by experts provided by the vendor.
- A mix of class time and on-site experience provided a depth of understanding and expertise.

The students had an opportunity to practice what was taught in the first two days with practical hands-on experience in the mill under the tutelage of competent instructors.

Feedback: An Essential Ingredient

No lubrication program is complete without a feedback program. The feedback program must cover two time frames: (1) What is being done? (2) What results are occurring?

Oiler notes, work orders, completed computer lubrication checklists, readings from electromechanical devices, and personal inspection will monitor what is being done. Periodic inspection of the equipment for wear, such as preventive maintenance and predictive maintenance activities, will yield much data on the success of the lubrication program. Oil sampling and analysis (more fully described in chapter 12) can be an important assist.

The elimination of unexpected downtime caused by inadequate lubrication, the wrong lubricant, and the buildup of high concentrations of contaminants is the goal. Ongoing follow-up and inspection can prevent each. The challenge is to optimize machine and system performance. This can be achieved when an effective lubrication program is in place.

References

Akhavein, M. 1985. Lubrication Program Pays Off for Champion. *Southern Paper and Pulp* (February).

Barnes, T. C. 1983. Nine Common Lubrication Errors. Maintenance. Maintenance Practices. Part C. Lubrication. Plant Engineering Library. Barrington, IL: Cahner's Publishing Co.

Carson, B. 1983. Seven Steps Lead to Efficient Plant Lubrication. Maintenance. Maintenance Practices. Part C: Lubrication. Plant Engineering Library. Barrington, IL: Cahner's Publishing Co.

Garretson, R.C. 1983. The Merits of Standardization in a Lubrication Program. Maintenance – Maintenance Practices – Part C – Lubrication. *Plant Engineering Library*. Barrington, IL: Cahner's Publishing Co.

Good, W. R. 1980. Proper Lubrication of Paper Machine Bearings Cut Replacement Costs. *Maintenance Methods for the Pulp and Paper Industry*. San Francisco: Miller Freeman.

Guyer, R. A., Jr. 1988. Why Bearings Fail. *Plant Engineering* (May 12): 52–55.

———. 1985. How to Make Your Equipment Last. *The Logger and Lumberman* (March): 48, 50.

Marinello, R. L. 1983. Interchangeable Lubricants. *Plant Engineering* (June 9).
Schaefer, W. L. 1987. Using Antiseize Lubricants. *Plant Engineering* (February 12): 54–56.
———. 1980. Selecting the Correct Lubricant for Use in Woodyard, Pulp and Paper Mill Equipment. *Maintenance Methods for the Pulp and Paper Industry.* San Francisco: Miller Freeman.
———. 1985. Straight Talk about Never-Say-Die Myths. *Timber Harvesting* (April): 40–41.
Wheelock, L. 1980. Three-point Lubrication Program Improves Maintenance at Groveton. *Maintenance Methods for the Pulp and Paper Industry.* San Francisco: Miller Freeman.

CHAPTER 20

Selecting the Vendor

New technology and new world competition have created a new role for the vendor. The mill, as a customer, and the vendor, as a supplier, are compelled to work together toward a common goal.

"We want strategic partnerships with our suppliers that result in a competitive advantage," said Robert Bartley, procurement vice president for Whirlpool Corporation (Keller and Burgert, 1988, 7). Manufacturing appliances is something different than manufacturing forest products, but the goal of survival and profitability is the same.

The wise forest products operator will quickly abandon the traditional adversarial relationship and recognize the vendor as something more than a salesperson. The vendor has become an intregal participant within a mill's maintenance support group.

Searching for the Vendor

The accelerating pace of automation, innovation, product development, and heightened expectations of product quality and good service are providing an impetus for change. The forest products manufacturer is now seeking a vendor as a partner to help meet the needs of the ultimate customer.

In former years the original equipment changed little from year to year. The equipment manufacturer was the chief source of spare parts, including the spare parts of an outside supplier. Manufacturer-supplied spare parts lists and equipment manuals were about all that was needed for the mill maintenance person or purchasing agent to locate and purchase what was needed. Now all that has changed.

An increasing variety of replacement parts are being produced competitively by vendors who specialize in a particular component for a particular make and model of equipment. Innovations are added to improve the product. Often the replacement product is superior to the original component in cost, performance, delivery time, and new features.

These vendors are usually small entrepreneurs, or midsized companies with limited advertising budgets, few salespeople, and unsophisticated product promotion. Too often they are difficult to locate or the potential buyer is not aware of their existence. Let's look at a few ways to locate these vendors.

Reading and Literature Searches

Books, magazines, and other trade periodicals provide windows into what other manufacturers are doing and what is being developed by suppliers. A comprehensive and regular reading program that reviews both industry-specific and related processing information will provide clues and facts on what is available from who. Emerging trends, such as plastics as maintenance materials, have surfaced in this fashion within recent years.

In addition, a number of publications, such as *Forest Industries* magazine, provide an annual buyers' guide complete with a comprehensive listing of who manufactures or markets mill-specific equipment and parts. TAPPI, a papermakers' trade organization, publishes a monthly periodical that offers a comprehensive review of current maintenance materials for the forest products industry.

The TAPPI Information Resources Center also maintains a computerized suppliers file that lists a wide array of products. TAPPI members may also log onto the Information Resource Center computer file and search the file directly for maintenance materials.

Vendor Visits

Vendors often visit the customer; but a visit to the vendor is an even more productive way to communicate. The customer then meets the product designers and producers while reviewing product features and specifications. These visits benefit both the vendor and the customer, because each comes away knowing more about the other.

Trade Shows

Trade shows provide a showroom for a multiplicity of products; a show also provides a forum for competitors, both vendors and customers of those vendors. The individual business and the industry as a whole are the winners. The Ligna Show at Hannover and the Portland Show and Clinic of Miller Freeman Publications are the premier shows. Others, particularly those sponsored by industry trade organizations, are also useful.

Mill Visits

One manager has commented, "I've never visited another mill without paying for at least the price of the trip with one or more useful ideas."

Mill visits are a time-consuming way to pick up information, but they can be useful for a specific purpose such as observing a system or machine center equipped with innovative features. Existing low-cost innovations observed by others will often spur further innovation; both the visitor and the host gain from the exchange of questions and answers.

Qualifying a Vendor

Qualifying a vendor takes homework. The goal is to identify those vendors who can provide competitive prices, quality products, and timely service. Research will identify and rate the important attributes of a vendor when the following questions are asked and answered:

- Does the vendor understand the customer's real needs?
- Are the products thoroughly engineered, or does the customer become the tester without being told?
- What kind of warranty and service backup is provided? Are the delivery and service requests timely and on schedule?
- Does the vendor provide training? How available is it and what is the cost?
- Will the vendor be available when needed? Does the vendor stock the needed parts and materials? At what volume?
- How adequate is the documentation that describes how the product is to be used and maintained?
- Do the vendor's representatives make a first-time installation go smoothly? Do they stay with it until it performs to expectation?

The best way to answer these questions is to check with others in a like situation, then test the vendor with a pilot order.

Manufacturers then seek an even closer examination of a vendor; those that have an enviable record of performance become closely allied with their customers. Those that don't perform are out.

"We are reducing our supplier base by roughly 50 percent a year. We are continuing our goal to get only the best suppliers in the business" stated Ken Stork of Motorola (Keller and Burgert, 1988, 1). "Fewer and more committed" sums up what is happening in the industry as vendor relationships are being ever more closely examined.

The supplier is shedding the salesman image and emerging in the role of a teacher as a means of committing a customer to products and services.

"As maintenance systems become more sophisticated, the supplier is playing an increasing role in the training of mill staff; indeed, training is often the cornerstone of a supplier's marketing policy" (Marley, 1988, 23).

This trend in training will continue as products become more user specific. The maintenance manager's task is to provide the environment within which the vendor and customer work toward a common goal.

References

———. 1984. Eliminating the Production Bottlenecks in Finnish Mills. Wood Based Panels International, October/November/December.

Girouard, R. 1983. Selecting a Vendor? Do Homework First. *Forest Industries* (September).

Keller, E. L. and P. Burgert. 1988. Suppliers, Producers Forging New Bonds. *Manufacturing Week,* Issue 026 (February 22).

Marley, M. E. 1988. Maintenance Technology and Trends. *Focus on Predictive Maintenance* (August).

———. 1984. On the Stump. *Weyerhauser Maintenance Journal* 2 (January-February): 9.

CHAPTER 21

Stores and Spares Control

"In maintenance management, the only way to improve maintenance productivity is to reduce nonproductive activities," noted Edwin B. Feldman (1987) at a plant engineering and maintenance conference. There is nothing less productive than searching for parts that are not there and then figuring out how to make do until the just right parts and components are available. The task is to create a stores and spares program that is as complete, time efficient, and functional as possible.

An effective stores and spare control program will focus on three essential support activities: setting up and maintaining a stores facility, determining what and how many are to be stored in the facility, and disbursement and procurement of materials on an ongoing basis.

Establishing and Maintaining a Stores Facility

The squirrel is best known for stashing away stores for both real and anticipated needs. Stashing away is also commonly done by maintenance professionals in a mill that does not have an effective stores and spares program. This board plant in western Washington state is one such example.

A bearing, a critical component on the board former, broke down several hours into the afternoon shift. The entire board line was down until a replacement could be located. Unfortunately, a replacement was not available in the storeroom.

The bearing was a specifically designed component that required a three-week lead time to restock from the factory. One or more spares were usually kept on hand. Mill records indicated that three had been ordered the previous year, and only one of the three had been used. The other two were supposed to be in the storeroom, but they weren't.

The purchasing agent, called in from his home, personally searched the storeroom and the purchasing records. Finally, someone suggested that the day-shift millwright, who usually worked in the area, be called to determine if he could help locate the missing bearings. The day-shift man was notified, came to the plant, examined the bearing, and then dug a spare out of his personal toolbox, which was located in his locker. The elapsed downtime for the line was three-and-one-half hours.

A readily available bearing would have resulted in no more than a forty-five-minute repair period.

The millwright thought he was doing the right thing. He felt that the bearing stood a better chance of getting lost permanently in the unsecured storeroom than safely kept in his tool box "and being readily available just in case we need it."

This true story and its variations are played out periodically in any operation that does not have a secure storeroom with the right parts. Squirreling away of parts occurs because a well-intentioned maintenance person, or even a supervisor, believes that sole control of a tool, a part, or a material will prevent even longer downtime. The use of locally controlled satellite stores is another well-intentioned idea.

Satellite stores are sometimes located in strategic locations near or adjacent to the machine or system. Usually the area supervisor or maintenance leadman will control the access to these stores. It is not unusual to have these same personnel order the supplies and even negotiate with the vendor for price, quantity, and delivery dates without the purchasing agent being aware of the purchases.

Satellite stores and independent purchasing can create a costly uncoordinated purchasing effort that usually results in higher costs. It also results in unnecessary duplication of parts and materials. However, satellite stores may be a necessity because of the size of the complex. If so, access and control should reside with the central purchasing and stores function. Ideally, all the parts for both the central storeroom and the necessary satellites will be tallied within a central computer that provides a perpetual inventory report.

The following are time-tested recommendations for setting up or restructuring a stores facility:

1. Gain control of the purchasing process. One person, usually the purchasing agent, will be responsible for purchasing, delivery, and stocking parts and materials. The user should provide the specifications, quantity, usage rate, and delivery needs.
2. Establish a secure storeroom with limited access. A number of larger companies have found that the benefits far outweigh the costs of maintaining and staffing a storeroom open twenty-four

hours a day, seven days a week. Most have found that the price of a storeroom clerk is cheaper than the parts-chasing time spent by the millwrights or electricians.

Smaller operations will use a day-shift person and supplement that person with keys and locks assigned to key personnel who work the off hours. The keys and locks are periodically changed over time to prevent unauthorized access.

3. Centralize the stores function. Locate the "squirrel caches" and transport the materials to a central storeroom, as described earlier. Closets, desks, lockers, toolboxes, boneyards, and other assorted formal and informal storage areas will yield a cornucopia of parts, materials, and supplies.
4. Organize the storage function "with a place for everything and everything in its place." Catalogue motors, place bearings in a central location along with belts, valves, sprockets, and other families of parts and materials. Segregate specialized machine or process parts into separate, easy-to-audit shelves and bins.

The resulting stream of activities will result in a number of benefits: minimum stocking levels, timely access to a part or material, and economical purchasing. These benefits can only be fully realized when the real needs are established and documented. This initiates another stream of activities – determining and documenting real needs.

Determining Needs

The exact determination of what and how many are to be stocked can yield substantial savings. Lloyd B. Mitchell, a management consultant, describes the cost-cutting opportunities and then indentifies the questions to be asked as a vehicle to identify opportunities:

> In most facilities, spare parts investments in warehouses, maintenance shops, and private stashes range from a few hundred thousand to several million dollars. These inventories present major opportunities for effective management and significant profit and balance sheet improvements.
>
> When the manager assesses spare parts inventories, he should consider several questions: Are the inventories managed or are they simply warehoused? What is the total investment in spare parts in stores, maintenance shops, and separate stashes? How much inventory is active, dormant, or surplus? Why? Are material shortages causing plant shutdowns or contributing to lost productivity?
>
> Answering these questions requires an understanding of basic concepts related to spare parts management. (Mitchell, 1987)

Maintenance, repair, and operating (MRO) supplies, used to support the operation of the plant, are identified and categorized. These items are divided into two groups: spares, and commodity materials. Commodity materials are usually readily identifiable and equally readily available.

These materials (fasteners, pipe, fittings, and so on) can be used in a variety of situations. They are usually available with short and consistent lead times from local or regional suppliers. Their material value is generally low; reorder points are identified and the supply replenished when the reorder point is reached.

Spare parts are further categorized as stocking spares or critical spare parts. The first task is to identify just what is being used in the plant and handle the potential need as either a stocking spare or a critical spare. Figures 21.1 and 21.2 are examples of suggested methodology.

A schematic is prepared for the machine or area to be audited, such as in figure 21.1. A simple computerized line drawing is shown: This line drawing is then used as a work sheet to identify a particular category of potential needs, such as pneumatic cylinders and valves in this example.

The maintenance person and a purchasing representative thoroughly canvass the designated area. They locate each part, visually or with the assistance of an equipment manual or machine history file, and document it, as in figure 21.2.

This work sheet identifies the audit results. The number in the lefthand column corresponds to the number placed on figure 21.1 and

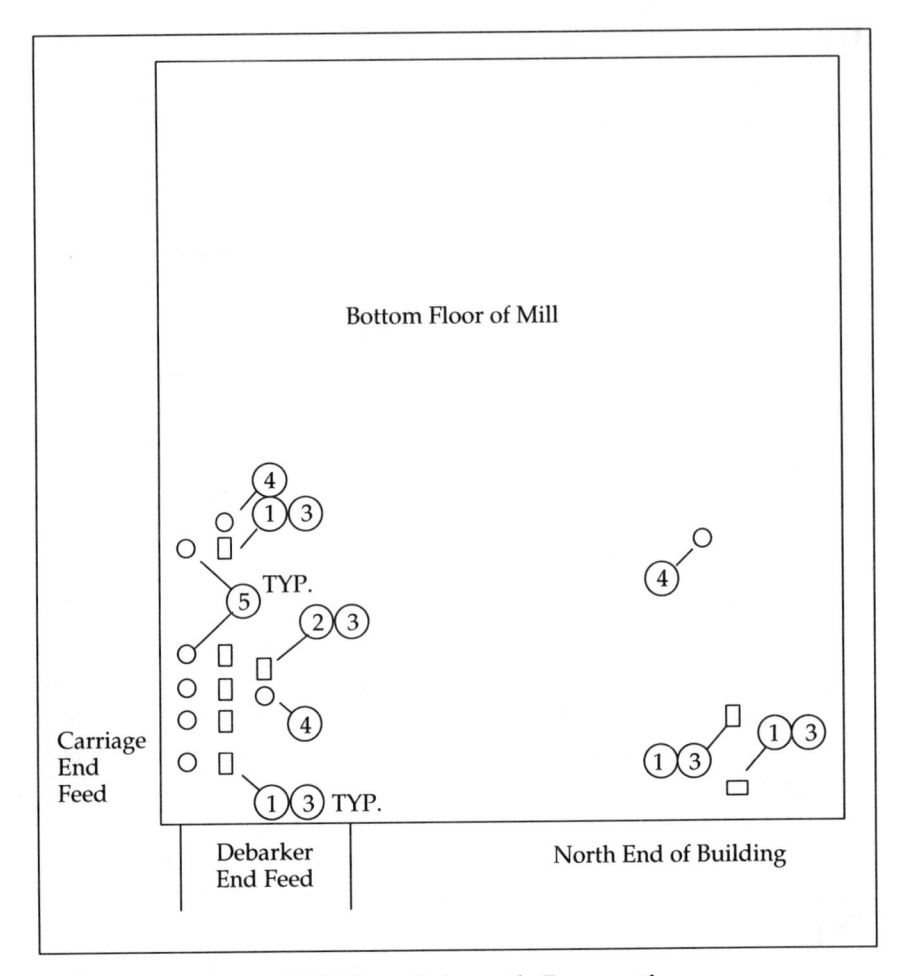

Figure 21.1 **Mill Floor Schematic Pneumatic Cylinders and Valves**

identifies the specific physical location of the component. The next column identifies the number of that specific part in use throughout the area being reviewed (figure 21.1). The manufacturer's assigned part number then follows in the column to the right. The part description then follows in the next column.

Work sheets are prepared for each area, system, or piece of equipment within the plant and its supporting facilities. Next, a usage history is compiled from the individual machine history file and a double check of the purchasing records. The differences are reconciled to determine an agreed-upon stocking level.

The stocking level will be influenced by the present or expected usage level and the availability from the vendor. A nearby stocking vendor plus a past history of few failures will provide the combination of least risk and lowest on-site stocking level. Frequent failures, long lead times, and a nonstocking vendor situation will necessitate the highest level. Most stocking decisions will identify the correct amount as somewhere in between. The decision will be an economic one; an on-shelf item costs about 1.5 percent of its purchased price for each month a part lays idle on the shelf. The benefits of stocking must outweigh the costs or risks.

Whether or not to stock an item and how many to stock will often be determined by the answers to the following questions:

- Is the particular part in use the best one for the task?
- Is there a preferred alternative that will yield lower costs, improved delivery times, and superior performance?
- Can a single make and model take the place of a number of brands and types? What modifications have to be made? What will be the benefits?
- What is the expected life of the particular spare part? What has the historical usage been? How does the latter compare to the expected? Is the difference significant? Why or why not?
- Is this a stocking spare or is it a critical spare part? What is the definition of a critical spare part? How can we match the definition to the part?

Figure 21.3 identifies what is and what is not a critical spare part. Clearly, the bearing and the board plant illustration cited earlier in the chapter met all the criteria for a critical spare part. The bearing described in the illustration "would cause a substantial shutdown of all or a significant part of a primary production line if the existing part were to become defective."

Each part or component is reviewed within the framework of figure 21.3. Is it a critical spare or just a stocking spare? The vital few of the many will be identified as critical spares and handled as follows:

1. Form a critical spares committee at the location. This committee should consist of the operations/plant manager, the local purchasing representative, the maintenance manager/superintendent, and others as required.
2. Review each service or machine center and identify the critical few parts as defined in figure 21.3.
3. The operations/plant manager, local purchasing representative,

3	6506BG	Atlas Cylinder Series "M"
5	N.N.	Arrow Lubricator
4		
5		
6		
7		
8		
9		
10		
11		
12		
13		
14		
15		
16		
17		
18		
19		
20		
21		
22		
23		
24		

Stores and Spares Control 273

NO.	QTY.	Part Number	Description
3	16	EDF258	Del-Trol Easy Read Needle Valve
2	1	L645-49-102	Schrader Bellows Valve
1	7	L645-89-102	Schrader Bellows Valve

Date: 10/12/88

Customer Name: Marysville Lumber
Address:
City: Marysville
State & ZIP: Cal.
Phone & Area Code:
Purchase Order #: 880193 Saw Mill Bottom Floor
Drawing Number:

Figure 21.2 Spares Listing Pneumatic Cylinders and Valves

Figure 21.3 *Critical Spare Parts: A Definition*

A part or component which would cause a substantial shutdown of all or a significant part of a primary production line if the existing part were to become defective is a critical spare part.

Critical Spares Are:
1. Based on the concept that 20% of the machine components will create 80% of the downtime. The vital few of the many.
2. Based on 1, above, the 20% that are truly critical are:
   a. Not easily repairable within an acceptable time frame.
   b. Sometimes a custom made or proprietary part that requires long lead time.
   c. The part may be only available at a distant location and is not usually stocked locally.
   d. Usually a component for a critical machine that does not have a backup system.

Critical Spares Are Not:
1. Normal replacement parts that are readily available; these parts are handled as part of normal warehouse inventory.
2. Usually not components for equipment that can remain idle until the part is received without impacting mill operations.

Source: Baldwin 1981, 282

and maintenance manager/superintendent further screen the list to determine if all entries are indeed critical spares, based on possible contingencies and the probability of occurrence. For example:

- A part may be critical but the probability of its unexpectedly becoming defective is extremely low. Therefore, rather than stocking the part, a periodic preventive maintenance audit is scheduled.
- A part may be critical for a machine but the machine may not be critical to the operation. Therefore the required part may be stocked only as a part of the normal inventory.

4. The local purchasing manager evaluates the list to determine the following:

- Is it necessary to stock the part in house or can an agreement be made with a reliable local vendor to retain the part in stock?

- Do other reliable sources (mills with like equipment) have the part readily available? Can an agreement be made with them to stock the part?
- What are the acceptable stocking limits for the part (minimum and maximum quantities)?

5. The operations manager and the purchasing representative then determine the expenditures required and the timing of the expenditures.
6. The local purchasing representative then implements the plan:

- An approved list is typed up and put in a red looseleaf binder. Each inventory sheet is covered with plastic so that a grease pencil can be used to keep a dated running inventory on each part. A minimum and maximum inventory is identified for each part; the minimum level is usually the reorder point.
- The incoming critical spare parts are put in a central location, with department identification marked in large letters that are easy for all maintenance personnel to see.
- A tag (color-coded by machine or department) is attached to each part; the item purchase order description is on the tag (Baldwin, 1986).

The critical spares program was developed from necessity during mill startups, turnarounds, and downtime reduction efforts generally over the past twenty-five years. It supports the management thesis that the manager's two worst enemies are unplanned events and the lack of a second way to go. The critical spares program answers the need of both.

A stocking spare, as differentiated from a critical spare, also goes through a review process. The review process is rigorous and comprehensive, but lacks the more rigid stocking disciplines characteristic of the critical spares program.

Disbursement and Procurement of Spare Parts

Parts are catalogued and stored for ease in locating, monitoring, and replenishing. Minimum/maximum levels are agreed to and purchase orders prepared as needed when the minimum level is reached. Blanket orders supplement the individual purchase orders for parts or supplies used in periodic and predictable quantities.

Normally the stores manager should achieve four to six turns a year on the stocking spares. Anything less than this indicates an overstock condition that is costly to maintain and more time consuming to track on a continuing basis.

Access to the storeroom is tightly controlled to provide the information needed to maintain the optimum supply of needed parts and supplies. Unrestricted access to a storeroom virtually assures both overstocking and frequent stockouts.

A number of computer software programs have been written to assist the purchasing and storeroom function. The benefits from this software and the overall benefits available to the maintenance program and the mill can only be achieved with well-established procedures and controls. An effective stores and spares control function can improve maintenance productivity dramatically.

References

Baldwin, R. F. 1986. *Operations Management in the Forest Products Industry*. San Francisco: Miller Freeman.

——. 1981. *Plywood Manufacturing Practices*. Rev. 2d ed. San Francisco: Miller Freeman.

Feldman, E. B. 1987. The Second Law of Maintenance Productivity. *Intech* (December).

Mitchell, L. B. 1987. Spare Parts Inventories: Uncovering the Cost Reduction Opportunities. *Plant Engineering* (May 28).

PART SIX

WORKER PARTICIPATION

CHAPTER 22

Innovation, Involvement, and Quality Circles

Innovation is a familiar word in the forest products industry. However, the term conjures up images of an entrepreneur, or at most two or three partners, who develop a vision into a reality. The individual proceeds in a Horatio Alger fashion to develop a new business opportunity. Heine Anderson was one of those.

> In 1938–39 Anderson, who always seemed to know what and where the bear did it in the buckwheat, noticed a steady increase in house-building and also an increase in California and East Coast demand for western lumber: this with the knowledge that 16-foot 2 × 4s brought from $3.00 to $5.00 more per thousand than any other length because they could be cut in two for studs (eight-foot 2 × 4s). Why cut 16-foot lumber into eight-foot studs? Anderson mulled the question, finally concluding it was worth a try to get retail yards to stock studs. (Von Syckle, 1980, 37)

Anderson then converted a money-losing eight-foot hardwood mill into a stud mill . . . and made lots of money.

Involvement and quality circles were once totally unfamiliar terms—and, if understood, would have been unwelcome strangers. The forest industry focus has always been on the dynamic decision making leader and not on the group. In addition, contemporary management literature also recommends a detail-oriented directive approach to the maintenance function: "The smooth operation of a controlled maintenance force is achieved by everyone doing his assigned job. In a functioning unit, the daily operation proceeds along these lines . . . " (Criswell, 1983, 23). The author then details exactly how the maintenance activity should be performed, who communicates with whom, and the precise sequence of activities.

This system has functioned successfully for years; but times are changing. An increasingly perceptive workforce is seeking something more than a job and a paycheck.

279

Changing Perceptions

Change is usually painful; it is particularly painful in an industry where tradition is the norm. It often takes a major upheaval to develop an industry-wide questioning attitude and the search for change. The early 1980s was a period of major upheaval for the forest products industry, as it was for many industries:

> Corporations are being forced to make many difficult adjustments involving limited natural resources, environmental constraints, governmental regulation, rising interest group power, and other well-recognized problems. As a result, the jobs of most employees increasingly involve difficult problemsolving responsibilities of a rather complex, professional nature, rather than simple clerical or technical tasks. (Halal and Brown, 1981, 20–21)

The role of the mill maintenance person, and how the maintenance task was carried out, changed with the times at a number of forest products locations. Simpson Timber's sawmill at Korbell, California, was an example.

"We have done some neat things with maintenance at Korbell; people have ideas and we are using those ideas. Overall we have achieved a 70 percent increase in total man-hour productivity," commented Paul Everett, as he described the quality circle activities at this location in 1983.

Paul's efforts and the efforts of other Simpson employees created a marked change at Simpson. Similar efforts were being made at other companies and other locations. The payoff was survival; the by-product was involved employees who began to contribute something more than time and routine.

Participative Management

The more successful programs have recognized that sound employee involvement programs must have certain features.

> Sound participation is a tough, no-nonsense relationship that places great demands on subordinates through the skillful use of profit, cost, or production center concepts, performance evaluation systems, financial incentives, or other means of ensuring accountability. A sound strategy for implementing participative management should first aim to control performance outcomes effectively, which will then permit subordinates greater freedom to employ their discretion. (Halal and Brown, 1981, 30)

The maintenance supervisor's role changes; directive activities are replaced with facilitative tasks. The maintenance manager's job also changes. The predominant concern for operational details is refocused on a larger role of organization development, maintenance skill upgrading, and maintenance program strategy. These refocused activities provide the time and resources to cope with increasingly complex maintenance problems.

Group activities such as involvement and quality circle participation are part of the participative management process. Each emphasizes the team approach. Decisions and activities, formerly accomplished by the supervisor or manager, are considered fair game for group participation.

There have been notable participative management successes; there also have been failures. Unfortunately, the successes of the participative management process have been overblown in the literature, speeches at industry meetings, and other trade communication.

Complex people problems have been encountered, the process has been time consuming, the resulting decisions sometimes mediocre, accountability muddled, and the people problems far-reaching. On balance, the industry has made progress in transferring the decision making process to the workers, including the maintenance staff. Certain steps, however, will increase the probability of success.

Successful Program Ingredients

The maintenance organization must have leadership that demonstrates strong maintenance appreciation. Maintenance appreciation then translates into a supportive effort to obtain improved results. No less important is the organization structure.

The flatter the organization structure and the wider the span of control, the greater the opportunity for top management to seek an increased role from the hourly and salary workers. A flat organization enhances communicaton; fewer supervisors doing more creates a need. Each is a basis for a successful participative management program.

Participative management and the use of quality circles is not for everyone. The demands of greater participation in decision making frequently result in employee turnover in the early stages of a program implemented in an established operation. Recruitment and selection of personnel is important when establishing a program in a new operation; this prevents turnover and insures the success of the program.

Don't attempt to go it alone. Even a modest program needs assistance from outside the group. In-house resource people can be a help in organizing and structuring the effort. In addition, a number of credible outside consultants have gained valuable experience in the forest products industry. Each can establish and coach a tailor-made program that will meet the site-specific needs of an organization. Most successful programs have adopted the top-down approach using in-house or outside consultants.

The location management group is introduced to the program. Frequently, this same group is organized into a team. The experience gained as a team member translates into team support as the hourly workforce is introduced to the participative process.

The maintenance department can be organized into a separate team, or each maintenance worker can be a member or a production team. The concept of a maintenance team with each team member also participating in a production team has worked well at a number of locations.

The mission statement, described in chapter 3, should be prepared and the objectives established. An organization with an existing mission statement and objectives should introduce these to the new teams. This provides the basis for reviewing and reworking the objectives. Participation in this task then provides the charter for further team activity.

Five major elements need to be in place to support the subsequent team activities:

1. Each individual team member must share a common vision.
2. The organization leader must believe that the team can make a valuable contribution.
3. The individual team member must believe that he or she can make a valid contribution.
4. An information system must be in place to provide feedback on results achieved.
5. Training and skill enhancement for each team member should be provided on a continuing basis.

Most people who have gone through team building and development recognize that the skills to participate fully only come with time and individual effort. Companies that have gone through the participative management process—such as Simpson Timber, Champion International, Weyerhaeuser, Scott Paper, and others—recognize that it takes at least six months to witness any change at all.

It takes no less than about two years before the participative management process becomes a cultural norm for a mill or a company. A commitment to the process at all levels and a sustained effort to make it happen will determine whether or not this happens.

References

Brownell, P. 1982. The State of the Art Participative Management. *The Wharton Magazine* 7, no. 1 (Fall).
Criswell, J. W. 1983. Planned Maintenance for Productivity and Energy Conservation. Atlanta: The Fairmont Press.
Dixon, N. 1984. Participative Management: It's Not as Simple as It Seems. *Supervisory Management* 29, no. 12 (December).
Making the Most of What You Have. 1987. *Forintek Review* (January).
Halal, W. E. and B. S. Brown. 1981. Participative Management: Myth and Reality. *California Management Review* 23, no. 4 (Summer).
Hamlin, R. 1986. Choosing Between Directive and Participative Management. *Supervisory Management* 31, no. 1 (January).
Van Syckle, E. 1980. *They Tried to Cut It All*. Seattle: Pacific Search Press.

CHAPTER 23

Designing Away From Maintenance

Reliability/maintainability engineering is the art and science of designing away from maintenance. It identifies improved ways to minimize the length and cost of downtime when it occurs; it also extends the lifetime of the equipment components and assemblies.

"I have a plain old household refrigerator that falls into this category. We purchased it in 1950, so it has lasted twenty-seven years and survived six moves, yet it has not cost us one red cent or one hour of repair labor in those twenty-seven years, they selected a door gasket material that would live as long as the compressor, likewise hinges, latches, and finish," wrote M. R. Rivers, a Georgia Pacific maintenance engineer, in an unpublished memo to his company colleagues in 1977.

He continued,

> The lack of good system design is exemplified by the roof of my home. The roof is a thick-butted hand-split cedar shake roof which is known to last at least fifty years. What really tears me up is that they installed galvanized sheet metal gutters that only have an expected life of five years and nearly 20 percent of my roof will have to be torn up to replace these short-lived gutters. They would have only increased the roof costs by 3 or 4 percent if they would have installed PVC gutters or stainless steel so that the gutters would last as long as the shakes.

Most mill and maintenance managers are well acquainted with "sheetmetal gutter"-type situations built into their mills. The example of others indicate that reliability/maintainability can be built into a mill.

The Swedish Experience

Forest industry mills are being designed and redesigned to run longer and faster with relatively less maintenance. This phenomenon is occurring worldwide as capacity increases, trade barriers fall, and previously underutilized forest resources are tapped for higher-valued products. Nowhere is this more apparent than in Sweden's pulp and paper industry.

"In Sweden, the number of paper mills decreased from 74 in 1970 to 58 in 1986; the average mill size increased from 89,000 metric tpy to 145,000 metric tpy," cited Rolf Eidensten, president of Jaako Poyry AB, during a speech in April 1987.

"The percentage of maintenance personnel to total personnel slowly increased between 1974 and 1985: from 27% to 35% for pulp mills, from 20% to 25% for integrated paper mills, and from 12% to 15% for nonintegrated papermills" (Sward, 1987).

It becomes apparent that the Swedish maintenance effort has changed, but has grown in a much smaller proportion when compared to the increase in capacity and the resulting automation. A similiar situation has occurred elsewhere in the world in both site- and industry-specific situations.

Developing better, more focused maintenance organizations with improved organizational structures, upgrading the crew selection and training process, and structuring ways to more effectively communicate has helped. The hidden dimension has been the formal and informal emphasis on reliability/maintainability engineering.

Formal versus Informal Methods

Both formal and informal methods are effective in designing away from maintenance. Each has its role; each shares much in common with the other. Both methods require the full participation of the design engineer and other engineers, other technical skilled personnel, mill repair and maintenance people, and the operations representatives.

The formal approach tends to be best suited for large complex projects; the informal method tends to focus on the relatively smaller projects or projects of a repetitive design. The informal approach tends to operate closer to the site, with the resulting design heavily influenced by the inducer.

The Informal Method

Sierra Pacific Industries calls this method "home cooking." A design, engineering, and construction department has been created to serve the needs of fourteen lumber manufacturing plants scattered in Northern California from Arcata to Loyalton. Twenty-five welders, fabricators, machinists, electricians, and computer technicians staff the department.

"We feel that we have better control of the end product when we produce it 'in house,' and we are able to react faster to a need at one of the mills," commented Greg Waalkes, construction department manager.

"We are involved in the design, development, and installation of the equipment, and when it is in place we are familiar with it and able to get it into operation faster."

The staff works closely with the mill during the design stage. Layouts that work well in one mill tend to be repeated in similar situations. Components are selected on the basis of mill experience; reliability and simplicity rank high as a basis for selection.

A paper mill maintenance engineer comments,

> Other things that the engineers can do for us during the design stage are to specify the pump seal we have found works best, the steam trap we find works best, nonlubricated couplings, tilt pad bearings on high speed equipment, mist lubrication, numerous grease fittings piped out to a common easily accessible point, increased service factor for gear reducers, branch shut-off valves, nonabsorbent insulation, circumferentially corrugated metal jackets, Dodd bar brackets for high-speed equipment, standardize wherever possible on gears, motors, pumps, and seals, first-class painting, and use proximity probes instead of microswitches.

The informal method is effective, but it is not without its pitfalls. One pitfall may be created by the limited knowledge of the decision makers; another may be created by the impromptu changes that occur in an operating mill to "make things better."

Mill-related technology is changing at a rapid pace. It takes a specialist to stay current with the emerging technology, which extends from the smallest system component to the overall process. Without this input a process, a machine, or a component may be out of date before it is installed. This pitfall can be avoided by recognizing local limitations and then obtaining outside assistance and review before proceeding with a project.

Impromptu changes are expensive and often difficult to control. This situation occurs at most mills, but it occurs most frequently at mills that use and encourage the informal methods of designing away from maintenance.

A better way is discovered during ongoing operations or a downtime occurrence. The change is made, and sometimes it works well . . . and sometimes it doesn't. Sometimes the change is documented in the machine history file and redlined on the working drawings . . . and sometimes it isn't. The result can be chaos rather than improvement. The best bet is to require one-over-one approval for change or, in participative organization, a consensus. Then document the change.

The Formal Method

The formal method skews the design and engineering responsibility to the professional rather than the mill person. Some companies welcome little mill participation in the project design, although an operational representative is welcomed as a liaison person. Whether or not the system works depends in large measure on the process and operational expertise of the engineering professional and his or her informal communication with the mill. Most companies are finding that the input of the operational and maintenance professional is indispensable, from concept to installation. The formal approach is still centered on the professional, but more input is requested and expected.

Life cycle cost (LCC) is one formal methodology. Logisticians work closely with maintenance engineers and other knowledgeable personnel to study a system. The operations or maintenance situation is simulated through the use of calculations.

The goal is to identify cost and technical difficulties, and redesign and respecify as appropriate. The knowledge gained from this formal approach is invaluable in understanding a problem or situation. It acts as a training tool, in addition to its immediate benefits of usually lower project costs and improved reliability and maintainability.

Computer-assisted design (CAD) is bridging the gap between the formal and informal approaches. The needed hardware and software, available either in-house in a large company or at an outside engineering firm for a smaller company, projects the design on a computer screen. Capacities can be tested and design parameters closely examined. Alternatives can be selected and evaluated, changes can be made in seconds. The resulting design is immediately reproduced onto a hard copy original line drawing.

Timing and Results

Reliability/maintainability engineering can occur from the conceptual phase of a project and continue throughout its life. The least-cost results are achieved in the earliest phases. Figure 23.1 illustrates the effect of timing.

The vertical axis represents the percent completion for an average project. The horizontal axis indicates the cost index on a scale of 1 to 1,000 with one being the conceptual phase and 1,000 occurring sometime during installation.

The bold trend line indicates the magnitude of future operating and maintenance costs that have been locked in as decisions are made or not made during a particular project phase. The dotted trend line indicates the total investment of time and resources made at that point in the project.

Design changes and modification are inexpensive to implement in the early stages of the project. Parato's Principle prevails during the design phase; about 80 percent of the future operating and maintenance costs are locked in while 20 percent or less of the investment has been made. The obvious time to change is in the early part of the project, even if the cumulative costs of respecifying and reengineering push the project cost upward.

During the early phases of the project the following questions should be asked and answered:

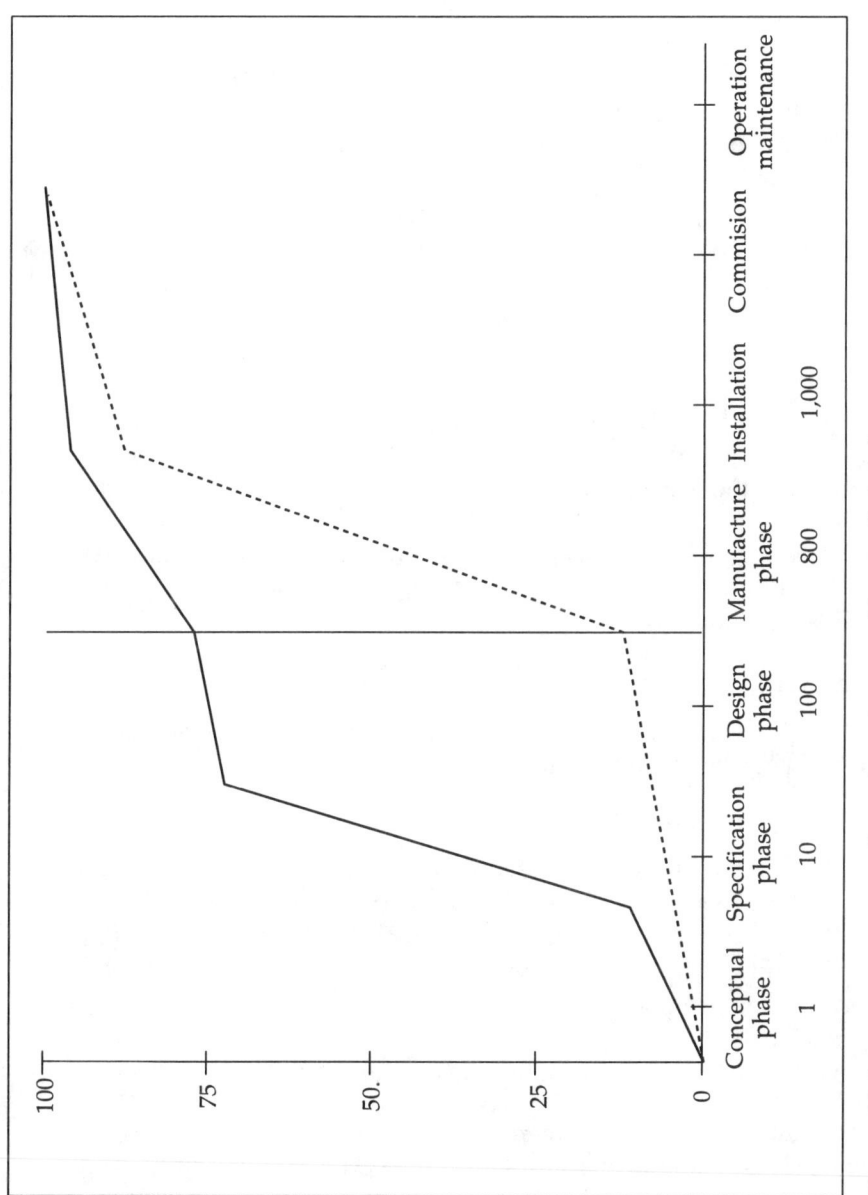

Designing Away From Maintenance 289

Figure 23.1 Investment versus Future Operating and Maintenance Costs
Source: Sword, 1987

New Equipment Process

- Does it stack up to the state-of-the-art technology? Why or why not?
- Has the design had sufficient input from engineering, maintenance, operational, and other personnel? What is new in the design? Why is it different than other tested designs?
- Is the new equipment or process to be maintained by existing maintenance personnel? What needs to be done to improve maintenance staffing?
- Who has "lived with" a similar system? What are their opinions or recommendations?
- Does the design follow recommendations of manufacturing management? Why or why not?
- Is the design stout enough? What allowances have been made for the unexpected?
- What has been done to minimize the maintenance effort while maximizing performance?
- What is the cost and availability of spare parts? What is the expected usage rate?
- Have field drawings been checked closely? Will there be surprises during installation? Have the field dimensions been compared to the equipment prior to installation?
- Has housekeeping been designed into the system? What more needs to be done?
- What can be expected in future expansion? Future updates? How will each be accommodated?

Existing Equipment

- What is the current maintenance cycle? Where and why? What can be done to simplify or stretch out this cycle?
- What is the current reliability in operation? What is downtime currently? What should it be?
- What can be done to enhance quality, promote safety and increase production?
- What can be done to simplify the operation?

Designing away from maintenance will occur as these questions and others are asked and answered. And the answers are not always easy. Sometimes an answer is so significant in our lives that we still reminisce about it years later. A veteran maintenance manager tells the following story:

I was a start-up Manager of UM&E at Crown Zellerbach's brand new 600-ton-a-day bleach market pulp mill in Fairhaven, California. Shortly after we started it up we broke the shaft that ran through the driven head sheave on the bale conveyor to the warehouse. They put the sheet from the machine into the dry end slusher for a while, but soon ran out of capacity in the broke tank as we scrambled to make a new shaft and get it installed. The shaft had snapped at the diameter reduction where it entered the drive sprocket.

Figuring that they had not allowed enough radius on this stress concentration point, we machined the new shaft with a greater radius at this point and got the conveyor going as soon as we could. About a month later the shaft snapped again at exactly the same point, and we figured this time there was more load on the conveyors than the designers had accounted for. So this time we used a higher-strength steel. This lasted about two months and it broke again.

Obviously, this time we were very angry and frustrated. We called in the vendor, threw our hats on the floor and stomped our feet, and replaced the shaft again with the same high-strength steel to get going.

As I reflected back over the day's activity and this failure in particular, it occurred to me that something other than the obvious must be wrong. I went to the engineering supervisor and requested a full-time dedicated engineer to live with this problem until he solved it. Whether it took a day, a week, or a month, we had to have an answer.

Well, it only took the guy twenty minutes to come up with the answer of what was wrong—the conveyor was running twenty feet a minute faster than the conveyor it fed, and it was a very simple task just to change the drive sprockets to obtain the correct speed.

This story makes it clear that designing away from maintenance is anything but an exact science. It sometimes takes more than knowledge to accomplish the task; courage and perseverance help, too.

References

BoardTalk 9, no 4. 1988. Sierra Pacific Industries Employees' Newsletter (September).

Bowman, L. 1987. Designing a Process Cooling Water System. *Plant Engineering* (May 14).

Dhillon, B. S. 1983. *Reliability Engineering in System Design and Operation*. New York: Van Nostrand Reinhold.

Sward, K. 1987. Reliability and Maintainability Engineering Is Key to Productivity. *Pulp & Paper* (December).

Veranth, J. M., P. E. 1987. Designing Plant Modifications That Fit. *Plant Engineering* (May 14).

CHAPTER 24

The Coupling of Maintenance and Manufacturing: Getting Started

The forest products industry is indeed changing. A relatively low-tech industry is being restructured and transformed into a capital-intensive world competitor. New machines, new processes, and new products are demanding a new approach to the maintenance task. The industry products, heretofore thought of as unglamorous undifferentiated commodities, are being more closely identified with consumers' needs and wants. Each gut-wrenching industry shakeout or Goldsmith-type restructuring brings the point home to those who survive and prosper in this industry: A mill cannot survive without low costs and desirable products.

And how does this relate to the maintenance effort? Low costs and desirable products cannot be obtained without it.

Maintenance: The Linkage

Maintenance is the linkage between the raw material and the customers; it is an assurance that the former is processed efficiently and the latter get what they want, and when they want it. The maintenance process is intertwined with the people ingredient—so much so that one far-sighted manager told me, "We don't have maintenance problems; we only have people problems. Downtime is a direct reflection of people's attitude and capability!"

As this manager and others shared experiences, it became apparent that the more successful operations—success defined from such outward signs as the condition of the facility and the demonstrated capability to weather the sometimes turbulent economic environment—were managing maintenance as something akin to the management of physical health. Those who manage their health well make it a continuing process characterized by adequate planning with occasional outside help. Periodic preventive or predictive checkups are the basis for action. A mill is no different.

People's attitude and capability are readily visible in a maintenance program. This lumber operation is a good example: Eleven production workers and two millwrights produced about 20 mbm to 22 mbm per operating hour when the mill operated; frequently, however, it did not. The two millwrights had little time to do anything more than repair equipment, unplug jam-ups, and wish for the end of the shift. An observation of how the equipment was being handled indicated little regard for the equipment... or the millwright. The millwrights were preceived as barriers rather than partners. A machine operator would pull the whistle cord and wait for a millwright. The employee attitudes and capability were frightening; so were the shift results.

Another mill had like equipment but unlike results. One shift was quite like another, with predictable results. Something else was predictable: the relationship between maintenance and production. Production managed maintenance with formal preventive and predictive maintenance supplementing a basic maintenance program that had the active participation and support of the individual equipment operator. The resulting notes from this mill expressed the manager's and my own summation of what I was seeing and hearing: "Downtime is no accident or happenstance... it can be prevented if the maintenance and related people activities are in control. Each is certainly in control in this mill."

Getting Started

This book outlines and details specific activities to effect a total maintenance (TM) program in a mill. Often an out-of-control situation needs to be remedied before the formal implementation steps can occur. In other words, "You don't give swimming lessons to a drowning person."

The following steps can be taken quickly. Each will buy the operator time to implement the full program. The sequence of activities will disrupt the break-it/fix-it cycle long enough to gain sufficient control to take the permanent steps.

1. *Establish a Leader* Too often poor attitudes and equally poor capabilities are a mirror image of the supervisor. If this is the case, then change leadership quickly. This allows the mill operator to obtain hands on and removes a barrier to the problem; it also demon-

strates that the past is past. The incumbant, ideally an in-house promotion or one who has survived and prospered through one or more turnaround situations, will need to be a take-charge individual who is long on people skills and short on patience for equipment abuse and overlooked details. The new leader will need to readily accept and coordinate outside assistance in a purposeful fashion.

2. *Identify Resources, In-house and Outside* The leader will think through the conceivable problems, including support systems problems. The high-visibility problems are usually just the tip of the iceberg; other problems are usually hidden, time-consuming to fix, and costly. Next, identify in-house capability and available staff assistance, outside consultants and vendors, and other suppliers of expertise and tangible services. Establish an effective critical spares program immediately to provide parts and component backup.

3. *Audit Each System and Subsystem* This detailed audit will establish maintenance needs, both fix-it needs and training needs. This procedure is not unlike a preflight inspection; it may actually require a link-by-link chain inspection, for example. The result is

usually a lengthy fix-it list. Ideas are also accumulated to minimize further deterioration—such as an improved lubrication program, a better method of equipment usage, or reducing operating hours.
4. *Prioritize Needs* Prioritize the resulting maintenance needs. The prioritization process will take into account the timing and probability of failure; it will also take into account the allocation of available resources. Then address the prioritized list and follow up on a timely basis.
5. *Commit Resources* Avoid the "penny wise and pound foolish" syndrome. Commit resources in large enough quantity and high enough quality to avoid more costly unscheduled downtime. You cannot spend your way out of trouble . . . but there is a balance.
6. *Obtain and Keep Control* Audit closely during walk-abouts and over-the-shoulder inspections until confidence is gained in individual assigned maintenance and production person.
7. *Train and Develop* Train, train, train! And follow up, follow up, follow up! The first few days, weeks, and months are critical in changing attitudes and skills. Patience is required and necessary.

Getting started is just that: getting started. The task is to gain a respite from the downtime and then move on from there. Moving on should mean initiating the sequential steps outlined in this book in installing a TM program.

As Bruce Mallory, then operations manager of Snow Mountain Pine in Burns, Oregon, said, "The day of the haywire artist is about over . . . the industry has been slow in moving into the new era in maintenance." We need to hasten the pace and move into a TM program. Our task is to anticipate and respond to new needs, new customer demands, and new technology. Our goal is a stable and profitable operation. This goal cannot be achieved without an effective maintenance program.

Index

ABC/MM, 65
Accelerometers, 118–119
Air leaks, 178–179
Alumax, 35, 49, 156
American Petroleum Institute (API) standards, 123
American Society for Testing and Materials (ASTM), 254
American Society of Lubrication Engineers (ASLE), 254
Analyzers, 123
Anderson, Heine, 279
Ansul Company, 100
Antiseize lubricants, 256–257
Antiwear protection, of lubricant, 255
Apple Computer, 93
Area maintenance organization type, 37–38
Assignment, specific task, 74–75
A. T. Kearney, Inc., 34
Automated expert systems, 92–93

Babcock, Frank, 64
Bartley, Robert, 262
BC Hydro, 183
Bingham, Charles W., 3
Boise Cascade, 4, 6, 95–96, 105
Bonneville Power Administration (BPA), 183
Bowering, Cliff, 42
Break it/fix it maintenance programs, 17–18
Brookhaeuser, Byron, 9
Budgeting and forecasting, 157–162
Buell, Tom, xiii
Burlington Industries, 24

Carroll, Hatch and Associates, 183
Central maintenance organization type, 36–37
Central shop, deemphasis of, in maintenance organization, 32–33
Champion International, 4, 6, 10, 117, 259, 283
Chargeable Time Summary, 67
Checklists
  preventive maintenance (PM), 151
  vehicle operator's, 100, 101, 164, 166

Cleanliness, importance of, 35–36
Coffren, Dick, 129
Combine, in budgeting, 159
Combined rolling and sliding wear, 136
Commodity materials, 269
Complete engineering, steps to, 190–192
Compressed-air systems, and energy conservation, 178–181
Computer-assisted design (CAD), 64, 191, 288
Computer-assisted maintenance (CAM), 19, 63–72, 80–81
  examples, 65–68
  make or buy decision, 70–71
  selection and design of program, 68–70
  tasks, 64
Computerized modeling, 137
Congressional Record, 96
Conservation, energy. *See* Energy conservation
Consultants, outside, use, 22–23, 25, 281–282
Container Corporation of America (CCA), 35
Contamination and dilution, oil, testing, 134
Controlling, importance in maintenance, 14–16
Cost tracking, 154–156
Critical spare parts, 269, 271, 274–275
Crown Zellerbach, 291
Cutting and welding permit, 98–100
Cutting wear, 136

Daily individual maintenance report, 57–59, 152
Daily job planning, 60–61
Day, John, 49
DC high-potential testing, 132
Decision Dynamics Inc., 64
Decision making, in maintenance organization, 33–34
Demulsibility, of lubricant, 255
Department of Energy, 176
Departmental maintenance organization type, 38–39
Dersin, Pierre, 92

297

Design, computer-assisted (CAD), 64, 191, 288
Designing away from maintenance, 284–291
Detergency, of lubricant, 255
Diagonal Data Corporation, 67, 68
Dickson, Bob, 147
Dilution, oil, testing, 134
Downtime, 84–85, 292–293
  reporting, 76–79
Drawings, redlined, 152
Dubal, Beck, Harris & Humphries, Inc., 66
Du Pont. *See* E. I. duPont de Nemours

Economics of maintenance, 141–148
  assessing the cost, 142–143
  changing perceptions, 141–142
  as common sense, 147–148
  the heavy envelope, 145–147
  organization and systems investment, 143–144
Eidensten, Rolf, 285
E. I. duPont de Nemours, 95–97, 102, 105
Electrical-powered production systems, and energy conservation, 181–182
Electrician, rating system for skills evaluation, 44–45
Eliminate, in budgeting, 159
Emergency management planning, 59–60
Employees
  role in maintenance organization, 31–34
  selection and placement, 73–74
Energy conservation, 175–186
  eliminate overcapacity and redundancy, 177–178
  new gadgets and methods, 178–185
  role of maintenance person, 175–176
  turn off when not in use, 176–177
Energy, Department of, 176
Engineer, role of, 187–193
  as problem solver, 187–188
  as project designer and manager, 188–190
Engineering, steps to complete, 190–192
Engineer's Digest, 68
Equipment History file card, 164
Equipment record system, 75–77
  use in planning, 54
Everett, Paul, 280
Expert systems, 90–92
  automated, 92–93
Exxon Corporation, 196

Facility
  assessment of, 23, 28–30
  stores, establishing and maintaining, 266–268
Failure, defined, 84–85

Federal Paper Board, 117
Feedback program, in lubrication, 260
Feldman, Edwin B., 266
File
  machine history, 152, 153
  master drawing, 152
File card, equipment history, 164
Filterability, of lubricant, 255–256
Flat organizational structure, in maintenance organization, 32, 281
FMC, 105
Foam resistance, of lubricant, 255
Forecasting and budgeting, 157–162
Forest Industries, 196, 263
Formalized vs. standardized methods, in maintenance organization, 33
Fuel soot, testing, in lubricant, 135

Geisel, Charles E., 35
GEMS Systems, 68
Geneen, Harold, 53
General Electric, 183
Georgia Pacific Corporation, 4, 6, 127, 284
Greases. *See* Lubrication, lubricants

Hahn, T. Marshall, 127
Handrail sitting, 187–188
Harvard Business Review, 13
Harvey, Paul, 95
H. B. Maynard and Company, 45
Helicopter maintenance program, 86–87
Herbaty, Frank, 160
Hewlett Packard, 76
High-efficiency motors, and energy conservation, 182–185
High-frequency surge testing, 132
High-potential testing, DC, 132
Honey, Greg, 67
"How to Manage Maintenance," 13
Hypercard software, 93

IBM, 34
Imaging, infrared, 128–129
Implementation of total maintenance program. *See* Total maintenance program, implementation of
Implementation steps, of predictive maintenance, 112, 114–115
"Industrial Liquid Lubricants—ISO Viscosity Classification," 254
Industry Week, 34, 41
Infrared imaging, 128–129
Innovation, 279
Inspection, safety, 102–103
Interchangeable lubricants, table, 196–253
International Organization for Standardization (ISO) standards, 123, 254

Index

International Paper, 3–4, 6
Inventory and stores control, 80

Jaako Poyry AB, 285
James G. Biddle Company, 131
Japan Institute of Plant Maintenance (JIPM), 24
Job planning, 103–105

Kaibab Forest Products, 66–67
Kirkham, Kevin, 8
Kress, Howard A., 95
Kuper, George H., 7

Lacquer deposits, oil, testing, 135
Laminar particles, 136
Laser shaft alignment system, 125–126
Leadership, committed, importance to maintenance organization, 14, 15, 32
Lewis, John L., 141
Life cycle cost (LCC), 287–288
Ligna Trade Show, 263
Lists, parts and materials, use in planning, 55
Literature search, for vendor, 263
Load reduction, 185
Location manager, attributes needed to create maintenance program, 25
Lockout procedures, 98
Long-range planning, 62
Loss prevention. *See* Safety and loss prevention
Louisiana Pacific, 4, 6
Lubrication, lubricants, 194–261
  choosing a lubricant, 195–257
  feedback program, 260
  how to use lubricants, 257–259
  interchangeable lubricants, table, 196–253
  training, 259–260
  types of lubricants, 194–195

Machine, changing expectations of the, 10–11
Machine history file, 152, 153
Macmillan Bloedel, 7–8
Maintenance
  appreciation, importance of, 32, 281
  costs, 4–7, 157–162
  defining the task, 12–21
  Management (software), 76
  organization, building, 31–46
  person, role in energy conservation, 175–176
  planning and scheduling, 49–62
  program, starting, 22–30
  program, total. *See* Total maintenance program

  programs, types, 16–21
  repair, and operating (MRO) supplies, 269
  schedule board, for mobile equipment, 166, 167
Make or buy decision, for software, 70–71
Mallory, Bruce, 295
Manager
  engineer as, 188–190
  location, attributes needed to create maintenance program, 25
Managing, 53
Manufacturing Studies Board, 7
Marshall, Edwin L., 80
Marshall & Little Inc., 80
Master drawing file, 152
Master equipment list, 76, 77
Materials and parts lists, use in planning, 55
Maxey Electronics, 10
Maxey, Wanda, 10
Mayers, Gene, 5
McQueen, Reggie, 10
Megger tester, 131
Megohmmeter, 131
Meters, 122
Meyer, Gene, 33
Mill visits, 264
Miller Freeman Publications, 196, 263
Millwright
  rating system for skills evaluation, 44–45
  role in safety, 96–97
Mission Statement, 23, 26–27, 282
  coordination with, 34
Mitchell, Lloyd B., 269
Mitchell, Robert, Jr., 183
Mobil, 259
Mobile equipment
  Maintenance. *See* Rolling stock maintenance scheduling and cost control
  maintenance schedule board, 166, 167
  monthly repair and cost report, 170–172
  repair/cost form, 168–172
  replacement schedule, 164, 165
Modeling, computerized, 137
Monitors, 122–123
Monthly repair and cost report, for mobile equipment, 170–172
Moore International, 116
Mora, Michael E., 34
Motorola, 264
Motors
  failure prevention, 131–134
  high-efficiency, and energy conservation, 182–185
Multicraft skills, importance in maintenance organization, 33

Naisbitt, John, 8
National Academy of Sciences, 7
National Aeronautics and Space Administration (NASA), 89
Needs, determining, for stores and spares, 269-275
Nitration, oil, testing, 135
Nolden, Carol, 111
Noncontact probe, 120-122

Objectives, establishing, 23, 27-29
Oils. *See also* Lubrication, lubricants
  sampling and analysis, 134-135, 166
Orders, work, 55-57, 151
Organization types
  area maintenance, 37-38
  central maintenance, 36-37
  departmental maintenance, 38-39
  emerging, 39-42
  flat, 32, 281
Organizing, importance in maintenance, 14, 15
Outside consultants, use of, 22-23, 25, 281-282
Overcapacity, eliminating, for energy conservation, 177-178
Oxidation stability, of lubricant, 255

Parato's Principle, 288
Parrish, Dick, 95-96
Participative management, 280-283
Particle analysis, wear, 135-137
Parts and materials lists, use in planning, 55
People. *See* Employees
Performance ratio, 145-147
Permit, cutting and welding, 98-100
Pickups, velocity, 119-120
Planner, 51-54
Planning and scheduling, maintenance, 49-62
  importance of, 113-115
  planner, 51-54
  planning horizons, 59-62
  planning ingredients, 54-59
  task of, 49-51
Plant Engineering, 42, 111, 196
Portland Show and Clinic, 263
Potlatch, 6
Power factor, 181-182
Predictive maintenance
  infrared imaging, ultrasonic testing, and other techniques, 128-138
  overview, 20, 109-115
  vibration monitoring and analysis, 116-127
Prevention of problem, 86-87

Preventive maintenance (PM)
  checklist, 151
  programs, 18-20
Probe, noncontact, 120-122
Problem cycle, 84-86
Problem solving, 84-94
  as engineer's task, 187-188
  prevention, 86-87
  techniques, 89-93
  troubleshooting, 87-89
Process information, use in planning, 55
Proctor & Gamble Cellulose, Ltd., 65-67
Project designer, engineer as, 188-190
Protective devices, 97-98

Qualifying a vendor, 264-265
Quality-awareness program, 7-8
Quality circles, 279-281
Questionnaire, for facility assessment, 29-30

Rating systems, for skills evaluation, 44-45
Ratio, performance, 145-147
Rearrange, in budgeting, 158
Record keeping, maintenance, 149-153
  importance of, 149-150
  the system described, 150-153
Records, equipment, use in planning, 54
Redlined drawings, 152
Reduction, load, 185
Redundancy, eliminating, for energy conservation, 177-178
Renewal, organizational, in maintenance organization, 34-42
Repair and maintenance costs, 4-7
Repair/cost form, for mobile equipment, 168-172
Replacement schedule, for mobile equipment, 164, 165
Report, daily individual maintenance, 57-59, 152
Request, work, 151
Results, implementing, 23, 30
Rivers, M. R., 284
Rolling fatigue, 136
Rolling stock maintenance scheduling and cost control, 163-172
Rubbing wear, 135-136
Rust protection, of lubricant, 255

Safe Control, 110
Safety analysis, of equipment, 103-105
Safety and loss prevention, 95-106
  as a culture, 105-106
  job planning, 103-105
  millwright's role, 96-97
  safety inspection, 102-103

Index

safety tasks and protective devices, 97–102
Safety Training Observation Program (STOP), Du Pont, 96, 97
Satellite stores, 267
Saybolt Universal Seconds (SUS), 254
Scheduling and planning, maintenance, 49–62
  importance of, 13–15
  planner, 51–54
  planning horizons, 59–62
  planning ingredients, 54–59
  task of, 49–51
Scott Paper, 283
Scuffing of gears, 136–137
Sensors, 88, 118–122
Service manual, importance of, 9
Shop, central, deemphasis of, in maintenance organization, 32–33
Short-range planning, 61
Should-be costs, in budgeting, 158–159
Sierra Pacific Industries, 285
Simplify, in budgeting, 158
Simpson Timber, 280, 283
Skills
  mulitcraft, importance in maintenance organization, 33
  rating system to evaluate, 44–45
Sliding wear, 136
Small Business Administration, 3
Sneak analysis (SA), 89–90
Snow Mountain Pine, 295
Software, make or buy decision, 70–71
Solids content, oil, testing, 135
Soot, testing fuel oil, 135
Southern, Jerry, 7
Spall particles, 136
Spares and stores control, 80, 266–276
  determining needs, 269–275
  disbursement and procurement of spare parts, 275–276
  stores facility, 266–268
Specific task assignments, 74–75
Spherical particles, 136
"Standard Recommended Practice for Viscosity Systems for Industrial Fluid Lubricants," 254
Standardized vs. formalized methods, in maintenance organization, 33
Standards, setting, for vibration monitoring and analysis, 123–125
Standing work order, 151
Statistical reports, use in budgeting, 159–161
Stocking level, determining, 270–275
Stocking spares, 269, 275
  disbursement and procurement, 275–276

Stores and spares control. *See* Spares and stores control
Stork, Ken, 264
Surge testing, high-frequency, 132

TAPPI, 196, 263
Task assignment, specific, 74–75
Teresko, John, 34, 41
Teresstic N, 196, 254
Testing, ultrasonic, 130–131
Thermograph, 128
Timber Processing, 145
Time card, 152
Time-of-flight tip defraction, 130
Timing, in design, 288–291
Total acid number (TAN), oil, testing, 135
Total base number (TBN), oil, testing, 135
Total maintenance program, implementation of, 73–83
  benefits of, 81–82
  computer-assisted maintenance, 19, 63–72, 80–81
  equipment record system and downtime reporting, 75–79
  overview, 20–21
  people selection and placement, 73–74
  specific task assignment, 74–75
  steps to get started, 293–295
  stores and inventory control, 80, 266–276
Trade show, for vendor selection, 263
Training and development, importance of, 42–45
Transducers, 118–122
Transimatics, Inc., 92
Trickle down, 164
Troubleshooting, 87–89

Ultra-high molecular weight (UHMW) wear plate, 185
Ultra Image III, 130, 131
Ultrasonic Predictable Maintenance, 130
Ultrasonic testing, 130–131
Union Camp, 6, 67
Union Carbide, 28–29

Variable frequency drive, 180
Vehicle operator's checklist, 100, 101, 164, 166
Velocity pickups, 119–120
Vendor, selecting the, 262–265
Vibration monitoring and analysis, 116–127
  equipment systems and components, 117–123
  establishing standards, 123–125
  overview, 116–117
  vibration prevention, 125–126

Viscosity, lubricant, 254–255
  testing, 134
Visits
  to mill, 264
  to vendor, 263

Waalkes, Greg, 286
Wear particle analysis, 135–137
Wear plate, ultra-high molecular weight (UHMW), 185
Weekly job planning, 61
Welding and cutting permit, 98–100

Westerkamp, Thomas, 45
Weyerhaeuser, 3–6, 13, 23, 33, 42, 64, 117, 129, 130, 147, 283
Whirpool Corporation, 262
Wilkinson, John T., 12, 13
Willamette, 6
Work orders, 55–57, 151
Work request, 151
WORKSMART, 65
World Wood, 196

Yeater, Tom, 105